MOSAIK'S PHOTOGRAPHIC KEY TO THE TREES AND SHRUBS

OF GREAT BRITAIN AND NORTHERN EUROPE

A new system for identifying trees by their leaves and needles

MOSAIK'S PHOTOGRAPHIC KEY TO THE TREES AND SHRUBS

OF GREAT BRITAIN AND NORTHERN EUROPE

A new system for identifying trees by their leaves and needles

Jean – Denis Godet

Translated by Clive King and Helen M. Stevenson

Additional material by Alan Mitchell

Mosaik Books

The Viables Centre
Harrow Way, Basingstoke,
Hampshire RG22 4BJ

First published in Great Britain 1988 by William Collins Sons & Co. Ltd.
London . Glasgow . Sydney . Auckland . Toronto . Johannesburg
under the title:
COLLINS PHOTOGRAPHIC KEY TO THE TREES

ISBN 3 – 576 – 80004 – 2

Typeset by Ace Filmsetting Ltd, Frome, Somerset
Printed and bound in Belgium by Brepols Fabrieken N.V., Turnhout

To My Mother

Contents

Foreword

My first book, 'Trees of Europe in Four Seasons', demonstrates the wide variety of important trees in Central Europe. My next two books, the pocket guides to 'Buds and Twigs' and 'Flowers', were identification guides to indigenous and introduced species of trees and shrubs from autumn through to early summer. This, my fourth book, is a guide for the summer season. As with the other two pocket guides, particular attention is paid to the introduction. In the second section, the most important species are described, in each of the four seasons, and an indication is given of their significance in and influence on our culture.

For the purposes of identification, only those features are described which are visible to the naked eye or with the use of a good magnifying glass. To ensure that the fine details do not cause the reader to lose sight of the general picture of the tree, a short description of the tree in question is highlighted against a grey background in the 'key' section.

In the main section of the book, 260 species and varieties are described in detail with full colour illustration. An English and a Latin index at the end of the book allow the user to locate references to species known by name.

I should like to thank, for all their guidance and stimulation over the one and a half years during which I wrote this book, all the staff at the Botanic Gardens in Basel, Bern, Geneva, St Gallen and Zurich. I hope this book will be a reliable guide and a good companion to all who use it and that it will play its part in preventing the beauty and variety of our trees from being forgotten, for they play a vital role in the formation of our countryside's character.

Bern, December 1986 — Jean-Denis Godet

1. Introduction

1.1. Preface

In order to identify a tree or shrub during the summertime, when flowers and fruits are often absent, it is only the leaves which are of any practical value. It is important to describe these with precision at the beginning so that mistakes may be avoided at a later stage. With this in mind, only those characters have been used here which can be seen with the naked eye or with the aid of a good lens.

1.2. Structure of leaves

1.2.1. Leaf-forms and age of leaves

A leaf consists of a flat, usually green blade (lamina) and often a shaft-like stalk (Fig. 1–3). The point where the leaf is attached to the shoot is called the leaf-base, and in some species this may be enlarged.
In Butcher's Broom (*Ruscus aculeatus*) the typical leaf-blade is absent, but in its place is a flattened, leaf-like lateral shoot known as a cladode (Fig. 5). At the base of the cladode are modified leaves, reduced to small scales. Flowers arise from a point on the upper surface of the cladode, in the axil of a small, scale-like bract (Fig. 6).
Where the leaves are without stalks (sessile) the base of the blade is attached directly to the shoot (Fig. 4).

Leaf with blade, stalk and leaf-base

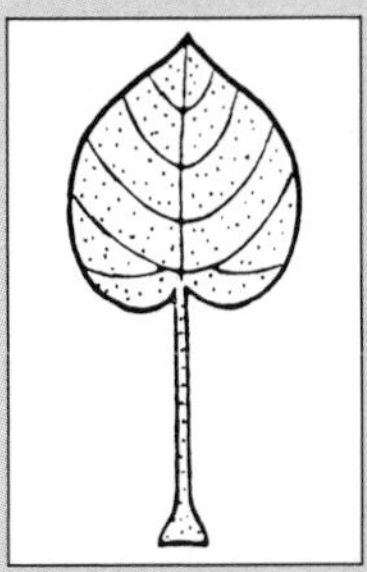

1 **Schematic representation**

Stalked leaf

2 ***Prunus avium*** **Wild Cherry**

Stalked leaf

3 ***Cercis siliquestrum*** **Judas Tree**

Sessile leaf

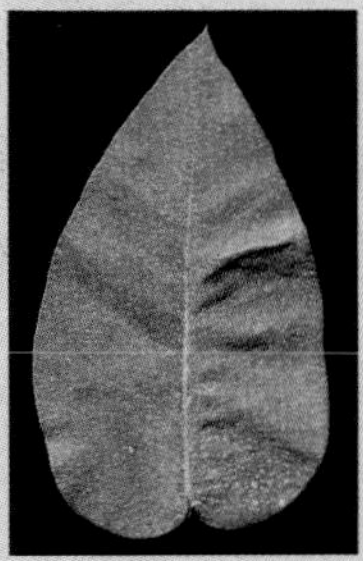

4 ***Eucalyptus globulus*** **Blue Gum**

Cladode

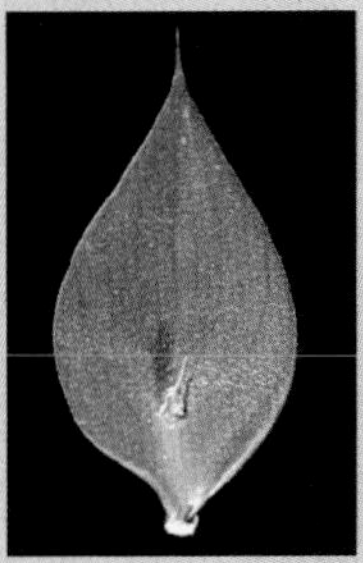

5 ***Ruscus aculeatus*** **Butcher's Broom**

Cladode with flower

6 ***Ruscus aculeatus*** **Butcher's Broom**

Three kinds of leaves may be found on the shoot:

1. Scale leaves	Simple leaves which, in woody plants, are usually found only as coverings for the winter buds.
2. Foliage leaves	Most of the leaves on a shoot are of this kind.
3. Bracts	Simple leaves, situated above the foliage leaves, especially frequent in the floral region. Since they are often coloured, they frequently resemble petals.

The life-span of a leaf can vary considerably:

One year	Leaves are green in the summer, and are shed at the end of the first foliage period.
Winter-green	Old leaves are only shed when the new ones appear.
Two years	Leaves are shed at the end of the second foliage period.
Evergreen	These leaves remain throughout several periods of growth, and as they do not all fall off at the same time, the tree or shrub appears evergreen.

1.2.2. Shape of the leaf-blade

Oblong leaf-blades

In oblong leaf-blades the ends may be obtuse or acute (Fig. 7–10):

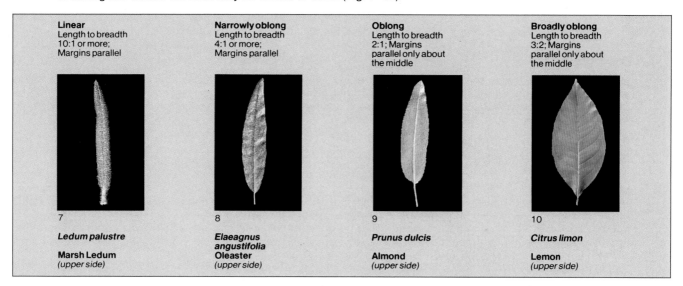

Linear
Length to breadth 10:1 or more; Margins parallel

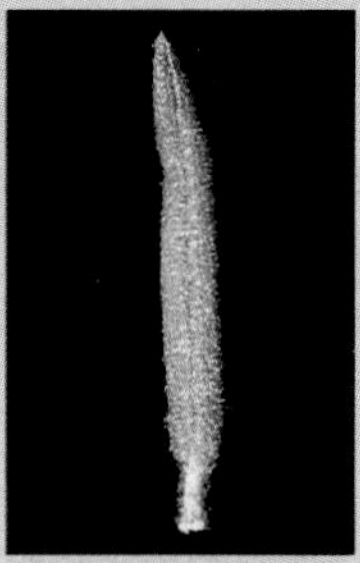

7

Ledum palustre

Marsh Ledum
(upper side)

Narrowly oblong
Length to breadth 4:1 or more; Margins parallel

8

Elaeagnus angustifolia
Oleaster
(upper side)

Oblong
Length to breadth 2:1; Margins parallel only about the middle

9

Prunus dulcis

Almond
(upper side)

Broadly oblong
Length to breadth 3:2; Margins parallel only about the middle

10

Citrus limon

Lemon
(upper side)

Lanceolate leaf-blades

The greatest breadth is always below the middle of the blade. The base is usually rounded and the tip usually pointed (Fig. 11–14):

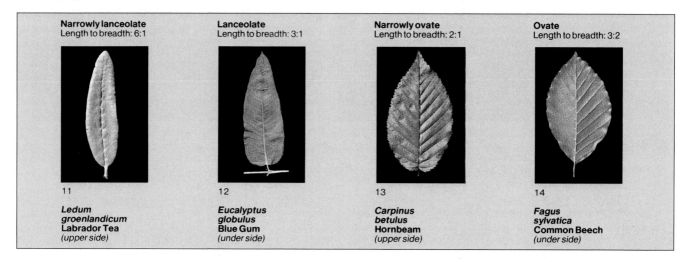

Narrowly lanceolate
Length to breadth: 6:1

11

Ledum groenlandicum
Labrador Tea
(upper side)

Lanceolate
Length to breadth: 3:1

12

Eucalyptus globulus
Blue Gum
(under side)

Narrowly ovate
Length to breadth: 2:1

13

Carpinus betulus
Hornbeam
(upper side)

Ovate
Length to breadth: 3:2

14

Fagus sylvatica
Common Beech
(under side)

Elliptic and orbicular leaf-blades

The greatest breadth is always at the middle of the blade. The ends are usually pointed (Fig. 15–18):

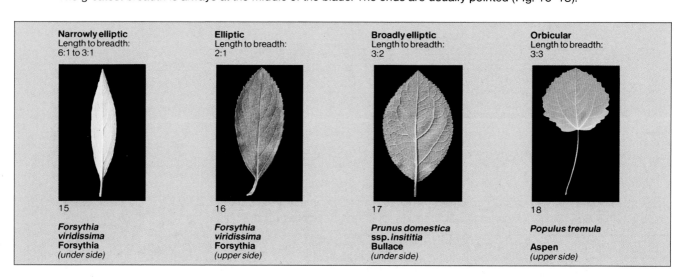

Narrowly elliptic
Length to breadth: 6:1 to 3:1

15

Forsythia viridissima
Forsythia
(under side)

Elliptic
Length to breadth: 2:1

16

Forsythia viridissima
Forsythia
(upper side)

Broadly elliptic
Length to breadth: 3:2

17

Prunus domestica* ssp. *insititia
Bullace
(under side)

Orbicular
Length to breadth: 3:3

18

Populus tremula

Aspen
(upper side)

Obovate leaf-blades

The greatest breadth is above the middle of the blade. The base is usually pointed, but the tip is rounded (Fig. 19–22):

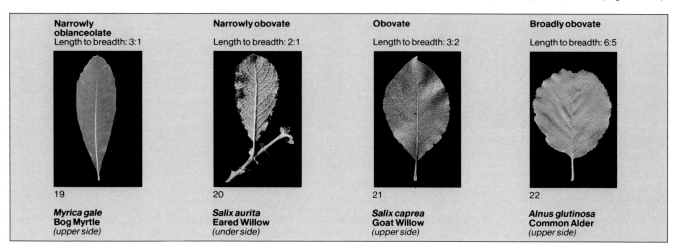

Narrowly oblanceolate
Length to breadth: 3:1

19

Myrica gale
Bog Myrtle
(upper side)

Narrowly obovate
Length to breadth: 2:1

20

Salix aurita
Eared Willow
(under side)

Obovate
Length to breadth: 3:2

21

Salix caprea
Goat Willow
(upper side)

Broadly obovate
Length to breadth: 6:5

22

Alnus glutinosa
Common Alder
(upper side)

Other kinds of leaf-blades

Heart-shaped

23

Tilia cordata
Small-leaved Lime
(upper side)

Quadrangular

24

Liriodendron tulipifera
Tulip Tree
(upper side)

Triangular

25

Populus nigra
Black Poplar
(upper side)

Kidney-shaped

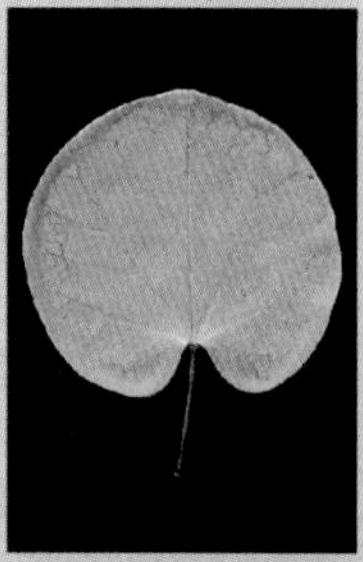

26

Cercis siliquastrum
Judas Tree
(upper side)

1.2.3. Venation (veining)

Parallel-veined leaves*

The numerous, equally strongly formed veins run parallel or in a curve from the base of the blade to its tip. There is no prominent midrib. This kind of venation is found mainly in monocotyledonous plants (Fig. 27).

* The example shown is of a cladode.

27

Ruscus aculeatus
Butcher's Broom

Net-veined leaves (pinnately veined)

A characteristic feature of the leaves of most dicotyledonous plants is the prominent midrib, from which lateral veins run to the leaf-margin. These are connected to each other by smaller veins forming a close network (Fig. 28–40).

28

Salix caprea
Goat Willow
(under side)

Net-veined leaves

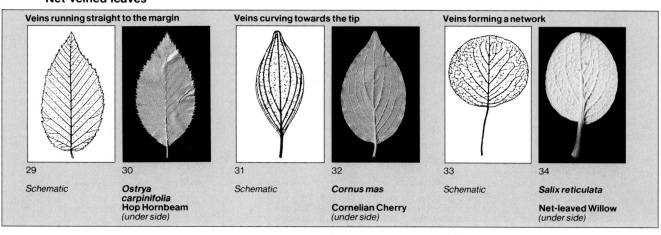

Veins running straight to the margin

29

Schematic

30

Ostrya carpinifolia
Hop Hornbeam
(under side)

Veins curving towards the tip

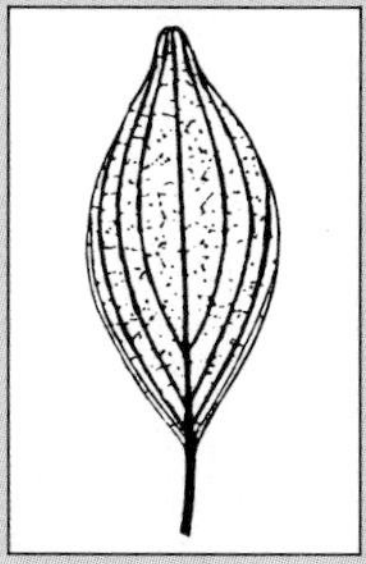

31

Schematic

32

Cornus mas
Cornelian Cherry
(under side)

Veins forming a network

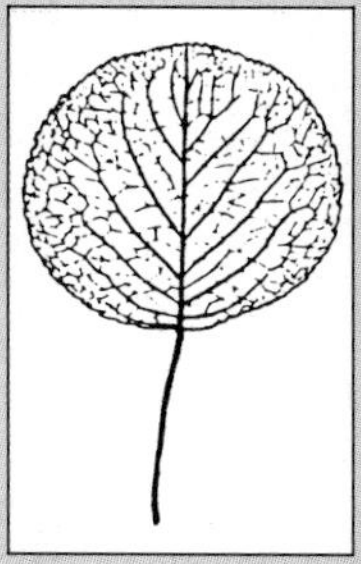

33

Schematic

34

Salix reticulata
Net-leaved Willow
(under side)

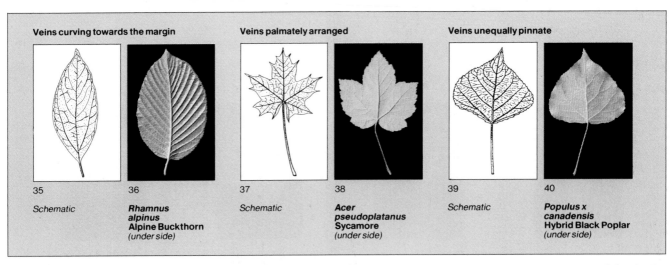

Veins curving towards the margin

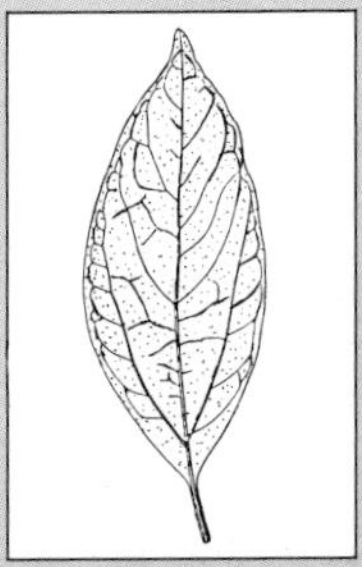

35

Schematic

36

Rhamnus alpinus
Alpine Buckthorn
(under side)

Veins palmately arranged

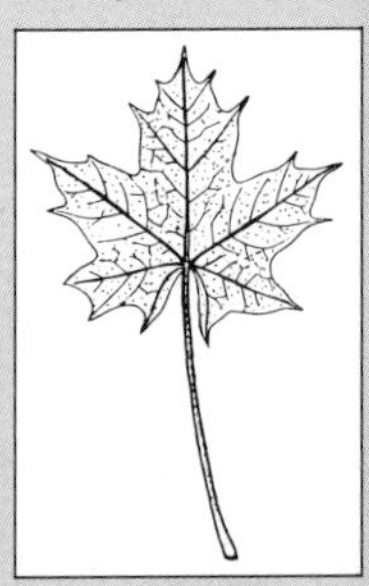

37

Schematic

38

Acer pseudoplatanus
Sycamore
(under side)

Veins unequally pinnate

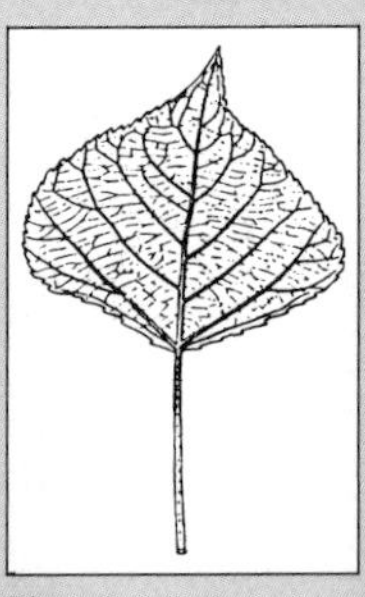

39

Schematic

40

Populus x canadensis
Hybrid Black Poplar
(under side)

Digitate or palmate venation represents a modification of pinnate venation. It occurs when several prominent lateral veins radiate from the base of the leaf-blade like the fingers of a hand (Fig. 37, 38).

1.2.4. Margin of the leaf-blade (leaf-margin)

The margin of the leaf (or leaflet in the case of compound leaves) may be entire or it may be indented in various ways as follows (Fig. 41–56):

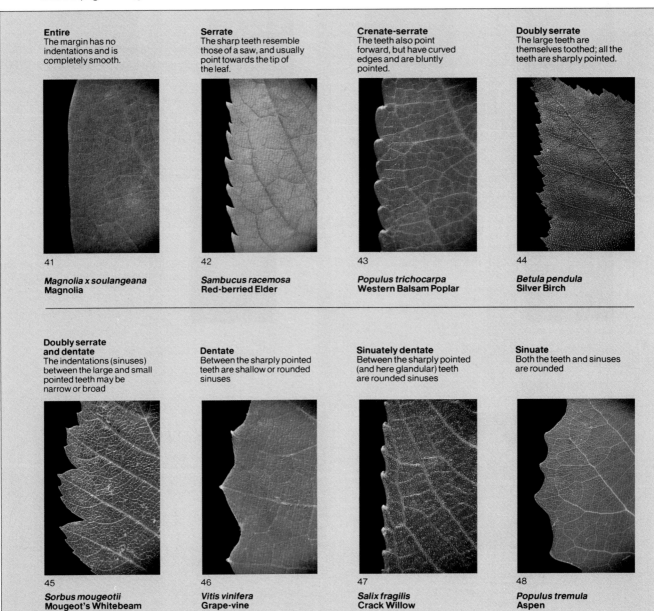

Entire
The margin has no indentations and is completely smooth.

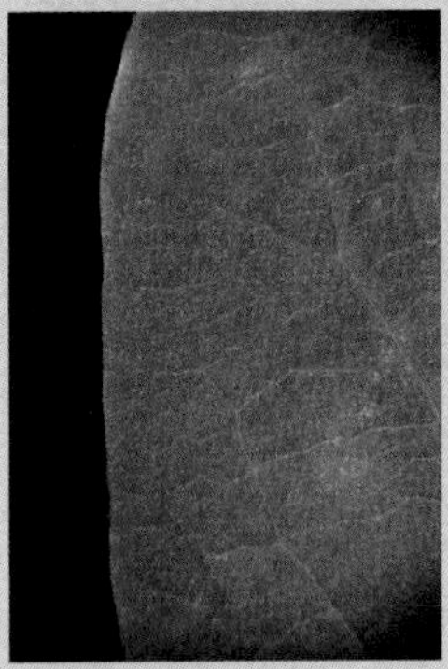

41

Magnolia x soulangeana
Magnolia

Serrate
The sharp teeth resemble those of a saw, and usually point towards the tip of the leaf.

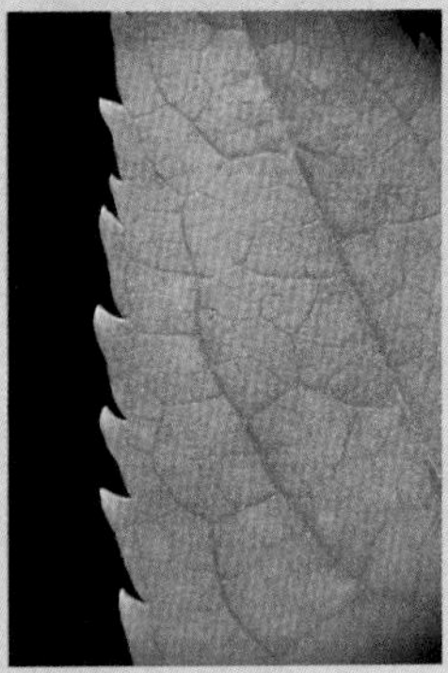

42

Sambucus racemosa
Red-berried Elder

Crenate-serrate
The teeth also point forward, but have curved edges and are bluntly pointed.

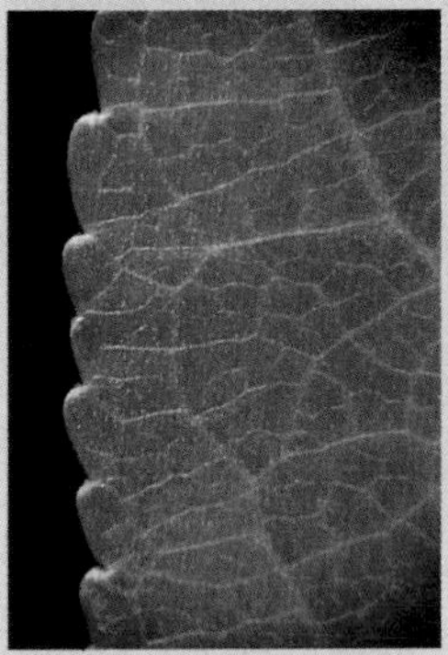

43

Populus trichocarpa
Western Balsam Poplar

Doubly serrate
The large teeth are themselves toothed; all the teeth are sharply pointed.

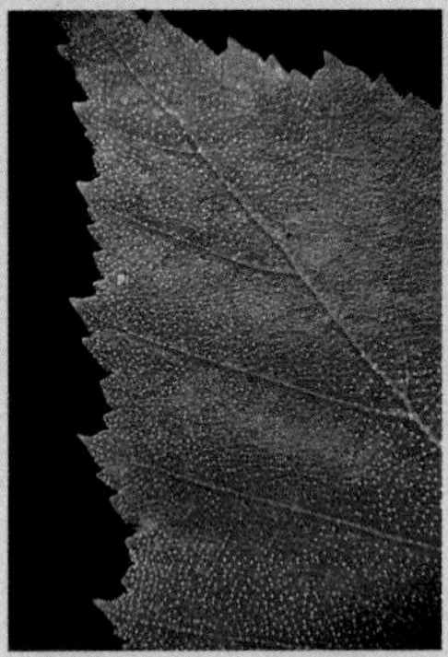

44

Betula pendula
Silver Birch

Doubly serrate and dentate
The indentations (sinuses) between the large and small pointed teeth may be narrow or broad

45

Sorbus mougeotii
Mougeot's Whitebeam

Dentate
Between the sharply pointed teeth are shallow or rounded sinuses

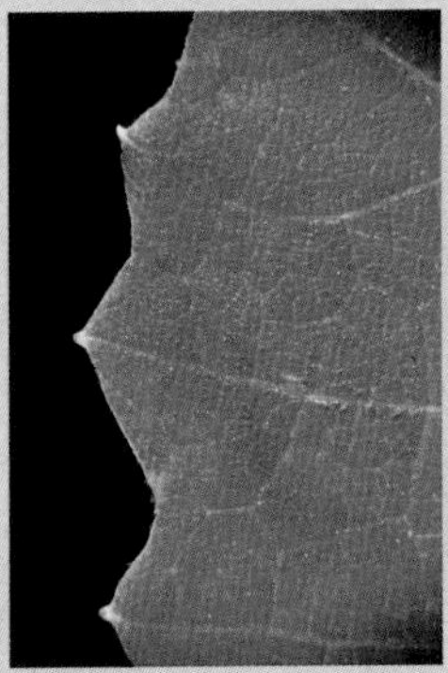

46

Vitis vinifera
Grape-vine

Sinuately dentate
Between the sharply pointed (and here glandular) teeth are rounded sinuses

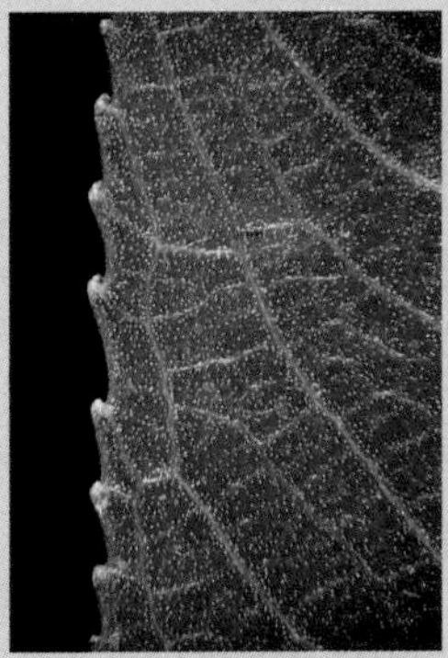

47

Salix fragilis
Crack Willow

Sinuate
Both the teeth and sinuses are rounded

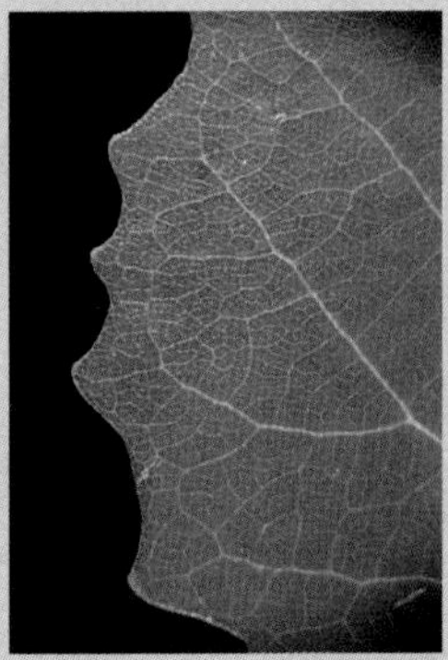

48

Populus tremula
Aspen

Bristle-toothed
Long-pointed teeth with rounded sinuses in between

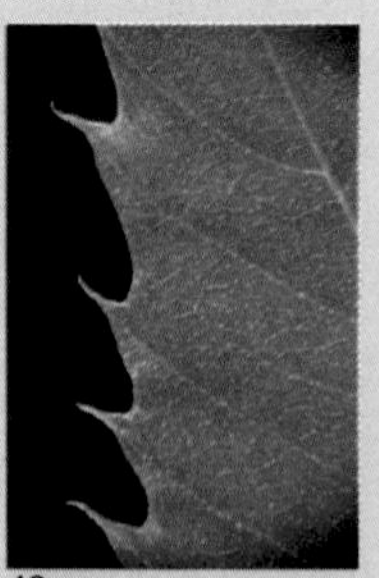

49

Castanea sativa
Sweet Chestnut

Spring-toothed
Sharp, spiny teeth with rounded sinuses of varying size between them

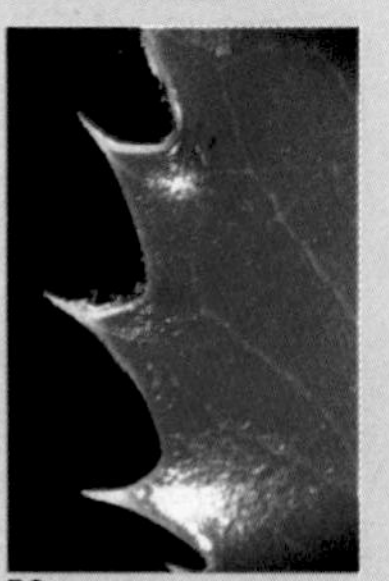

50

Ilex aquifolium
Holly *(young leaf)*

Undulate
Margin in the form of a wavy line

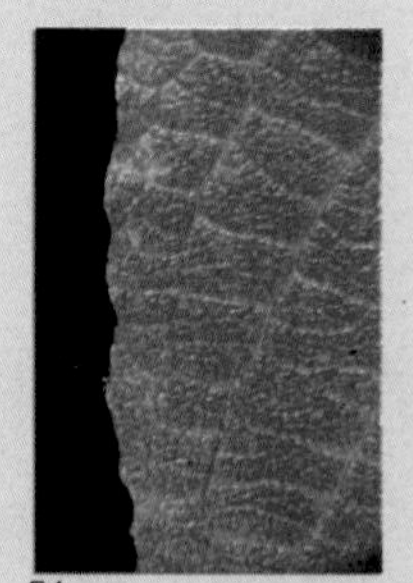

51

Salix caprea
Goat Willow

Crenate
Rounded teeth separated by narrow sinuses

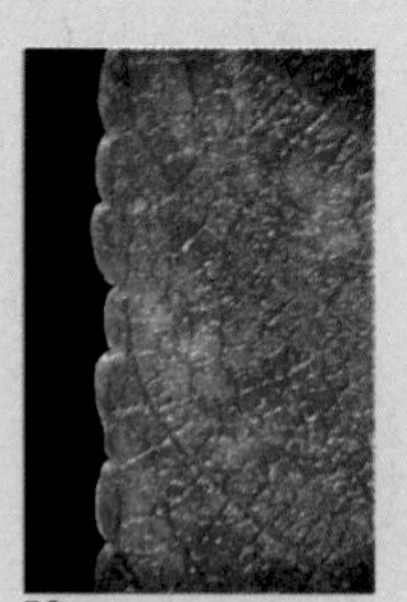

52

Rhamnus alpinus
Alpine Buckthorn

Ciliate
Margin fringed with hairs to a greater or lesser extent

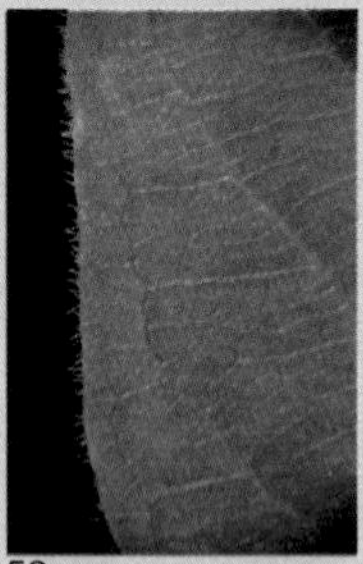

53

Lonicera alpigena
Alpine Honeysuckle

Lobed
The leaf-blades are deeply cut into lobes, which may themselves be sharply or bluntly pointed or rounded

54

Acer platanoides
Norway Maple

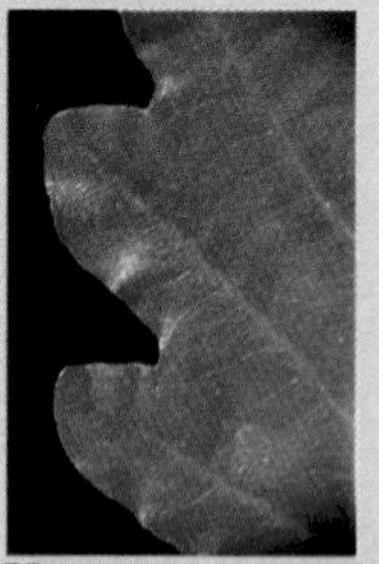

55

Quercus pubescens
Downy Oak

Recurved
Margin of leaf-blade curled under

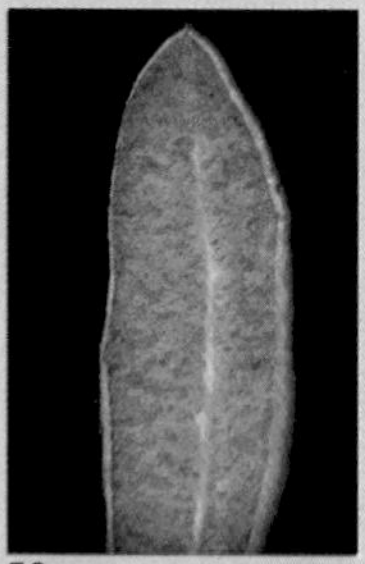

56

Ledum palustre
Marsh Ledum

1.2.5. Apex of blade (= tip of leaf)

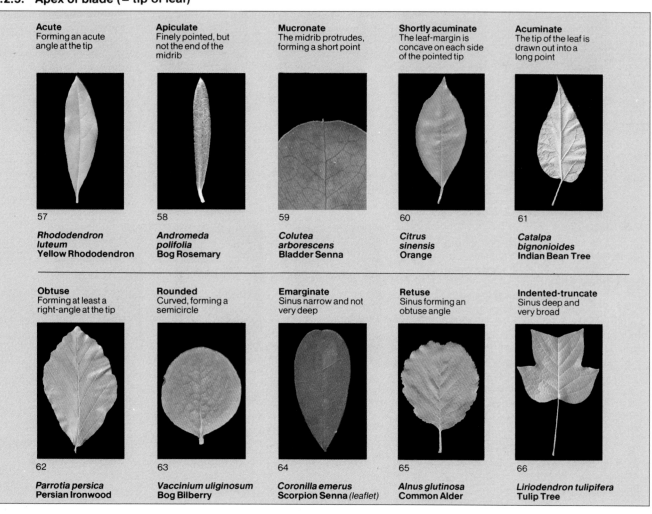

Acute
Forming an acute angle at the tip

57

Rhododendron luteum
Yellow Rhododendron

Apiculate
Finely pointed, but not the end of the midrib

58

Andromeda polifolia
Bog Rosemary

Mucronate
The midrib protrudes, forming a short point

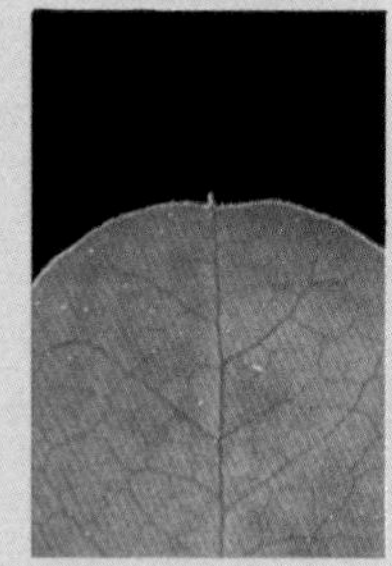

59

Colutea arborescens
Bladder Senna

Shortly acuminate
The leaf-margin is concave on each side of the pointed tip

60

Citrus sinensis
Orange

Acuminate
The tip of the leaf is drawn out into a long point

61

Catalpa bignonioides
Indian Bean Tree

Obtuse
Forming at least a right-angle at the tip

62

Parrotia persica
Persian Ironwood

Rounded
Curved, forming a semicircle

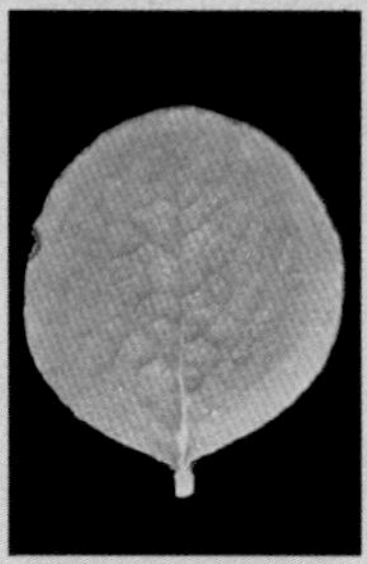

63

Vaccinium uliginosum
Bog Bilberry

Emarginate
Sinus narrow and not very deep

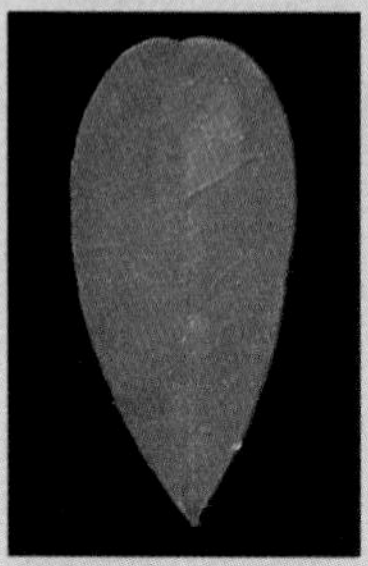

64

Coronilla emerus
Scorpion Senna *(leaflet)*

Retuse
Sinus forming an obtuse angle

65

Alnus glutinosa
Common Alder

Indented-truncate
Sinus deep and very broad

66

Liriodendron tulipifera
Tulip Tree

1.2.6. Base of blade

In stalked leaves the base of the blade is immediately above the leaf-stalk. In sessile leaves it forms the lower end of the leaf and is joined directly to the shoot. It can be formed in the following ways (Fig. 67–76):

Cuneate (wedge-shaped)
Leaf-margins straight, forming an acute angle at the base

67

Prunus domestica
Plum

Obtuse
Leaf-margins forming a right angle or an obtuse angle at the base

68

Populus nigra* var. *italica
Lombardy Poplar

Truncate
Appearing as if cut off at right-angles to the midrib

69

Populus alba
White Poplar

Rounded
Leaf-margins of the 2 halves of the blade forming a semicircle

70

Prunus lusitanica
Portugal Laurel

Asymmetrical
The 2 halves of the blade unequal in size

71

Ulmus laevis
Fluttering Elm

Oblique
One side of the blade extends further down than the other, though both are about the same size

72

Tilia cordata
Small-leaved Lime

Heart-shaped
Semicircular at the base with a deep sinus

73

Tilia cordata
Small-leaved Lime

Auriculate
Each half of the blade is extended at the base into a small lobe

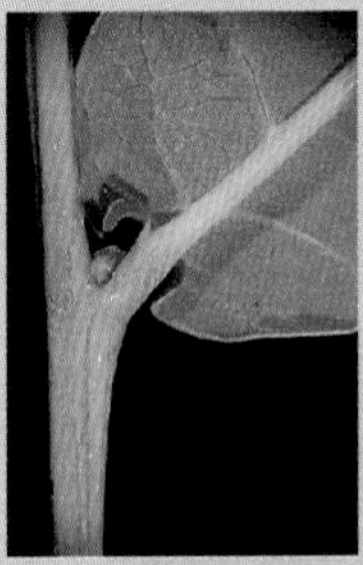

74

Quercus robur
Common Oak

Connate
The leaves lying opposite each other are joined together

75

Lonicera caprifolium
Perfoliate Honeysuckle

Decurrent
(in needles)
The lower part of the leaf is prolonged down the shoot

76

Taxus baccata
Yew

1.2.7. Leaf-stalk (petiole)

Between the leaf-base and the blade is the leaf-stalk, a cross-section of which may be circular or laterally compressed. It may sometimes also be grooved. If its formation is suppressed the leaves are described as sessile.

1.2.8. Leaf-base

The leaf-base is the part of the leaf that is joined to the shoot. In sessile leaves it is the base of the blade, while in stalked leaves it is the lower part of the leaf-stalk.
In many species of plants the leaf-base is not clearly distinguished from the leaf-stalk. There may be only a slight broadening at the base (Fig. 77) or even none at all. By contrast, plants in the Rosaceae and other families develop large stipules which last throughout the entire life of the leaves (Fig. 78). In the case of the Hornbeam, Hazel, Lime, Poplar, amongst others, they quickly fall and are therefore of no use as a character in identification. In the Robinia the stipules are converted into spines (Fig. 79).

77

Lonicera caerulea
Blue Honeysuckle

78

Rosa canina
Dog Rose

79

Robinia pseudoacacia
False Acacia

1.2.9. Hairiness of leaves

Both shoots and leaves may be hairy. They may be described as sparsely hairy, slightly hairy, densely hairy, silky, felted, or woolly according to the degree of hairiness. Often only certain parts of an organ have hairs, as for example the veins of a leaf, the axils of the veins (axillary tufts) or one of the surfaces. It is not uncommon for these hairs to disappear during the growth period.

1.2.10. Form of leaves

Leaves may be classified as simple (undivided) or compound (Fig. 80–92):

Simple leaves

The leaf-stalk bears only a single blade. If it is absent, the base of the blade is joined directly on to the shoot. The following forms can be distinguished according to the depth of the sinuses between the lobes:

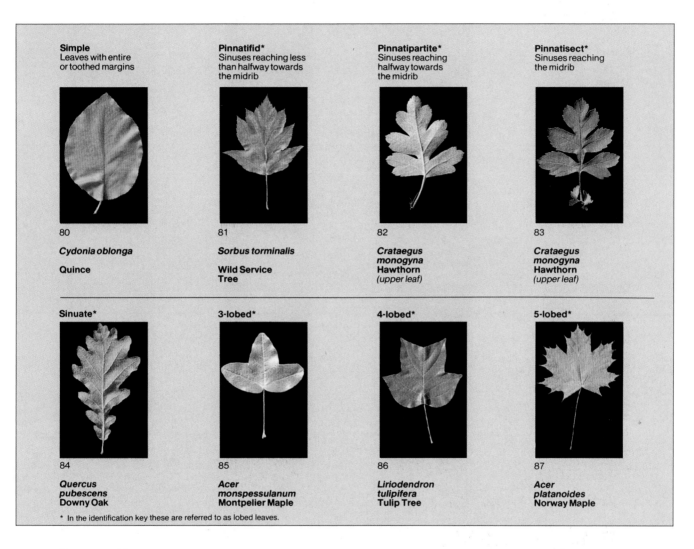

Simple
Leaves with entire or toothed margins

80

Cydonia oblonga

Quince

Pinnatifid*
Sinuses reaching less than halfway towards the midrib

81

Sorbus torminalis

Wild Service Tree

Pinnatipartite*
Sinuses reaching halfway towards the midrib

82

Crataegus monogyna
Hawthorn
(upper leaf)

Pinnatisect*
Sinuses reaching the midrib

83

Crataegus monogyna
Hawthorn
(upper leaf)

Sinuate*

84

Quercus pubescens
Downy Oak

3-lobed*

85

Acer monspessulanum
Montpelier Maple

4-lobed*

86

Liriodendron tulipifera
Tulip Tree

5-lobed*

87

Acer platanoides
Norway Maple

* In the identification key these are referred to as lobed leaves.

Compound Leaves:

Each leaf is composed of 2 or more blades (leaflets) attached to a common axis – the leaf-stalk:

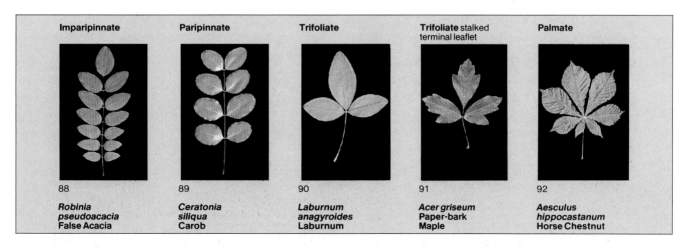

Imparipinnate

88

Robinia pseudoacacia
False Acacia

Paripinnate

89

Ceratonia siliqua
Carob

Trifoliate

90

Laburnum anagyroides
Laburnum

Trifoliate stalked terminal leaflet

91

Acer griseum
Paper-bark Maple

Palmate

92

Aesculus hippocastanum
Horse Chestnut

1.2.11. Heterophylly

In certain trees and shrubs leaves on the same plant may have a different shape according to their position on the shoot. If the leaves at the same level are different in size, the condition is known as anisophylly (Fig. 93–100):

Example 1: Sycamore

Cotyledons, juvenile and adult leaves show a difference in shape.

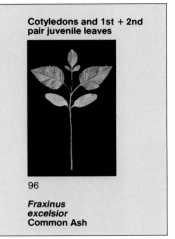

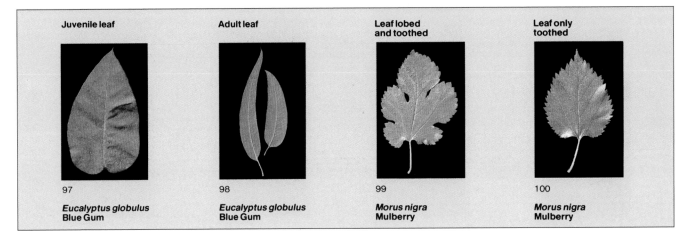

Cotyledons and 1st pair of juvenile leaves

93

Acer pseudoplatanus
Sycamore

1st and 2nd pair of juvenile leaves

94

Acer pseudoplatanus
Sycamore

Adult leaf

95

Acer pseudoplatanus
Sycamore

Example 2: Common Ash

Cotyledons and 1st + 2nd pair juvenile leaves

96

Fraxinus excelsior
Common Ash

Example 3: Blue Gum

The juvenile leaves are very different from the adult leaves.

Example 4: Mulberry

Adult leaves can show considerable variation in the shape of the leaf-blade.

Juvenile leaf

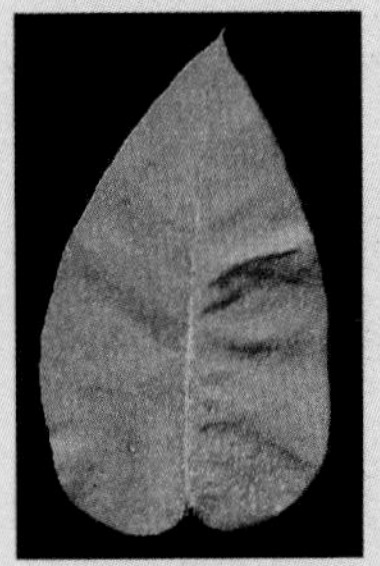

97

Eucalyptus globulus
Blue Gum

Adult leaf

98

Eucalyptus globulus
Blue Gum

Leaf lobed and toothed

99

Morus nigra
Mulberry

Leaf only toothed

100

Morus nigra
Mulberry

1.3. Arrangement of leaves on the shoot

Leaves may be arranged on the shoot in the following ways (Fig. 101–112):

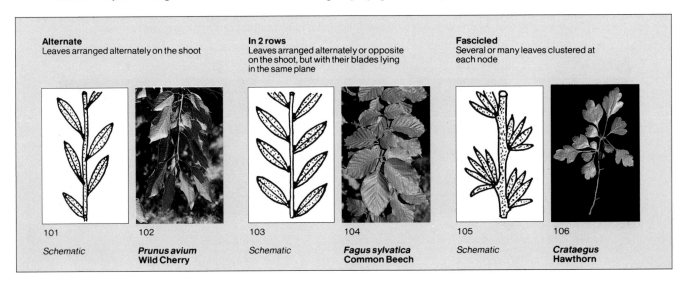

Alternate
Leaves arranged alternately on the shoot

101

Schematic

102

Prunus avium
Wild Cherry

In 2 rows
Leaves arranged alternately or opposite on the shoot, but with their blades lying in the same plane

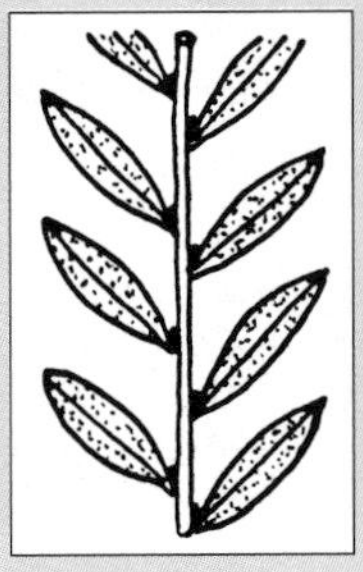

103

Schematic

104

Fagus sylvatica
Common Beech

Fascicled
Several or many leaves clustered at each node

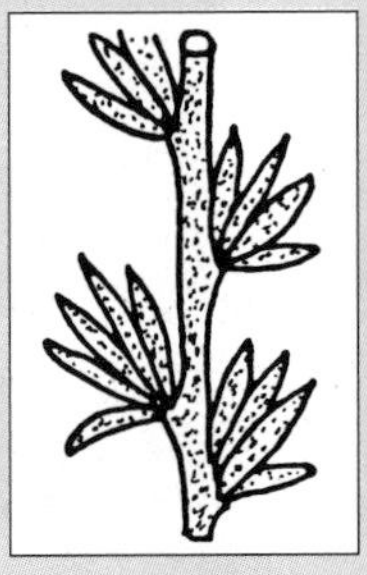

105

Schematic

106

Crataegus
Hawthorn

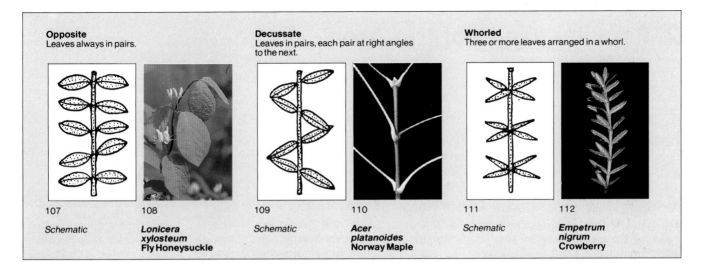

Opposite
Leaves always in pairs.

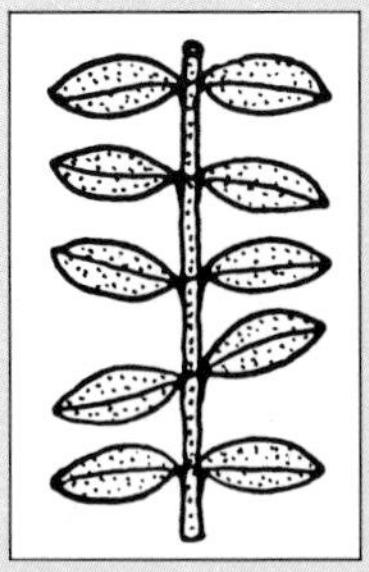

107

Schematic

108

Lonicera xylosteum
Fly Honeysuckle

Decussate
Leaves in pairs, each pair at right angles to the next.

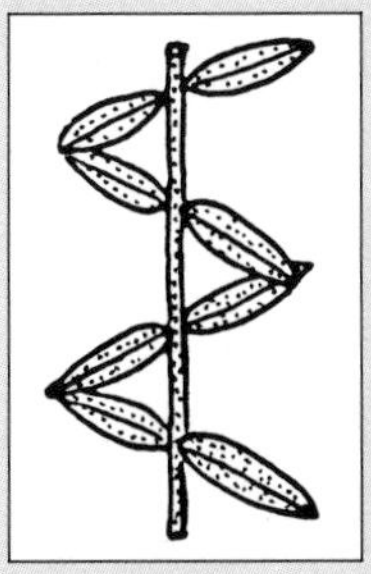

109

Schematic

110

Acer platanoides
Norway Maple

Whorled
Three or more leaves arranged in a whorl.

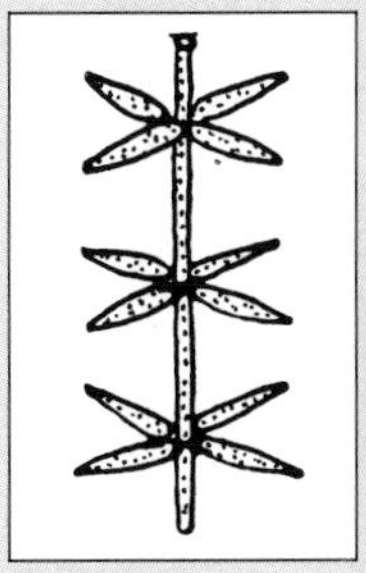

111

Schematic

112

Empetrum nigrum
Crowberry

1.4. Structure of needle-like leaves

Leaves of conifers differ considerably in their external and internal structure from those of deciduous trees. In addition to flat leaves with an upper and an under side, there are needles which are triangular, square or circular in cross-section. Most needles are evergreen, stout, and xeromorphic. Some exceptions with deciduous needles mentioned in this book are Larches, Swamp Cypress and Dawn Redwood.
The scale-like or needle-like leaves may be in a spiral, opposite, whorled or imbricate (overlapping) arrangement.

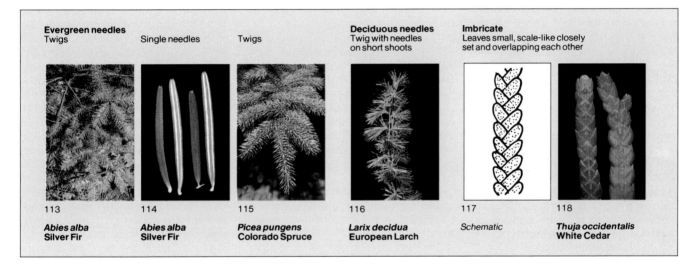

Evergreen needles
Twigs

113

Abies alba
Silver Fir

Single needles

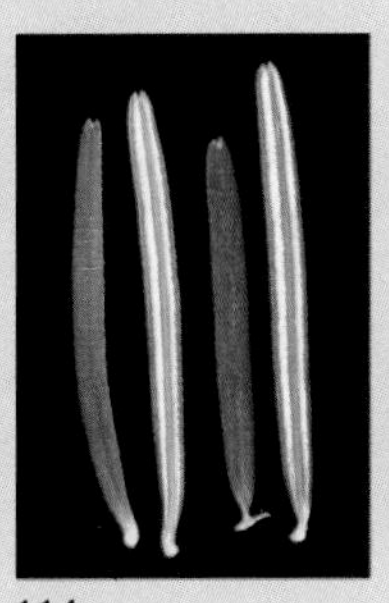

114

Abies alba
Silver Fir

Twigs

115

Picea pungens
Colorado Spruce

Deciduous needles
Twig with needles on short shoots

116

Larix decidua
European Larch

Imbricate
Leaves small, scale-like closely set and overlapping each other

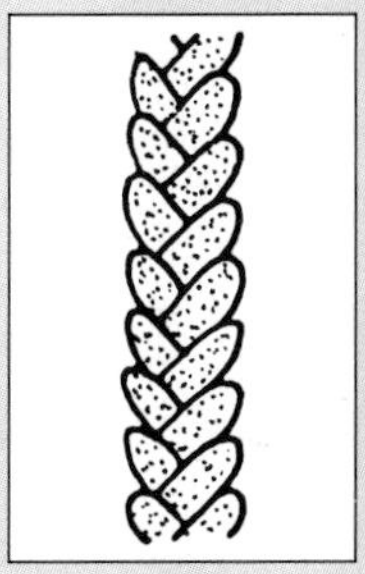

117

Schematic

118

Thuja occidentalis
White Cedar

1.5. Fan-shaped leaves with forked veins

The Maidenhair Tree (Fig. 119–122) is the sole surviving representative of the genus *Ginkgo*, which appeared in an abundance of forms from the Triassic to the Cretaceous period and had a world-wide distribution. It was cultivated in China and Japan, and in this way was protected from extinction. Nowadays it is planted throughout the world in gardens and parks. From a seedling with two cotyledons the Ginkgo grows into a branched, deciduous tree up to 40m high.

119

Leaves
Schematic

120

Single leaf

121

Leaves on long shoots

122

Leaves on short shoots

2. Familiar Trees of the Area

Norway Maple

Acer platanoides L.

Erable plane
Spitzahorn

Pages 85, 150, 151

The Norway Maple is a medium-sized tree, growing to a height of 20–30m. Its trunk is slim and straight, with a diameter of 1m. Its crown is domed, densely leaved, and, in the case of free-standing trees, becomes increasingly spherical with age. Its growth is very similar to that of the oak, but its twigs are glabrous, shiny brown, thinner and attenuate and, when damaged, emit a white, milky juice. This juice is only soluble in ether or pure alcohol, is highly acidic, and is easily dyed. It grows much more rapidly than the Sycamore Maple (Scots Plane), but does not reach such a great height. Even at their oldest (and the Norway Maple may live for up to 200 years), the two species of maple are easily distinguishable.

Inside the brown-black, longitudinally cracked, non-scaly bark, which is sometimes used for tanning, is to be found a yellow to pinky white, fairly hard, elastic, resistant, finely grained, sticky, easily split wood, which will preserve well only under dry conditions. One cubic metre of seasoned, chopped wood weighs 500–650kg. Because it has a marked tendency to snap and warp, it should be dried with particular care. There is also a risk, as with all other woods, of fading. It is easily and securely held together by glue, nails and pins, and is generally held to be a good joinery timber.

It is only durable, however, if kept dry. As it is not inclined to contract or warp, it is very suitable for making veneers for knives, light-coloured living room and bedroom furniture, chairs, tables, kitchen utensils, table tops and musical instruments. It sharpens well to a point, so can be used for skewers, but it in inferior to the wood of the Sycamore, which is preferred for all kitchen tools used for food.

Its buds are usually dark red to reddish brown, and smooth. Many-flowered panicles appear in April or May, a few days before, or at the same time as the leaves unfurl. The flowers may be male, female, or hybrid. All flowers have five independent greenish yellow sepals, 3–5mm in length, and five greenish yellow, roughly ovate, independent petals, 5–6mm in length. All eight anthers are smaller than the petals and lie on the outer edge of the disc.

The ovary consists of two fused carpels and develops into a schizocarp with two separate achene. The achene are flat, about 4cm long, each with very slightly curved husks, projecting more or less horizontally. They are glabrous on the inside and heavily veined.

The trees only begin to flower after 15–20 years. The Norway Maple is an excellent source of food for the Honey Bee, as it yields large quantities of flower and leaf honey.

At the end of the stalk, which may be up to 15cm long, lies the blade, which is 10–20cm long, and the same again wide. It is orbicular, reniform, or broadly ovate in outline, with 3–5, or 7 dentate lobes.

In contrast to the dark green glabrous superior surface, the inferior surface is pale green, with tufts of hair at the vein axils.

The leaves are golden yellow to scarlet in autumn and are arranged in opposing pairs along the branch.

The Norway Maple favours deep, wet to damp, calcareous soil, and thrives in humid conditions. It is, however, less demanding of light, warmth and nutrients than the Sycamore Maple. It is also less susceptible to the risks posed by long-term flooding.

It is at its best when growing not alongside the Sycamore Maple but amongst mixed lime woodland, where oaks, limes and elms predominate. Today such woods are to be found in only a few places, for example in the mountains of Southern France and in Alpine valleys, such as the Rhone. It predominates only occasionally, in patches, in the Turinmeister mixed lime woodland. Otherwise it is found interspersed amongst beech woods. It is dispersed throughout most of Europe, from the mountains of Northern Spain and the Pyrenees, through France, southern Belgium, Germany, Denmark, Norway, Sweden, Central Finland, spreading eastwards right up to the Urals. The species has been planted in the USA.

The Norway Maple was introduced to Britain in the seventeenth century. The first reference to it is in the list made in 1683 by Sutherland of plants he had moved from Holyrood Palace to reform the Royal Botanic Garden of Edinburgh. It is likely that at the time this list was compiled, Sutherland's tree was already some 20 years old.

This species is indigenous to hilly and mountainous regions. However, it has been planted very widely throughout the British Isles in gardens and parks, and also occasionally in shelterbelts and small woods – rarely as a forest tree. It has been freely used in the Salisbury Plain chalklands for landscaping and sheltering purposes. It grows equally well in the high rainfall areas of western Scotland and in the dry East Anglian brecklands. In fact, few large gardens or city parks are without it.

Thanks to its modest requirement of light, and its ability to put out shoots, it is well suited to existence within, as well as on the edge of mixed woodland of European Ash and Sycamore Maple. The rapid decomposition of its leaves encourages biological activity.

According to folklore, the maple offers protection against witches. For this reason, in Hinterpommern, it is the custom to decorate doors and inner walls with maple wood. In Mecklenberg, plugs of maple wood were driven into walls and doorsteps as a safeguard against witches.

123 Norway Maple in spring

124 Erect, many-flowered panicles

125 Male flowers, with 5 sepals and petals, 8 anthers and a disc

126 Cross-section through a male flower

127 Norway Maple in summer

128 10–20cm long, lobed leaves, arranged in opposing pairs

129 Superior leaf surface, dark green and glabrous

130 Inferior leaf surface, pale green at first, with tufts of hair in vein axils

131 Norway Maple in autumn

132 Fruit clusters

133 Schizocarp with two separate achenes

134 Whitish, often slightly pinkish, elastic, resistant wood

135 Norway Maple in winter

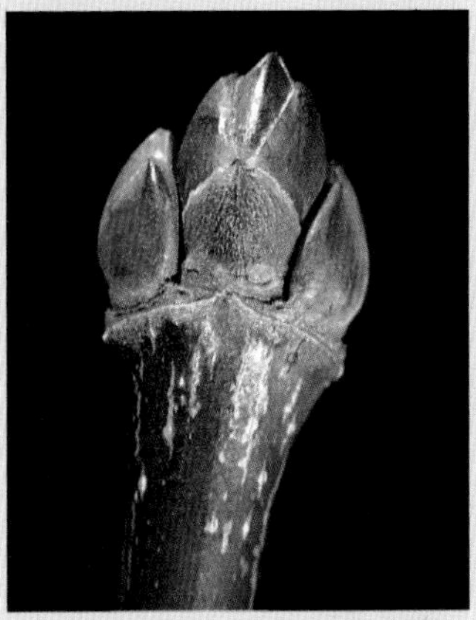

136 Broad-ovoid, pointed, terminal buds dominating the side buds

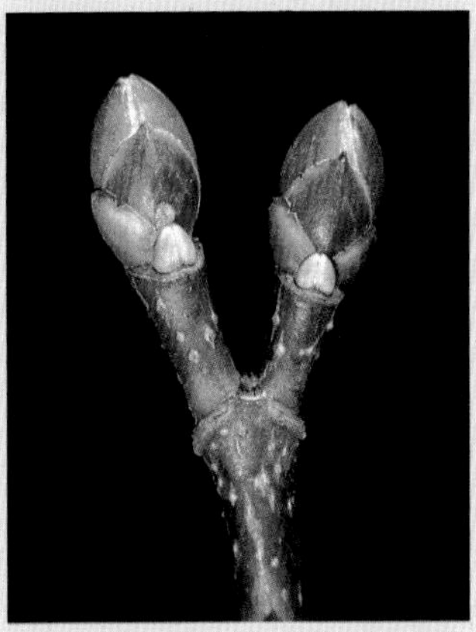

137 Narrow-ovoid, lateral, wine-red, terminal buds

138 Straight, cylinder-shaped trunk with longtitudinally cracked, dark brown bark

Sycamore

Acer pseudoplatanus L.

Erable de montagne, Erable sycomore
Berg Ahorn

Pages 87, 154, 155

In pastureland at alpine and sub-alpine levels, where the ground is wet to slightly damp, and rich in nutrients, the Sycamore develops a huge crown, which broadens out with age. In woodlands, where it grows more upwards than outwards, its slim, straight trunk bears its first branches quite a long way up its length. In mixed woodland, together with the Mountain Ash, it reaches a maximum height of 40m.

This species of maple, which, together with the Norway Spruce and the Mountain Ash, frequently occurs on the edges of a wood, is usually planted in the hill zone. They are also found in avenues, parks and forests.

The Sycamore spreads rapidly on fertile, damp soils and its seedlings arise in dense masses, soon shading out shrubs and flowers in woodland. It is extraordinarily robust in conditions too severe for most trees. It dominates in central parks of industrial cities because it could prosper when sooty fogs were frequent. It is planted for shelter on high, exposed farmlands on chalk and limestone hills and succeeds there better than any other broadleaf tree. Although its natural range is nowhere near the sea, it stands up against the salty sea-winds along our west coasts where all native trees are deformed and low.

The bark, which, on young trees, is light brown, later develops flat plates, which tend to taper at the bottom. When they eventually drop away, they expose fairly smooth indentations of reddish brown colour. As a result of this process, the trunk become multi-coloured. The trunk of an old tree will have developed a very patchy, light and dark brown patterned bark. The maximum age of a Sycamore is around 500 years. The Sycamore can yield a naturally white, top-quality wood. In order to achieve this, the bark must be removed shortly after the winter felling and the wood immediately sawn up. Immediately after this the planks are brushed clean of sawdust and stacked upright. As a result of the air movement through them the wood is evenly and gently dried. If it is necessary for the wood to be dried artificially, this should be done as soon as possible, to avoid splitting and discolouration.

Sycamore wood is thick, shiny, has no colouration, contracting only slightly, dries extremely well, and, if it is done carefully, to a dazzling white shade. One cubic metre of cut, naturally dried wood weighs 650–750kg.

It is easy to work, polish, carve, and particularly to stain. Thanks to these excellent properties it is highly valued for making furniture and veneers. Kitchen equipment, billiard cases, table tops, parquet floors and parts for musical instruments are made from this wood. In its peculiarly gnarled form, as so-called tone- or resonance wood, it is much beloved of violin makers.

The timber itself has little resistance to weather conditions. For this reason it is not very suitable as a building material. Its light-coloured medullary rays appear in cross-section as bright, shiny lines and lengthways as dark patches or stripes. The timber was used for the rollers in wool mills and grown for this purpose in Yorkshire.

Shortly before the tree blossoms, out of large, green, opposite buds, emerge the five-lobed leaves. In summer they grow up to 15–30cm long and 10–16cm across. The individual lobes are coarsely dentate, or notched, each separated from the next by a pointed sinus. In autumn they turn a golden yellow colour.

Once the leaves have appeared, dangling, grape-shaped racemes, 5–15cm long, emerge out of the many separate buds.

The five or so petals and sepals are 2–6mm long. Each of them is independent, and is at first hairy on the inner surface and glabrous on the outer. Around the inside edge of the receptacle lie 8 stamens, which can be up to 2 or 3 times the length of the petals. The superior ovary is covered with long hairs and consists of 2 fused carpels. Once flowering has finished they form two small bumps, which, during the development of the fruit, grow into large seed-wings.

The fruits – schizocarps, each with two separate achenes – are constructed in such a way that when they fall they spin earthwards with a sort of propeller-like flight. This increases the time it takes for them to reach the ground, and depending on the air currents which take them up, they are often carried quite some distance from the parent tree.

The Trojan horse (Troy: the town celebrated by Homer on the north-west point of Asia Minor) was fashioned out of maple, although not out of Sycamore Maple. The story goes that Epios, on the advice of Odysseus, and with the aid of the goddess Athena, built a wooden horse. Inside the horse the Greeks hid a troop of hand-picked heroes. The enormous wooden beast was then left standing outside the gates of Troy and the army sailed away. Heedless of the warnings of Laakoon and Cassandra, the Trojans tore down a portion of the walls and brought the horse inside the city. Typically for that age, they were convinced that this animal, being visible for miles around, would make their city sovereign over all of Asia Minor and Europe.

Under cover of night, the Greek army returned. The heroes emerged from the horse and after a short battle the town which hitherto had been unconquerable was completely destroyed.

The strong and powerful wood was greatly prized not only in the heathen age, but also by Christians in the Middle Ages. If a large tree was to be felled, it was done so bare-headed and on bended knee with votive offerings and invocations.

In certain parts of Europe the Sycamore is considered a safeguard against evil spirits. Plugs of maple wood, driven into walls and doorsteps, will ward off witches. To the same end, branches of Sycamore are piled up against doors and windows. This is also thought to act as a safeguard against lightning.

In Scotland, the Sycamore was occasionally used as the 'Dool Tree', the tree from which those unfortunates who fell foul of the laird were hanged. This would be a large tree with branches suitable for the task, and near the castle. One such tree still stands at Blairquhan in Ayrshire.

The celebrated Martyrs' Tree at Tolpuddle is a Sycamore, measuring 18m by 183cm. To this day the cost of maintaining it is met by the Trade Union Congress.

This species was unable to spread to England after the Ice Ages because it did not grow on the lowlands near the French end of the land-bridge. It has been suggested that it was brought by the Romans, but this is rather unlikely. The first trees were probably planted in Scotland after 1500. One near Edinburgh is reputed to date from the Reformation, which spanned many years around 1550.

139 Sycamore in spring

140 Dangling racemes with male and female flowers

141 Older bisexual flowers with young schizocarp; wilting stigmae

142 Older bisexual flowers with young schizocarp; stigmae and styles no longer present

143 Sycamore in summer

144 8–20cm long, lobed leaves, arranged in opposite pairs

145 Superior leaf surface, dark green and glabrous

146 Inferior leaf surface, bluish green, villous at first, later glabrous

147 Sycamore in autumn

148 Fruit clusters

149 Schizocarp with two separate achenes

150 Well-treated wood, dazzling white, compact, hard

151 Sycamore in winter

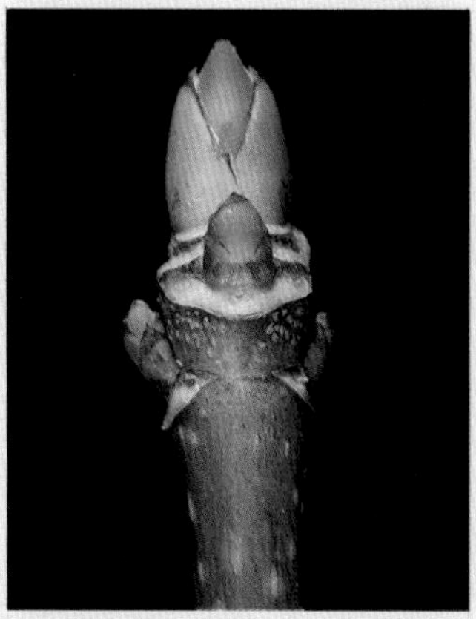
152 Newly formed stigma on pointed-ovoid terminal bud dominating side buds

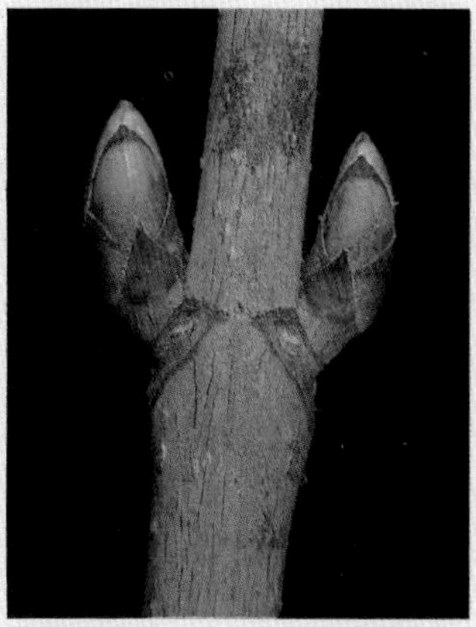
153 Pointed-ovoid, often projecting yellow-green to green side buds

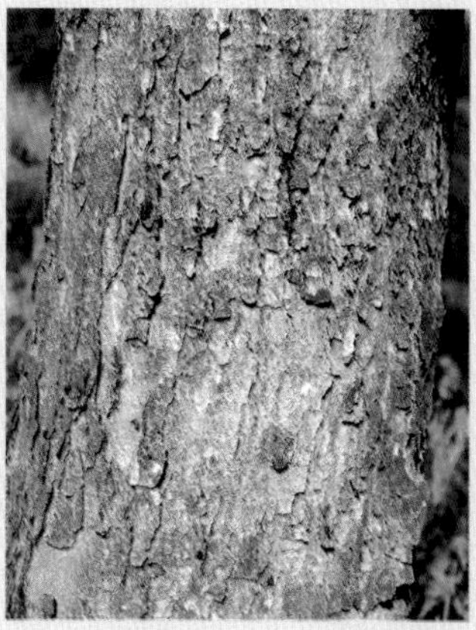
154 Crumbly grey bark flaking away; bare patches usually brown

Horse Chestnut

Aesculus hippocastanum L.

Marronier d'Inde
Gemeine Rosskastanie

Pages 81, 144, 145

The Horse Chestnut grows to a maximum height of 30–35m. Its trunk is usually short, strong, woody and always has a spiral grain to the right. Its crown is broad and dome shaped, with gnarled branches and abundant foliage. Its thick leaf coverage affords a good deal of shade.

It is grown throughout the British Isles and has long been the traditional tree of village greens and rectory gardens. It occurs at woodland edges only near habitation from which it has escaped. It is frequent as a large specimen in grazed parklands and in avenues there, as well as in town and city parks. It grows equally well in all parts given good soil. Some of the biggest and finest trees are: Hurstbourne Priors Church, Hants., 36m × 213cm; West Dean House, Sussex, 26m × 197cm; The Rectory, Much Hadham, Herts., 37m × 181cm; Castle Ashby, Northants., planted 1762, 31m × 171cm, with widely layered branches; Preston House, Midlothian, 26m × 186cm; and Grays House, Dundee, 36m × 140cm.

The bark of the young tree is light grey or greyish brown and smooth. Later this turns to dark grey bark, with coarse, cracked plates. The new, young shoots are very strong, almost a finger thick, very long, light brownish in colour, with pale lenticels.

The underlying wood is nothing if not colourful – whitish yellow to pale pink, fine, soft, supple, easily chopped, with a dull sheen. One cubic metre of seasoned wood weighs 500–600kg. It is easy to handle, to carve, and chisel. Since it stains easily, it should be dried very soon after felling. Once dry, it warps and distorts very little, and is therefore excellent for making furniture. It is used for carving, and for making clogs, kitchen equipment, toys and pianos.

In April or May, palmate leaves, which will eventually grow to 10–30cm in length, emerge from very sticky, shiny red-brown buds. The stalks are long and grooved. The 5–7 leaflets are long-obovate, being at their widest in the outer third, abruptly acuminate, 8–20cm long, and irregularly serrate.

Once the bud-scales have fallen off, the erect, many-flowered panicles start to grow. They reach a length of up to 30cm and a width of 8–12cm and produce mostly bi-sexual flowers. The bell-shaped calyx has 5 lobes. The white, ovate petals, of which there are usually 4 or 5, are 10–15mm long, and curl back at the edges.

The nectaries are found in the heart-shaped base. They are yellow to begin with, turning red after pollination by the bee. The superior ovary consists of two fused carpels.

Once the stigma has been pollinated by insects and the ovules fertilised, the fruit capsules appear, each up to 6cm thick, with flexible spines. Inside the green husk lie 1–3 shiny, brownish red horse chestnuts.

The outer rind contains *saponin*, the fluorescing glucoid aesculin, tannic acid, resin, fatty oil and starch. Aesculin is able to intercept ultra-violet rays and is therefore used in sun-shields for the skin. The chestnuts themselves contain a large amount of starch, fatty oil and, above all, *saponin*.

The extract from chestnut bark strengthens the veins and accelerates the blood flow, thus preventing blood-blockages. The use of this extract is also advocated for the treatment of varicose veins (blood blockages, haemorrhoids, abscesses on the tibia). Before the Ice Age, the Horse Chestnut was indigenous throughout central Europe, and, retreating in the face of the ice, found its only refuge in a very small area of the Balkan peninsula.

The area of main concentration is centred around southern Albania, northern and central Greece, either side of the Pindus Mountains, where it is found in the lower pine zone, as well as in the mixed deciduous woodland of Epitus and at sea level.

In this region it is found together with the Common Alder, the Common Walnut, the European Ash and the Norway Maple, all trees which prefer damp soil.

A second, but important area of distribution is in Northern Bulgaria, on the north side of the Little Balkan, to the south of the town of Preslav. Whereas most Greek locations are in mountainous areas, the Bulgarian *refugium* is distinctly lower lying. Where at first the Horse Chestnut occurred only in isolated patches in wild-flower and mixed-woodland habitats above 380m, it is now dominant here, although it nevertheless abruptly yields to the Common Beech at 500m. In spite of the dense leaf canopy, there is still a good deal of undergrowth and a varied herbaceous layer.

Two main factors militated against a return to the original areas of indigenous growth. Firstly, the weight of the fruit, and secondly the extensive dry regions lying between the tree's refuge areas and central Europe, in which the Horse Chestnut is unable to compete with other species.

In 1557 the Turks introduced the Horse Chestnut to Constantinople. In 1569 it reached Italy, 1625, France and 1629, England. It did not arrive in America until the mid-nineteenth century. Many people take exception to its abundant shedding of leaves and fruit in the autumn. But what a delight it is for children to go collecting conkers. This alone should provide sufficient reason for planting the Horse Chestnut. When it is planted on the edge of a wood, though, it needs the protection of the forester as the Red Deer uses it to scratch against and the stag for rubbing the velvet from its antlers.

155 Horse Chestnut in spring

156 20–30cm long racemes, erect or projecting at an angle

157 Individual racemes; nectary yellow at first, red later

158 Two flowers; flowers often become monosexual as they mature

159 Horse Chestnut in summer

160 Leaves 10–30cm long, with 5 or 7 leaflets

161 Superior leaf surface, dark green and glabrous

162 Inferior leaf surface, pale bluish green at first, with brownish tufts in the vein axils

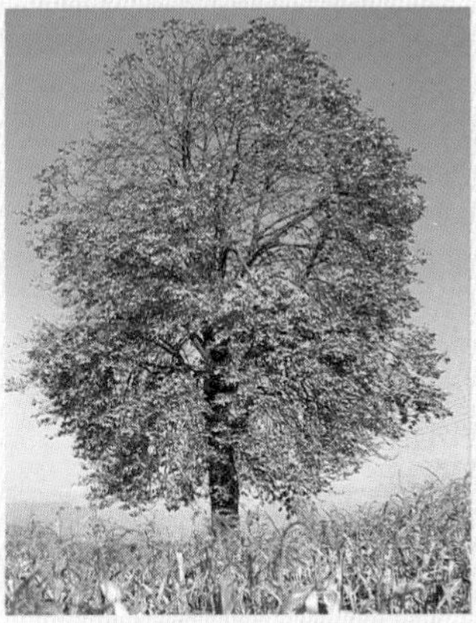
163 Horse Chestnut in autumn

164 Inside the prickly, green case lie 2 or 3 horse chestnuts

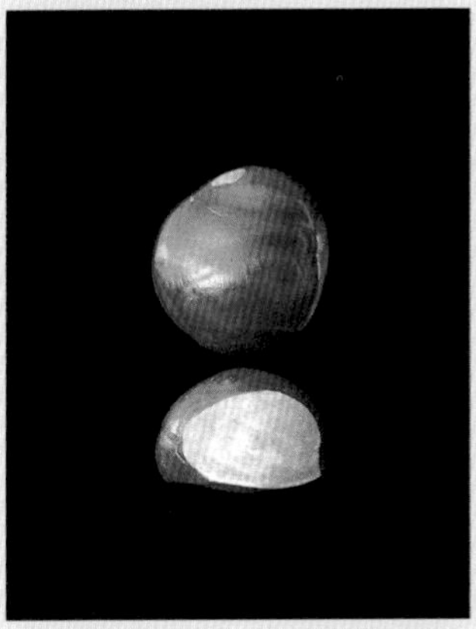
165 Shiny red-brown horse chestnuts

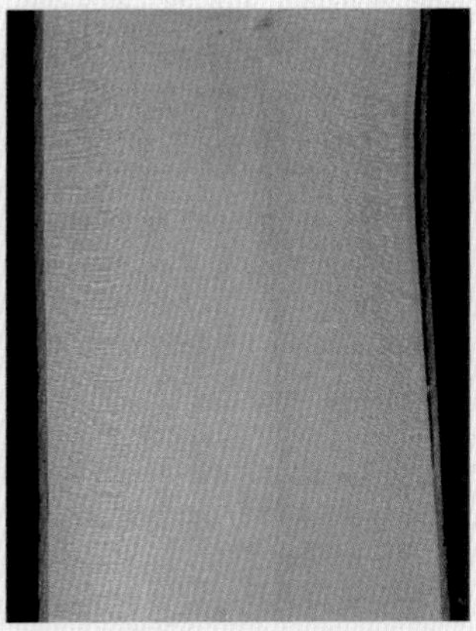
166 Consistently coloured whitish yellow, very fine, soft wood

167 Horse Chestnut in winter

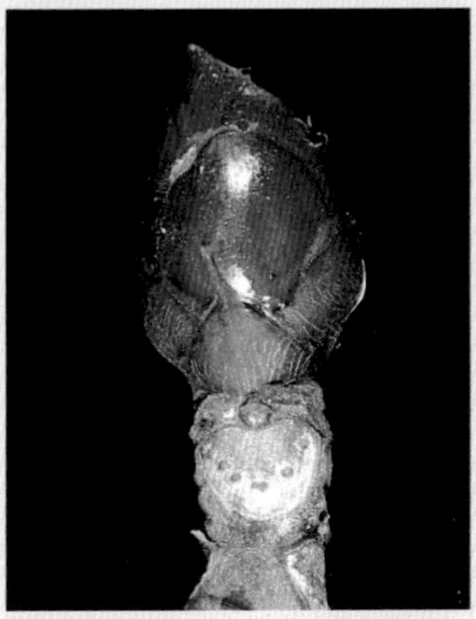
168 Broad-spherical, sticky, terminal bud

169 Pointed-ovoid side buds in opposing pairs

170 Fairly short trunk; dark brown to black bark, cracked into thin plates

Common Alder

Alnus glutinosa (L.) Gaertn.	**Aune glutineux** **Schwarzerle, Roterle**	**Pages 13, 15, 108, 188, 189**

After the first year, during which the process of growth is very slow, rapid and hearty growth takes place until around the twentieth year. But the Common Alder's fine, sparsely leaved, broadly conic crown does not develop until after some 4–5 years of growth, formed out of the narrow trunk, which grows right up to the treetop, and almost horizontal, outward-stretching branches.

If it is to reach its maximum height of 30m and maximum age of 120 years, the Common Alder needs soil which is high in humus content and rich in nutrients, deep and water-logged, or at least with a constantly available water supply; it also requires a good deal of light and moist atmosphere. Acidic, marshy or calcareous soils are not really suited to the Common Alder. However, the alder does have nodules on its roots, where nutrifying bacteria live. It can therefore grow well on very poor soils so long as they are damp, and will enrich them by its leaf-fall. The roots grow into the open water beside which the tree is so often found, as dense masses of hard, dark red cords which hold the bank firm against spates and the wash of passing boats. It coppices well and sprouts from a stump can, with the big root system of the former tree supplying them, grow 2m in a year. It grows along spring-lines in oak woods and in damp hollows or on wet slopes in high rainfall areas, away from the waterside. One in an oak wood in Kent is among the biggest few in Britain, 31m × 126cm and the biggest trunk, 170cm in diameter, is on a hillside in Wester Ross.

No alder shows any autumn colour beyond the normal dark green, then the black of decay. The seeds attract flocks of Redpolls and Siskins, often mixed, and some Goldfinches, all through the winter.

Of all the alders this is the one most often found in hilly regions, along the banks of streams and rivers, in damp marshy woods and riverside woodlands. It is frequently employed in the afforestation of wastelands. In the Alps it is found up to a height of 1300m above sea level. As the tree very readily puts out shoots, it is also planted in lower woodlands.

The young bark is greenish or greyish brown, soon turning to dark grey-brown, cracked into square plates. Underneath is to be found the light, soft, pale reddish yellow, fairly firm, non-supple but rarely splitting wood. One cubic metre of seasoned wood weighs 550kg.

The wood makes a poor firewood but one of the best charcoals, which was formerly prized for gunpowder-making. It was also the wood for making soles of clogs because it not only holds nails well near its edge, but once dried, the wood is highly durable in alternating wet and dry conditions. It was therefore also used for small timbers in canal and bridge works.

As it is very low in fat content it is easy to stain. This often used to lead to its being used as a substitute for precious woods, particularly mahogany. It keeps well underwater and, under such conditions, turns black and hardens over the years. Because of this particular property it used to be used for building ships and water-taps.

Above the leaf buds are found the female cones, which remain bare throughout the winter, and the male 'catkins'. The tree flowers in February or March, that is, long before it comes into leaf. The female flowers come in the form of inflorescences of 2–8 many-flowered, 1–2cm long, greyish green, stalked cones, arranged side by side, like grapes, or ears of corn on a hairless stem.

The male flowers, consisting of 4 stamens and 2 outer and 2 inner perigynous leaves, are found in groups of three behind the 2 small inner and 2 larger outer sprout-leaves and the axil of a bract.

By autumn the female inflorescences have developed into brown cones. The small brown nuts, consisting of a flat seed and a narrow, opaque wing, fall in late autumn and winter. The cone remains on the tree long after this. It is often used for handicrafts or decoration.

After the flowering season, broad, obovate to roundish, sticky, emarginate and dentate leaves emerge out of the characteristically stalked, purplish-brown, long, alternate buds. They are 4–10cm long, and at the base of the blade they usually narrow inwards, forming a wedge shape. On their inferior surface, in the vein-axils, are whitish to rust-coloured tufts of hair.

Because the Common Alder grows on the edge of moors, and on the banks of insect-infested ponds, it should not surprise us that, particularly in centuries gone by, it was associated with evil spirits, the devil and witches. It was said that witches used alder wood to summon up storms.

The alder features in Greek mythology on a number of occasions. It is said to have grown in Kalypos's cave, as well as in that of the nymph loved by Odysseus, who detained him for 7 years. Only on the order of the gods did she release him. According to Virgil, the Heliades – the sisters of Phaeton – were changed into alders by Zeus. In Homer's Odyssey, the island of death, 'Aia', is skirted with alders belonging to the sorceress Circe. Alders also play a role in the business of fertility potions, because of their early flowering blooms.

Time after time, in Northern European folk legend, various afflictions are cast out and absorbed by the alder; for example, fever, toothache, and warts. Alders and ashes play a special role in rural superstition. During the sowing seasons, on Good Friday, people place tiny pieces of alder in their mouths, or receive the sacrament through a ring woven out of alder. This is supposed to keep sparrows away from the fields. Mice and moles are shooed away by placing chips of alder wood in all four corners of the field or barn on Good Friday.

171 Common Alder in spring

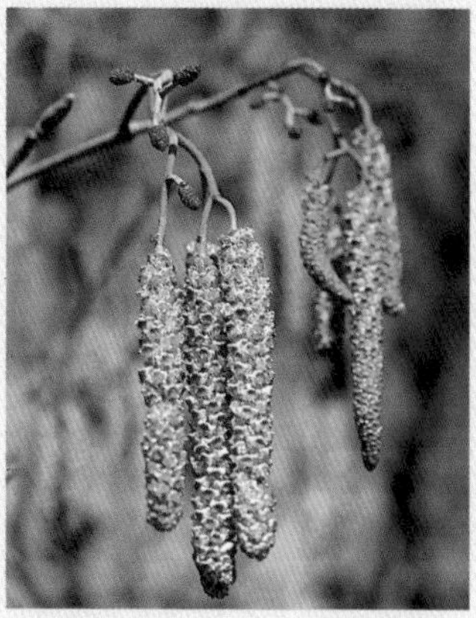

172 Male catkins, 3–12cm long, drooping; female flowers in small cones

173 Stalked, female inflorescences (= cones)

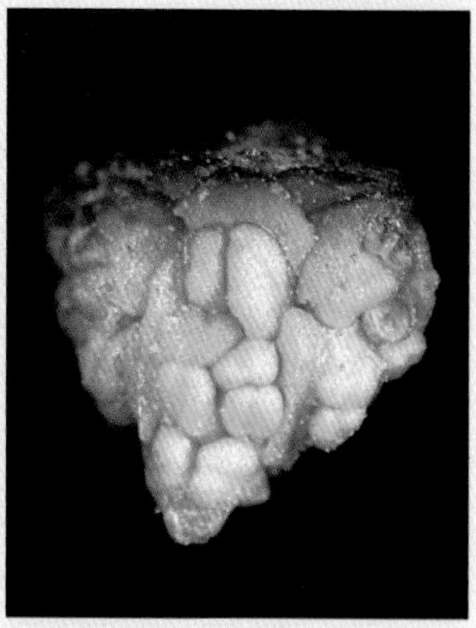

174 3 male flowers on a bract

175 Common Alder in summer

176 4–10cm long leaves arranged alternately

177 Superior leaf surface, mid- to dark green and glabrous

178 Inferior leaf surface, light green, with whitish to rust coloured tufts in the vein axils

179 Common Alder in autumn

180 7 cone-shaped fruits

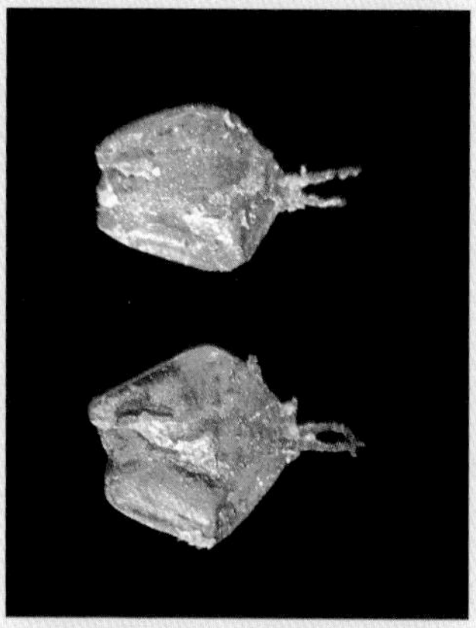

181 Nuts, each with a flat seed and opaque wing

182 Yellow-white wood; discolours to yellow-red to dark red when exposed to light or air

183 Common Alder in winter

184 Narrow side buds, each stalked with 2 visible scales

185 Young bark, grey-brown to greenish brown

186 Dark brown, cracked bark on old trees, flaking away in vertical plates

Silver Birch

Betula pendula Roth, *Betula verrucosa*

Bouleau verruqueux
Hängebirke, Weissbirke

Pages 108, 188, 189

The Silver Birch is a graceful and charming tree which grows to a height of 20-30m. Its trunk is slender and supple, reaching a maximum diameter of 40-60cm. Its crown is at first narrow, conic, and pointed, eventually assuming a rounded, dome-like or irregular shape.

The rate of growth slows down once the tree reaches the age of 20 years. Growth in height ceases altogether after 50-60 years. It is not unusual to find birch trees over 100 years old. It used to be very common to find brooms made from their long, dangling twigs. On the lower part of the trunk the bark is bulging, cracked, dark brown to black and has small white patch-marks. Between the white patches lie large, gnarled, deeply cracked, black, diamond-shaped patches. The rest of the trunk and the branches have a smooth, silvery white to yellowish, shiny outer rind, overlain by separate grey-white cross-strips. The bark is structured in two layers. It is from the originally snow-white strips which peel off horizontally that we derive birch tar and, by a process of distillation, birch oil. The tar forms the basis of a good conserving agent for leather and wood, and is often used to make car polish. The inner part of the bark, because of its high tannin content, is often used as a tanning agent, particularly in northern European countries. The whole bark, which is almost totally waterproof, is also used as an underlay for doormats, roof coverings and balconies. Even today, many roofs in Scandinavia are covered with birch bark and sealed with a layer of tar. The North American Indians used to construct lightweight canoes and wigwams from birch bark.

Boreholes, 2-5cm deep, are made in older trees in April. Birch juice pours out of these holes and ferments to make a foamy drink known as birch wine. In 4 days, 50 tree trunks with a diameter of 40-50cm would yield around 175kg of birch juice. This alcoholic birch water was known to Albertus Magnus as early as 1240 BC.

Underneath the bark is a slightly shiny, supple, sticky wood, which is extremely difficult to chop and is a yellowish white shade, turning reddish near the medulla. It is quite difficult to distinguish the heartwood from the sapwood. One cubic metre of seasoned wood weighs 600-700kg. It must be dried slowly. There is a danger, during drying, of discolouration and the formation of irregular patches. As this wood cannot support a great deal of weight it is not very good for use in building. It is, however, popular for use in making bobbins, reels, trays, bowls, boxes and tool-handles. It is also commonly used to make plywood. Because it contains ethereal oil, birchwood oil burns well and produces a rapid heat. It is therefore a popular firewood.

Birches begin to flower after 20-30 years. Birches bear both male and female flowers. Male catkins appear in autumn at the tips of many branches. Between March and May they increase gradually in size until, several days after the leaves emerge, they are up to 10cm long. They are long and cylindrical in shape, hang downwards, but have no stalk. The female catkins are also formed in autumn and are preserved in buds until the first growth movements. They are cylindrical, stalked, 2-4cm long, covered in tiny flowers and bright green. During the flowering season they are mostly erect and project outwards; once the flowers fade they start to droop.

In very early autumn the fruit cones are already a brownish colour. The protective fruit scales enclose the light brown nuts, with their propeller-like attachments. After the fall these are carried large distances by the autumn wind.

The Silver Birch was a very early colonist in Britain but was preceded a little by the White or Downy Birch. This has no hanging shoots but a crown of confused shoots and its bark has horizontal bands and patches of grey speckling. It ranges north into Orkney and the Shetlands, beyond the Silver Birch, but is also found all over the country on damper sites, often among Silver Birch, which keeps more to drier places like sandy heaths. In the Highlands, the glens have Silver Birch along the steep, often rocky, well-drained hillsides and White Birch along the bogs and ditchsides of the valley bottom. Both will grow on clays and are in many town and city parks.

The birches coppice well and seedlings grow fast, as a pioneer species needing rapidly to overtop competitors.

Placenames derived from birch are numerous: Birchington, Kent; Bartley, Hampshire; Berkhampstead, Buckinghamshire; Much Birch, Herefordshire; Berkeley, Gloucestershire; Birkenhead, Cheshire; Birks Bridge, Lancashire; Birkhill House, Fife; and Birkhall, Aberdeenshire.

187 Silver Birch in spring

188 Dangling male catkins; female catkins erect or projecting

189 Erect female inflorescence

190 Section of a female inflorescence with yellow stigmae

191 Silver Birch in summer

192 3-7cm long leaves, arranged alternately

193 Superior leaf surface, dark green and glabrous

194 Inferior leaf surface, pale grey-green and glabrous

195 Silver Birch in autumn

196 Brown, long-stalked, fruit cones, up to 3cm long

197 Fruit scales enclosing small nuts, each with a transparent fruit wing

198 Yellowish white to reddish, fairly soft, elastic wood

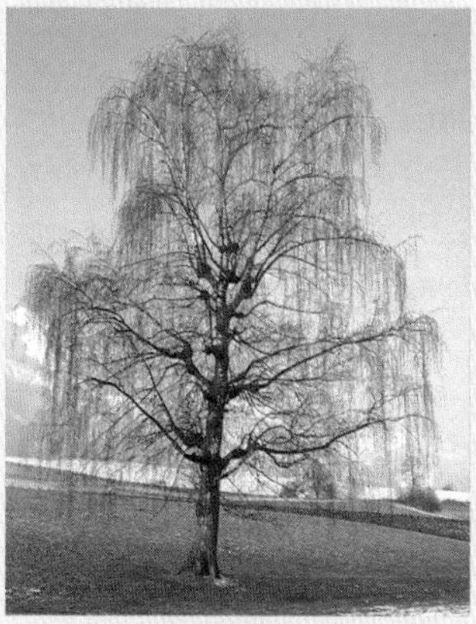

199 Silver Birch in winter

200 Side buds and hibernating male catkins

201 (left) Young and (middle and right) older side buds

202 Young bark, white, smooth, peeling away in thin, horizontal strips

Common Beech

Fagus sylvatica L.

Hêtre
Buche, Rotbuche

Pages 101, 178, 179

On this medium to large tree, branching starts very close to the ground where the tree stands in the open, and relatively high up the trunk where it stands in the forest. It has a straight, nearly cylindrical trunk, which reaches a height of 25–30m over a period of 120 years. The crown is narrow in young trees, but broadens out with age into a vaulted dome. Beeches over 300 years old grow as tall as 45m, with a diameter of 1.5m.

Woodland beeches have a heavily foliaged crown, which allows only a small amount of light to pass through. For this reason only very early-leafing and shade-bearing trees are able to flourish in beech forests, which are usually very dark.

The bark is grey-green, later turning to ash grey, and even in old age remains thin, smooth and silver-grey. It is rare for the beech to develop ridged bark. If trees which have grown up in a forest are abruptly transplanted into open spaces, or if a tree in a wood is suddenly exposed, the bark can suffer 'sunburn'. If the bark is over-exposed in this way it may loosen and the vascular cambium is likely to dry up.

The beech is a mature wood tree. The heartwood is differentiated from the sapwood only by its hardness and firmness, not by its colour.

The diffuse-porous wood is whitish grey to reddish yellow in colour, tough though not very supple, but even so, pretty strong, heavy (one cubic metre of seasoned wood weighs between 650kg and 800kg), contracts significantly, is resistant to pressure and preserves excellently under water.

The steaming process gives it its well-known reddish hue, but also has the disadvantage of inducing a certain amount of cracking, contracting and warping. If the drying process is carefully and slowly carried out these problems can for the most part be minimised.

The medullary rays are broad and well-spaced. The pores are not visible to the naked eye; on the other hand, the growth zones can be recognised as annual rings in the end-of-season wood, which has noticeably few pores.

If the wood is stored in damp conditions it will soon be attacked by insects and fungi.

It is easy to work, handle, stain and polish.

In the Chiltern Hills in Buckinghamshire, the trade of 'bodging' was plied until as recently as the 1950s. The bodger would fell a beech tree, saw and hew it into pieces which could be transformed on the spot into chair legs with the use of a hand-made lathe.

It is used particularly for cabinet-making and carpentry, for making chairs, tables, kitchen equipment, toys, staircases, work benches, school desks, plywood and railway sleepers (which will last for up to 40 years), for veneering, trimming and edging. It can also be processed to make plywood boards and compressed wood.

Because it produces a high degree of heat it is also very popular as a firewood. Recently it has been widely cultivated for the production of cellulose and the manufacture of artificial fibres. The quality of the wood starts to deteriorate once a 'false' heartwood starts to develop. At the same time as the leaves start to appear in May, flower buds also appear, supporting female and male inflorescences. The female ones are spherical, stalked, more or less erect, and always have two flowers. These are contained inside a slightly prickly fruitcase, the cupule, which is covered in scales at the base. The male inflorescences are also round, supported by 3–5cm-long stalks, bearing many flowers and covered in villous hairs. Each of the flowers has a 5–7 part perigone and 6–15 anthers, which protrude from the hairy flower case.

In the autumn each of the 20–25mm long fruits contains 2 reddish brown seeds, usually triangular in section, and rich in oil. These 'beech-nuts' fall from their cases until well into the autumn and are then collected and eaten by coal-tits, chaffinches, bramblings and wood-pigeons. If these animals leave nuts lying on the ground instead of eating them they contribute considerably to the propagation of the beech.

A heavy 'mast year' usually follows a hot summer in the previous year.

The buds are up to 2cm long, spike-shaped, reddish brown and pointed. They stand erect, are scaly and alternate. In May they put out stalked leaves. The blades are 5–10cm in length, elliptic or ovate in outline, very slightly cuspidate, with an entire margin tapering or rounded at the base. When young they bear soft hairs and have wavy margins.

Common Beeches favour alkaline, damp, loose, well-ventilated soil and a relatively humid atmosphere. They will avoid low-lying ground, where the soil may be water-logged. As beeches are very sensitive to winter cold, late frosts, drought and heat, they do not occur in regions with a 'continental' climate, in the far north or in hot areas with low precipitation. As well as in central Europe, where they are particularly common on plains and at mid-altitude, they are also found in the southern parts of the Scandinavian peninsula, in England, in the higher regions of Italy and at the tip of Greece. The Common Beech is widespread throughout most of the central band of Switzerland and in many valleys on the northern side of the Alps. Here it can occur as high as 1500m above sea level.

Although the Common or European Beech was not indigenous to Ancient Greece, Theophrastus refers to it by the name of 'oxya'. Roman writers knew it as 'fagus'. Macrobius Theodosius compliments the tree in noting that its wood is especially good for making sacrificial urns. The Gauls used the ashes of the beech to make soap.

As a late-comer crossing the land-bridge across the chalk ridge from France, the beech did not prog ess very far as a native tree, reaching probably the Usk Valley in South Wales and perhaps to the Pennines but not into Scotland. It is, however, well suited to the climate there and is planted everywhere, in extensive shelterbelts in the Southern Uplands and as a roadside and parkland tree in the Highland glens. Many of the biggest beeches are in Scotland, the tallest, 46m tall, on the Perthshire–Angus border and the biggest good bole, 220cm diameter, in Inverness-shire, and many nearly as big, especially in the Lothians.

Although traditionally a tree of the chalk hilltops, which seem so dry, the beech is a thirsty tree and thrives there only because it roots powerfully into the fissures in chalk and reaches the water which this rock holds so abundantly. It is also perfectly at home on sands and clays where the surface soils are quite acid and where foxgloves and rhododendrons may grow. Beech pollards well and many of the old woods like Burnham Beeches were pollarded to grow smallwood beyond the reach of browsing deer.

Numerous place-names are derived from 'beech', for example: Bookham, Surrey; Boxted, Essex; and Long Buckby.

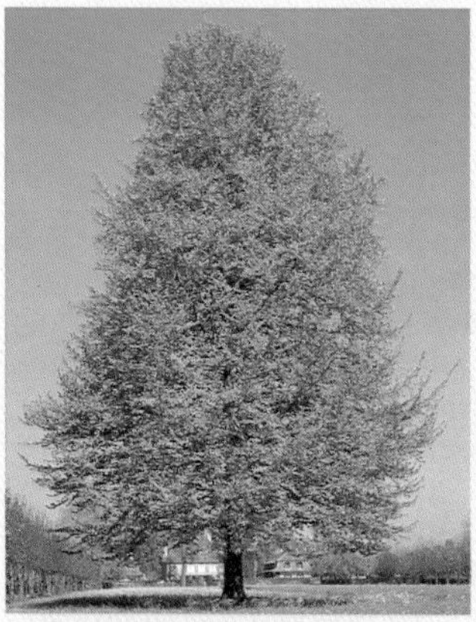
203 Common Beech in spring

204 Male inflorescences with long stalks and many flowers; female inflorescences stalked, more spherical

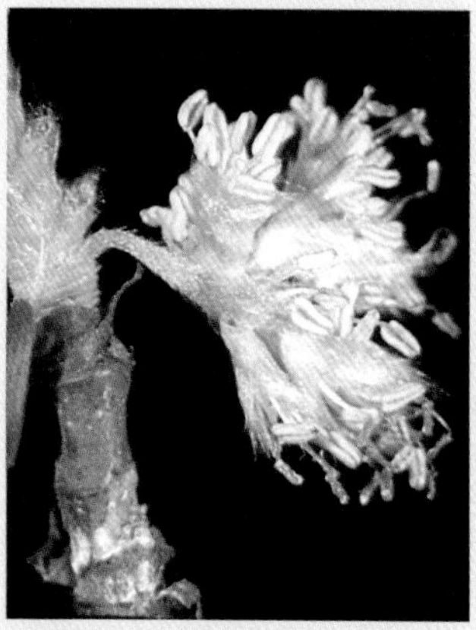
205 Male inflorescences with numerous flowers

206 Female inflorescences (from above); stigma lobes yellowish green and curved

207 Common Beech in summer

208 5–10cm long leaves, alternately arranged

209 Superior leaf surface, shiny, dark green, glabrous at first

210 Inferior leaf surface, pale blue-green, with tufts in the vein axils

211 Common Beech in autumn

212 Young fruits with soft brown barbs

213 Seeds, triangular, red-brown, with high oil content

214 Yellowish red hard wood

215 Common Beech in winter

216 Very long, spindle-shaped terminal and side buds

217 Softly barbed fruit cases and spindle-shaped side buds

218 Long, straight, cylinder-shaped trunk; grey-silver bark, smooth and thin

Common Ash

Fraxinus excelsior L.

Frêne commun
Gemeine Esche

Pages 78, 138, 139

The ash is one of the taller of the indigenous trees, usually growing to a height of around 40m. The crown of younger trees is very open with ascending branches. In older trees it is ovoid or spherical, being broadest at the summit.

It shoots upwards at a remarkable rate until its 50th year. Once over a hundred years old it ceases to increase in height, whilst continuing to expand outwards. Old trees can be up to 1m in diameter. Where the environment is favourable, it can live for 200 to 300 years. The greenish-coloured outer bark is smooth for the first 30 years. Thereafter it develops longitudinal ridges and furrows, forming a lattice-like pattern, turning grey to brown-black with age.

In many museums are to be found lances, spears and javelins, all made from highly pliable, long-fibred, non-brittle, extremely supple and hard ash wood. This would explain why as early as the Middle Ages the ash was frequently planted near to towns.

Inside the light-coloured, wide, tough and very useful sapwood is to be found the heartwood. This darkens considerably with age, has large pores set in rings, is very strong, with long, straight fibres, and very pliable.

One cubic metre of naturally dried, cut wood weighs 700-780kg. It usually dries fairly successfully. If it is to be artificially dried, it is advisable not to hurry the process, otherwise the wood will crack.

The wood is commonly used for making tool handles, wheels, skis, gymnasium equipment, hockey sticks, furniture, table tops and wooden floors. As it stains well, it is often used by cabinet makers. A distinction is made between chalk, water, wood and garden ashes. The chalk ash grows on dry, stony slopes, has fibres, is brittle and consequently of little practical use. The garden ash yields the hardest, firmest wood.

Ashes first flower and fruit at some point between their 30th and 40th years. The many-flowered panicles emerge in April, before the leaves, out of spherical, slightly pointed, black side-buds, which project somewhat from the twig. The flowers have neither petals nor sepals, are wind-dispersed and either bisexual or single-sex. The male flowers consist of 2 or 3 anthers, whose pollen sacks are originally violet-red. Female flowers have an ovary. a two-lobed style and 2 spatula-shaped staminodes (sterile anthers). The anthers do not open until 2 to 4 days after the styles have matured. This feature is designed to preclude the possibility of self-pollination. The closed fruits are gathered together in overhanging clusters. They are elongated, slightly twisted, and, in the early stages, green in colour. They only begin to turn brown towards the end of autumn. They may become detached from the panicle at any time up to the early spring.

Inside the oblanceolate, flat, elongated fruit-wing, or 'key', lies an elongated, pointed nut. Once the tree has flowered, the large, pinnately compound leaves appear. The individual pinnate leaflets are oblong to ovate, 3-12cm long, acuminate, irregularly serrate, with woolly hairs along the veins on the inferior surface of the leaf. The leaves are arranged in opposite pairs along the twig.

The ash is only able to develop its magnificent crown when it grows in deep, fairly damp, mineral-rich soil in a place where it will not experience late frosts, and where the atmosphere is not too warm or humid. It grows less successfully on completely dry slopes with a thin soil layer and a deficient supply of ground water. It is most frequently found on river banks, in meadow and valley woodland, with rich ground-level vegetation, and in mixed deciduous woodland between the hilly and montane zones.

The ash requires a lot of light - about the same amount as the oak.

When the tree is grown commercially it is often planted in narrow passes, to encourage it to grow to maximum height.

The manuscript of Edda, written in the second half of the 13th century, contains references to a large number of gods and heroes. This is just about the only piece of evidence we have on which to base our notions concerning the religious beliefs of the Teutons. Here we can read of the mythological ash, 'Yggdrasil', whose roots were anchored in the abyss of the underworld, and watered by the streams of wisdom and fate; its trunk was supported by the earth, and its crown touched the arc of heaven. Mythical animals lived in the tree and fulfilled particular roles which contributed to the successful perpetuation of life on earth. And each day the gods would come over the bridge of the rainbow and hold court under its shade.

Earlier still, ash wood was considered efficacious when applied to fresh flesh wounds. The leaf sap was used as an antidote to snake bites and the distillation of young shoots produced an excellent cure for earache and unsteady hands.

Many Slavic people believe that snakes are afraid of the constantly shifting shadow of the ash tree. A traveller should therefore be able to rest at ease under its generous shade.

English place-names derived from 'ash' include: Ascot, Berkshire; Ashton, Northamptonshire and other counties; Ashton-under-Lyne, Lancashire.

219 Ash in spring

220 Erect panicles with bisexual flowers

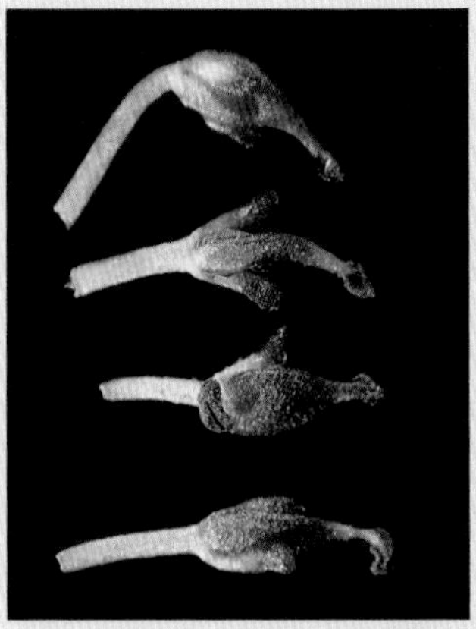

221 Wilted bisexual flowers with young fruits

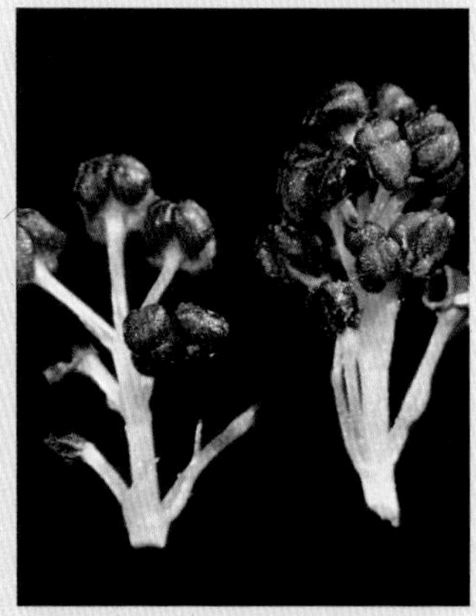

222 Part of an all-male panicle

223 Ash in summer

224 20-30cm long leaves, in opposite pairs, usually pinnate

225 Superior leaf surface, dark green, glabrous

226 Inferior leaf surface, light green with red-brown hairs along the veins

227 Ash in autumn

228 Numerous fruits clustered in overhanging panicles

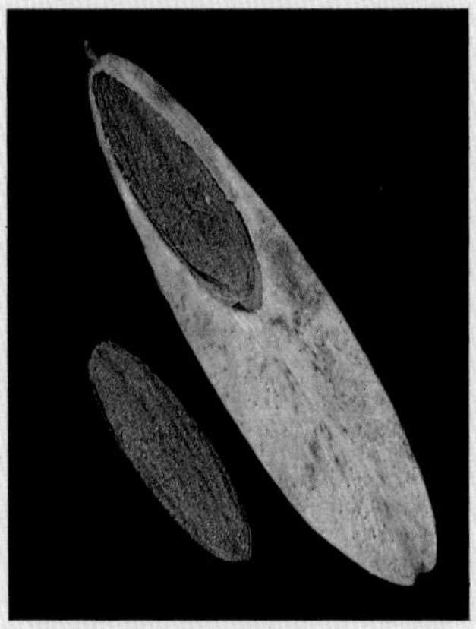

229 Narrow, dark brown seed, enclosed by flight organ

230 Heartwood turning brownish with age

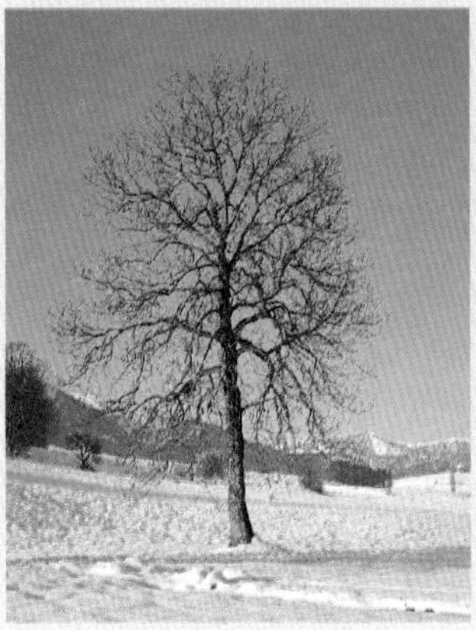

231 Ash in winter

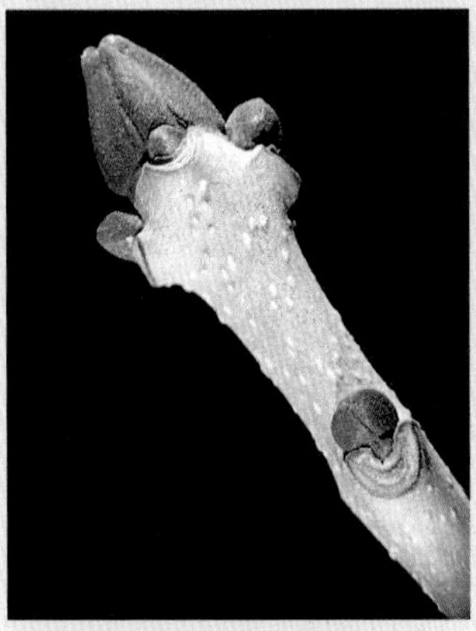

232 Pyramid-shaped, black, terminal buds, larger than roundish side buds

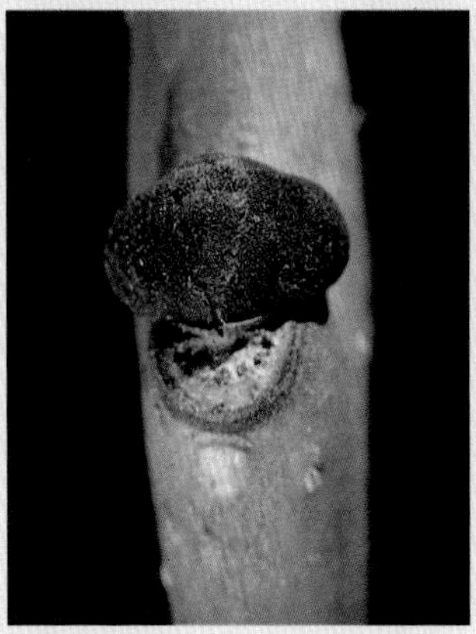

233 Black side buds with leaf stigma

234 Older bark, grey, pitted with 'plaitted' grooves

Common Walnut

Juglans regia L.

Noyer
Gemeiner Walnussbaum

Pages 76, 136, 137

The Common Walnut is a sturdy, well-proportioned tree. Growing singly it has an open, roundish crown and is well endowed with foliage. Its maximum height is 30m, diameter 1.5m, and it can live for up to 400 years. Given the right habitat it can grow to 15-20m by the time it is between 60 and 90 years old.

It thrives best in loose, porous, deep soil which is rich in nutrients, and in the gentle climate of the wine-growing regions. Particularly fine examples may be found in hollows on sheltered valley bottoms and gently sloping hillsides.

The young Common Walnut has a smooth, ash grey to grey-brown outer rind. With age this changes into a deeply fissured, grey bark.

Within the white to grey-white sapwood, which can be very wide in young trees, lies a grey to dark brown, heavy, fairly hard, tough and not very pliable heartwood. Its pith is shot through with dark stripes.

The increasing demand for walnut wood can easily be explained. Seasoned wood is very durable and has a beautiful colour, which contributes to its increasing rarity. The colour and the structure of the wood can vary a great deal according to climate, habitat and composition of the soil. Thus it is possible to distinguish Italian walnut from the German or Swiss walnuts by its more lively structure and its slightly more reddish tinge. Growing in the Caucasus region, on the other hand, the walnut has a pronounced black colouring. One of the most beautiful woods for drawing on and staining comes from France.

Since walnut wood is so easy to handle, to cut, and to polish, it is commonly used to make house furniture (for bedroom furniture it is particularly the darker, burnished woods whch are used), in interior fittings, for building organs and pianos, for tableware, bread-boards, toast-racks, carvings and, by way of long tradition, for making shields and rifle-butts and stocks, the last because it is very stable and will not move or warp.

The valuable veneers, with their superbly intricate figures, are taken from the axis of the branches, the lower part of the trunk, or from the root knots. Walnut trees are therefore felled not by sawing through the trunk above the ground, but by cutting below ground level. The buttressed bases are used to make very valuable veneered furniture. One cubic metre of dried wood weighs 650–750kg. The drying process is usually fairly straightforward and there is little danger that the wood will develop fissures.

In spring the young leaves unfold, odd-pinnate and still orange-brown in colour. By summer they have grown to 20-50cm in length and are strongly aromatic when crushed. The pinnate leaflets are elongated and elliptic to ovate, 6-15cm long, with an entire margin and, with the exception of the terminal leaflet, sessile.

The leaves - known as 'folia juglandis' - contain, amongst other things, walnut tannin and ethereal oil and are used in natural medicine as an antidote to poison, intestinal worms and skin disorders. A decoction of the leaves is supposed to produce a good mouth wash, and a mixture of linseed oil and walnut leaves to be an effective laxative for cattle. Common Walnut trees usually flower for the first time after 15–20 years. The male catkins dangling from the previous year's shoot emerge from the axis where the leaves have fallen. Their flowers have a six- sided case consisting of 4 perigynous leaves, 2 sprout-leaves and 6-30 anthers. The female inflorescences lie near the tip of new twigs and bear 1-3 and sometimes 5 flowers. Each of the perigynous leaves is fused with the receptacle. Their styles possess fringed stigmas. The fruits begin to ripen in September. They are incomplete, 2 or 4 layered stone fruits, enclosed inside a green, smooth, tough and fleshy outer case which turns brown upon ripening. Underneath lies the light brown, furrowed, rock-hard nut-case, with its thick seam. Inside all this is a 2–4 layered seed with large, fleshy, folded, tasty shoots, containing a good deal of oil. Trees aged 50–100 years give the best yields. The largest plantations are to be found today in France (the Grenoble walnuts are well known), Italy, Hungary and Yugoslavia. Ripe nuts are edible and are used to make salad oil. This is done by crushing the edible part of the nut, which is bright yellow and has no smell. It is also used to make soap and oil-based paints. The leaves, rind and fruit case are dried and aloes are added to them to make brown dyes for wood, wool and hair. The name 'walnut' came from the old English 'wahlnut', literally meaning foreign nut, probably a translation of the Vulgar Latin phrase 'nux Gallica' (Gaulish, hence foreign nut). The Gauls, the people who inhabited France, were known to the Teutons in the Middle Ages as Walchen or Welsche.

The tree was originally indigenous from South-West Asia to China, and was dedicated to Jupiter. The Romans called it 'jovis glans', meaning 'the nut of the great god Jove [or Jupiter]'. From this is derived its scientific name Juglans.

Excavations in Carinthia, and of stilt buildings in northern and southern Italy, have shown that the Romans were not the first to introduce the walnut tree to central Europe. Grafted varieties were brought to Italy by the Greeks and then later taken northward by the Romans. But the Walnut did not achieve a wide distribution in Europe until the time of Charlemagne.

The Common Walnut was probably introduced to Britain by the Romans, and is now grown everywhere northwards, at least to Skye, where there is a fair tree at Armadale Castle, and to Easter Ross. Some of the best trees surviving the search by timber-scouts are in Yorkshire and the Midlands, but growth is faster where summers are hotter in the south and south-east. The best tree now, as it was in 1900, is at Gayhurst, Newport Pagnell, a near perfect stem and 21m × 195cm, but many trees collapse before reaching that size. Good growth is only likely in deep, rich soils like those found along the edges of lowland alluvial valleys, and particularly where these are in chalk country.

The old tag about women, dogs and walnut trees has a certain validity for walnut trees at least, for unhindered growth can be too lush for the production of much flower and fruit. The old scheme was to collect the fruit by beating and bending the branches, and the slight wounding acted like root-pruning in slowing down leaf-production and increasing flowering.

235 Walnut in spring

236 Male catkins on previous year's shoots

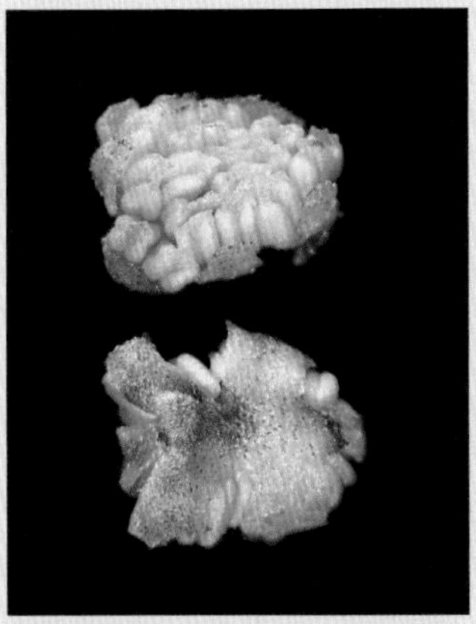

237 Male flowers; (above) from the front, (below) from behind

238 Two female flowers with feathery stigma

239 Walnut in summer

240 20–50cm long, unequally pinnate leaves

241 Superior leaf surface; leaflets unequal in size, mid green in colour

242 Inferior surface of a young leaf

243 Walnut in autumn

244 Green stone fruits on new shoots

245 Light brown 'wooden' nut inside fruit case

246 Brown-grey heartwood with dark stripes

247 Walnut in winter

248 Terminal buds and two male inflorescences

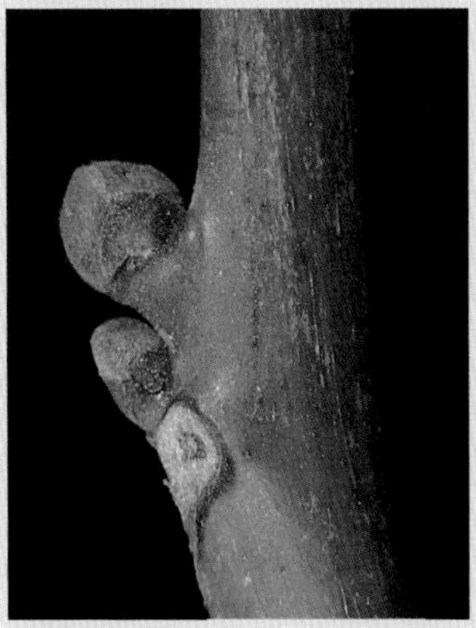

249 Side buds on a long shoot

250 Short trunk with pale grey bark, vertically ridged

European Larch

Larix decidua Mill.	**Mélèze** **Europäische Lärche**	**Pages 70, 128, 129**

Larch trees grow to a height of 40m and to around 1.5m in diameter. They are found in regions with warm summers and cold winters, where there is little fog. The soil should be rich in nutrients, loamy and porous, and reasonably deep. Trees are less likely to flourish as well on steep, slippery slopes, or on mountainsides in the sub-alpine zone. Even so, planted larches are often found in these regions. Where they have been planted in large towns their growth is usually very poor, as they are unable to withstand the damaging effects of toxins in the atmosphere.

Originally the larch was found only in the western and central Alps (where they formed the outer edge of the forest region), in eastern parts of the Sudetan, the Tatra mountains and on the Polish plain. However, because its wood is very valuable, its distribution has been extended far beyond these original confines. It was already well established in the European uplands by the 16th century.

The first larches in Britain were a few trees grown in the gardens of botanical enthusiasts a few years before 1629. It remained very rare until after 1700. In 1727 the Duke of Atholl had two at Dunkeld, Perthshire, and these grew remarkably well. In 1737 he had a hamper of larch plants brought up from London to plant five at Dunkeld and a dozen at his home, Blair Castle. The carrier, John Menzies, dropped off a few at some estates on his way, notably at Linley, Shropshire, and Monzie Castle, Crieff, and kept a few for his home at Meggernie Castle. Any big old larch in Scotland is now reputed to have come from that hamper, by various, sometimes devious means, and several probably did, like two each at Kinloch House, Angus, and Gordon Castle, Moray. The Atholl trees, eight of which survive, grew with remarkable vigour and soon convinced the Duke that this was the tree to plant on a large scale for the Navy. Which he did, all down the Tay Valley, which he owned, planting several million trees between 1750 and 1780.

From this example, larch became the one forest tree to rival the Scots Pine as a plantation tree in Scotland. Larch forestry quickly spread to England and Wales, and until the conifers from north-western America arrived in adequate quantity to compete, after 1860, the larch was supreme as the exotic conifer in forestry. It was also used much in shelterbelts and parks. It is popular again now both for financial reasons, with its very early yield of marketable timber, and for its value in amenity as a deciduous tree with fine spring and autumn colours, and its attraction for wildlife. The Scottish Crossbill moves into larch from the Scots Pine, where it nests, in September because the larch seed can be extracted and eaten then, a month before that of Scots Pine. Small finches, Bullfinches and Sparrowhawks nest and feed in larch, and tall old larches are favoured for nest sites by Buzzards.

When the needles fall in the autumn, they very quickly improve the quality of the soil, which in turn improves the survival chances of more demanding species such as the Norway Spruce and the Swiss Stone Pine. The larch is therefore acknowledged to be a particularly useful 'pioneer' tree.

The European Larch requires a good deal of light and has a narrow-conic, regular and massively branched crown, which in old age becomes somewhat flatter and more open. In between the irregularly spaced main branches grow smaller, almost horizontal, bow-like branches, tending slightly upwards. The young shoots are pale yellow and surrounded by pulvini. They usually bear numerous little twigs and droop heavily. The young tree has a smooth, greenish bark. This later turns into a 10cm thick, vertically ridged, scaly bark which is grey-brown on the outside and red-purple underneath. It encases a narrow, yellow-brown layer of sapwood and the inner red-brown heartwood, which later turns much darker.

Of all the indigenous conifers, the European Larch yields the hardest and most hard-wearing wood. Because of its high resin content it is weatherproof and is therefore unbeatable for use in building, for constructing bridges, pit-props and other kinds of equipment. It is also used for making railway sleepers, fence posts, exterior doors, staircases and floors. Many tubs and containers used in the chemical industry are made from larch (because of its resistance to acid). But it is also used to make interior fittings and furniture. The larch is industrially processed to make fretwood and veneers. This wood can present difficulties to the manufacturer when he encounters particularly stubborn branches. The drying of the wood is usually successful, although it does occasionally have a tendency to split and warp. It is pliable, tough, easily hewn and weighs around 600–750kg/m^3.

The sulphurous yellow male inflorescences are roundish, ovoid catkins, about 5–10mm in length. Even before the end of the winter they are visible in the form of enlarged buds. The numerous male flowers are disposed radially, and their anthers comprise a short stalk, a scaly tip and two pollen sacks, located on the underside.

The female inflorescences are a vivid dark red, 10–25mm long, and are usually found on 2-year-old needle-bearing shoots. They consist of surface scales arranged in a spiral pattern and the small yellowish seed- or fruit-scales, each of which contains two ovules. When the inflorescence turns into a cone, these seed scales (megasphorophyll) grow vigorously and later form the round-shaped adjacent, slightly curled, cone scales with their very fine tracery of lines. The bracts, on the other hand, have arrested growth, and in the mature cone are visible only at the base of the fruit scales.

The triangular, light brown, 3–4.5mm long seeds are equipped with a 5–6mm wide 'wing' and ripen in September or October of the first year. At any time between then and the following spring they can be shed from the cone. The gestation period of the seed is about 4–5 weeks, and it is fertile for 4–5 years.Only after about 4–5 years do the cones drop, together with the dried twigs. On 2-year-old or older branches, the needles occur in tufts, on small bunches of short shoots; in the case of the new long shoots, they are found singly and are arranged spirally. The individual needles are straight, 1.5–3cm long, soft, slightly flattened, with a blunt or shortly pointed tip. In the autumn they turn golden yellow and drop before the start of winter.

In Scotland, the best timber is used for boatskins and in the building of trawlers, where the great strength is essential for the strains of trawling. The early returns come from the use of thinnings for garden fences and pergolas when small, and pit- props and estate work, especially fence-stobs when a little larger. It is remarkably durable in the ground.

251 Larch in spring

252 Male inflorescences, spherical, yellow, projecting outwards

253 Female inflorescences (cones), dark red, erect

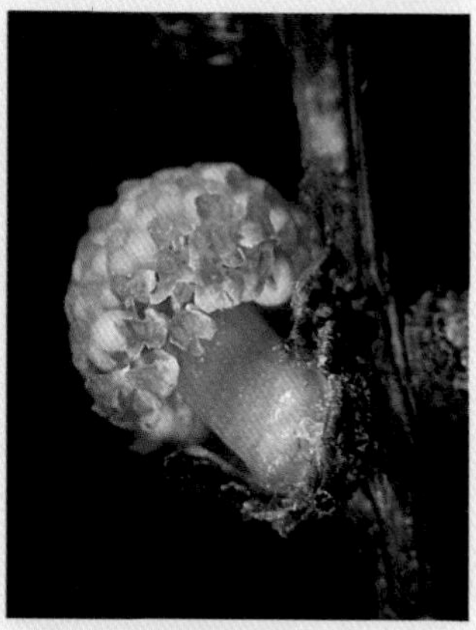

254 Side view of a male inflorescence with stalk

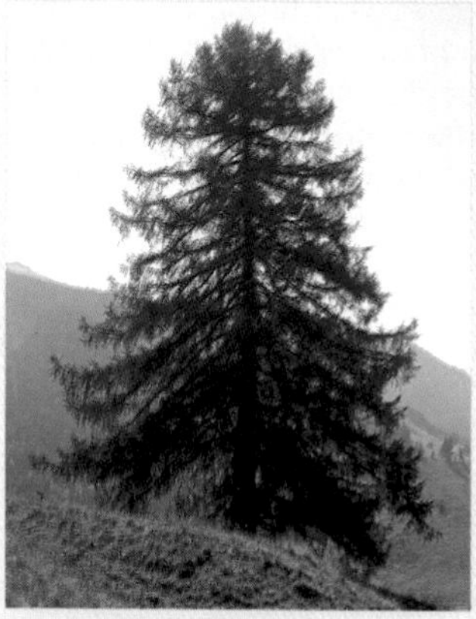

255 Larch in summer

256 Needles in clusters on short shoots; arranged singly on long shoots

257 Section showing old (brown) and new parts of twig, with clustered and single needles

258 Needles, 1.5–3cm long, narrow-linear, soft, flattened, with rounded or slightly pointed tip

259 Larch in autumn

260 Cones 2–4cm long, broad, grey-brown in colour

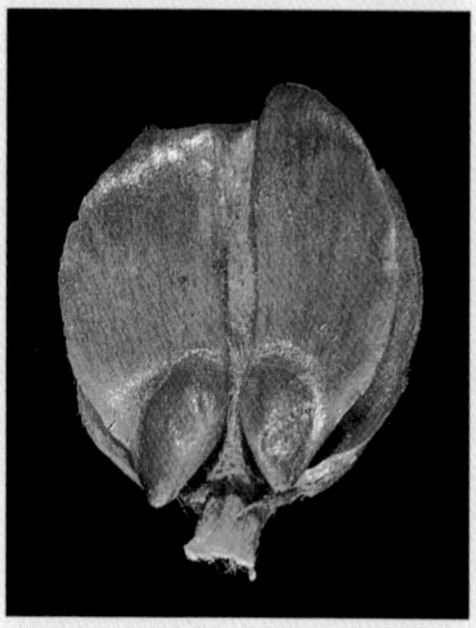

261 Triangular seeds, light brown, enclosed by wing

262 Within the yellow sapwood lies the tough, resinous, brown-red heartwood

263 Larch in winter

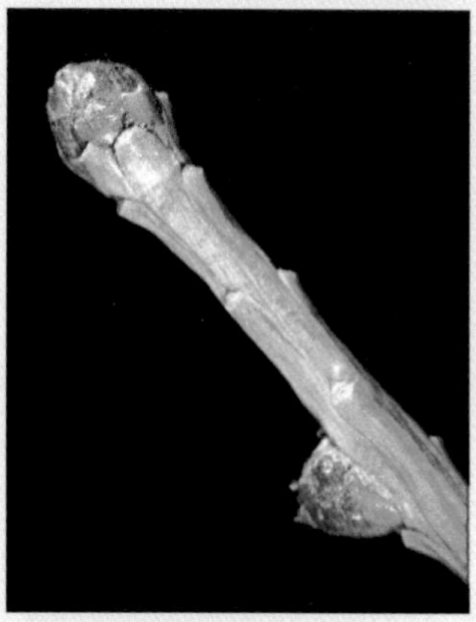

264 Half-spherical to wedge-shaped, brown, terminal and side buds

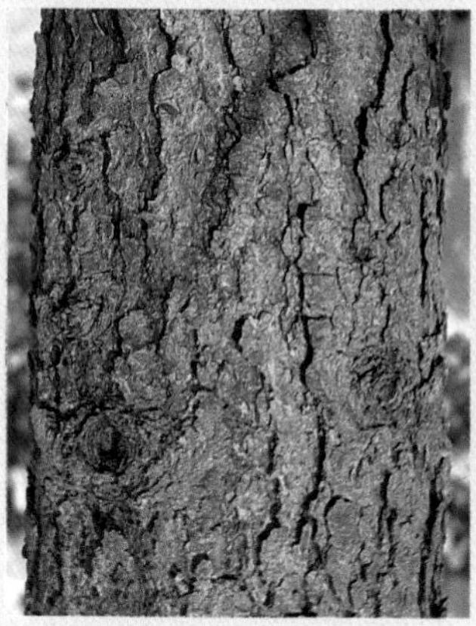

265 Young tree with medium to deeply furrowed brown-red bark

266 Old tree with thick, grey, deeply furrowed bark

Crab Apple

Malus sylvestris* ssp. *domestica (Borkh.) Mansf.

Pommier
Apfelbaum

Pages 112, 196, 197

Large, twisting branches, thick foliage and a broad crown are the identifying features of the Crab Apple. It rarely grows above a height of 10m.

The young tree has a light grey, smooth bark. Later in its life this turns grey-brown and cracks into small, square plates. The underlying wood consists of broad, light reddish sapwood and brownish red, medium-heavy (one cubic metre of dried, sawn wood weighs 700–850kg), extremely valuable heartwood. The wood is hard, dense, difficult to cut, often with twisted fibres, contracts severely and will not withstand damp. It dries slowly and is inclined to crack and warp. The annual rings are distinctive for the wavy lines of the end-of-season wood. The wood is very hard and turns and polishes excellently but is available only in small sizes. It is used for chessmen, tool-handles and mallet-heads.

Erect umbels appear at the tips of the short shoots, known as 'spurs', together with the leaves, in May or June. Their hermaphrodite flowers possess a 1.3cm long stalk, which has a felt-like covering of hairs. Each calyx has about 5 sepal tips and is a green-brown colour, with a similar felt-like covering of hairs. Between them are found the obovate to round, acutely pointed petals. They are white, tipped with a faint pink shade at the edges and up to 25mm long. The 10–20 anthers, with their yellow pollen sacks, surround and shelter the ovary. The ovary has a fine covering of hair and slightly stunted or only half-grown styles. When the fruit develops, the ovary becomes the parchment-like casing. The flesh of the round, green, yellow or red fruit, the apple – which is in fact only a pseudocarp or 'false fruit' – is actually formed from the receptacle, not the ovary.

The alternate leaves are elliptic to ovate in outline and have stalks. The blades have a delicately notched or serrate margin and curved reticulate veins running towards the tip of the leaf.

In hilly regions, where the ground is rich in minerals and chalky, and there is plenty of sun, Crab Apples produce plentiful fruit. Areas which experience late frosts are ill-suited to the Crab Apple.

Unlike the Greeks, who knew only a few varieties of apple tree, the Romans cultivated about 29 different sorts. In central and northern Europe the cultivation of the apple tree can be traced back to the Stone Age. However, many of the varieties with which we are familiar today are not descended from the trees of the plough builder, but, like so many other types of fruit, were introduced by the Romans.

The mythological role of the apple is obscured by the fact that when the Greeks passed down their word for 'apple', the fruits of the quince and the pomegranate trees were included under the same name. Thus the interpretation of the 'golden apple' which plays an important part in the judgement of Paris can vary. In this story, Eris is said to have thrown a golden apple bearing the inscription 'to the fairest one' into the midst of three goddesses attending the wedding of Peleus and Thetis – Hera, Athene and Aphrodite. Since each of the three claimed the apple as her own, a hefty argument broke out. At first, no one could come to an agreement. In the hope of finding a solution, Paris was chosen to act as arbiter. Each of the three goddesses promised him valuable gifts. Eventually Paris chose Aphrodite, who had promised to give him Helen. Thus the fruit became the symbol of love.

The 'Golden Apples of the Hesperides', which Gaia caused to burst forth as a wedding present for Hera, must actually have been pomegranates. These fruits had the power to bestow immortality. They were watched over by the Hesperides and the dragon Ladeu. Heracles, the most popular of the Greek heroes, and prototype of all masculine strength, broke into the gardens, killed the hundred-headed dragon and seized the fruit.

Like so many symbols, the apple is ambivalent. We should not forget the story of the Fall or of Persephone, Snow White, William Tell or the Imperial apple. In the story of the Fall, the apple was the block over which Adam and Eve stumbled. After they had eaten of the forbidden fruit of the tree of knowledge they were denied access to the tree of life, and thus to immortality. Thus the apple has become the symbol of knowledge and sin. Persephone was abducted and taken down as a bride to the underworld of Hades. When Hermes came to fetch her back, Hades gave his spouse an apple to eat before she left. Through doing so she became forever bound to the underworld. In the fairy story 'Snow White', the apple conceals the deadly poison, in the tale of William Tell it becomes the symbol of hope and freedom, and in the case of the Imperial apple of the German Kaiser – the work of a goldsmith – of power and sovereignty.

The Crab Apple is native to England but uncommon, found mainly on the edge of old woodlands in the most rural areas and becoming scarce towards the north. In all parts the true native tree is less often seen than seedlings arising from domestic apples. These are most frequent beside roads and come from cores ejected from passing vehicles. The true wild tree has some thorns in its shoots and has pure white flowers. A tinge of pink in the flowers shows a tree to be a domestic seedling and it will be found to lack thorns completely.

Associated place-names include Appledore, Devon and Kent; Appledram, Sussex; Appletreewick, Yorkshire; Appleby, Cumbria; and Apley, Lincolnshire, Shropshire, Somerset and Isle of Wight.

267 Apple tree in spring

268 Several flowers in erect panicles

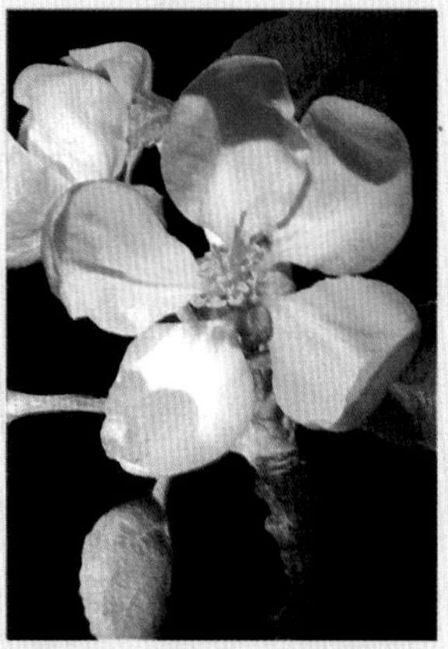
269 Single flower viewed from above

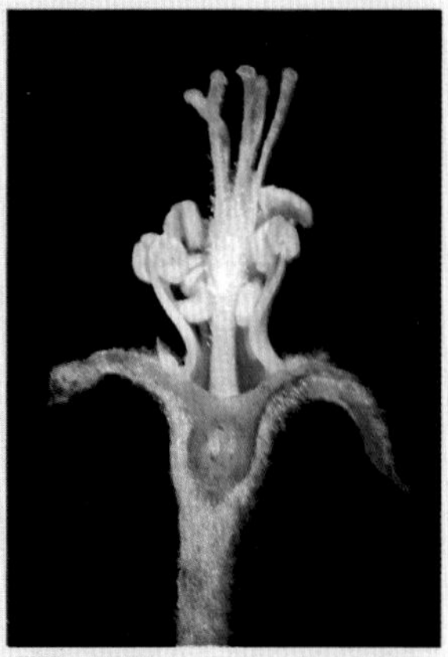
270 Vertical section through an apple flower: ovary, 5 styles (fused at the bottom) and anthers

271 Apple tree in summer

272 Leaves 5–9cm long, arranged alternately

273 Superior leaf-surface, often slightly wavy and glabrous

274 Inferior leaf-surface, pale, grey-green, villous at first

275 Apple tree in autumn

276 Apples

277 The fruit

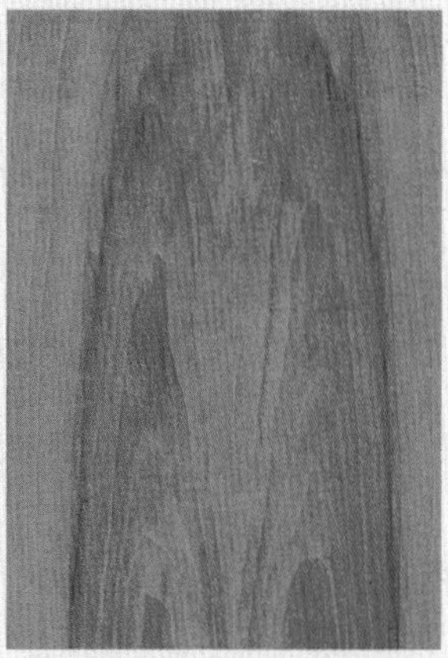
278 Brown-red heartwood, very hard, heavy and valuable

279 Apple tree in winter

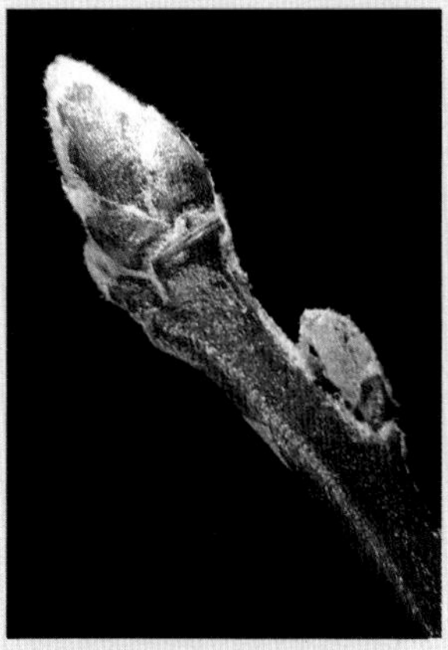
280 Terminal bud, ovoid to spherical, dominating the side buds

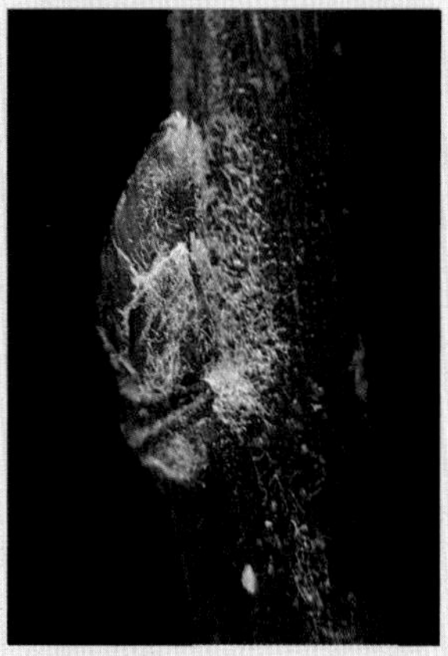
281 Side bud, narrow-ovoid, clinging to the twig

282 Older tree with grey-brown bark, flaking in thin plates

White Poplar

Populus alba L.

Peuplier blanc
Weisspappel

Pages 86, 152, 153

In Britain, the average height of this rather straggly tree, with its initially dome-shaped but later broader crown, is something like 15-18m (10-30m in other parts of Europe). Under favourable conditions the trunk will grow to a circumference of around 60cm.

The White Poplar is a relatively small, bushy, suckering tree that grows rapidly when young. It is much confused with the altogether finer tree, the Grey Poplar, *Populus canescens*. It can be told apart from it by its smaller, bushier or leaning growth and, by direct comparison, the pure snowy white of the underside of the leaf. That of the Grey Poplar is less bright and tends towards pale grey. Both the White and the Grey Poplars bear lobed leaves when young but they are more marked and persist longer in the White Poplar while the Grey soon has only rounded aspen-like leaves. The White Poplar is short-lived and rarely achieves 18m before dying or being blown down. The Grey Poplar, however, can live for over 200 years and grows rapidly into an imposing tree of 35m or more with a straight, long bole and a few stout, spreading branches.

The bark of the young White Poplar is whitish grey to grey-green and turns with age into coarse, dark grey, cracked bark, which is deeply furrowed and ridged down its length. Underneath is to be found a wide layer of sapwood and an evenly constructed and stable, red to brownish yellow core of heartwood. Corresponding to the rapid growth, the annual rings are very wide. The pores are small to medium sized and, like the very fine medullary rays, are not visible to the naked eye. The very lightweight wood (one cubic metre of dry wood weighs 400-500kg) has a smooth and somewhat sandy surface. It distorts and contracts very little, and is very soft, but tough. It is elastic, but will not resist pressure or bending.

It is easy to work, to glue, to stain, but not to polish. When freshly cut this wood has a rather acidic smell. The largest user of poplar wood is the plywood industry. Plywood and joiner's boards made from this wood are very light and stable.

In addition, this wood is used for making boxes, firewood baskets, wooden tiles, drawing boards, wood-carving and for making cellulose.

Perhaps because by the time they are 30-40 years old, Grey Poplars are already 20m high, and within that short time produce a great yield, their place in folk traditions is all the more prominent. In terms of their size, both Black and Grey Poplars, as well as the numerous other strains, outstrip all other species of indigenous tree.

Poplars thrive in soil which is rich in minerals, deep, loose, damp, sandy to loamy or sandy-humus, rich in calcium, and where the level of the water table is high. This group of trees is therefore one of those most frequently encountered in softwood meadows and riverside woodland. Where they grow in dry, deficient soil, White Poplars often have a slightly deformed, rather bush-like appearance. Of all the poplars growing in these kind of conditions, however, the White Poplar is most able to tolerate the dryness of the soil.

This tree, which first arrived from southern Europe in the Middle Ages, is a typical representative of the hilly zone. It can, on the other hand, be found growing at up to 1500m above sea level. We find it not only on the banks of the larger rivers, but more and more often as a decorative tree in parks and urban streets. Thanks to its hairy, felt-like leaves, the tree traps a lot of the dust in the atmosphere, and this helps to keep town centres clean. The dust, which sticks between the hairs, is usually washed away by heavy rainfall, so that even in heavily polluted areas the tree will not suffer any damage.

Both the White and the Grey Poplar are of southern and central European and west Asiatic origin and were brought in by early settlers long before records of such things were kept. Any tribes moving across to England very soon after the ice had retreated would have valued the White Poplar to grow for shelter in the loose sands and glacial outwash where there were no trees, and the Grey Poplar for more substantial shelterbelts in broad valleys. The best Grey Poplars today are in the wide, shallow valleys in chalklands in Hampshire and Wiltshire and on the limestones of central Ireland. Like the White Poplar, this tree can grow well on dune sand even where its roots must be in brackish water at high tide. A fine example of its resistance to sea winds, sea water, poor soil and northern extremes is a fine 30m tree on the tideline at Dunrobin Castle, Sutherland.

The White Poplar is local on farmland, by roadsides and behind sand-dunes and sometimes as an ornamental tree in town parks, in which it grows well. The Grey Poplar is much more frequent in all parts, with some big trees lining roads in the Highlands and many in farmland valleys in the chalklands of England as well as in town and city parks. It resists industrial pollution well.

Some trees have male inflorescences, others female. These emerge in March or April, before the leaves, from spherical, slightly pointed, very large buds.

The male catkins are 3-7cm long, up to 1.5cm thick, bearing innumerable flowers, at first narrowly ovoid and protruding, later narrowly cylindrical and dangling. Each flower has an irregularly dentate and villously haired bract and numerous anthers (at first crimson, later yellow).

The female flowers are also attached to long, greenish yellow catkins. The bracts are again irregularly dentate and have villous hairs.

The ovary is greenish coloured, has a short stalk, is conical and elongated. The two stigmas are also yellow-green. After the flowering season, whitish leaves with dense hairs on both surfaces unfold from pointed-ovate to conical end- and side-buds. Later they grow to 5-12cm in length, are oval or three-lobed, have a 2-4cm long stalk and at the base of the blade are either rounded or truncate. The superior surface is shiny dark green and is by now no longer hairy. The inferior surface remains thickly coated with white hairs.

In Greek mythology the tree not only receives frequent mention, but is even dedicated to a specific god - Hades, the god of the underworld. The tree owes its very existence to Hades' passion for the beautiful daughter of Okeanos, the god of the seas, whose name was Leuke. After the death of Leuke, Hades, by way of tribute to the dead woman, caused the White Poplar to grow in the Elysian fields, where the souls of the departed reside, and regarded it as a sacred tree. It was also sacred to the wife of Hades, Persephone. It was chosen to grow in the underworld on the banks of the Lake of Remembrance. Since, at that time, everyone was quite convinced of the idea that the White Poplar grew in the underworld, it was often planted in cemeteries and next to memorials.

According to another legend, the Heliades, the daughters of the sun god Zeus, froze with grief for their murdered brother Phaeton, and were turned into poplars (Virgil, Aeneid 10, 190; Ovid, Epistulae ex Ponto 1, 2, 33v). The poplar is also mentioned in connection with the cult of Dionysus. (Dionysus was the god of wine and fruitfulness and encouraged his followers to bear witness to the power of nature.) Anyone initiated into

283 White Poplar in spring

284 Many flowered, narrow-cylindrical, 3–7cm long, drooping male catkins

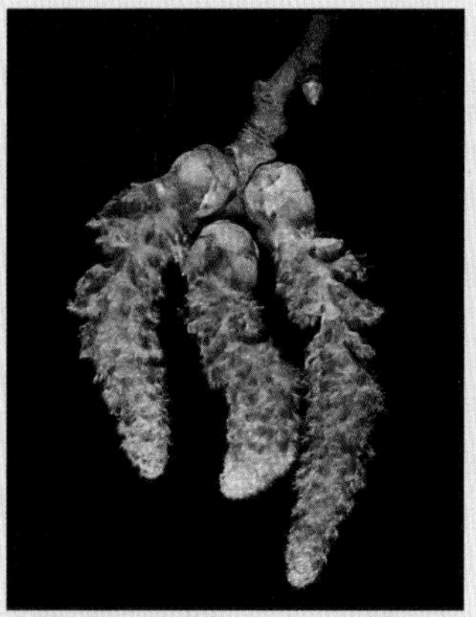
285 Young, still narrow-ovoid, male catkins

286 Male flowers: (above) from the front, (below) from the back

287 White Poplar in summer

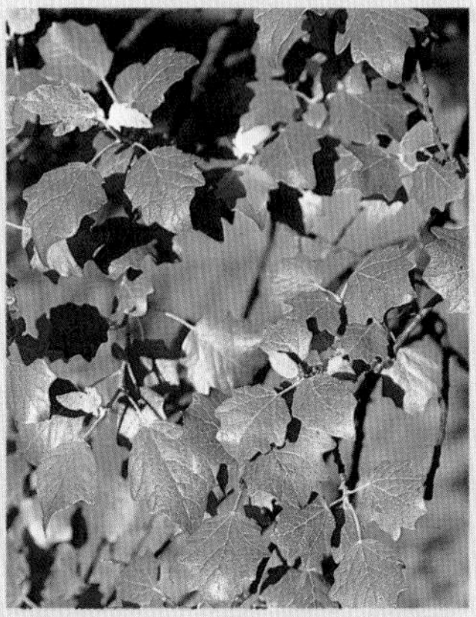
288 Leaves, 5–12cm long, lobed or dentate

289 Superior leaf surface, shiny, dark green, becoming glabrous

290 Inferior leaf surface, retains dense white hair layer

291 White Poplar in autumn

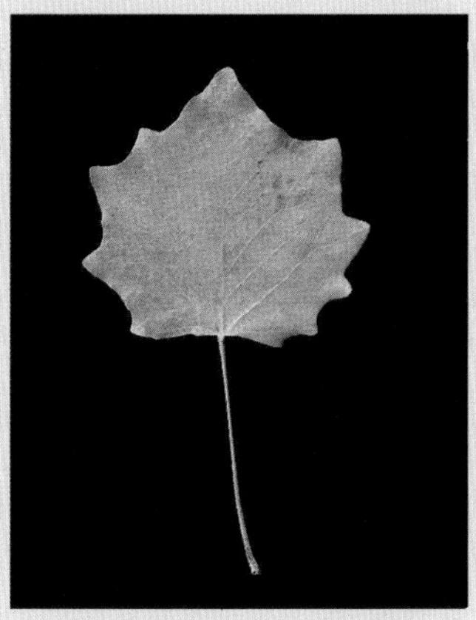
292 Round shaped autumn leaf

293 Untreated wood: whitish sapwood (right) and reddish brown heartwood (left)

294 Wood treated with linseed oil: pale sapwood (right); dark reddish brown heartwood

295 White Poplar in winter

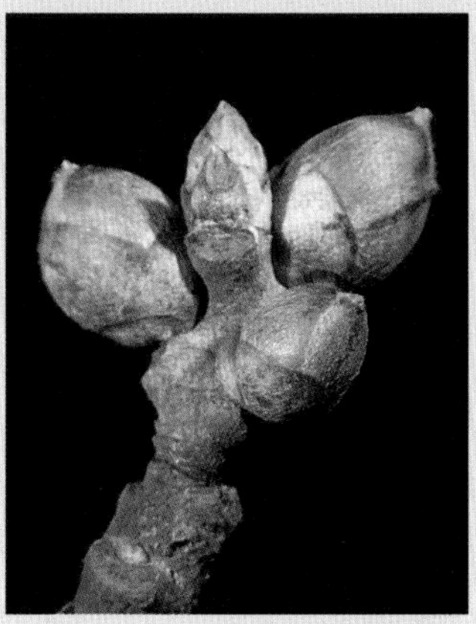
296 Broad-ovoid to spherical flower buds and pointed-ovoid leaf bud

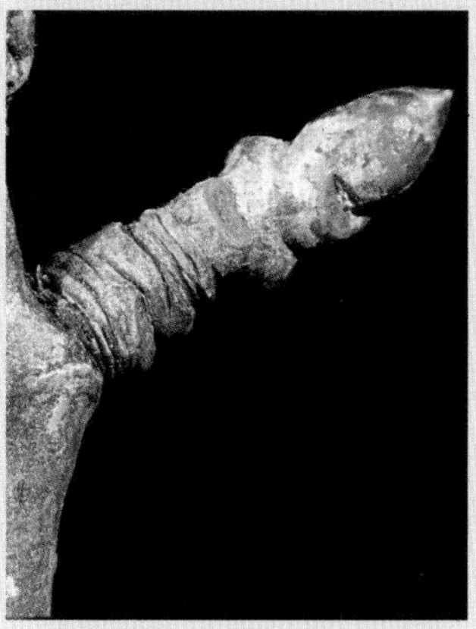
297 Wedge-shaped side bud on short shoot

298 Originally smooth, grey-green young bark; older bark black and ridged

this cult was crowned with a ring of poplar leaves. For Dionysus, like Hades, is a chtonian god. The chtonian gods (the earth gods) rule over life and death – Hades reigns in the kingdom of the dead and Dionysus represents all the energy of the life-force. The poplar thus bears a relationship to both life and death.

In another legend we learn that Heracles (the Greeks' favourite hero) returned from the underworld with a crown of White Poplar leaves. The White Poplar was his favourite tree. The practice at Olympia of using poplar branches to weave the victor's crown has been traced back to him. It is said that when Heracles erected an altar to Zeus, the only wood which was permitted to be burned on it was that of the White Poplar. Such traditions as the ritual burning of poplar wood and the weaving of victors' crowns from White Poplar branches obviously came about because of the silvery surface of the leaf.

Lombardy Poplar

Populus nigra* var. *Italica Muenchh.

Peuplier de Lombardie
Pyramidenpappel

Pages 107, 188, 189

The Lombardy Poplar grows over 30m tall and acquires a 3m-thick trunk. Its branches grow directly upwards and its crown is narrow-columnar or extended-conical in shape. Even in trees over several hundred years old this only measures up to 2m at the most across.

The tree is a particular growth-form of the Black Poplar. Beneath the thick, cracked, ridged, ochre bark lies a whitish layer of sapwood and the grey-yellow to light brown heartwood. The annual rings are usually pretty wide and easily distinguished because of the dark end-of-season wood lines. The light-coloured wood has large fibres, is very soft, spongy, easily hewn and weighs little (mass of dry, cut wood is 400-550kg/m^3). It contracts little and is not very durable when dry. It is used principally for making boxes, drying barrels, blind wood and in the match and cellulose industries.

These dioecious poplars produce female or male flowers in March or at the beginning of April out of brown, broadly conical buds.

The male inflorescences are up to 7cm long, 0.4–0.8cm across, heavy with tiny flowers and dangling. The flowers have a triangular, hairless, palmate bract and 12–30 anthers with red pollen sacks. After pollination these turn purple or black.

The female trees, have 12cm-long, many-flowered, dangling catkins. Next to the palmate bract, the flowers each have a two-carpelled ovary, at the base of which the nectar is produced. When it ripens, the two folds of the ovary open up to release very small seeds. Being equipped with a small tuft of hair, they can be carried quite long distances away from the parent tree.

The leaves only open after the flowering season. At first they are a reddish bright green colour; later on, the superior surface turns dark green and the inferior surface grey-green. Both surfaces are hairless from the start. When fully grown they are 4–8cm long, broadly wedge-shaped at the base of the blade, with a sinuately serrate, dentate margin and a 1–3cm long stalk, slightly tinged with red.

This tree is often planted on river banks to stock up the vegetation on the water's edge, near farmhouses, as protection against lightning, on country roads, in rows to form a windbreak, and near churches and homes for decoration.

The poplar is most widespread in hilly regions, and is rarely found in the mountains. Where it does occur this high it usually does so in 'bush' form.

In ideal ground conditions – in damp, humus-rich soil – the Lombardy Poplar can grow to a height of 20–25m within the first 40–50 years. If, though, as a result of changes in the water supply, the soil loses its humidity, not only does it cease to grow, but also starts to become sickly, the first sign of which becomes apparent when the topmost branches turn dry and brittle. It is much more sensitive to frost and cold than the Black Poplar.

This species of poplar did not find its way from Persia to the Mediterranean region until the end of the 17th century. And it is a very late arrival in central Europe. The true Lombardy Poplar is a male clone. In 1740 a male tree from Lombardy is said to have been planted in a park in Worlitz bei Dachau. Many of the trees growing in central and East Germany are thought to be descended from this tree. Female examples, of unknown origin, were found for the first time in 1859 in Karlsruhe and Vienna, and again in 1870 in Frankfurt am Oder.

The Lombardy Poplars in France, Alsace and western Switzerland are supposed to be of French origin, because Napoleon I is thought to have had a fondness for them and to have planted them along his armies' routes.

The true Lombardy Poplar was brought to England from Turin in 1758 by the Earl of Rochford and planted at his home, St Osyth Priory in Essex, where it still is, split into two trunks, each with several young stems growing to 21m. This tree is very common in all settled areas except parts of the Highlands. It is often 30m tall even in very open, exposed places, and many are now over 35m. It is remarkably windfirm, but the 1987 hurricane blew down the tallest, which was 40m tall, in Marble Hill Park, Twickenham.

299 Lombardy Poplar in spring

300 Male catkins up to 7cm long, many-flowered, drooping

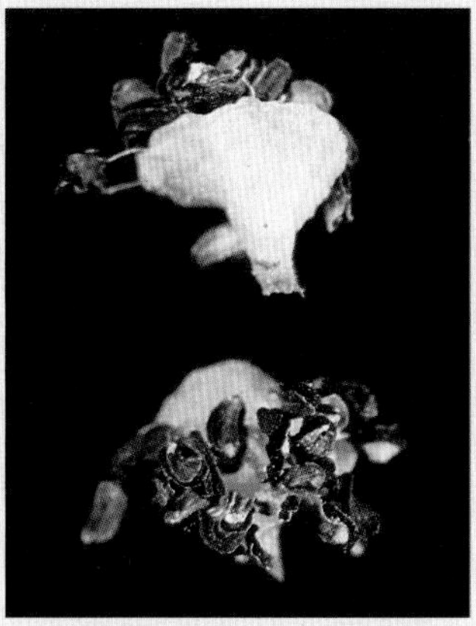

301 Male flowers: (above) from behind, (below) from the front

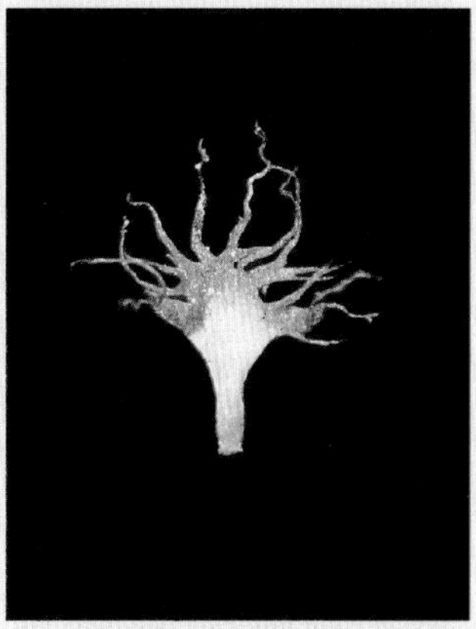

302 Flower bract, markedly palmate

303 Lombardy Poplar in summer

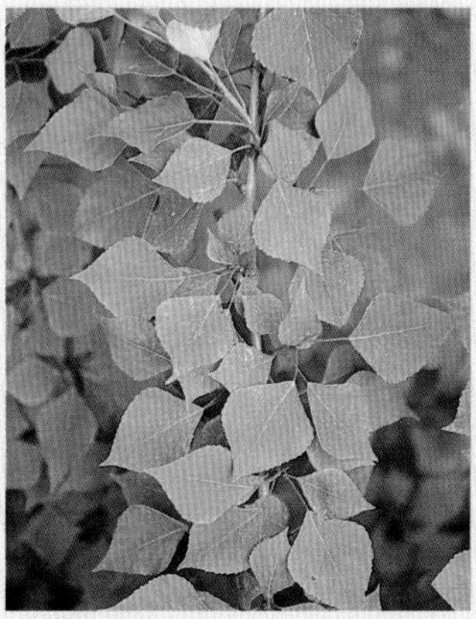

304 Leaves 4–8cm long, diamond-shaped in outline, arranged alternately

305 Superior leaf surface, grey-green, glabrous

306 Lombardy Poplar in autumn

307 Lombardy Poplar in autumn

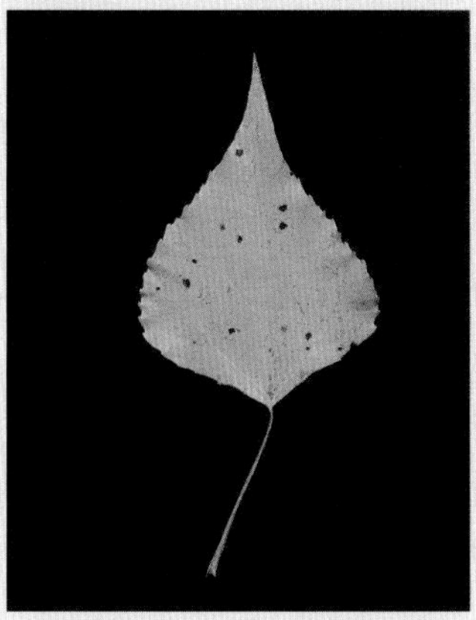

308 Diamond-shaped autumn leaf

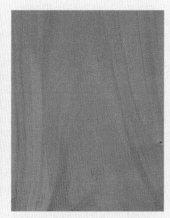

309 Poplar wood treated with linseed

310 Young tree with ochre-coloured bark, with occasional deep furrows

311 Lombardy Poplar in winter

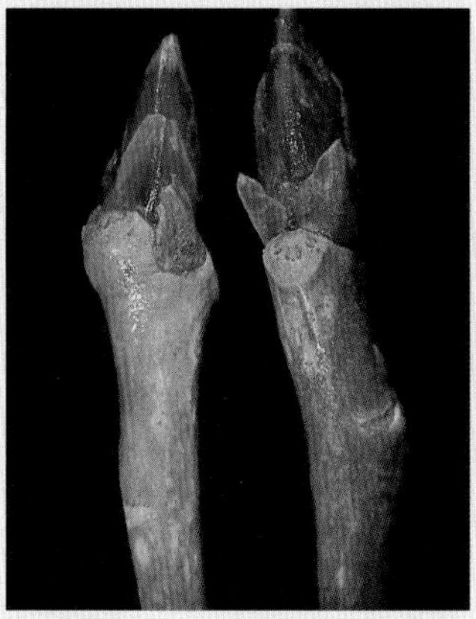

312 Narrow-spherical terminal buds

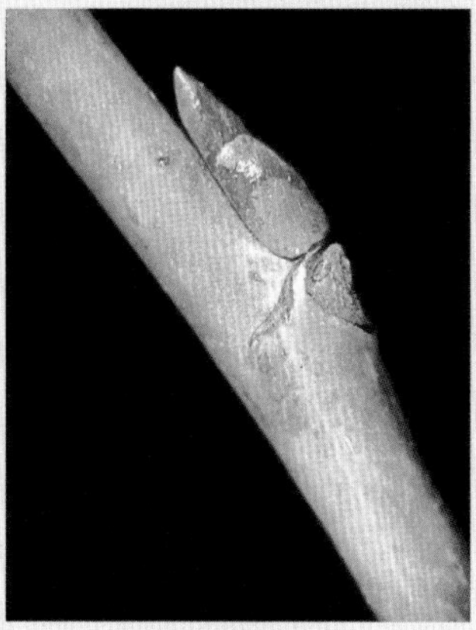

313 Narrow-ovoid, pointed side bud

314 Older tree with thick, cracked, grey bark

Common Pear

Pyrus communis* var. *sativa L.

Poirier
Birnbaum

Pages 112, 196, 197

When growing singly, the pear tree can reach a height of 20m. It has a straight, slender stem with a reasonably broad, conic crown, which is largely formed of ascending branches. Its light grey to blackish bark is cracked into small squares by horizontal and vertical lines. All single trees produce small, early-ripening fruits, which are usually used for making fruit juices or wine. Certain grafted varieties of pear tree, yielding large quantities of fruit, require a protected site. An increasing preference is developing in the fruit industry for trellis and 'bush' varieties, as opposed to fully grown trees, as they are much less expensive to harvest, prune and protect from disease. Bushes, being closer to the ground, have a stronger defence against dehydration and frost than tall trees.

The Common Pear is one of the mature woods. Sapwood and heartwood are scarcely distinguishable.

The heartwood is light brown, with a reddish tinge, fairly hard, very compact, difficult to hew, not very supple, often wavy-grained, very durable in its dry state, and, compared to the wood of the apple tree, has fairly fine fibres. One cubic metre of naturally dried wood weighs 650–750kg. As it has a strong tendency to warp, it must be dried very slowly. If it has been well dried it is easy to handle, to carve, polish and cut. It readily accepts the application of varnish and staining agents. Pear wood is one of the finest indigenous woods. It is used to make furniture, musical instruments, letter-openers, rulers, casting moulds, and precision instruments. As it also reacts well to being steamed and painted black, it is used for making piano keys by way of a substitute for ebony.

The leaves are alternately spaced along the twigs, and are up to 8cm long, elliptic, ovate or orbicular, with a slender stalk. Their margin is finely serrate or entire in places. In autumn they turn yellow to dark red.

Between May and June, up to 9cm long panicles appear on the end of short, leaf-bearing shoots. The individual flowers each have 5 triangular, greenish sepals, both surfaces of which are hairy, and 5 ovate to orbicular petals, both surfaces of which are white.

The 20–30 anthers on the young flowers are dark red in colour. The inferior ovary, with its 5 free-waving styles, which are often hairy at the base, consist of 5 carpels.

During the last 2–4 days of the female flower's development, the insect pollination takes place. The first thing that happens is that the anthers, inside the flower, which up until now have been pointing inwards, turn outwards and release their pollen grains. This phenomenon (known as heterostyly) precludes the possibility of self-pollination. In rare instances, though, it does nevertheless occur. However, the resulting fruit is usually not very healthy.

Common Pear trees grow very slowly. They will only reach a height of 20m when growing in deep, damp, calcareous soil, in a position which is exposed on the south side. When the climate and soil conditions are not appropriate the tree will have stunted and often rather deformed growth.

The Common Pear is indigenous to hilly and mountain regions and can actually be sown at very high altitudes.

As early as the Stone Age, man was gathering the fruit of the pear tree. He actually began to cultivate it at a much later stage, in Persia and Armenia. From there it spread to Greece, then to Rome, and thence to northern Europe. Several varieties were already known at the time of the Romans. We can be sure that the early Greeks were familiar with the cultivated pear tree from the epic poem about Tantalos. He was one of the sons of Zeus, and at first was in good favour with the gods. But later he sinned, and was condemned to eternal atonement in Hades. He was made to stand in water, and was afflicted with an unquenchable thirst. If he bent down to drink, the source dried up. If he stretched upwards, the branches of the overhanging pear trees would shrink out of his reach. At the same time, a boulder was poised just above his head, threatening to crash down on top of him at any moment.

In ancient Greek, the word for the Common Pear was 'Apion' or 'Apies'. According to Athenaios, the archipelago of the Peloponnes was known as the Apia, that is, the land of the pear tree.

As we learn from Pliny, the ancient Romans were already familiar with 35 different varieties of pear.

In the Middle Ages, new varieties were cultivated on country estates and in monasteries.

The pear tree plays a less prominent role in cultural tradition than the apple tree. From time to time, however, it does crop up as a symbol of fertility.

In Britain, the only truly wild pear is *Pyrus cordata*, a small, spiny, bushy tree in Devon and Cornwall, where it is very rare and was discovered in 1865. The widespread, apparently wild trees frequently found in hedgerows are seedlings of introduced cultivated forms. In Gloucestershire and Herefordshire there are still many trees surviving in fields that were formerly perry orchards. They often carry large bunches of mistletoe. In the Vale of Evesham, Worcestershire, some hedges retain many trees from older orchards of eating pears, and these are a feature in autumn when the leaves turn bronze, orange and dark red.

The wood is too knotty and inferior to have any uses, and is even useless as fuel.

315 Pear tree in spring

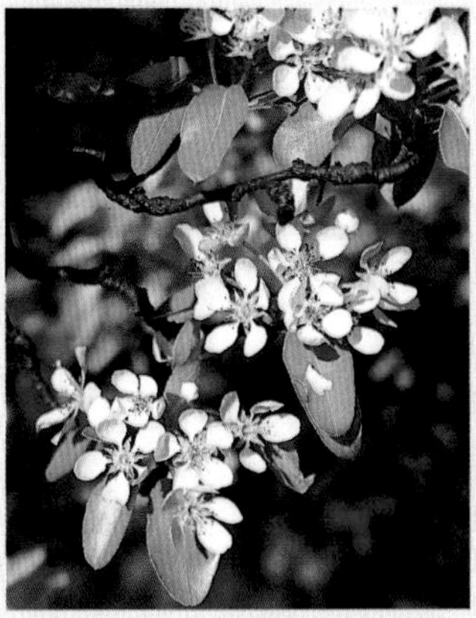
316 Flowers with stalks up to 3cm long in panicles of 3–9

317 Young flower seen from above: anthers still red

318 Vertical section of a flower

319 Pear tree in summer

320 Leaves up to 7cm long, arranged alternately

321 Superior leaf surface, pale green and glabrous

322 Inferior leaf surface, pale green and glabrous

323 Pear tree in autumn

324 Fruit at end of September

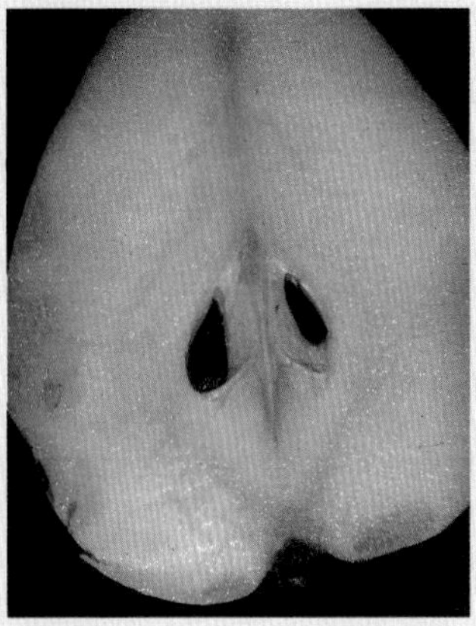
325 Cross section through a pear with core and flesh

326 Brownish red pear wood (treated with linseed)

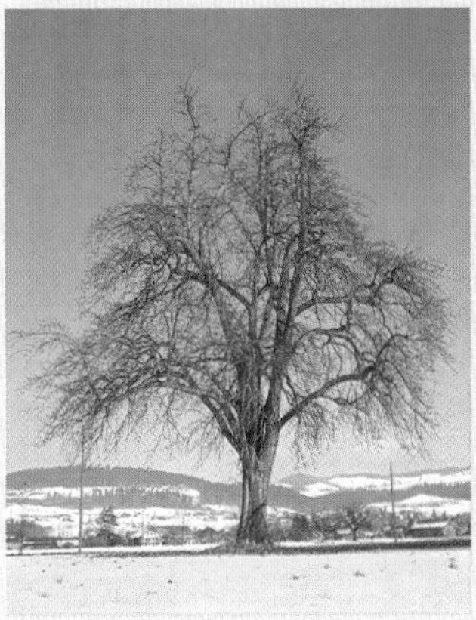
327 Pear tree in winter

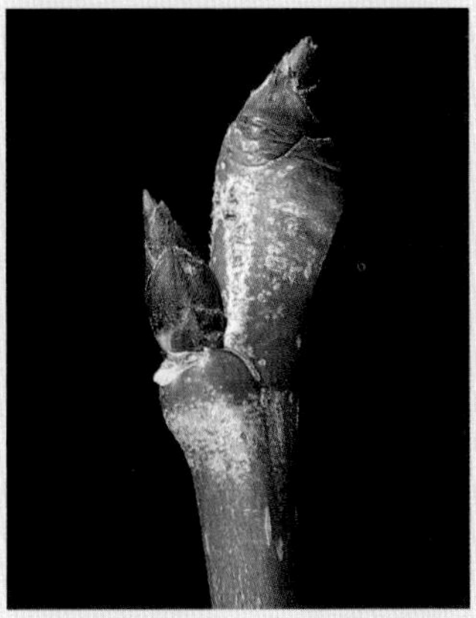
328 Narrow- and broad-ovoid side and terminal buds

329 Projecting side buds on a long shoot

330 Grey-black bark cracked into small squares by vertical and horizontal lines

Wild Cherry, Gean

Prunus avium L.

Cerisier
Kirschbaum

Pages 118, 204, 205

When growing in woodland, the Wild Cherry has a long, straight trunk with thick branching arising from its upper reaches, and will grow to a maximum height of 25m. When growing in the open, on the other hand, it has a short, almost circular bole, with ascending branches.

Its crown is whorled like that of a pine or spruce, a ring of branches at the end of each year's growth. Since young trees usually grow 0.8m or so in a year, the whorls are this much apart, making a very open crown. In later years growth slows down and the crown becomes more dense, the lower crown from lateral shoots. Trees are often over 22m tall and occasionally over 27m but their lives are usually short and 1m is a good diameter before decay sets in. One tree, however, at Studley Royal in Yorkshire, was 144cm in diameter in 1966 and, when it should have been dead in 1984, it was a robust 170cm.

The outer rind is smooth, leathery, shiny and silvery grey. It peels away in horizontal strips, and is therefore known as ring bark. It later develops lengthwise ridges and turns black.

Underneath the bark is a narrow band of reddish white sapwood, enclosing the reddish yellow heartwood. Over the course of the year, the sapwood soon comes to look very similar to the heartwood, and they are therefore fairly interchangeable. As a result of exposure to light over the years, Wild Cherry wood gradually darkens in colour. It becomes increasingly attractive, to the point where it achieves its unique and unparalleled red-brown shade. It is a very valuable wood. It is hard, pliable, difficult to chop, compact, fine-fibred, supple, heavy (600-700kg/m^3), not weatherproof, but very tough. The reason it is so difficult to chop is that its fibres are so fine and its composition so compact.

It is often used to make very expensive veneers for interior fittings. Also, as basic material for brush and knife handles, for arts and crafts, and musical instruments. Wood with an attractive grain is always very much sought after for use in marquetry.

Wild Cherry wood is easily combined with other woods such as fir, maple and larch. It is often used in these combinations in the furniture industry.

If the bole is not to be artificially dried, it should really be left for 2-3 years inside the bark, somewhere dry, with good air circulation. During this time the initial tendency to sharp contraction will be overcome and the wood will settle. After the first incision has been made, the bark is stripped off and stored carefully in a barn. Sometimes green stripes may appear during the drying process. As long as these are not too severe, they can be treated with hydrogen peroxide. Wild Cherry wood does have rather a tendency to crack and contract. The wood of Wild Cherry trees growing in woodlands is usually darker than that of a tree growing out in the open.

Characteristic of Wild Cherry wood are its very straight, light-coloured, medullary rays.

There is a special and very limited market for this wood in England. The best trees grow on or near the chalk downs and a group of estates on the southern slopes of the Chiltern Hills across the Buckinghamshire–Hertfordshire border are organised to supply it.

In April or May, umbellate clusters of white flowers break out from the round, chubby terminal buds left by the previous year's shoots. Their stalks are 3-5mm in length and either protrude or droop. The 5 sepals are ovate, short-acuminate, with, for the most part, entire margins. They are usually slightly bent backwards. Between them lie the 5 white, ovate to orbicular, slightly emarginate, 10–15mm long petals.

Shortly before the end of the flowering period, or immediately after it, obovate leaves with a wedge-shaped or rounded base unfold from ovate, pointed, reddish-brown buds. The leaf stalks support 2–4 large red nectar glands. Apart from at the tip of the leaf, the margin is sharply serrate. The leaves are 6–15mm long, alternate along the branch, and turn yellow or red in the autumn.

The cherry is a stoned fruit. Its flesh is yellow-red, red or black, and encloses a hard, usually one-seeded stone. The Wild Cherry does not always yield as much fruit as it might, owing to damage caused by birds, rain, hailstones and the cherry fly.

For it to be able to grow naturally and produce large quantities of fruit, the Wild Cherry tree needs warm, deep, porous, nutritious soil. Since the tree flowers early it is very susceptible to late frosts, so it is often planted on slopes at fairly high altitudes, or on upland plains, where cold air is less likely to accumulate. It is hardly ever found more than 1000 feet above sea level.

All varieties of Wild Cherry are related to the Bird Cherry which, as fossils and prehistoric discoveries have shown, has always been indigenous to central Europe. (Excavations of Neolithic or Bronze Age sites on the edges of the Alps have revealed that its wood was used to make props for early 'stilt' houses.) Grafted varieties were, however, unknown in Europe before the Roman period, but were to be found in Asia Minor.

According to Diphylos and Theophrastus, assorted varieties of Wild Cherry were familiar to the Greeks as early as 400 BC. The Romans, on the other hand, from the time of Servius until the introduction of the grafted varieties of Wild Cherry by Lucullus, only knew the wild varieties, with their bitter fruit.

An important centre for the cultivation of the cherry tree was to be found on the Pontos coast of Asia Minor, near the town of Kerasos. When this town was destroyed, Lucullus (a Roman commander, 79–37 BC) brought fruit from the grafted species back to Rome.

Cultivation of domestic cherry trees was common in the time of Lysimachos of Pella (c. 360–281 BC, a high-ranking officer under Alexander the Great).

The Romans took grafted varieties of cherry over the Alps, as is proven by discoveries in numerous Roman settlements.

This tree crossed the land-bridge to England not so long before that eroded and when it was a chalk ridge, but long enough to have spread into Scotland, where it is called the 'gean'. It spreads rapidly because thrushes, blackbirds and starlings eat the little fruit avidly and the passage through their highly acidic stomachs makes the seeds ready to germinate. The lack of place-names of Anglo-Saxon origin involving the cherry and the first mention of it as a wild tree being as late as 1634 has made it possible to dispute that it is a native and to credit the Romans with its introduction. Its early spread to all parts is easy to explain if even a very few were grown in remote gardens, but it seems likely that such a tree would come here unaided.

This tree has been much planted lately because of its value as a fast-growing ornamental tree, on chalk and clay soils, its abundance of spring flowers being followed in autumn by yellow, orange and crimson colouring, and its value to birds.

331 Cherry tree in spring

332 Flowers 3-5cm long, single or in clusters

333 Flower seen from above: petals white, obovate and emarginate

334 Vertical section through a cherry flower

335 Cherry tree in summer

336 Leaves 6-15cm long, arranged alternately

337 Superior leaf surface, dark green, glabrous, often wrinkled

338 Inferior leaf surface, pale green, slightly villous when young

339 Cherry tree in autumn

340 Red fruits

341 Black fruits

342 Reddish heartwood, turning darker on exposure to light

343 Cherry tree in winter

344 Terminal buds on a long shoot

345 Heaped leaf and flower buds on a short shoot

346 Older tree with vertical ridges and grey-black bark

Common Oak, Pedunculate Oak

Quercus robur L.

Chêne pédonculé
Stiel-Eiche Sommer-Eiche

Pages 89, 158, 159

The English Oak has a strong, irregular, heavily branched crown, with protruding, horizontal branches. It usually has a life span of around 500 years, although 700 to 1200-year-old trees are sometimes to be found. It can grow to a height of 30–35m, or, exceptionally, even 60m. Its long, deep-reaching and very strong central root accounts for the oak's resistance in the face of storms. Young oak trees grow very quickly, but this rate slows down after about 100–200 years. They continue, however, to increase in thickness, if not in height. Numerous branches often erupt from the trunk only a few metres above the ground, and this can lend the tree an almost 'two-tiered' aspect.

The English Oak was later to arrive after the Ice Ages than the Sessile Oak and this would tend to explain the largely southern and eastern occurrence today of English Oak woods, and the northern and western preponderance of Sessile Oak woods. In the clay lowlands, the English Oak soon replaced the Small-leaved Lime as the main element in the woods and has been ever since, the commonest tree in woodlands other than those on the chalk hills.

Climate and soil also take a part in the current distribution of the two oaks common in England. The Sessile Oak prefers a humid site with high rainfall but fairly rapid drainage and therefore grows well on mountainsides from rocky ghylls to shaley slopes in the cool of the heights of Dartmoor, Exmoor, the Welsh hills, Cumbria and the Highlands. It has occasional outliers on gravels and clays in the high-lying parts of the Weald of Surrey and Sussex and throughout Enfield Chase, the area along the west side of the lower River Lee. The English Oak can tolerate warmer, drier air but needs as much moisture at the root, so it grows where the soil is retentive, in thick clays and valley bottoms. It may prefer humid air as well, as the English Oaks in the bottoms of Highland glens, especially in Perthshire and Angus, are much taller than those in eastern England, 30–35m being far from rare heights, when elsewhere trees are seldom much above 25m. Growing where it can reach moisture, the English Oak is not reported as having ever suffered from drought, even in 1976. It often spreads, through acorn-planting by jays, far on to sandy heaths but makes there only low, bushy trees.

The comparative uselessness of the narrow, brownish-white sapwood is made up for by the yellow-brown heartwood, which has a pattern of broadly spaced medullary rays and is superior in strength and durability to any other European wood. It is hard, easy to split and to work with, very heavy (670–1400kg/m^3), and preserves well under water. It is used as building wood for overground structures, foundations, ship-building, for making barrels, railway sleepers and parquet as well as other kinds of floors, boat frames, window ledges and water wheels. Oak veneers are also much sought after.

The most common flaws in oak wood are frost cracks, and the holes made by the lichen bock. After felling, the trees are cut into beams and then left lying out in the open for several years to allow them to dry out. They are then brought inside to dry out completely.

From time to time we come across the name 'bog oak'. This is not a new variety of tree, but wood taken from the English Oak which has lain for many years in marshland or water. This not only makes it heavier, but also gives it a beautiful dark brown, almost black colour.

Clusters of alternate, short-stalked leaves, each 5–16cm long, are found at the tips of the new shoots. Their blades each have 4–5 elliptic, round-ended, irregularly formed lobes, each with its margin entire; the two bottom-most lobes each have small but perceptible auricles.

At the same time as the leaves, that is, in May, loosely flowered, 2–5cm long, yellow-green, narrow, dangling male catkins emerge from the previous year's shoots. Each flower bears 6–10, usually 8 anthers. Above them, several leaves appear on the new shoots shortly afterwards, after which come the female inflorescences. Their flowers are found singly or in groups of 2–5 at the end of a common stalk, each in the axil of its own scaly bract. They consist of 6 perigynous sepals and a three- layered, three-styled ovary. A small, bowl-shaped, small-scaled cupule encloses the simple flower case.

At the end of summer the egg-shaped fruits start to ripen. They have a high starch and tannin content. They used to be roasted to make a kind of coffee substitute, or to fortify spirits and, in cases of dire necessity, to make bread. In many regions they also constituted a major part of the pig's diet, and in the forest at Kew this was in fact the case until quite recently. These fruits are commonly known as acorns.

If there is a heavy fall of acorns in autumn this, according to long-standing belief, is a sign of a hard winter to come. Similar conclusions are drawn from such signs as the oak tree keeping its leaves for longer than usual, or the acorns being particularly deep-set inside their cups.

If the oak trees are heavy with fruit this is thought to indicate that the harvest will be good. This is a rural belief which can be traced right back to antique times. In those days a heavy crop of acorns on the Holm Oak also meant that the field harvest would be plentiful.

Reference to the benefits of a plentiful harvest of acorns is made in more immediately practical terms in Gilbert White's 'Journals'. In his entry for 12 October 1783 he records: 'The crop of acorns is so prodigious that the trees look quite white without them; and the poor make, as it were, a second harvest of them, by gathering them at one shilling per bushel. At the same time not one beech-mast is to be seen. This plenty of acorns has raised store-pigs to an extravagant price.'

Traditionally the oak is regarded as the king of trees. In Greece and Italy it was known as the 'first tree', to which the origin of man could be traced back. The oak acquired a special significance through its close association with the gods. Thus in Greece it was dedicated to Zeus, in Roman Italy to Jupiter and in Teutonic Germany to the god of thunder and lightning, Donar. The reason for this is no doubt that of all indigenous trees the oak is particularly frequently struck by lightning – and this has actually been confirmed by scientific tests.

Any oak within an oak wood to be found with mistletoe hanging from it was considered holy by the Gauls. They believed that when a god singled out any particular tree for attention, he would leave mistletoe hanging from its boughs.

For many Indo-Germanic peoples, the oak was the most sacred of all trees. The reason for this, apart from its powerful appearance, may have been that it served in early times as a source of human food. Perhaps even at that very early stage in its history it was looked upon as a kind of totem. An echo of this cult of the oak can be found in the numerous tales of holy oaks which are common in many parts of Europe. Presumably because of its early function of providing nourishment it is often seen as a symbol of fertility and fruitfulness.

As the English navy grew, between the 16th and 18th centuries, the oak, which had always been considered the

347 Oak in spring

348 Male catkins, 2–5cm long, drooping

349 Section of a catkin; individual flowers with 6–10 anthers

350 Female flowers, 2–5 on a common villous stalk; stigmae yellowish or red

351 Oak in summer

352 Leaves 5–16cm long, lobed, arranged alternately

353 Superior leaf surface, shiny, dark green and glabrous

354 Inferior leaf surface, blue-green, slightly villous

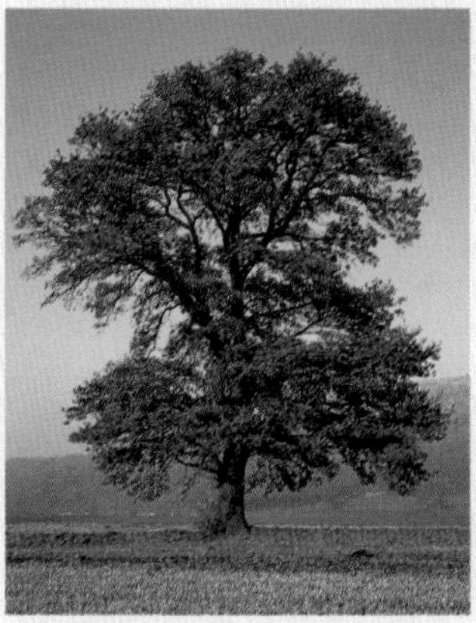
355 Oak in autumn

356 Fruit clusters

357 Individual fruits, stalks 3–6cm long

358 Untreated yellow-brown to dark brown, very hard wood

359 Oak in winter

360 Fat, ovoid-spherical terminal buds heaped at the tip of a twig

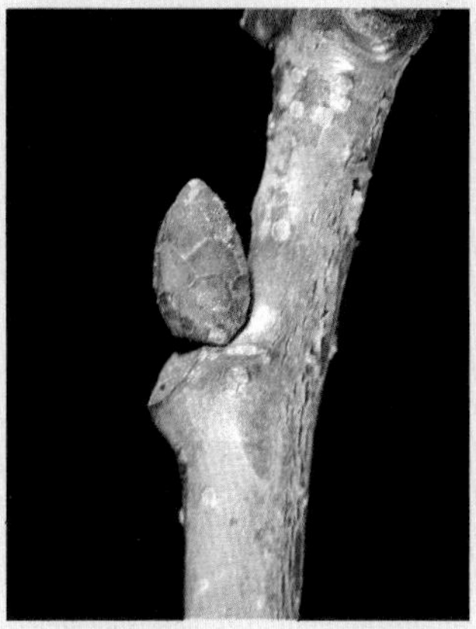
361 Pointed-ovoid side buds projecting from the twig

362 Older Oak with brown-black, deeply ridged bark

king of trees in this country, became something of a national symbol. So loyal, indeed, were the British people to this symbol, and its associations of strength, solidity, vigour and masculinity, that they refused to acknowledge the inferiority of its timber to that of other species, a vanity which was not altogether in the best interests of national security, considering that the English navy was largely constructed from it.

The many veteran oaks in the British Isles, some with names and legends attached, are all English Oaks except for some in Powys, the 'Capon Tree' at Jedburgh, a few more in Scotland, and the 'Michenden' or 'Chandos Oak' near Enfield. The most famous and one of only two trees marked on the standard Ordnance Survey maps, is the Major Oak near Ollerton, Nottinghamshire, 329cm diameter. It was 295cm in 1906 and this, together with other dated measurements, shows that it is unlikely to be more than 450 years old or less than about 400. Contrary to local belief, it is certainly not, by a good margin, the biggest oak in Britain, nor the oldest, and connections with Robin Hood are as mythical as he was. The biggest is at Bowthorpe, Lincolnshire, 383cm and very hollow with a large entrance, while 'Majesty' at Fredville Park, Kent, is 369cm with a good, apparently solid bole. The 'King's Oak' at Sparkford, Somerset, is also sound but has big, low branches and is 334cm. At Lydham Hall, Shropshire, one which is solid burrs all round is 374cm.

Place-names abound which are self-evidently derived from oak, like Sevenoaks, Kent; Hatfield Broad Oak, Hertfordshire; and Oakham, Rutland; and there are many less obvious, like Acton and the Yorkshire Acklam, and even Aigburth, near Liverpool.

White Willow

Salix alba L.

Saule blanc
Silberweide, Weissweide

Pages 119, 208, 209

In the absence of human interference the rapidly growing White Willow will reach a height of 20-25m. Branching begins quite near to the base of the trunk. By the time the tree is 80 to 100 years old the trunk can have a diameter of up to 1m and bear an irregularly formed and billowing crown.

Advocates of this tree as the best source of beating rods very often support their case with the argument that it bears knotty protuberances along the length of its twigs. Although these knots soon become hollow, they continue to put out shoots from the thin layer of bark. These are not only used to make baskets, but also for tying up the shoots.

Inside the initially smooth, white-grey skin, which later turns into a thick brown bark with longitudinal fissures, is to be found the brownish-white sapwood and reddish heartwood.

In the process of whitening leather, the young bark is used to make 'Russian leather' and 'Danish glove leather'.

The fine vessels are numerous and dispersed and create fine delicate cracks in the lengthwise-cut wood.

The wood is very soft, with coarse fibres, and is spongy and pliable. One cubic metre of seasoned wood weighs 400–500kg. It dries quickly, is easy to work with, to stain and varnish but not to polish. It is mostly used to make boxes, baskets, wooden shoes, wood wool, in boat construction and in the matchwood and paper industries. This kind of willow wood is also very good for making drawing boards and, of course, cricket bats.

In April or May the flowers appear, at the same time as the leaves.

Male trees develop 3–6cm long, slender, stalked, slightly curved catkins. Their flowers are composed of a bract, an ovary and a gland.

As the White Willow flowers so early in the year, it is a useful source of honey. After the pollination of the ovules has taken place, the ovaries develop into oblanceolate capsule fruits, covered with a film of grey hairs. When the fruits ripen these flap open and release numerous seeds, each with a white tuft of hair. Out of the leaves unfold tiny buds, which are pressed close to the twig, at exactly the same time as the flowers. In the young tree, both surfaces are covered with a thick, silvery layer of hair. Later in the year the superior surface turns dark green and loses most of its hairs. The inferior surface retains its silvery coating. The leaves are 5–10cm long, narrowly lanceolate to lanceolate, and their margin is finely and regularly serrate. In order to reach the stately height of 25m, White Willows require damp to wet soil, and a lot of light. These requirements are most easily met along river banks, at the edges of ponds and lakes, in marshy ground and in meadow woodlands. They can also survive for a long time in water, or with part of their trunk submerged, without incurring any damage. Its roots enable it to keep the mounting deposits on the bank at bay and it is therefore useful in gradually extending the river foreshore.

We come across the willow in Greek mythology. For example, it is found in the underworld, in Persephone's grove (wife of Hades, the god of the kingdom of the dead), and at the entrance of the cave on Crete in which Zeus's child was raised. In traditional folklore the willow is associated with sinister spirits and witches. According to an old tale, love-smitten witches disappear into the hollows of willow trees, reappearing later in the form of hissing cats to frighten the village folk.

Traditional medicine recommends the administering of a decoction of leaves and pieces of young bark as a cure for fever.

This is probably a native tree except in the north and west of Scotland, but doubts have been expressed because it is found only near habitations. Since riversides, in the north at least, were the obvious centres of early settlers, this association is inevitable and probably without further significance. Nevertheless, it may well have been restricted to the south, for today all the big specimens are in the southern half of England. None of these is very old, and the big hulks noted 30 years ago have all gone. The biggest now plainly were planted, and probably within this century. One in the Home Park Private at Windsor was 148cm diameter in 1972; one in the University Parks, Oxford, is 24m × 110cm, while the biggest of many on The Fen, Cambridge, is 25m × 116cm.

The Bat Willow is the form grown commercially and seen by field ditches

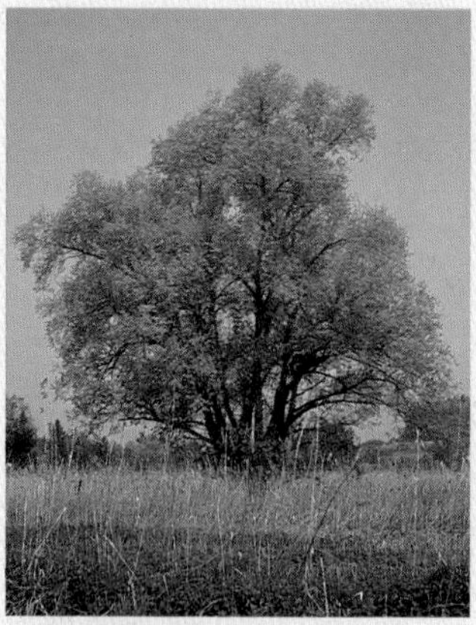
363 White Willow in spring

364 Many-flowered female catkins, 3-6cm long

365 Many-flowered male catkins, 4cm long

366 Female flowers, 4mm long: ovary at the base, roundish gland, elongated bract

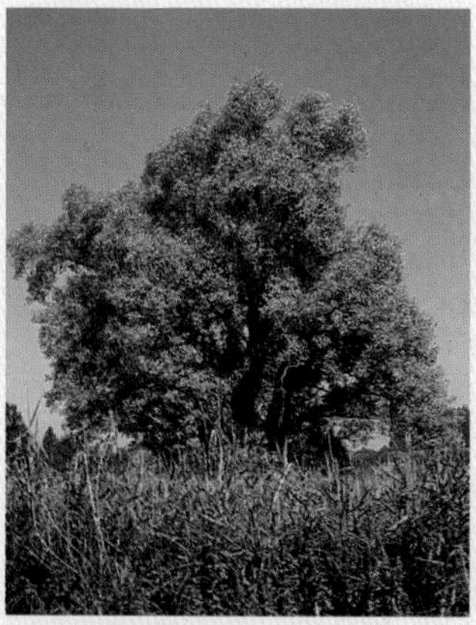
367 White Willow in summer

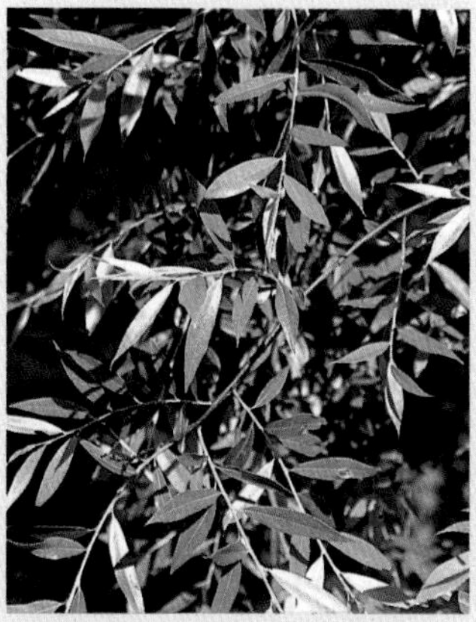
368 Leaves 5–10cm long, narrow-lanceolate, alternately arranged

369 Superior leaf surface, dark green with slight hair covering later

370 Inferior leaf surface with permanent silver-white hair covering

371 White Willow in autumn

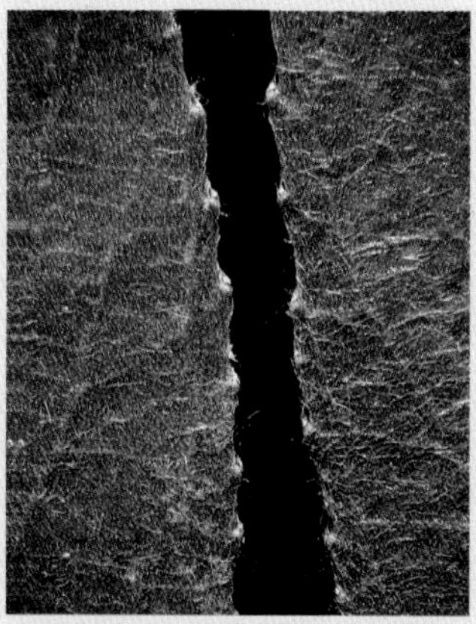
372 Leaf margin, serrate, with fine glands

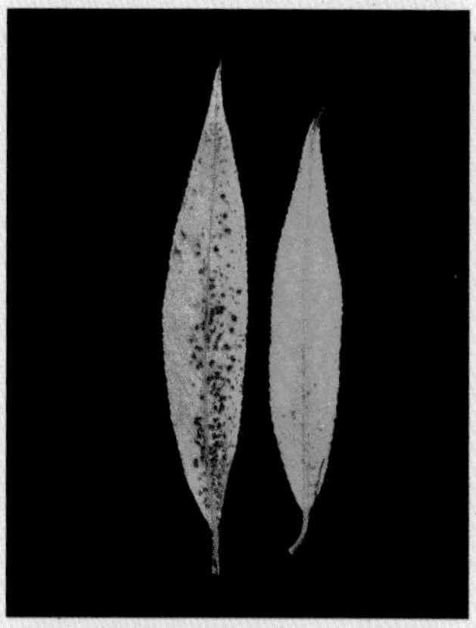
373 Lanceolate autumn leaf

374 Wood with brownish white sapwood and reddish heartwood

375 White Willow in winter

376 Narrow-ovoid villous terminal and side buds

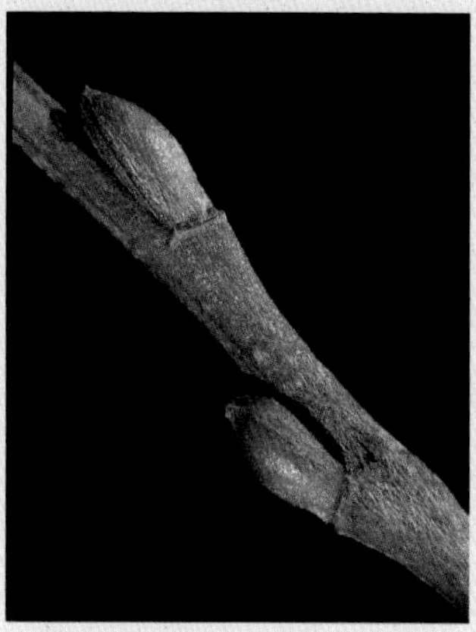
377 Side buds lying close to twig

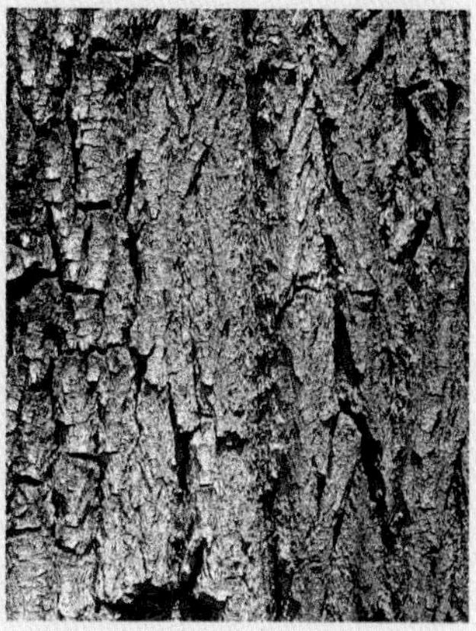
378 Ochre-grey old bark, deeply furrowed with distinct fluting and ridging

in Kent and East Anglia but also in some town parks. It grows remarkably fast and trees of nine years have been measured 14m × 38cm; trees of 16 years, 21m × 61cm. At Thorp Perrow, Yorkshire, one 52 years old is 25m × 108cm; and an undated tree in Marble Hill Park, Twickenham, was 31m × 127cm.

Place-names derived from willow mainly refer to the Osier *Salix viminalis* rather than the White or Crack Willow, and many come from the same root as *Salix* and Sallow, as in Salhouse, Norfolk, and Sale, Cheshire, while more derive from 'withy', the cut shoots of the Osier, as in Withington, Cheshire and other counties, and Wythburn, Cumbria.

Rowan, Mountain Ash

Sorbus aucuparia L.

Sorbier des oiseleurs
Vogelbeerbaum

Pages 78, 138, 139

The bush-like Mountain Ash may grow to anything between 5m and 10m. Its maximum diameter is around 40cm, and its maximum age around 120 years. Its crown is ovoid to spherical. Because of its far-reaching and deeply embedded network of roots, it is particularly well suited to the role of holding together the sides of mountains which might otherwise be prone to avalanches. The one thing it cannot tolerate, though, is being water-logged.

It thrives best in fresh, damp, loose, fertile soil. It is, however, one of the least demanding of all trees and will also grow where the bottom soil is dry and of poor quality. It will also tolerate a good deal of shade, which means it will also willingly take root in shady exposed and windy positions.

On the edges of woodland, the Mountain Ash affords shelter for young conifers in bad weather conditions. We find it growing wild in mountainous and subalpine regions, where it is almost always found in company with the Norway Spruce. But it is also found in many places above the tree-line.

In the far north it crops up again, to the north of the enclosed coniferous forests, where it occurs together with the Aspen Poplar and dwarf species of the birch and willow.

Apart from in the areas of southern Europe where the forests have been destroyed by man, the distribution of this Euro-Siberian species is spread throughout Europe.

A very early colonist of Britain, this tree ranges to the far north, and being also hardy and rugged, it grows at up to 900m on the mountains, which is higher than any other tree. It is common on the edges of lowland woods and on sandy heaths and hills. It will grow quite well on clays and with paving over its roots, so it is frequently seen in streets and city parks. It is not long-lived, and trunks 80cm diameter are rare and have little future, but in their prime some trees are 18m tall.

The name 'Mountain Ash' arises from the compound leaf resembling slightly that of the true Ash, but the tree is in the Rose Family and the Ash is quite unrelated to it, in the Olive Family. Many people, and all with botanical leanings or an interest in keeping old words alive where appropriate, call it the Rowan, from Old English, *roan*.

Each year the soil is enriched with the leaves of the Mountain Ash. These decompose very quickly to produce an excellent humus. This tree also works as a weed controller and since wild deer are able to feast on the Mountain Ash to their hearts' content it is in a position, to a certain extent, to protect other species from such attack. The ash itself reacts by rapidly putting out numerous new shoots.

The silvery grey, shiny, young bark produces a lot of tannin and is therefore used in the tanning process to give leather its lovely brown colour. With age the bark toughens, turns grey-black in colour and develops longitudinal ridges. This is wrapped around a wide band of reddish-white sapwood, inside which is the light brown, slightly red-streaked heartwood.

The wood is fairly pliable and supple, not very durable, extremely difficult to chop, with a diffuse pattern of pores, weighing 600–700kg/m³. It is easy to carve, plane, polish and stain and it dries fairly normally. It is used by carpenters and cartwrights. Selected pieces are especially sought after for fine woodcarving and making craft objects. The annual rings are sharply defined by lovely brown end-of-season wood marks, which considerably enhance the appearance of the wood. The alternate leaves, each 10–25cm long, are oddpinnate and bear 4–9 pairs of leaflets. These are oblong-lanceolate, 2–6cm long and, with the exception of the terminal leaflet, touch the rachis directly, or, at least, have only very short stalks.

Tea can be made from the leaves. It is not particularly pleasant tasting, because of its high tannin content, but is thought to be effective against intestinal and stomach problems.

The foliage is supposed to be particularly good fodder for goats and sheep.

In May, or, in higher regions, in June, the many-flowered cyme appear. The flowers are 4–7mm in diameter and are composed of 5 small, yellow-green, triangular, villous or glabrous sepals, each 1.5–1.8mm long, 5 orbicular or ovate shaped, yellow-white petals, numerous anthers and an ovary with 2–4 styles. The ovary is fused with the inner wall of the cup-shaped, hollow flower axil. Inside the berry, which is initially yellow, later turning bright red, lie the flat, narrow, pointed, reddish-coloured seeds. The berries provide food for birds and cattle, as well as being a source of vinegar, spirits and liqueurs. The dried fruit is also supposed to be effective in combating diarrhoea.

Many legends speak of so-called 'blood trees', grown from the blood of innocents who had been wrongly hanged. Along with the blood, the victim's soul also entered the tree. An old Icelandic tale has it that a rowan tree sprang from the blood of two innocents, a brother and sister falsely accused of incest. Every Christmas Eve, lights could be seen on every branch, which could not be extinguished, not even by the strongest gale.

The rowan has more folk-names than any other tree and was regarded as singularly potent against witchcraft. Miles Hadfield wrote that until the 1950s on May Day, branches were placed around farm buildings, and possibly they still are today.

379 Mountain Ash in spring

380 Flowers in erect cymes

381 Flower from above: petals white and rounded to broad-ovate

382 Vertical section of a flower: 3–5 styles

383 Mountain Ash in summer

384 Leaves 10–20cm long, unequally pinnate, alternately arranged

385 Superior leaf surface, dark green, with silver-grey hairs

386 Inferior leaf surface, felt-like grey green; later becoming glabrous

387 Mountain Ash in autumn

388 Ripening clusters of fruit

389 Pea size berries, first yellow, later coral red

390 Young trunk with yellow-white sapwood; heartwood later light brown

391 Mountain Ash in winter

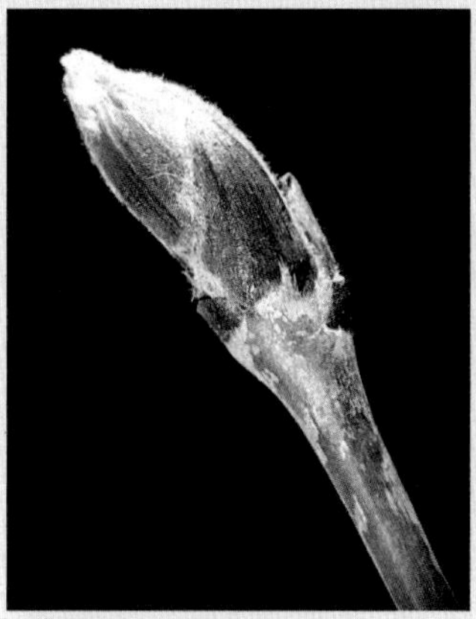

392 Terminal bud, pointed-ovoid and larger than side buds

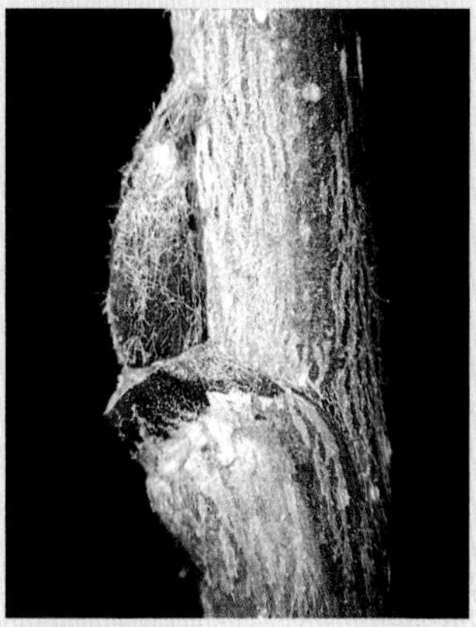

393 Side bud lying close to long shoot

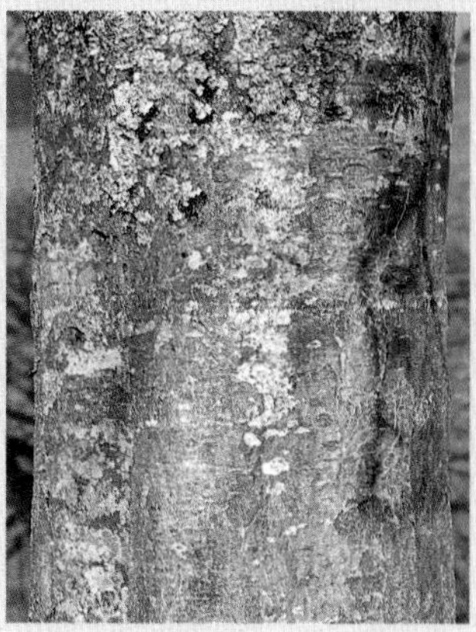

394 Yellow-grey shiny bark, becoming grey-black and vertically ridged with age

Large-leaved Lime

Tilia platyphyllos Scop.

Tilleul à grandes feuilles
Sommerlinde

Pages 106, 186, 187

In fresh, deep, well-aerated, calcareous soil, the Large-leaved Lime will grow to a height of 40m. Its short, straight, thick trunk bears a low-set, broadly dome-shaped, thick crown, supported by strong, gnarled branches.

Up to its 60th year, it does not grow particularly quickly. Thereafter, however, it suddenly spurts upwards, reaching its maximum height when it is around 150 years old. It continues to expand outwards even after this. It is said of the lime tree that it grows for 300 years, stands still for 300 years and takes 300 years to die.

The young bark is smooth, grey-green, with vertical wavy streaks. In between there are dark brown fissures. In old trees, the bark is coarse, ridged and dark brown, with a fine rhomboid pattern. In times gone by the young bark was often used for basketry and roof-covering.

This species of tree is one of the mature woods, and has a fairly broad layer of sapwood. Because it does not have a distinctly coloured heartwood, or pith, the wood is the same colour throughout. It can be whitish, yellowish or sometimes light brown or reddish. Between its green and its dried conditions (dried wood weighs 450–550kg/m^3) it contracts moderately to severely. Once dried it is easy and clean to handle. Because it is very high in protein it is often attacked by woodworm.

Lime wood is tough, stable, pliable, but not very supple, and, cut lengthways, exposes very fine, delicate cracks. It is not very durable in harsh weather conditions or when exposed to water. It is therefore not very well suited for use in external construction. Because it is so soft, it is good for making drawing boards, toys, small boxes, barrels and chests. It also makes good wood-wool, excellent veneers and high quality charcoal. Because lime wood was so commonly used by masters of wood-carving in the Middle Ages to make figures of Christ on the cross, the Virgin Mary or the Apostles, it came to be known as 'sacrum lignum'. When the peoples of Europe first started to settle, they had no metal from which to make axes or saws. With simple stone axes they were unable to work on hardwood, and were restricted to using softwoods only. Lime, as a major softwood, was used widely to build primitive houses and shortly after that to make hunting bows. Shields made of several layers of interwoven lime phloem were also able to withstand very heavy blows. With the invention of the metal axe it became possible to peel off the bark of lime trees in strips and thus to obtain the necessary bast for housing and clothing requirements. A tree trunk with a diameter of around 35cm would yield around 45kg of phloem. This was sufficient to make, for example, 10–12 mats.

In May or June the Large-leaved Lime begins to flower. The flowers are found in clusters of 3–6 in a cyme. The first half of the stalk is fused with a wing-like, leathery bract. It later serves as a flight aid for the multiple fruit. The five sepals are ovate, yellow-white and 3–4mm long. The five petals are elongated, 5–8mm long and also yellow-white. The very hairy superior ovary is surrounded by 30–40 anthers. The flowers have pharmacological properties, and in this context are known as 'flores tiliae'. They contain a lot of mucilage, sugar, wax, tannin and traces of ethereal oil, which contains the aromatic fern oil. As early as the 16th century, herb books mentioned lime-flower tea as an antidote to fever in sufferers from cold or 'flu.

Out of the green ovary develops a spherical, 4–5-ribbed, hard, wood-like nut, with a velvety covering of hair. It falls in autumn or winter, and is a welcome source of food for small rodents, during what is otherwise a very lean period.

In Continental Europe, almost all the big, named and famous lindens or limes are trees of Large-leaved Lime or Small-leaved Lime, but in the British Isles this is not so. They are all the Common Lime, the hybrid between these two species, which may have been brought from Europe before 1600 or may have arisen in England. It is known to reach 46m tall and over 200cm diameter. The Large-leaved Lime, or Broadleaf Lime, was a late-arriving native, found now apparently only on limestone cliffs by the lower River Wye and in Yorkshire. It is widely planted in parks, gardens and streets, favoured by those who know that it is a much more shapely and cleaner tree, very rarely growing sprouts round the base and never on the stem. It flowers a week or more before the Common Lime and three or four before the Small-leaved, with fewer and bigger flowers in each cyme. The bracts from which the flowers hang are also bigger, paler, nearly white, and more prominent. In the autumn it is distinguished by retaining on the lower, outer crown, many browned bracts and their fruit. It is rarely over 30m tall, although one tree at Knightshayes, Devon, and another at Scone Palace, Perth, are 37m. Two trees at West Dean House, Sussex, are 180cm in diameter, but an extraordinary tree at Pitchford House in Shropshire is 236cm and has a house with a table and chairs over 2m up where three immense branches spring, which is reputed to have been put there in 1600.

On newly emerged foliage, the dense soft hairs on the shoots and leaf-stalks distinguish the species, and fully developed leaves retain soft fine hairs over the upper surface and longer more sparse hairs on the veins beneath. By autumn, most of the hairiness has gone from the shoot, but a little usually remains near the tip. A form seen in streets and gardens has rather smaller leaves with dense hairs on the stalk and around the base of the blade.

According to Greek legend, Philemon and his wife Baukis, despite being very poor, led a happy and contented life. When Zeus and Hermes took on the form of earthly men and visited their village it was to this couple that they came for hospitality. During the meal, the couple realised the identity of their guests when the wine in the jug failed to run dry. As a punishment to the other villagers for their hard-heartedness, Zeus sent a flood to destroy the village. Only Philemon and Baukis's hut was left standing. This he transformed into a magnificent temple. The two hosts were also allowed one wish. They asked that when the time came they should be allowed to end their lives together. After their deaths, Philemon was turned into an oak and Baukis into a lime.

This is where the lime tree acquired its feminine character. This is reinforced by another association – the use of lime leaves to weave garlands for the goddess Aphrodite – the Greek goddess of sensual love and beauty.

Place-names have been derived via linden, as in Lyndhurst, Hampshire; Lindal, Lancashire; Linsheels, Northumberland; and Lindley, Yorkshire.

395 Large-leaved Lime in spring

396 Stalked flowers in groups of 2–5 in cymes

397 Flower from above showing numerous anthers, 5 short sepals and 5 long petals

398 Vertical section through lime flower: superior ovary with many hairs

399 Large-leaved Lime in summer

400 Superior leaf surface, dark green, somewhat hairy

401 Inferior leaf surface, with pronounced veins

402 Inferior leaf surface with small, white tufts of hair in the vein axils

403 Large-leaved Lime in autumn

404 Spherical nuts, with 4–5 ribs and long stalks

405 (left) Young, still green, spherical nut; (right) older nut with 5 ribs

406 Soft, light wood, yellowish white to reddish

407 Large-leaved Lime in winter

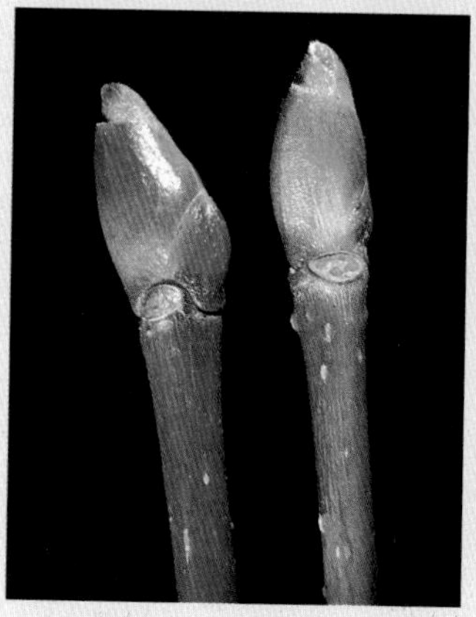

408 Terminal buds, narrow- to broad-ovoid, tinged with red on sunny side

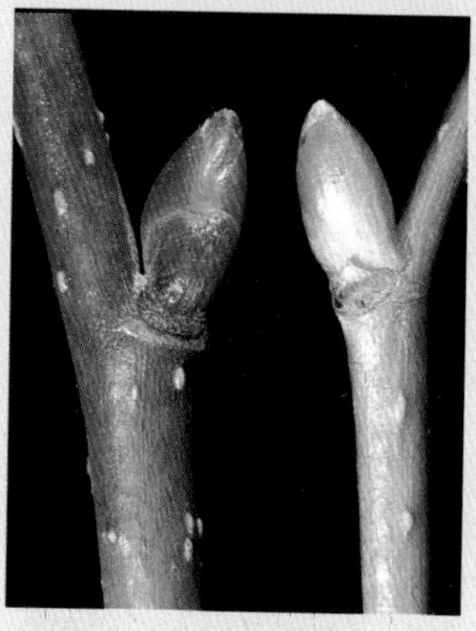

409 Side buds, narrow- to broad-ovoid, pointed, slightly flattened

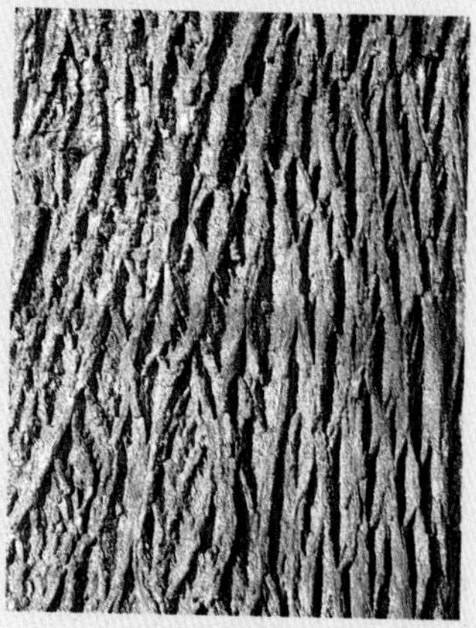

410 Coarse, furrowed bark, grey-brown, with diamond pattern

Wych Elm

Ulmus glabra Huds. emend. Moss

Orme de montagne
Bergulme, Bergruster

Pages 109, 192, 193

The young Wych Elm grows very quickly. Within 30 years it can grow up to as much as 90% of its maximum height. Once it is 60 years old, it more or less stops growing upwards. It is not rare to find Wych Elms around 30m high. They only grow to between 30m and 40m where there is a sufficient supply of light, warmth and little frost, and where the water in the soil is rich in nutrients. Such favourable conditions as these are most commonly found in mixed lime woods. In sycamore-ash or beech-hornbeam woods, elms are also quite able to establish themselves.

The crown is usually smoothly rounded and regular. The trunk may continue all the way up, or may branch out in the region of the crown. It reaches its maximum height after around 500 years. Elms of this great age may by this time have a circumference of 6-7m at a point 1.5m above the ground.

A strong and deeply embedded system of roots anchors the tree to the ground. On the side of the tree exposed to the wind it is often provided with lateral roots which make the tree more stable and secure.

The young bark is silvery grey to brownish and smooth. This later develops into grey to dark brown bark, with longitudinal ridges. The phloem used to be used for binding, knitting and basket weaving. Underneath the bark the sapwood is yellow-white, contrasting with the brown heartwood. In between is a layer of mature wood. It is because of this that the elm is classified as a mature heartwood.

The heartwood is very decorative, and is one of the most attractive of European woods. It is hard, resistant to pressure, but not to tension, moderately supple, tough, pliable and durable. As it has a marked tendency to crack and warp, the drying process should be carried out very carefully and slowly. Dried, sawn wood weighs between 550 and 850kg/m^3. It is not difficult to work. The treatment of the surfaces should not present too many problems either. It is easily joined, using glue, screws or nails. The wood is also easy to shave, cut and plane, but very difficult to split.

It is principally used for indoor fittings and for making furniture and parquet. Decorative elm veneers are very much sought after. Wood taken from the roots, with its lovely grain, is particularly popular with the carver. It used to be a common practice to stain elm wood and use it as a substitute for walnut and mahogany.

It is almost as good a firewood as beech, but it is far less popular for this purpose, as it is so difficult to chop. The cause of the death of so many elm trees has been *Ceratocystis ulmi*, a fungus, which first came to Europe in about 1920. The beetle eats out a path underneath the rind and thus allows the spores of the fungus to penetrate through to the vascular bundles inside the trunk. The fungus causes the cell walls to form blister-like protrusions. These growths then block up the water routes and upset the water balance to such an extent that within a very short time the twigs and branches begin to wither. Very shortly after, the whole tree dies. If measures are to be taken to combat the disease they must be directed at the beetle.

In hilly and mountainous regions the Wych Elm favours nutritious, particularly damp soil, avoiding dry, stony mountainsides. When the level of the water table sinks this can actually be detected in the drying up of the tip of the tree. Like the Sycamore, this tree really belongs in the company of the beech and will either welcome the chalk in the ground or be indifferent to it. Compared to other forest trees, elms are not prolific, and self-contained stands are rare. Usually they are found scattered individually, or at most are found in thickets. They are also frequently found in hillside or valley woodlands, together with the European Ash and the Sycamore.

Spherical inflorescences unfold from spherical and many-scaled terminal and side buds in March or April. The numerous flowers are 3-6mm long and consist of 5 reddish-purple or greenish perigynous petals, 5 anthers and a superior ovary. After pollination, this develops into an ovoid, green, winged fruit. This can ripen as early as June. The oval seed lies at the foot of the elm, enclosed inside a now brown, wiry case. Only every second or third year is there a really good fruit crop.

The leaves do not sprout until after the tree has flowered. When fully grown they are 5-16cm long, elliptic, ovate or obovate in outline, usually broadest in the upper third of the leaf, often irregularly triangular, with a 3-6mm long stalk. This is often slightly hidden by one half of the blade. The tip of the leaf is sharply pointed, its base very slightly asymmetric, and the leaf margin coarsely doubly serrate. Each of the teeth curves forward. The superior surface is dark green and perceptibly rough to the touch. The inferior surface is a somewhat lighter green and on the larger veins, delicate white tufts of hair appear.

Unlike the Smooth-leaved Elm, with its 12 pairs of side veins, the Wych Elm has 14-20 pairs. The European White Elm has a similar number. The leaves of the latter two species are easily distinguished from each other in having completely different laminal bases (the two halves of the blade in the European White Elm are completely asymmetric).

In Ancient Greece the elm was dedicated to the messenger god Hermes – who watched over merchants and thieves. The winged elm fruits also accompanied the souls of those who were brought before the Lord of Judgement by Hermes. Shady elms were planted by nymphs in remembrance of fallen heroes.

In the south of France the elm takes on the role normally played by the lime. Once upon a time, under its shadow, right was meted out and God's word preached.

The Wych Elm is the only elm with undisputed claims to be native in Britain. There are grave suspicions about the English Elm, which was most likely to have been brought by Iron Age tribes, and does not set viable seed here. The Wych Elm came early and was among those trees to spread early far to the north, where it is common by streamsides deep in the Highlands of Scotland and in the Pennine Hills. It was less common in the English lowlands and has now all but disappeared south of Cumbria. Elm disease is currently spreading into Scotland where the city parks rely greatly on Wych Elm, notably in Glasgow and Edinburgh, as it was able to flourish where industrial fogs were thick and frequent. Today there are still some trees in rural Yorkshire 35m tall, but near Dundee in Angus a group with some 40m tall died in 1986. Not far from those, one 220cm diameter was in good health in 1987.

Place-names with the prefixes 'Wych-', 'Wyke-' and 'Wick-' are widespread, but there are pitfalls in what is dubbed 'folk- etymology' since such names may have derivations from quite other words than Wych Elm.

411 Wych Elm in spring

412 Flowers in spherical bundles, appearing before the leaves

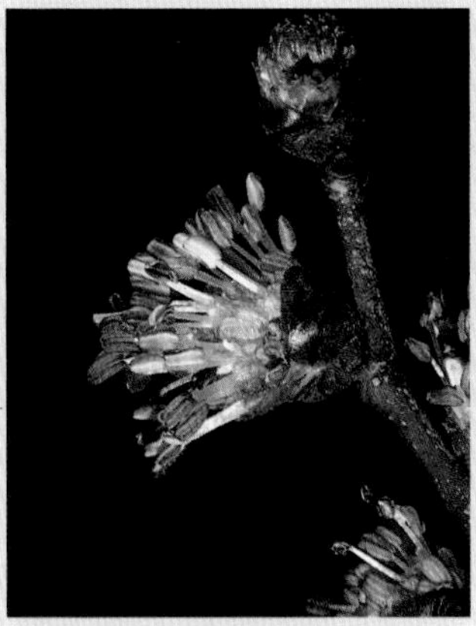
413 Spherical inflorescence with numerous flowers

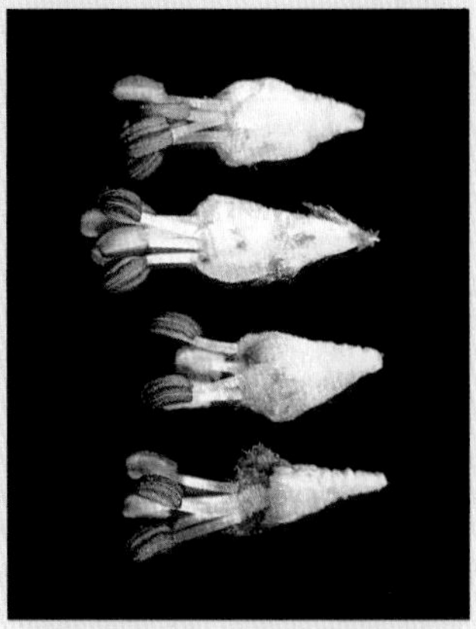
414 4 young, individual flowers

415 Wych Elm in summer

416 5–16cm long leaves, arranged alternately

417 Superior leaf surface, dark green and coarse

418 Inferior leaf surface, mid green, with fine hairs along larger veins

419 Wych Elm in autumn

420 Older flower with young, winged fruit

421 Young, winged fruits, with oval seed at the centre

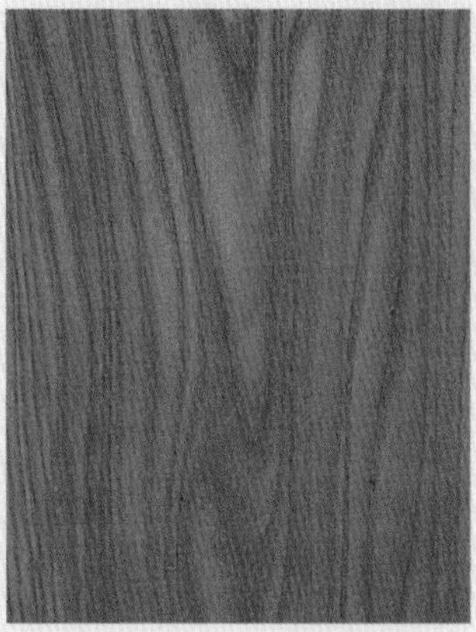
422 Heartwood light to dark brown or reddish brown, darkening with age

423 Wych Elm in winter

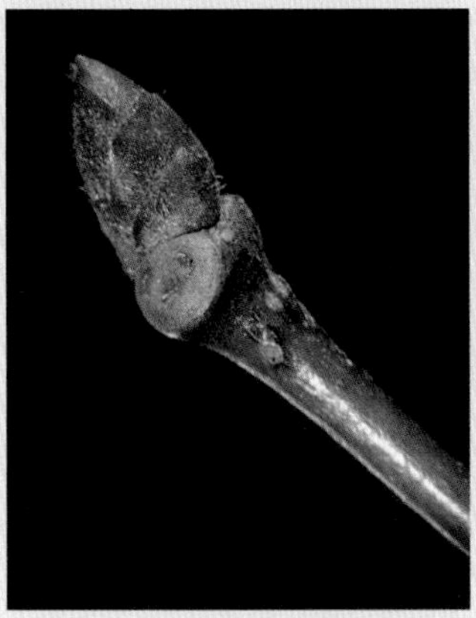
424 Narrow-ovoid, pointed terminal bud (here a leaf bud)

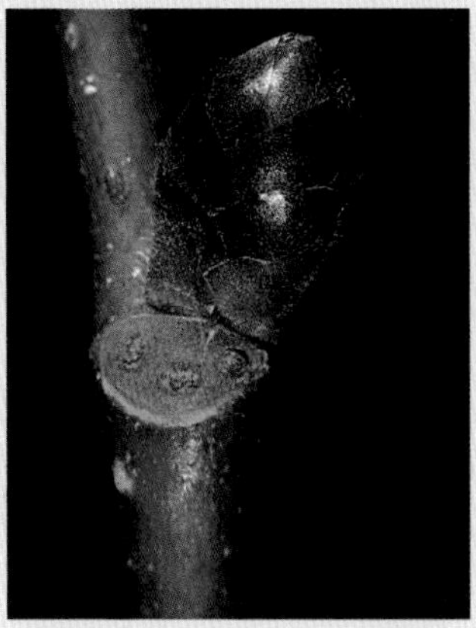
425 Spherical flower bud at an angle to the twig

426 Bark on older tree, with long furrows and dark brown flaking plates

Common Silver Fir

Abies alba Mill.

Sapin pectine
Weisstanne

Pages 66, 120, 121

Growing in a commercial forest, the Common Silver Fir will live to an age of 180–200 years, and grow to a height of 30–40m, with a diameter of 1m. But in a natural forest it can live for up to 500 years, reaching a height of 55m and a diameter of 1.5m. An elderly tree will have a central root leading down from the trunk, and a 'stork's nest', flattened crown. It is able to develop this shape only because the growth of the side branches is more rapid than the growth of the summit branches. If a summit branch breaks off, a side branch will grow upwards to replace it.

The outer bark is smooth, whitish grey, sometimes with a reddish tinge. Inside it is found the lightweight, soft, easily chopped wood. It is almost white in colour, with a yellowish or reddish tint. It is similar to the wood of the Norway Spruce, but of a slightly paler shade. The sapwood and heartwood are not sharply differentiated. It is very quickly dried, and there is only a slight danger of warping, but it is inclined to crack. One cubic metre of dried, cut wood weighs, on average, around 550kg. Nowadays it is mainly used to make furniture, wooden containers, matches and kindling.

The needles are up to 3cm long, flattened, usually rounded at the tip, narrowing towards the base, attached to the twig by a circular base. The superior surface is dark green, the inferior surface, with its 2 white, narrow bands, a paler green. After 6–11 years, the needles drop. Since the leaf-scars left after the fall are flat and not raised, the branches feel completely smooth.

Trees growing singly start to flower around their 30th year; those in stands after some 60–70 years. Male flowers grow on the lower surface of the previous year's shoots, in cylindrical, downward-pointing catkins. The female flowers are found on the top branches inside 6cm-long, light green, erect cones. By the time the seed is ripe, it is between 10cm and 18cm long. The seeds fall in October and the spindle remains on the branch. The dark brown seeds are large, triangular, with a high turpentine content and a large wing attachment. The tree will yield a large quantity of seeds only once every 2–6 years.

The Common Silver Fir is a very demanding mountain tree, found largely in central and southern Europe. It favours damp, slightly acidic, deep, loamy to clay, fertile soil, and grows best in a sheltered position. These requirements are met particularly on westerly and northern slopes in areas of high altitude. It rarely occurs as high up as the subalpine zone, but is often planted in the hill zone. This tree is seldom found in soil which has a high acidic content, is dry, or completely flat.

The first Silver Fir recorded as being planted in Britain was one in Edmonton in 1603, but the first introduction may have been a little earlier. During the 18th century there was a great deal of it planted as a forest and estate tree, especially in the mountain areas of Wales and Scotland, where it grows particularly well and seeds itself freely around, but also in England on good oakwood soil. Before 1800, the biggest trees in Britain were Common Silver Firs.

Norway Spruce

Picea abies L. (***P. excelsa*** Link)

Epicéa
Fichte, Rottane

Pages 67, 122, 123

The Norway Spruce grows to a height of 30–40m when standing alone and up to 60m when growing in a stand. It usually has a conical crown and a flattened, wide-reaching root system.

The branching of the spruce can vary greatly from one tree to another. The most common form is perhaps the 'comb spruce', with its curtain-like, downward sweeping twigs. In close proximity to this is often found the 'bush spruce', which has much shorter twigs, arranged in a bush-like pattern, and at a higher level, the 'leaf spruce', whose twigs are disposed more or less horizontally. Another variation is the 'hazel spruce', which is characterised by having particularly fine quality wood.

The bark of the young tree is usually red-brown, smooth, with small scales. It turns grey-brown with age, and flakes off in the form of little round scales. It encloses consistently white to bright yellow, resinous, soft, light, elastic, sturdy wood which warps only moderately and is reasonably weatherproof. The annual rings are sharply defined by the difference between the lighter spring wood and the darker end-of-season wood. It dries quickly and easily. One cubic metre of dried, cut wood usually weighs around 450kg. Planed and sanded surfaces have a beautiful shine to them. This wood can be put to many different uses.

The needles are very stout, spirally arranged, four-sided, 5-25mm long, slightly crescent-shaped, almost square in cross-section, and rather obtuse to pointed. They can last 5-7 years.

Single trees first start to flower after 30–40 years. Once the tree is sexually mature it will produce a healthy crop of seeds every 3-4 years (every 6–12 years in colder climates).

The female inflorescences, found on the tip of the previous year's shoots, are a luminous purple-red in colour, cone-shaped, 4–5cm long and erect.

The male flowers, which are found in amongst the needles of the leaves, have attached to their axil a scale-like leaf, above which are found the numerous anthers.

Each anther has a short stem and a scale-like, curved tip, underneath which are located the two pollen sacks.

At first the flowers droop downwards, but when they come into bloom they straighten up and display their reddish colouring.

Ripe cones are 10–15cm long, 3–4cm wide, and brown in colour. The topmost and bottom-most scales are sterile. The seeds are pointed-ovoid, dark brown, 4–5cm long, and equipped with a light brown, translucent wing. By the following spring they have become detached. Once this has occurred the entire cone drops off the tree.

The date of introduction to Britain cannot be known, as it was already common when first mentioned in 1548. By 1800 it was, with the Scots Pine and European Larch, a main component of plantation forestry and common in shelterbelts, shelterwoods for game birds and in gardens. It holds its own today in forestry in inland areas too liable to late frosts, by reason of altitude or being in a frost-hollow, for the normally preferred Sitka Spruce to be grown.

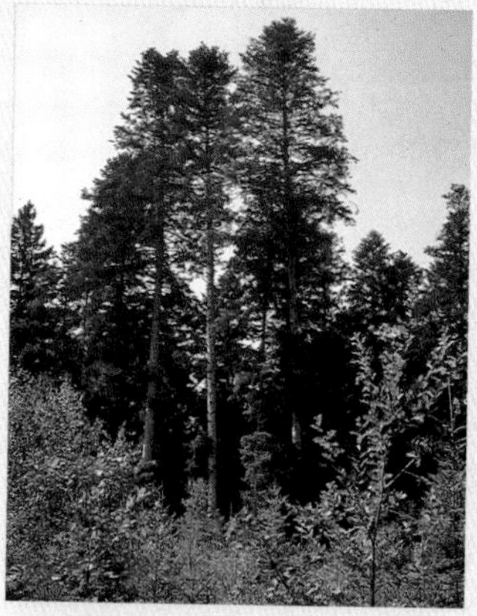
427 Common Silver Fir in summer

428 Fir twig with new shoots, still pale green

429 Male catkins in upper region of crown

430 Female flowers in 2-6cm long, light green, erect cones

431 Cone 10-18cm long, cylindrical, erect and light brown

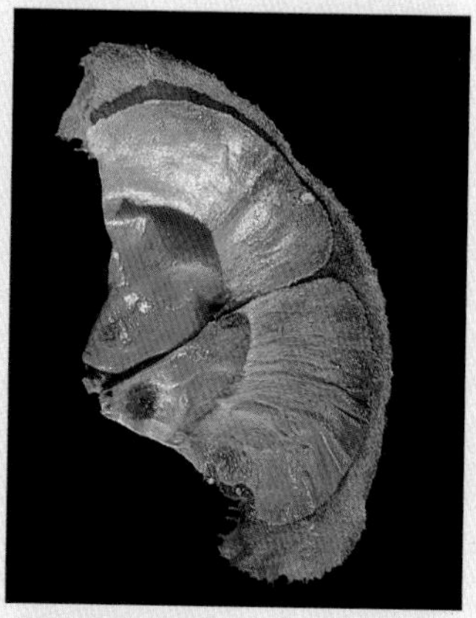
432 Dark brown seed, large, triangular, fused with a broad wing

433 Heartwood reddish white, easily split, containing no resin

434 Young bark, light to dark grey and smooth; older bark with uneven vertical furrows

435 Norway Spruce in summer

436 Spruce twig with pale, green, young shoots

437 Male flowers in spherical catkins, which grow up to 2-3cm

438 Female flowers in erect cones, 2-4cm long, later drooping

439 Ripe, brown cones, 10-15cm long, drooping

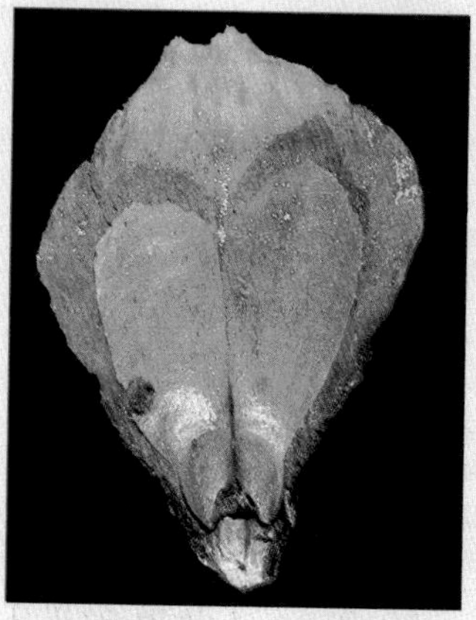
440 Dark brown seed, pointed-ovoid, with light brown wing

441 Yellowish white, soft, strong wood

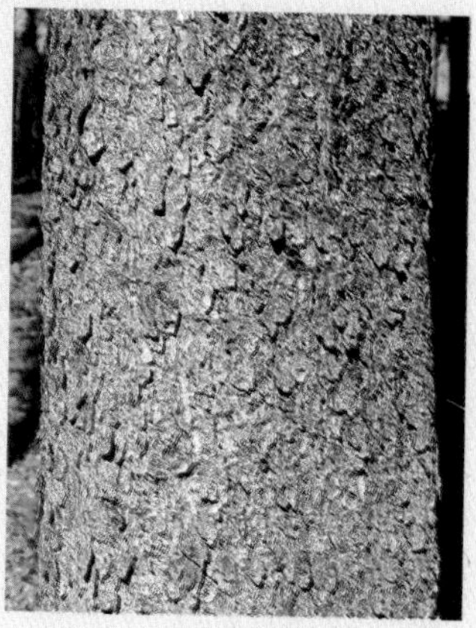
442 Grey-brown bark on an older tree, working loose in round flakes

Swiss Stone Pine, Arolla Pine

Pinus cembra L.

Arole, Pin cember
Arve, Zirbelkiefer, Zirbel

Pages 70, 128, 129

In a favourable environment, the Swiss Stone Pine can grow up to a height of 25m, 1.5m across and can live for up to 600 years. After some 200 years its upwards growth is almost complete; however, it does not cease to expand outwards until the tree itself dies.

The crown of the young tree is conical, but as it grows older it assumes more of a cylindrical shape. As its roots are flat and deep, the pine has a good deal of resistance to severe and stormy weather conditions.

The young bark is silver-grey and smooth. This later develops into scaly bark which is grey-brown on the outside and red-brown on the inside. It darkens quickly on exposure to light and encloses the yellow-white sapwood and the light red to yellowish heartwood. Characteristic of the Swiss Stone Pine are its numerous, firm, red-brown branches. The wood is very light and soft, with delicate fibres. It is durable, but will not bear a lot of strain. One cubic metre of cut wood weighs 400–500kg. It is used in carpentry for making furniture, floorboards, panels etc.

The stiffly erect, pointed needles are found in bundles of five on the short shoots. They are 5–12cm long, fairly straight and triangular in cross-section. They usually last for around 5 years.

The trees do not begin to flower until some time between the 60th and 80th years of growth (cultivated trees flower as early as after 25 years, but the resulting seeds are incapable of germination). The male catkins appear in June, July or August, depending on altitude, and are reddish coloured, gradually turning yellow. The flowers are 10–15mm long, sessile and ovoid. The female flowers are found in erect, violet-coloured conelets, at the tip of the new shoots. All the protective scales are more or less greenish in colour, touched with red, with slightly toothed edges. To each of the bluish-violet, downward-curving fruit scales is attached a small, weak keel. The cones ripen after two years, by which time they are egg-shaped, 5–8cm long, and cinnamon brown in colour. The plump, brown, hard-cased, unwinged nuts are edible. They ripen in October of the second year and fall with the cones in the spring of the third year.

The Swiss Stone Pine will also grow in damp, loose soil, in areas with warm summers and high humidity.

Since it is the only species of tree capable of withstanding the extremes of temperature encountered at very high altitude it is found in the central alpine region at an altitude of up to 2250m above sea level.

Pinus cembra, known here more generally as the Arolla Pine, was introduced in 1746 and is now uncommon but present in parks and gardens.

Scots Pine

Pinus sylvestris L.

Pin sylvestre
Waldkiefer

Pages 69, 126, 127

The Scots Pine grows to a height of up to 38m. It has a straight, woody trunk and a tall crown, which becomes dome-shaped with age, flattening out, umbrella-like, at the top.

Its strong central root is a continuation of the trunk itself, with numerous secondary roots leading off. Very old trees may have a diameter measuring as much as 1m. The young bark is rust red to grey-yellow, but as the tree ages it thickens considerably, turning grey-brown on the outside and red-brown on the inside. By the time it is 80 years old, the Scots Pine will have reached a height of 20–25m. In favourable conditions it may live for over 300 years.

Apart from requiring a good deal of light, it is a fairly undemanding tree. It will thrive on the edges of the steppes (warm, dry summers) and in Siberia (harsh, frosty winters) alike, and is found right through from the hilly zone to the subalpine zone, on sandy or rocky ground, in calcareous, gravelly or marly soil, or in wet marshland.

Next to that of the European Larch, the wood of the Scots Pine is the most resinous of any European tree. The sapwood is pink-white, the heartwood yellowish, darkening considerably after felling. The drying process should be quick and easy and the wood does not tend to warp, although it is inclined to crack. Well-dried heartwood will not distort, is very durable, and will stand up well to outside weather conditions. It chops well and is easy to work with. One cubic metre of naturally dried wood weighs around 600kg.

Floorboards, window frames, doors and table-tops are often made out of Scots Pine. It is also used to build ships and carts, and in the paper industry.

The 3cm-long needles grow in pairs on the short shoots. According to the variety of the tree they may stay on the twigs for anything between 2 and 7 years. The tree will begin to flower at some stage after its 30th year of growth. The female flowers are found at the end of new, long shoots, which will continue to grow into the second year. They are roughly egg-shaped and may occur singly or in clusters. At the end of the flowering season they are not yet ripe. They are green in colour, slightly curved, elongated, with clearly visible stalks. They will not ripen fully until the autumn of their second year.

During March or April of the third year, the ripe scales on the conical, elongated, drooping, female cone curve outwards and downwards to release 3–5mm-long, ovoid, light brown seeds, each of which is equipped with a 15–20mm-long wing. The seed contains a fatty oil, which is used in the preparation of varnishes.

The male flowers occur in place of needle-bundles amongst small scales at the base of one-year-old shoots.

Through a process of dry distillation, 'tar' can be extracted from the resinous wood. This may be used for coating ships' ropes or wooden fencing.

An early arrival among the native British trees, the Scots Pine moved to the far north and the population to the south mostly failed to hold its own against the invasion of various broadleaf trees. On some of the older estates, especially in Aberdeenshire and Moray, this is the predominant forest tree in plantations still, as it is south of the native range in Northumberland. When the Norfolk Brecklands were afforested after 1920, the Scots Pine was the main tree used, but growth deteriorated.

Although living for 300 years or more, growth becomes very slow and trees over 1.2m in diameter or 32m in height are scarce. Estates in Sussex and Kent have many big veterans, although most are likely to have perished in the October 1987 gale.

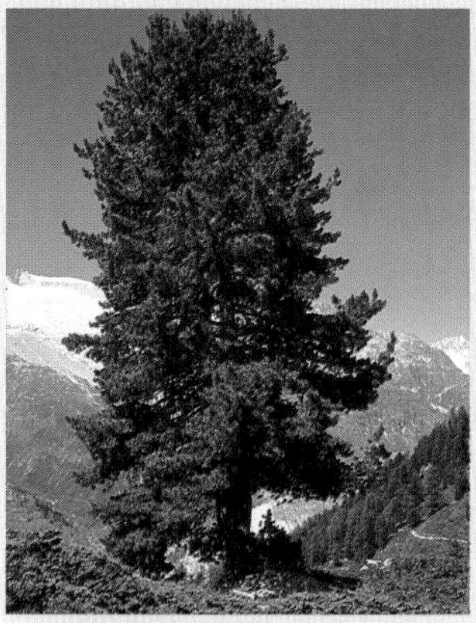
443 Swiss Stone Pine in summer

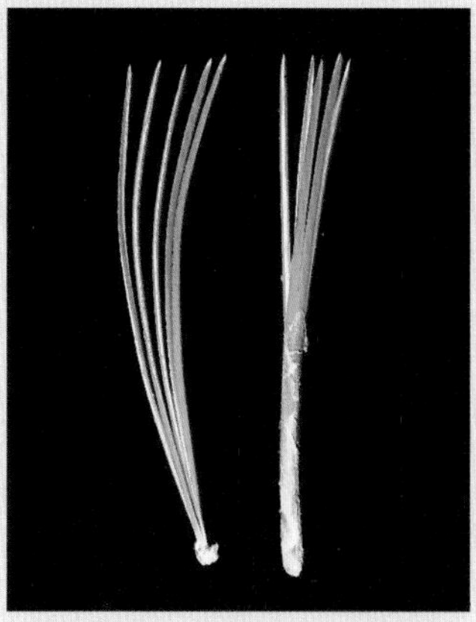
444 Needles 5-12cm long, found in tufts of 5, arranged spirally

445 Male flowers in 1-2cm long, ovoid, red catkins

446 Female flowers in violet, ovoid, stalked cones

447 Terminal bud, narrow-ovoid, often pointed

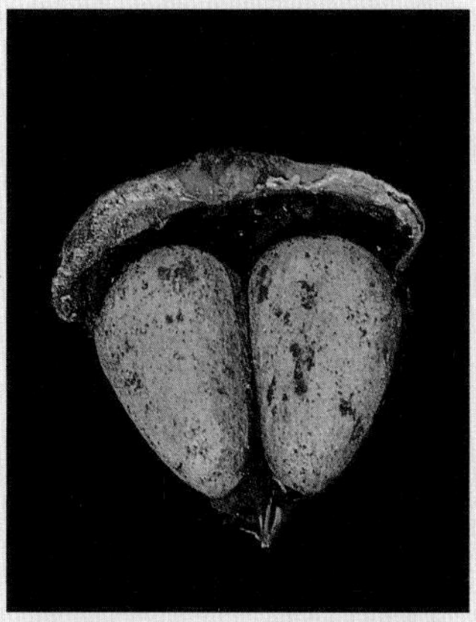
448 'Pine' nuts, fat, brown, edible, with hard shells

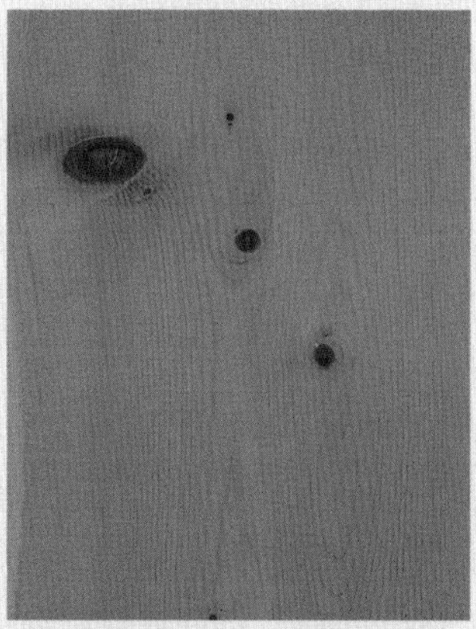
449 Yellowish red heartwood, high in resin, darkening rapidly on exposure to light

450 Flakey bark, grey-black on the outside, brown-red on the inside

451 Scots Pine in summer

452 Needles 3-7cm long, in pairs on short shoots, arranged spirally

453 Male flowers in 3-8cm long, narrow-pyramid catkins

454 Female flowers in ovoid, stalked, violet cones

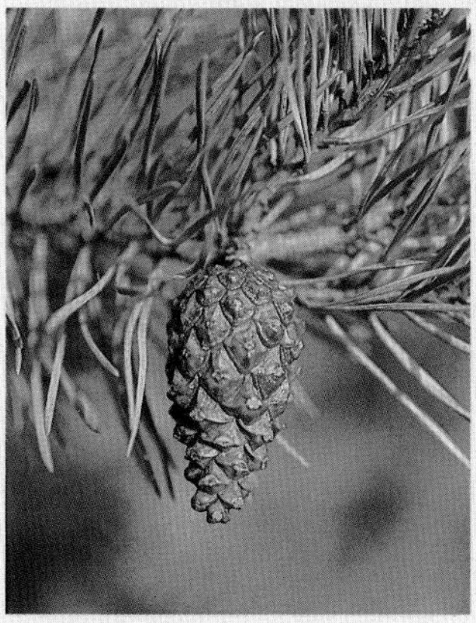
455 Young cones, elongated-ovoid, green, curving backwards

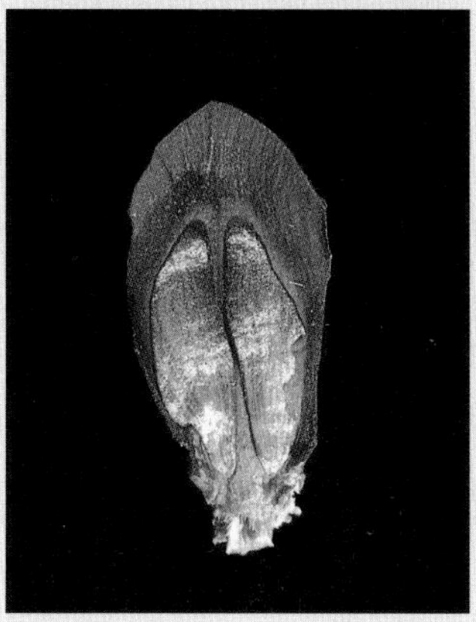
456 Seeds 3-5mm long, ovoid, light brown

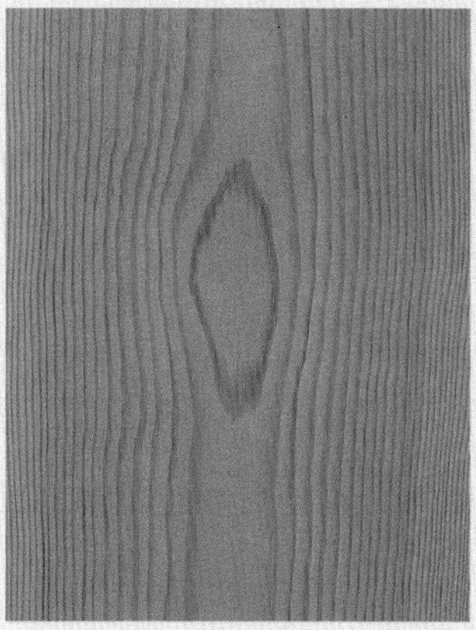
457 Resinous heartwood, yellowish in colour, with distinct, brown annual rings; darkening rapidly on exposure to light

458 Bark on older trees, reddish brown to violet, deeply furrowed, breaking away in flakes

3. Higher zones of vegetation

In climbing from the plain up into the mountain region where there is permanent snow and ice, it is possible to see how individual species and communities of plants occur only at certain altitudes. This is caused principally by:
1. A reduction in temperature
2. A shorter growth period
3. An increase in rainfall and wind-strength
4. A longer period under snow
5. An increase in direct, and especially short-wave, radiation

The more or less sharply defined zones are distinguished as follows:

1. Colline zone (hill zone)

- Up to a height of 600m hill region
  700m in Alpine foot-hills
  800 and 900m central and southern alps
- Average annual temperature between 8° and 12°C.
- Growth period more than 250 days
- Characterised by mixed deciduous woods
  - In lower regions mixed oak-hornbeam woods
  - In the warmest regions on calcareous soils downy oak woods
  - In dry regions pine woods
  - In higher regions mixed beech woods
  - At the southern foot of the alps on acid soils mixed oak woods; nowadays often replaced by chestnut woods.

2. Montane zone (lower mountain zone)

- Up to a height of 1200 and 1300m: On the northern side of the alps
  1300 and 1500m: central alps
  1500 and 1700m: southern alps
- Average annual temperature between 4° and 8°C.
- Growth period more than 200 days
- Characterised by
  - beech, beech-fir and fir woods
  - pine woods in the central alps
  - In more continental regions the spruce forms natural woods.

3. Subalpine zone (higher mountain zone)

- Up to a height of 1700 and 1900m: northern alps
  1900 and 2400m: central alps
  1800 and 2000m: southern alps
- Average annual temperature between 1° and −2°C.
- Growth period 100–200 days
- Characterised by
  - Spruce woods
  - In the inner ranges of the alps spruce woods pass into pine (Arolla) - larch woods
  - At the transition to the alpine zone dwarf shrubs such as the Alpenrose, Juniper and Green Alder (on steep, moist slopes); on calcareous soils stands of the erect or decumbent forms of the Mountain Pine

4. Alpine zone

- It comprises the treeless upper regions of the alps and extends from the tree-line to the natural snow-line (the line where the snow on horizontal surfaces melts in summer).
- The regions above the natural snow-line are often separated from the alpine zone and termed the nival zone.
- Climatic snow-line between 2400 and 3200m
- Characterised by
  - at the very bottom mainly stands of dwarf shrubs (e.g. Trailing Azalea)
  - above the swarf shrubs mainly grass

4. Identification keys

4.1. Guide to using keys I–V

- The key is built up from contrasting characters, and the character in question is shown by a large capital letter.

  Example: p. 65: **A =** **Leaves needle-like**

  Example: p. 74: **B =** **Leaves doubly pinnate**

  The contrasting character for the one given above is indicated by doubling the same letter.

  Example: p. 72: **AA =** **Leaves scale-like**

  In some cases, where the character has several forms, rather than merely 2, the relevant letter is used the appropriate number of times.

  Example: p. 65: **E =** **Needles flattened, and emarginate, obtuse, or rounded at the end**
  p. 66: **EE =** **Needles flattened, and pointed at the end**
  p. 67: **EEE =** **Needles 4-angled, pointed at the end, and attached at the base to a brownish, peg-like projection from the twig . . .**

  Example: p. 74: **B =** **Leaves doubly pinnate**
  p. 74: **BB =** **Leaves simply pinnate and leaflets . . .**
  p. 79: **BBB =** **Leaves simply pinnate with a terminal leaflet; the 3, 5, 7 or 9 leaflets coarsely toothed . . .**

- If the letter required for further description has already been used (e.g. for the description of a species) the same letter is followed by a small arabic numeral to avoid doubling the letter within the same key.

  Example: p. 65: **C =** **Description of the Yew**
  p. 65: **C_1 =** **Needles on long shoots always standing singly and arranged spirally or apparently in 2 rows; no real short shoots present**

  Example: p. 65 **F =** **Needles narrowing at the base into a stalk . . .**
  p. 67: **F_2 =** **Needles with narrow lines of stomata on each side . . .**
  p. 69 **F_3 =** **Needles not more than 10cm long . . .**

- Letters used for the first time for a character or the description of a species do not have an arabic numeral

- Each of the keys begins again with the letter **A** and the arabic numeral **1**
  (See p. 65, 74, 82, 90 and 105)

- Identification can be accomplished with the aid of the 5 keys (see p. 64)

4.2 Summary of the keys for identifying woody plants

Woody plants

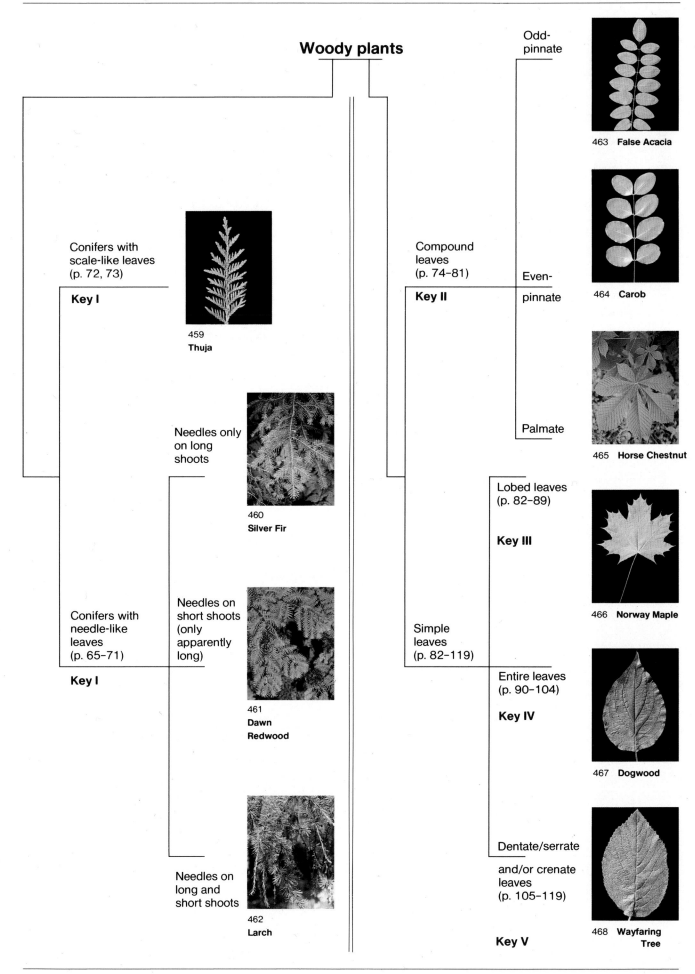

Conifers with scale-like leaves (p. 72, 73)

Key I

459 **Thuja**

Needles only on long shoots

460 **Silver Fir**

Conifers with needle-like leaves (p. 65–71)

Key I

Needles on short shoots (only apparently long)

461 **Dawn Redwood**

Needles on long and short shoots

462 **Larch**

Compound leaves (p. 74–81)

Key II

Odd-pinnate

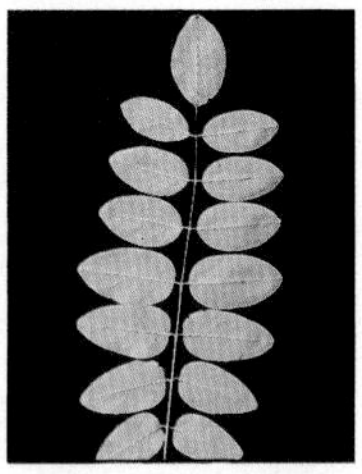

463 **False Acacia**

Even-pinnate

464 **Carob**

Palmate

465 **Horse Chestnut**

Simple leaves (p. 82–119)

Lobed leaves (p. 82–89)

Key III

466 **Norway Maple**

Entire leaves (p. 90–104)

Key IV

467 **Dogwood**

Dentate/serrate and/or crenate leaves (p. 105–119)

Key V

468 **Wayfaring Tree**

A Leaves needle-like (Fig. 469–519)
Correct, see **B** or **BB**
Wrong, see **AA** (p. 72)

B Needles not clearly distinguishable from the twig, but decurrent for 2–17mm, stalked or sessile (Fig. 469–471)
Correct, see **C**, **CC** or **CCC**
Wrong, see **BB** or **BBB** (p. 71)

Taxus – Yew

C

469 **Yew**

Taxus baccata L.
Yew
Fig. 469 – see p. 120/121

- Needles 1–3cm long, 2–3mm broad, linear, flattened, apiculate, entire and spirally arranged
- Stalk of needle 2–3mm long, green and decurrent
- Shiny dark green above with prominent midrib; pale or yellowish green beneath

Sequoia – Coast Redwood

CC

470 **Coast Redwood**

Sequoia sempervirens
(D. Don) Endl.
Coast Redwood
Fig. 470 – see p. 120/121

- Needles 4–20mm long, 1–2.5mm broad, linear to lanceolate, flattened, straight or slightly curved, abruptly pointed, entire and spirally arranged
- Needles decurrent
- Pale to dark green above and with 2 whitish bands of stomata beneath

Araucaria – Chile Pine

CC
C

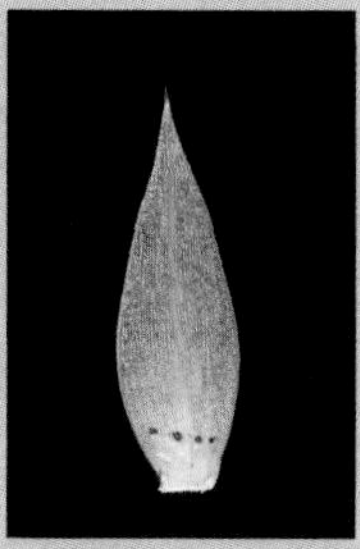

471 **Chile Pine**

Araucaria araucana (Mol.) K. Koch
Chile Pine, Monkey Puzzle
Fig. 471 – see p. 120/121

- Needles 2.5–5cm long, 1–2.5cm broad, triangular, stiff, ending in a sharp spiny point, entire, spirally arranged and overlapping each other
- Needles decurrent
- Both sides shiny dark green, glabrous and with parallel veins

BB Needles clearly distinguishable from the twig and **not** decurrent (Fig. 472–517)
Correct, see **C_1**, **C_1C_1** (p. 68) or **$C_1C_1C_1$** (p. 68)
Wrong, see **BBB** (p.71)

C_1 Needles on long shoots always standing singly and arranged spirally or apparently in 2 rows; no real short shoots present
Correct, see **D** or **DD** (p. 68)
Wrong, see **C_1C_1** (p. 68) or **$C_1C_1C_1$** (p. 68)

D Needles **not** stalked (Fig. 472–494); often somewhat narrowed towards the base
Correct, see **E** or **EE** (p. 66)
Wrong, see **DD** (p. 68)

472
Silver Fir

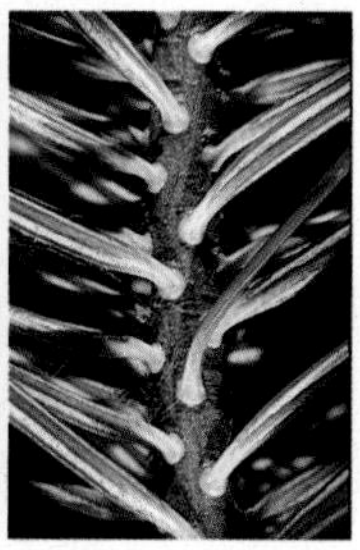

473
Caucasian Fir

E Needles flattened and emarginate, obtuse or rounded at the end
Correct, see **F** or **FF** (p. 66)
Wrong, see **EE** (p. 66) or **EEE** (p. 67)

F Needles narrowing below into a stalk and attached to the twig by a green, enlarged, disc-shaped base
Correct, see **G** or **GG** (p. 66)
Wrong, see **FF** (p. 66)

G Midrib of the needle broad, medium or dark green and clearly visible (Fig. 474, 475)
Correct, see **H** (p. 66) or **HH** (p. 66)
Wrong, see **GG** (p. 66)

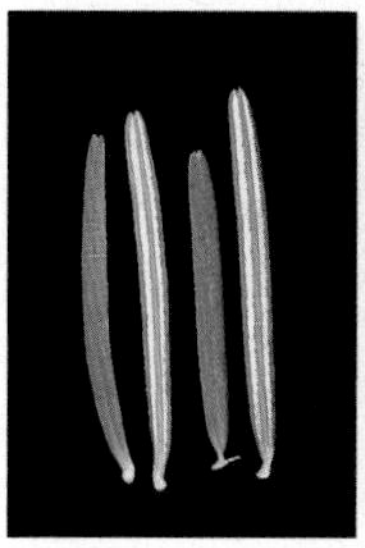

474
Silver Fir

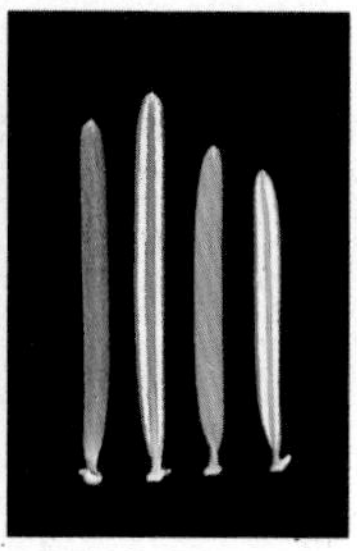

475
Caucasian Fir

Abies – Fir

H

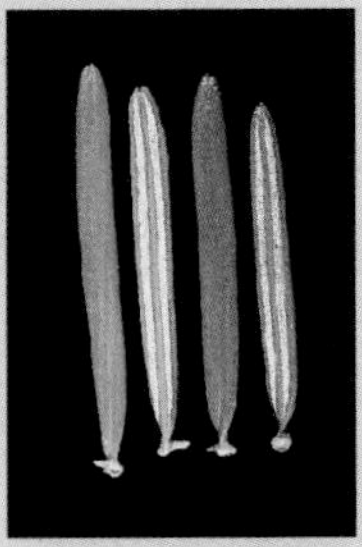

476 **Silver Fir**

Abies alba Mill.
Silver Fir

Fig. 476 – see p. 120/121

- Needles to 3cm long, 2-3mm broad, flattened, linear, obtuse but usually emarginate at the end, narrowing below, and attached to the twig by a circular base
- Margin of needle: entire
- Dark green above with a slightly impressed midrib; 2 broad bands of stomata beneath

HH

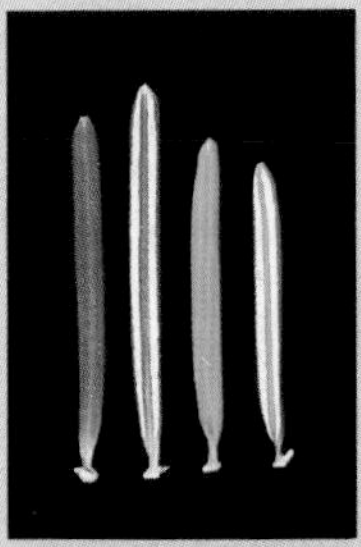

477 **Caucasian Fir**

Abies nordmanniana (Stev.) Spach
Caucasian Fir

Fig. 477 – see p. 120/121

- Needles 2–3.5cm long, 2–2.5mm broad, linear, stiff, firm, clearly furrowed, obtuse, rounded or slightly emarginate, twisted below and attached to the twig by a broadly elliptic to circular base
- Margin of needle: entire
- Dark green above with impressed midrib; the underside with a distinct green midrib and 2 broad, white bands of stomata

GG Midrib of needles somewhat whitish and therefore appearing less distinct than that of the 2 previous species (Fig. 478)

Correct, see **H_1**
Wrong, back to **G** (p. 65)

478 **Veitch's Fir**

Abies – Fir

H_1

479 **Veitch's Fir**

Abies veitchii Lindl.
Veitch's Fir

Fig. 479 – see p. 120/121

- Needles 1–2.5cm long, up to 2mm broad, linear, soft, often pointing diagonally forwards, brush-like, flat at the tip and distinctly emarginate, somewhat narrowed below, slightly curved and attached to the twig by an elliptic or more or less circular base
- Margin of needle: entire
- Medium to dark green above; bands of stomata on the underside chalky white

FF Needles not attached to the twig by an enlarged, disc-shaped base (Fig. 480, 481)

Correct, see **G_1** or **G_1G_1**
Wrong, back to **F** (p. 65)

480
Noble Fir

481
Douglas Fir

Abies – Fir

G_1

482 **Noble Fir**

Abies procera Rehd.
Noble Fir

Fig. 482 – see p. 122/123

- Needles 2.5–3.5cm long, up to 1.5mm broad, linear, firm, densely crowded, clearly curved upwards, usually obtuse at the end, and with the whole base (not enlarged) attached to the twig
- Needles abruptly curved upwards just above the base
- Margin of needle: entire
- Grey-green above, shallowly furrowed

Pseudotsuga – Douglas Fir

G_1
G_1

483 **Douglas Fir**

Pseudotsuga menziesii (Mirbel) Franco
Douglas Fir

Fig. 483 – see p. 122/123

- Needles 1.8–3.5cm long, 1–1.5mm broad, straight or slightly curved, flat, obtuse or somewhat pointed at the end and smelling of orange when rubbed
- Margin of needle: entire
- Medium to dark green and furrowed above; 2 silver grey bands of stomata beneath

EE Needles flattened and pointed at the end (Fig. 484–488)

Correct, see **F_1**, **F_1F_1**, **$F_1F_1F_1$** or **$F_1F_1F_1F_1$** (all p. 67)
Wrong, see **EEE** (p. 67)

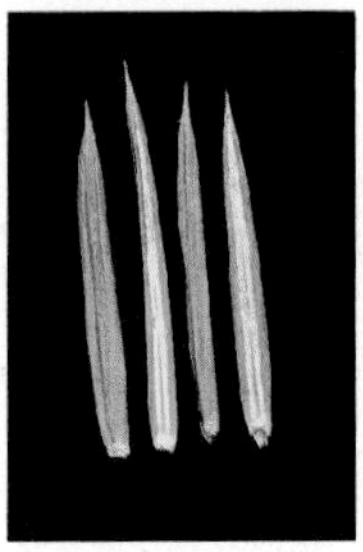

484 **Common Juniper**

Juniperus – Juniper

F_1

485 **Common Juniper**

Juniperus communis L.
ssp. *communis*
Common Juniper
Fig. 485 – see p. 122/123

- Needles 1-2cm long, 1-2mm broad, linear, straight, sessile, sharply pointed, somewhat prickly, attached to the twig by a broad base and usually standing out at right-angles from it
- Margin of needle: entire
- Slightly grooved above and with a white central band; green and keeled beneath

---

F_1F_1

486 **Dwarf Juniper**

Juniperus nana Willd.
Dwarf Juniper
Fig. 486 – see p. 122/123

- Needles 4-8mm long, 1-2mm broad, usually somewhat crescent-shaped, linear, sessile, shortly pointed, not prickly, and attached to the shoot by a broad base; whorls of needles close together
- Margin of needle: entire
- Dark green at the margins above with a broad band of stomata; dark green and somewhat keeled beneath

---

F_1F_1
F_1

487 **Savin**

Juniperus sabina L.
Savin
Fig. 487 – see p. 130/131

- Juvenile leaves needle-like, 4-5mm long, 0.5-1mm broad, arranged in whorls of 3, sessile, obtuse or pointed and attached to the twig by a broad base
- Leaf-margin: entire

F_1F_1
F_1F_1

488 **Chinese Juniper**

Juniperus chinensis L.
Chinese Juniper
Fig. 488 – see p. 122/123

- Juvenile leaves needle-like, 6-10mm long, 1mm broad, spreading and directed forwards, sessile, sharply pointed and arranged in whorls of 3 or opposite
- Margin of needle: entire
- 2 bluish green bands of stomata above; dark green beneath

EE
E

Needles 4-angled, pointed at the end and attached at the base to a brownish, peg-like projection from the twig, that remains as a stump after the needle has fallen (twigs rough!)

Correct, see **F_2** or **F_2F_2**
Wrong, back to **E** (p. 65)

F_2

Both sides of needles with narrow lines of stomata and therefore appearing medium to dark green

Correct, see **G_2** or **G_2G_2**
Wrong, see **F_2F_2**

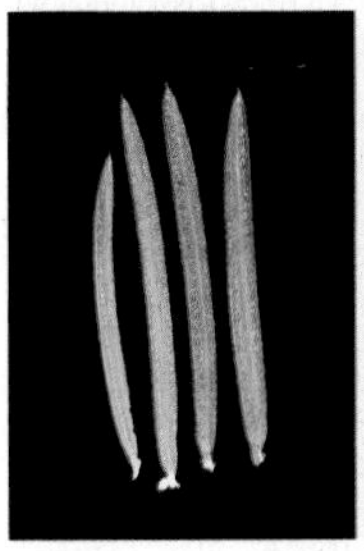

489
Norway Spruce

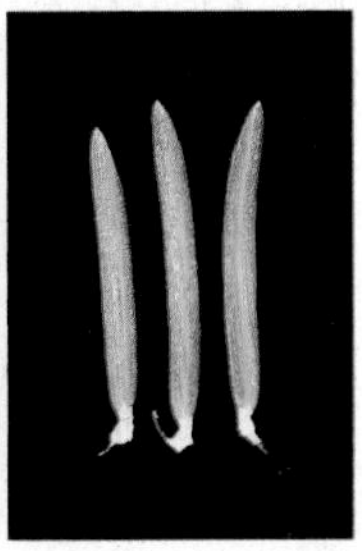

490
Oriental Spruce

Picea – Spruce

G_2

491 **Norway Spruce**

Picea abies (L.) Karst.
P. excelsa (Lam.) Link
Norway Spruce
Fig. 491 – see p. 122/123

- Needles 0.5-2.5cm long, up to 1mm broad, stiff, somewhat crescent-shaped, almost square in cross-section, somewhat obtuse to pointed and pointing diagonally forwards above the twig
- Margin of needle: entire
- Medium to dark green and with fine lines of stomata on all 4 sides

---

G_2
G_2

492 **Oriental Spruce**

Picea orientalis (L.) Link
Oriental Spruce
Fig. 492 – see p. 124/125

- Needles 5-11mm long, 1-1.3mm broad, straight or somewhat curved, shortly stalked, almost square in cross-section, obtuse, and set close together
- Margin of needle: entire
- Shiny dark green with white lines of stomata on all 4 sides

---

F_2F_2

Needles with very broad and distinct white bands of stomata and therefore appearing pale green and white (Fig. 493, 494)

Correct, see **G_3** (p. 68) or **G_3G_3** (p. 68)
Wrong, back to **F_2**

Picea – Spruce

G_3

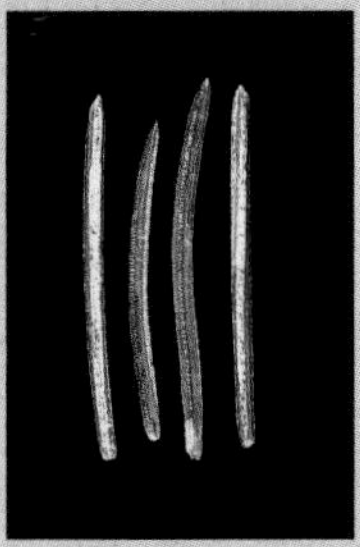

493 **Serbian Spruce**

Picea omorika (Panc.) Purk.
Serbian Spruce
Fig. 493 – see p. 124/125

- Needles 1–1.9cm long, 1.5–2mm broad, somewhat curved, distinctly flattened, closely pressed, keeled on both sides, obtuse or somewhat acute and pointing towards the end of the twig
- Margin of needle: entire
- Upper side becoming dark green: clearly visible bands of stomata on both sides of the keel below

G_3
G_3

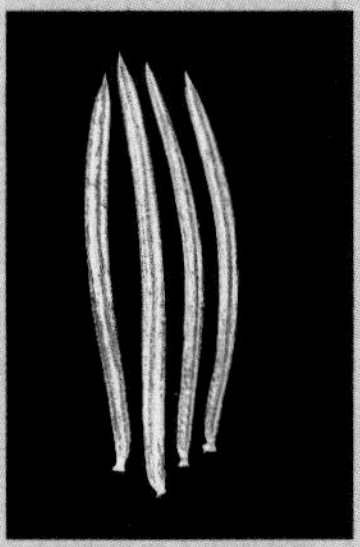

494 **Blue Spruce**

Picea pungens Engelm. **'Glauca'**
Blue Spruce
Fig. 494 – see p. 124/125

- Needles 1.5–3cm long, up to 1.5mm thick, stiff, 4-angled, often slightly crescent-shaped, with a short, sharp point
- Margin of needle: entire
- Needles bluish white with a whitish band of stomata on each side

DD Needles distinctly stalked (Fig. 495) — Correct, see **E_1**; Wrong, back to **D** (p. 65)

Tsuga – Hemlock

E_1

495 **Eastern Hemlock**

Tsuga canadensis (L.) Carr.
Eastern Hemlock, Canadian Hemlock
Fig. 495 – see p. 124/125

- Needles 7–15mm long, 1.5–2.5mm broad, flattened, tapering gradually towards the tip, rounded or truncate at the end with a distinct yellowish white stalk
- Margin of needle finely serrate; teeth far apart
- Dark green above; bluish green beneath with 2 silvery bands of stomata
- Needles along centre line of shoot often twisted

C_1C_1 Needles on short shoots (resembling long shoots) which fall together with the needles in autumn; needles pale green (Fig. 496, 497) — Correct, see **D_1** or **D_1D_1**; Wrong, see **$C_1C_1C_1$**

Metasequoia – Dawn Redwood

D_1

496 **Dawn Redwood**

Metasequoia glyptostroboides Hu et Cheng
Dawn Redwood
Fig. 496 – see p. 124/125

- Needles linear, flattened, soft, 1–4cm long and 2–3mm broad, rounded at the end or with a short point
- Needles on short shoots somewhat curved and falling in autumn with the short shoot
- Needles on long shoots falling individually in autumn
- Medium to dark green above

Taxodium – Swamp Cypress

D_1
D_1

497 **Swamp Cypress**

Taxodium distichum (L.) L.C. Rich.
Swamp Cypress
Fig. 497 – see p. 124/125

- Needles on short shoots 1–2cm long, 1–2mm broad, linear, flattened, somewhat pointed and falling in autumn with the green short shoot
- Arrangement of needles on short shoots alternate and in 2 rows; those on long shoots spirally arranged
- Margin of needle: entire
- At first fresh green, later pale to medium green and in autumn rusty brown

C_1C_1
C_1 Needles on long shoots usually standing singly, those on lateral short shoots in groups of 2–5 or forming a rosette of 10–40 — Correct, see **D_2** or **D_2D_2** (p. 70); Wrong, back to **C_1** (p. 65)

D_2 Needles long, thin, flexible and in groups of 2–5 on short shoots; the latter with a membranous sheath at the base which often falls away in the 1st year — Correct, see **E_2** or **E_2E_2** (p. 69); Wrong, see **D_2D_2** (p. 70)

E_2 Needles in pairs on short shoots (Fig. 498) — Correct, see **F_3** (p. 69) **F_3F_3** (p. 69) or **$F_3F_3F_3$** (p. 69); Wrong, see **E_2E_2** (p. 69)

498 **Mountain Pine**

F_3 Needles not more than 10cm long (2–8cm) and sheaths at the base of the needles on older shoots only short (Fig. 499, right) or falling early

Correct, see **G_4**
Wrong, see **F_3F_3** or **$F_3F_3F_3$**

Pinus – Pine

G_4

499 **Mountain Pine**

Pinus mugo Turra
Mountain Pine
Fig. 499 – see p. 126/127

- Needles 2–8cm long, 1–3mm broad, stiff, straight or somewhat crescent-shaped, semicircular in cross-section and shortly pointed
- Sheaths short even on older shoots
- Margin of needle finely serrate
- Dark green on both sides with numerous lines of stomata

F_3F_3 Needles not more than 10cm long and sheaths at the base of most pairs of needles several mm long and persistent (Fig. 500, 501)

Correct, see **G_5** or **G_5G_5**
Wrong, see **$F_3F_3F_3$**

Pinus – Pine

G_5

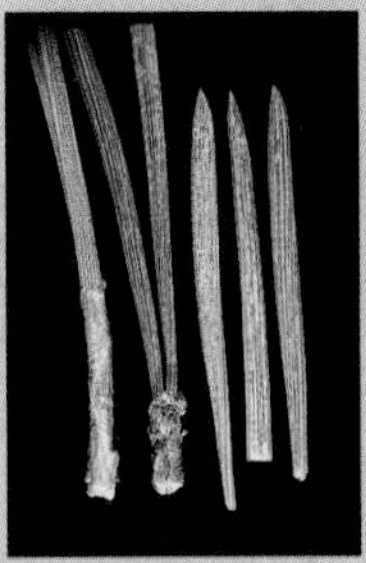

500 **Scots Pine**

Pinus sylvestris L.
Scots Pine
Fig. 500 – see p. 126/127

- Needles 3–7cm long, up to 2mm broad, usually distinctly twisted, semicircular in cross-section, pointed, and clustered at the end of the shoot
- Sheaths persistent
- Margin of needle finely serrate
- Bluish green or greyish green on both sides with very fine lines of stomata

G_5G_5

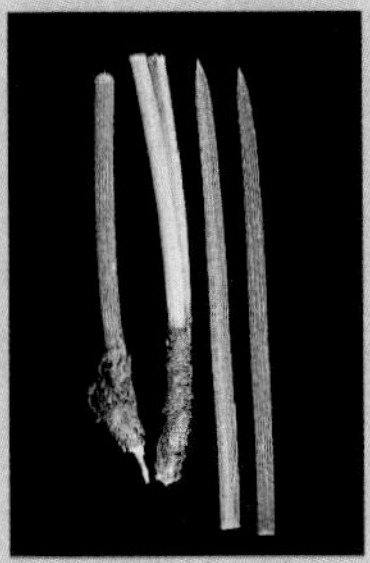

501 **Bosnian Pine**

Pinus leucodermis Ant.
Bosnian Pine
Fig. 501 – see p. 126/127

- Needles 6–10cm long, 1–2mm broad, often somewhat curved, semicircular in cross-section, pointed, and clustered at the ends of the shoots
- Sheaths persistent
- Margin of needle very finely toothed
- Dark green on both sides; bands of stomata over the whole surface

$F_3F_3F_3$ Needles between 10 and 25cm long and sheaths at the base of the needles persistent (Fig. 502, 503)

Correct, see **G_6** or **G_6G_6**
Wrong, back to **F_3**

Pinus – Pine

G_6

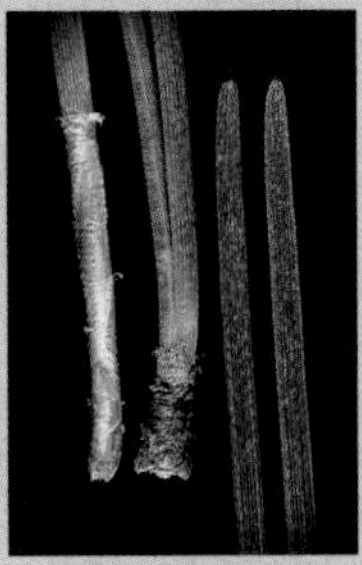

502 **Maritime Pine**

Pinus pinaster Ait.
Maritime Pine
Fig. 502 – see p. 126/127

- Needles 13–25cm long, 1–2mm broad, semicircular in cross-section, and sometimes in groups of 3 on younger trees
- Sheaths persisting until the 3rd or 4th year
- Margin of needle finely serrate
- Upper surface dark green or greyish green; fine lines of stomata present throughout

G_6G_6

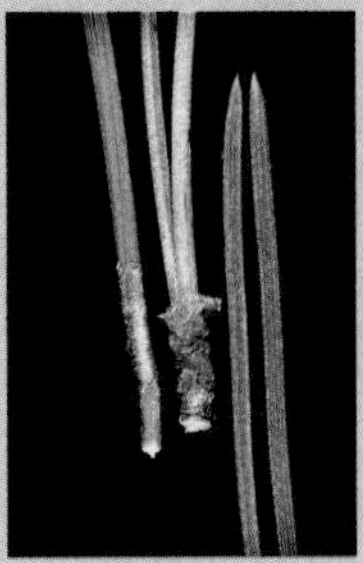

503 **Austrian Pine**

Pinus nigra Arnold **ssp. *nigra***
Austrian Pine
Fig. 503 – see p. 126/127

- Needles 10–18cm long, 1–2mm broad, usually somewhat curved, semicircular in cross-section, often somewhat flattened, pointed and fairly sharp
- Sheaths long and persistent
- Margin of needle finely toothed
- Whole surface dark green with lines of stomata

E_2E_2 Needles in groups of 5 (more rarely 3 or 4) on short shoots

Correct, see **F_4** or **F_4F_4** (p. 70)
Wrong, back to **E_2** (p. 68)

F_4 Needles with large, white spots of resin (Fig. 504)

Correct, see **G_7** (p. 70)
Wrong, see **F_4F_4** (p. 70)

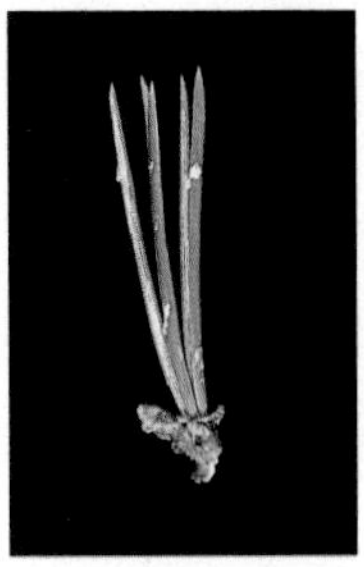

504 **Bristle-cone Pine**

Pinus – Pine

G_7

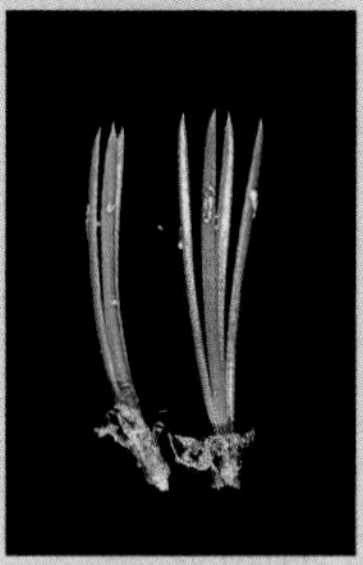

505 **Bristle-cone Pine**

Pinus aristata Engelm.
Bristle-cone Pine

Fig. 505 – see p. 126/127

- Needles 2.5–4cm long, 1mm broad, often curved, with white spots of resin, triangular in cross-section and narrowly pointed
- Sheaths persisting as reflexed lobes until the 4th year
- Margin of needle: entire
- 2 sides with lines of stomata; the 3rd side dark green without stomatic lines

---

F_4F_4	Needles without large white spots of resin	Correct, see G_8 or G_8G_8 Wrong, back to F_4 (p. 69)
G_8	Needles 4–7cm long and distinctly curved and twisted so that the twigs appear whitish and green	Correct, see H_2 Wrong, see G_8G_8

Pinus – Pine

H_2

506 **Japanese White Pine**

Pinus parviflora Sieb. et Zucc.
Japanese White Pine

Fig. 506 – see p. 128/129

- Needles 4–7cm long, 0.5–1cm broad, distinctly curved and twisted, triangular in cross-section, obtuse, and clustered brush-like at the ends of the twigs
- Sheaths falling away in the 1st year
- Margin of needle finely serrate
- Dark bluish green above; the two inner surfaces with whitish lines of stomata

---

G_8G_8	Needles 5–12cm long, not curved or twisted (Fig. 507, 508)	Correct, see H_3 or H_3H_3 Wrong, back to G_8

507 **Weymouth Pine**

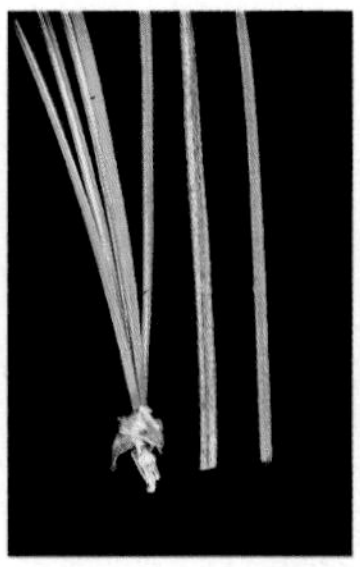

508 **Arolla Pine**

Pinus – Pine

H_3

509 **Weymouth Pine**

Pinus strobus L.
Weymouth Pine

Fig. 509 – see p. 128/129

- Needles 5–12cm long, slender and flexible, triangular in cross-section and with a pointed tip
- Sheaths falling away entirely in the 1st year
- Margin of needle very finely toothed
- 2 sides each with 2 or 3 bluish white lines of stomata; the 3rd side dark green in 2nd year

---

H_3
H_3

510 **Arolla Pine**

Pinus cembra L.
Arolla Pine, Swiss Stone Pine

Fig. 510 – see p. 128/129

- Needles 5–12cm long, 0.8–1.5mm broad, fairly straight, triangular in cross-section, stiffly erect and pointed
- Sheaths falling away in the 1st year
- Margin of needle very finely toothed
- 2 sides each with 3–5 bluish white lines of stomata; upperside dark green

---

D_2D_2	Needles on lateral short shoots forming a rosette of 10–40	Correct, see E_3 or E_3E_3 (p. 71) Wrong, back to D_2 (p. 68)
E_3	Needles soft, flattened and falling in autumn	Correct, see F_5 or F_5F_5 (p. 71) Wrong, see E_3E_3 (p. 71)

Larix – Larch

F_5

511 **European Larch**

Larix decidua Mill.
European Larch

Fig. 511 – see p. 128/129

- Needles 1.5–3cm long, 0.5–0.9mm broad, soft, flattened, obtuse or shortly pointed
- In groups of 30–40 on short shoots; singly, and fairly crowded on long shoots; young shoots not glaucous
- Margin of needle: entire
- Pale to dark green on both sides becoming golden yellow before falling in autumn

F_5
F_5

512 **Japanese Larch**

Larix kaempferi (Lamb.) Carr.
Japanese Larch
Fig. 512 - see p. 128/129

- Needles 1.5-3.5cm long, 1-1.5mm broad, soft, flattened, obtuse or acute
- In groups of 20-40 on short shoots; singly, and fairly crowded on long shoots; young shoots glaucous
- Margin of needle: entire
- Bluish green on both sides and golden yellow before leaf-fall

---

E_3E_3	Needles stiff or rather soft (not as soft as in larches), circular, 4-angled, rhombic or triangular and lasting for several years	Correct, see **F_6** or **F_6F_6** Wrong, back to **E_3** (p. 70)
F_6	Needles 2-6.5cm long, rather soft and circular or 4-angled in cross-section	Correct, see **G_9** Wrong, see **F_6F_6**

Cedrus - Cedar

G_9

513 **Deodar**

Cedrus deodara (D. Don) G. Don
Deodar
Fig. 513 - see p. 130/131

- Needles 2-6.5cm long, up to 1mm broad, whitish, circular or 4-angled in cross-section, finely pointed and rather sharp
- Margin of needle: entire
- Dark green on all sides with fine lines of stomata

F_6F_6	Needles 1-3.5cm long, stiff, triangular to flattened rhombic or 4-angled in cross-section and sharply pointed (Fig. 514, 515)	Correct, see **G_{10}** or **$G_{10}G_{10}$** Wrong, back to **F_6**

514
Cedar of Lebanon

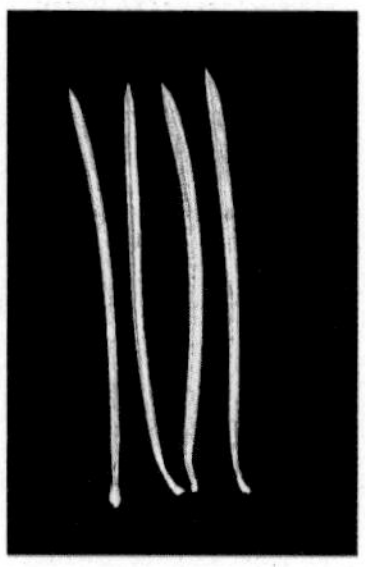

515
Atlas Cedar

Cedrus - Cedar

G_{10}

516 **Cedar of Lebanon**

Cedrus libani A. Rich.
Cedar of Lebanon
Fig. 516 - see p. 130/131

- Needles 1-3.5cm long, 1-1.2mm broad, stiff, sharp, triangular to rhombic in cross-section and because of the flattened surface always broader than high
- Margin of needle: entire
- Very fine lines of stomata on all sides; needles pale to dark green

---

G_{10}
G_{10}

517 **Atlas Cedar**

Cedrus atlantica
(Endl.) Manetti ex Carr.
Atlas Cedar
Fig. 517 - see p. 130/131

- Needles 1-3cm long, 1-1.3mm broad, stiff, somewhat curved and very shortly pointed, irregularly 4-angled in cross-section, thicker and stiffer than in the Cedar of Lebanon
- Margin of needle: entire
- Lines of stomata on all sides; therefore appearing pale bluish green

---

BBB	Needles with the lower part adhering to the twig, spirally arranged (forming 3 rows), pointed, and overlapping (Fig. 518)	Correct, see **C_2** Wrong, back to **B** (p. 65)

518 **Sierra Redwood**

Sequoiadendron - Sierra Redwood

C_2

519 **Sierra Redwood**

Sequoiadendron giganteum
(Lindl.) Buchh.
Sierra Redwood, Wellingtonia
Fig. 519 - see p. 128/129

- Needles 3-6mm long (on main shoots up to 12mm), 0.8-1.2mm broad, awl-shaped to lanceolate, pointed at the tip and attached to the shoot by a broad base
- Margin of needle: entire
- Dark green and somewhat rounded above; dark green and longitudinally furrowed beneath; with fine lines of stomata over the whole surface

AA Leaves scale-like (Fig. 520–533) — Correct, see **B_1** or **B_1B_1**; Wrong, back to **A** (p. 65)

B_1 Branchlets cylindrical or 4-angled and scale-leaves all similar — Correct, see **C_3** or **C_3C_3**; Wrong, see **B_1B_1**

Cupressus – Cypress

C_3

520 **Italian Cypress**

Cupressus sempervirens L.
Italian Cypress

Fig. 520 – see p. 130/131

- Scale-leaves 1–5mm long, closely pressed and overlapping on younger shoots, later somewhat spreading, pointed, but with a blunt tip on lateral shoots
- Leaf-margin: entire
- Dark green on both sides; with an oblong, often very indistinct gland on the back

Juniperus – Juniper

C_3
C_3

521 **Savin**

Juniperus sabina L.
Savin

Fig. 521 – see p. 130/131

- Juvenile leaves needle-like; adult leaves scale-like, overlapping and blunt or pointed
- Leaf-margin: entire
- Leaves of the upper and lower ranks dark green, with a whitish waxy line and an elliptical gland; leaves of the side ranks dark green with stomatic areas at the sides

B_1B_1 Shoots flattened and lateral scale-leaves different from those of the upper and lower ranks — Correct, see **C_4** or **C_4C_4**; Wrong, back to **B_1**

C_4 Younger shoots 4–8mm broad, shiny green above, with silvery white stomatic markings beneath and leaves of the side ranks not touching (Fig. 522) — Correct, see **D_3**; Wrong, see **C_4C_4**

Thujopsis – Hiba

D_3

522 **Hiba**

Thujopsis dolabrata
(L.f.) Sieb. et Zucc.

Hiba, Hiba Arbor-vitae

Fig. 522 – see p. 130/131

- Scale-leaves 3–8mm long, 1–4mm broad, flattened and leathery; leaves of the upper and lower ranks oblong-obovate and overlapping; leaves of the side ranks larger and keeled
- Leaves of the upper and lower ranks obtuse, those of the side ranks pointed
- Leaf-margin: entire
- Silvery white patches on the underside

C_4C_4 Younger branchlets at most 3–4mm broad and the lower to middle part of the leaves of the side ranks touching at the margins — Correct, see **D_4**, **D_4D_4** or **$D_4D_4D_4$** (p. 73); Wrong, back to **C_4**

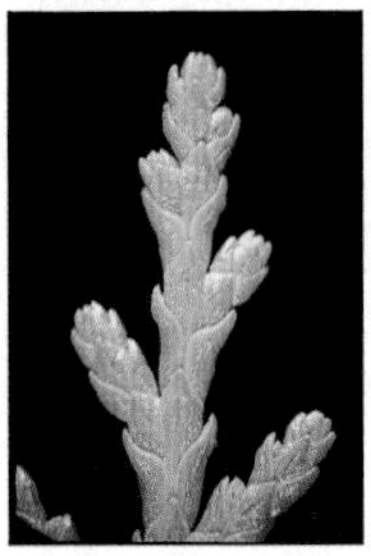

523 **Chinese Thuja**

D_4 Glands on the leaves of the upper and lower ranks inconspicuous and shoots same colour on both sides (Fig. 524) — Correct, see **E_4**; Wrong, see **D_4D_4** (p. 73) or **$D_4D_4D_4$** (p. 73)

Thuja – Arbor-vitae

E_4

524 **Chinese Thuja**

Thuja orientalis L.
Chinese Thuja

Fig. 524 – see p. 132/133

- Scale leaves 1.5–8mm long, closely oppressed to the shoots; leaves of the upper and lower ranks obtuse and overlapped on their margins by the leaves of the side ranks
- Leaf-margin: entire
- Both sides the same colour with scattered, white stomata; glands on the leaves of the upper and lower ranks inconspicuous

D_4D_4 Glands on the leaves of the upper and lower ranks clearly visible as small, oblong raised areas, and the upper and lower sides of the shoots a different colour (Fig. 525–529)

Correct, see E_5 or E_5E_5
Wrong, see $D_4D_4D_4$

525 **White Cedar**

526 **Lawson Cypress**

E_5 Leaves of the side ranks completely appressed to the leaves of the upper and lower ranks (Fig. 527)

Correct, see F_7
Wrong, see E_5E_5

Thuja – Arbor-vitae

F_7

527 **White Cedar**

Thuja occidentalis L.
White Cedar

Fig. 527 - see p. 132/133

- Scale-leaves 2–7mm long; leaves of the upper and lower ranks acutely obovate, appressed to the shoot, strongly compressed and somewhat overlapped by the elliptic to triangular, keeled leaves of the side ranks
- Tip of leaf obtuse or shortly pointed
- Leaf-margin: entire
- Leaves dark green above, those of the upper and lower ranks with a clearly visible resin gland

E_5E_5 Upper part of the leaves of the side ranks spreading away from the leaves of the upper and lower ranks

Correct, see F_8 or F_8F_8
Wrong, back to E_5

Chamaecyparis – False Cypress

F_8

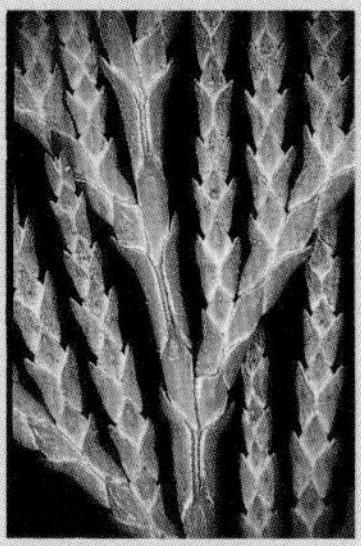

528 **Lawson Cypress**

Chamaecyparis lawsoniana
(A. Murr.) Parl.
Lawson Cypress

Fig. 528 - see p. 132/133

- Scale-leaves 1–7mm long; visible part of the leaves of the upper and lower ranks rhombic or narrowly elliptic with a conspicuous oblong resin-gland; leaves of the side ranks pointed and with 2 inconspicuous resin glands
- Leaf-margin: entire
- Dark to greyish green above; paler green beneath

Thuja – Arbor-vitae

F_8
F_8

529 **Western Red Cedar**

Thuja plicata Donn ex D. Don
Western Red Cedar

Fig. 529 - see p. 132/133

- Scale-leaves 2–8mm long appressed to the shoot; leaves of the side ranks covering the margins of the leaves of the upper and lower ranks
- Leaf-margin: entire
- Leaves of the lateral shoots rather blunt or somewhat pointed
- Leaves rich green above and with a gland on those of the upper and lower ranks; greyish green beneath and with stomata forming an almost triangular silver grey mark

D_4D_4
D_4 Leaves of the upper and lower ranks with glandular furrows (Fig. 530–533)

Correct, see E_6 or E_6E_6
Wrong, back to D_4 (p. 72)

530 **Nootka Cypress**

531 **Hinoki Cypress**

Chamaecyparis – False Cypress

E_6

532 **Nootka Cypress**

Chamaecyparis nootkatensis
(D. Don) Spach
Nootka Cypress

Fig. 532 - see p. 132/133

- Scale-like leaves of the upper and lower ranks overlapping; leaves of the side ranks triangular, somewhat keeled and with the upper part spreading
- All leaves pointed
- Leaf-margin: entire
- Dark green on both sides; leaves of the upper and lower ranks with a glandular furrow on the back

E_6
E_6

533 **Hinoki Cypress**

Chamaecyparis obtusa
(Sieb. et Zucc.) Endl.
Hinoki Cypress

Fig. 533 - see p. 132/133

- Scale-leaves obtuse or rounded; leaves of upper and lower ranks narrowly obovate, thickish, appressed to the shoot; leaves of side ranks crescent-shaped, closely overlapping and smaller than those of other ranks
- Leaf-margin: entire
- Shiny dark green above, those of the upper and lower ranks with a glandular furrow; greyish green beneath with white lines of stomata

A Leaves pinnate (Fig. 534–565) — Correct, see **B**, **BB** or **BBB** (p. 79) Wrong, see **AA** (p. 80)

534 Upper side
Common Ash

535 Upper side
Traveller's Joy

B Leaves doubly pinnate (Fig. 536) — Correct, see **C** Wrong, see **BB**

Acacia – Wattle

C

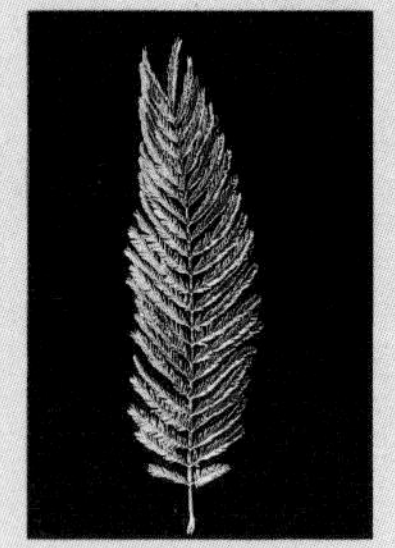

536 Upper side
Silver Wattle

Acacia dealbata Link
Silver Wattle, Mimosa
Fig. 536 – see p. 134/135

- Leaves 5–15cm long
- Leaf-stalk 1–3cm long
- Leaves with 15–25 pairs of leaflets, each leaflet with 20–40 pairs of smaller leaflets (leaflets of the 2nd order)
- Smaller leaflets narrowly linear, 3–5mm long, sessile, rounded or shortly pointed at the end and wedge-shaped or rounded at the base

---

BB Leaves simply pinnate and leaflets entire or finely serrate to dentate — Correct, see **C_1** or **C_1C_1** Wrong, see **BBB** (p. 79)

C_1 Pairs of leaflets mostly not exactly opposite each other (Fig. 537–539); leaflets rounded at the end with a short, sometimes bristly point — Correct, see **D** or **DD** Wrong, see **C_1C_1**

D Leaves up to 7cm long and with at most 12 leaflets, the latter with winged stalks (Fig. 537) — Correct, see **E** Wrong, see **DD**

Pistacia – Mastic Tree

E

537 Upper side
Mastic Tree

Pistacia lentiscus L.
Mastic Tree
Fig. 537 – see p. 136/137

- Leaves 3–7cm long
- Leaf-stalk 1–3cm long and winged
- Leaflets oblong to narrowly ovate, 2–4cm long, entire, usually rounded at the end with a short point and wedge-shaped at the base
- Leaves with or without a terminal leaflet

DD Leaves with 5–18 pairs of leaflets, 30–75cm long, without a winged stalk (Fig. 538, 539) — Correct, see **E_1** or **E_1E_1** Wrong, back to **D**

Juglans – Walnut

E_1

538 Upper side
Black Walnut

Juglans nigra L.
Black Walnut
Fig. 538 – see p. 134/135

- Leaves 30–60cm long
- Leaf-stalk 1–6cm long
- Leaflets lanceolate to narrowly ovate, 6–12cm long, irregularly serrate/dentate, usually entire in the lower part, broadly wedge-shaped at the base and with a shortly pointed tip

---

Ailanthus – Tree of Heaven

E_1
E_1

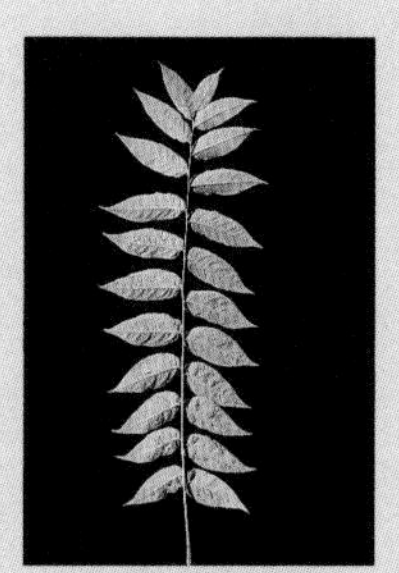

539 Under side
Tree of Heaven

Ailanthus altissima
(Mill.) Swingle
Tree of Heaven
Fig. 539 – see p. 134/135

- Leaves 40–75cm long
- Leaf-stalk 8–20cm long
- Leaflets oblong-ovate to obliquely elliptic, 5–15cm long, narrowing towards the pointed tip and broadly wedge-shaped or rounded at the base
- Margin of leaflets entire, except for 1–4 visually glandular teeth, and often fringed with fine hairs

---

C_1C_1 Pairs of leaflets mostly exactly opposite each other (Fig. 540–565) — Correct, see **D_1** (p. 75) or **D_1D_1** (p. 75) Wrong, back to **C_1**

D_1 Leaves without a terminal leaflet (Fig. 540) — Correct, see **E_2**; Wrong, see **D_1D_1**

Ceratonia - Carob

E_2

Ceratonia siliqua L.
Carob

Fig. 540 - see p. 134/135

- Leaves 10-20cm long
- Leaf-stalk 2-5cm long and tinged red
- Leaflets obovate or elliptic to oblong, 3-7cm long, entire, leathery, rounded and usually emarginate at the end, and rounded or broadly wedge-shaped at the base

540 Upper side **Carob**

D_1D_1 Leaves with a terminal leaflet (Fig. 541-565) — Correct, see **E_3** or **E_3E_3**; Wrong, back to **D_1**

E_3 Leaves 2-10cm long; leaflets obovate and emarginate at the end (Fig. 541, 542) — Correct, see **F** or **FF**; Wrong, see **E_3E_3**

F Terminal leaflet long stalked (Fig. 541) — Correct, see **G**; Wrong, see **FF**

Colutea - Bladder Senna

G

Colutea arborescens L.
Bladder Senna

Fig. 541 - see p. 134/135

- Leaves 4-10cm long
- Leaf-stalk 0.5-1.5cm long
- Leaflets elliptic to obovate, 1-3.5cm long, entire, distinctly emarginate at the end and rounded or wedge-shaped at the base

541 Upper side **Bladder Senna**

FF Terminal leaflet sessile or with only a short stalk (Fig. 542) — Correct, see **G_1**; Wrong, back to **F**

Coronilla - Crown Vetch

G_1

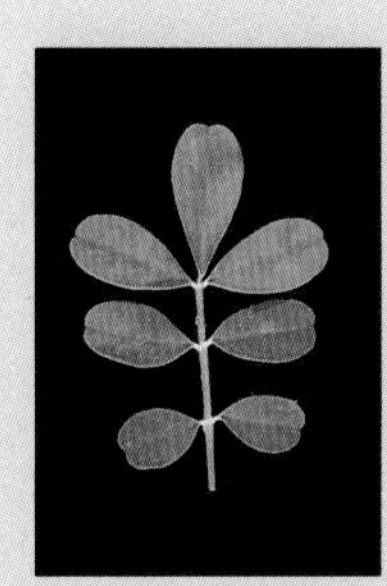

Coronilla emerus L.
Scorpion Senna

Fig. 542 - see p. 134/135

- Leaves 2-6cm long
- Leaf-stalk up to 1cm long
- Leaflets obovate, 1-2cm long, entire, usually emarginate at the end or more rarely rounded with a bristly point, and narrowly to broadly wedge-shaped at the base

542 Upper side **Scorpion Senna**

E_3E_3 Leaves much longer than 10cm; leaflets rounded at the end with a short or long point — Correct, see **F_1** or **F_1F_1** (p. 76); Wrong, back to **E_3**

F_1 Leaflets entire; in the Walnut these more rarely indistinctly serrate — Correct, see **G_2** or **G_2G_2** (p. 76); Wrong, see **F_1F_1** (p. 76)

G_2 Leaves with 3-12 pairs of leaflets; the latter oblong-elliptic to ovate, 3-6cm long and obtuse, rounded or indistinctly emarginate at the end (Fig. 543) — Correct, see **H**; Wrong, see **G_2G_2** (p. 76)

Robinia - False Acacia

H

Robinia pseudoacacia L.
False Acacia

Fig. 543 - see p. 136/137

- Leaves 15-30cm long
- Leaf-stalk 3-4cm long and enlarged at the base
- Leaflets oblong-elliptic to ovate, 3-6cm long, entire, shortly stalked, obtuse, rounded or indistinctly emarginate at the end and rounded or broadly wedge-shaped at the base

543 Upper side **False Acacia**

G_2G_2 Leaves with 2–6 pairs of leaflets; the latter oblong-elliptic to oblong-ovate, 6–15cm long and distinctly pointed at the end; leaves smelling of spice when rubbed (Fig. 544) — Correct, see **H_1**; Wrong, back to **G_2** (p. 75)

Juglans – Walnut

H_1

Juglans regia L.
Common Walnut
Fig. 544 – see p. 136/137

- Leaves 20–50cm long
- Leaf-stalk to 20cm long and thickened at the base
- All leaflets sessile except for the terminal leaflet; all pointed at the end and wedge-shaped or rounded at the base

544 Under side **Common Walnut**

F_1F_1 Leaflets finely to distinctly simply or doubly serrate or dentate — Correct, see **G_3** or **G_3G_3**; Wrong, back to **F_1** (p. 75)

G_3 The 3, 5 or 7 leaflets distinctly white-felted beneath (Fig. 545) — Correct, see **H_2**; Wrong, see **G_3G_3**

Rubus – Raspberry

H_2

Rubus idaeus L.
Raspberry
Fig. 545 – see p. 136/137

- Leaves 5–15cm long
- Leaf-stalk 3–8cm long, hairy and often prickly
- Leaflets elliptic to broadly ovate, 6–10cm long, simply and often even doubly serrate, pointed at the end, and heart-shaped, rounded or broadly wedge-shaped at the base

545 Underside **Raspberry**

G_3G_3 Leaflets not white-felted beneath — Correct, see **H_3** or **H_3H_3**; Wrong, back to **G_3**

H_3 Leaf-stalks with numerous curved prickles pointing towards the base of the stalk; leaflets broadly elliptic to obovate (Fig. 546) — Correct, see **I**; Wrong, see **H_3H_3**

Rubus – Blackberry

I

Rubus fruticosus L.
Blackberry
Fig. 546 – see p. 136/137

- Leaves 5–15cm long
- Leaf-stalk 2–6cm long and bearing numerous curved prickles pointing towards the base of the stalk
- Leaflets broadly elliptic to obovate, 3–8cm long, simply or doubly serrate, pointed at the end and rounded or truncate at the base
- Midrib of leaflets bearing small prickles

546 Upper side **Blackberry**

H_3H_3 Leaf-stalks without prickles or with only few (Rosa) and leaflets not broadly elliptic — Correct, see **I_1** or **I_1I_1** (p. 78); Wrong, back to **H_3**

I_1 Leaves without stipules at the base or, if present, stipules not like those of Roses (Fig. 547–562) — Correct, see **K** or **KK** (p. 77); Wrong, see **I_1I_1** (p. 78)

K Number of leaflets 5 or 7, more rarely 9 — Correct, see **L**, **LL** (p. 77) or **LLL** (p. 77); Wrong, see **KK** (p. 77)

L Leaflets sessile (Fig. 547) or very shortly stalked, finely serrate or dentate and pale bluish green beneath (Fig. 548) — Correct, see **M** (p. 77); Wrong, see **LL** (p. 77) or **LLL** (p. 77)

547 Upper side **Bladder-nut**

Staphylea - Bladder-nut

M

548 Under side **Bladder-nut**

Staphylea pinnata L.
Bladder-nut
Fig. 548 - see p. 136/137

- Leaves 15-25cm long
- Leaf-stalk 5-9cm long
- Lateral leaflets narrowly ovate to elliptic, 6-9cm long, sessile, shortly pointed at the end and wedge-shaped or rounded at the base
- Terminal leaflet long stalked

LL All leaflets very clearly stalked (Fig. 549) — Correct, see **M_1**; Wrong, see **LLL**

Fraxinus - Ash

M_1

549 Upper side **Manna Ash**

Fraxinus ornus L.
Manna Ash
Fig. 549 - see p. 138/139

- Leaves 15-30cm long
- Leaf-stalk 3-8cm long and often finely hairy
- Leaflets oblong-ovate 3-7cm long, irregularly serrate, distinctly stalked, pointed at the end and wedge-shaped or rounded at the base

---

LL
L Leaflets of the same leaf shortly stalked and sessile — Correct, see **M_2** or **M_2M_2**; Wrong, back to **L** (p. 76)

M_2 Leaflets lanceolate to narrowly ovate; stalks (if present) tinged red above (Fig. 550) — Correct, see **N**; Wrong, see **M_2M_2**

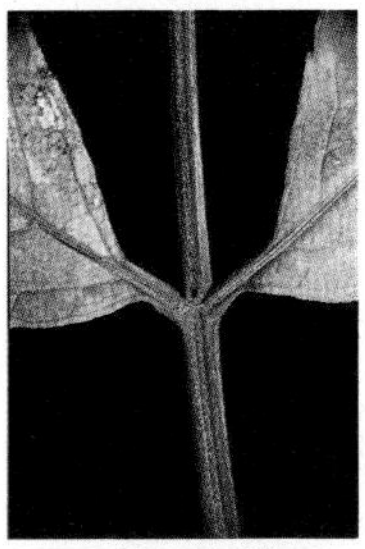

550 Upper side
Red-berried Elder, junction of leaflets with leaf-stalk

Sambucus - Elder

N

551 Upper side **Red-berried Elder**

Sambucus racemosa L.
Red-berried Elder
Fig. 551 - see p. 138/139

- Leaves 10-25cm long
- Leaf-stalk 7-10cm long
- Leaflets lanceolate to narrowly ovate, 4-8cm long, irregularly serrate, their stalks (if present) tinged red above, tips long printed and unequally narrowly or broadly wedge-shaped or rounded at the base

---

M_2M_2 Leaflets much broader (elliptic, ovate) than in the Red-berried Elder and their stalks (if present) not tinged red above (Fig. 552, 553) — Correct, see **N_1** or **N_1N_1**; Wrong, back to **M_2**

Sambucus - Elder

N_1

552 Upper side **Elder**

Sambucus nigra L.
Elder
Fig. 552 - see p. 138/139

- Leaves 10-30cm long
- Leaf-stalk 4-10cm long and grooved above
- Leaflets elliptic, 10-15cm long, irregularly coarsely serrate, shortly stalked or sessile, shortly pointed at the end and unequally or broadly wedge-shaped or rounded at the base

---

Fraxinus - Ash

N_1
N_1

553 Upper side **White Ash**

Fraxinus americana L.
White Ash
Fig. 553 - see p. 142/143

- Leaves 15-40cm long
- Leaf-stalk 5-12cm long
- Lateral leaflets ovate, 6-12cm long, serrate or in parts entire, shortly stalked, pointed at the end and rounded at the base
- Terminal leaflet long stalked and usually wedge-shaped at the base

---

KK Number of leaflets more than 9; if only 7, then very rare and only present in the Common Ash — Correct, see **L_1** (p. 78) or **L_1L_1** (p. 78); Wrong, back to **K** (p. 76)

L_1 Leaflets elliptic or lanceolate-ovate and shortly pointed; midrib and lateral veins beneath prominent (Fig. 554); veins beneath bearing reddish brown woolly hairs, often becoming glabrous late in the year — Correct, see **M_3** Wrong, see **L_1L_1**

Fraxinus – Ash

M_3

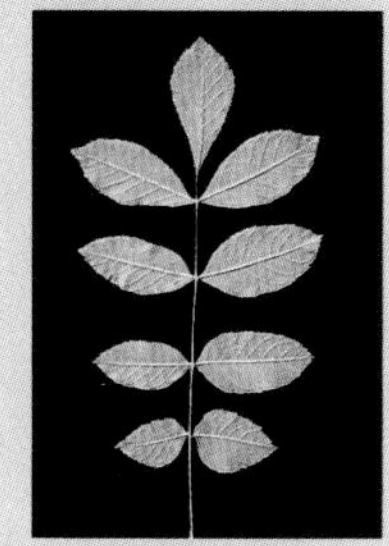

554 Under side **Common Ash**

Fraxinus excelsior L.
Common Ash
Fig. 554 – see p. 138/139

- Leaves 20–30cm long
- Leaf-stalk 3–6cm long
- Leaflets elliptic or ovate, 4–10cm long, unequally serrate and in most cases entire in the lower part, sessile or shortly stalked, shortly pointed at the end and narrowly or broadly wedge-shaped or rounded at the base
- Reddish brown woolly hairs along the veins beneath

L_1L_1 Leaflets oblong-lanceolate or oblong-elliptic; lateral veins beneath not very prominent; white hairs along the veins beneath (the whole surface hairy in young leaves) — Correct, see **M_4** or **M_4M_4** Wrong, back to **L_1**

Sorbus – Rowan, Service Tree

M_4

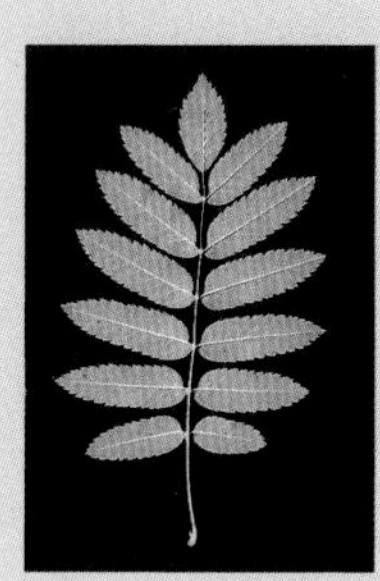

555 Under side **Rowan**

Sorbus aucuparia L.
Rowan, Mountain Ash
Fig. 555 – see p. 138/139

- Leaves 10–25cm long
- Leaf-stalk 2–5cm long, usually coloured alternately red and green above
- Leaflets oblong-lanceolate, 2–6cm long, simply and doubly serrate and in the lower quarter entire, pointed at the end and oblique at the broadly wedge-shaped or rounded base

M_4
M_4

556 Under side **Service Tree**

Sorbus domestica L.
Service Tree
Fig. 556 – see p. 138/139

- Leaves 10–25cm long
- Leaf-stalk 3–3.5cm long, green above and especially in young leaves bearing soft white hairs
- Leaflets narrowly oblong to narrowly elliptic, 3–8cm long, more finely serrate than in the Rowan and almost entire in the lower third, shortly pointed at the end and much more regularly wedge-shaped at the base than in the Rowan

I_1I_1 Leaves with long, narrow and pointed stipules at their base (Fig. 557–562) — Correct, see **K_1** or **K_1K_1** Wrong, back to **I_1** (p. 76)

K_1 Leaflets tinged dark red to pale purple beneath (Fig. 557) — Correct, see **L_2** Wrong, see **K_1K_1**

Rosa – Rose

L_2

557 Under side **Red-leaved Rose**

Rosa glauca Pourr.
R. rubrifolia Vill.
Red-leaved Rose
Fig. 557 – see p. 140/141

- Leaves 4–8cm long
- Leaf-stalk 1–4cm long and covered with a bluish purple bloom
- Leaflets elliptic to oblong-ovate, 2.5–4.5cm long, usually simply serrate, pointed at the end and wedge-shaped or rounded at the base

K_1K_1 Leaflets green or greyish green beneath — Correct, see **L_3** or **L_3L_3** (p. 79) Wrong, back to **K_1**

L_3 Leaflets oblong-elliptic and glabrous (only very rarely somewhat hairy); leaf-stalks reddish above — Correct, see **M_5** Wrong, see **L_3L_3** (p. 79)

Rosa – Rose

M_5

558 Upper side **Alpine Rose**

Rosa pendulina L.
Alpine Rose
Fig. 558 – see p. 140/141

- Leaves 5–10cm long
- Leaf-stalk 1.5–3cm long, predominantly reddish above, with slender stalked glands, and long, narrow, pointed stipules which broaden towards the end and spread outwards
- Leaflets oblong-elliptic, 1–4cm long, usually doubly serrate (teeth with stalked glands), printed at the end and wedge-shaped or rounded at the base

L_3L_3 Leaflets elliptic, ovate or roundish; leaf-stalk green (Fig. 559–562)
Correct, see **M_6** or **M_6M_6**
Wrong, back to **L_3** (p. 78)

M_6 Leaflets elliptic to ovate and glabrous on both sides, margin simply serrate and without glands (Fig. 559)
Correct, see **N_2**
Wrong, see **M_6M_6**

Rosa – Rose

N_2

559 Upper side
Dog Rose

Rosa canina L.
Dog Rose

Fig. 559 – see p. 140/141

- Leaves 6–11cm long
- Leaf-stalk 2–4cm long, somewhat prickly and broadened at the base
- Leaflets elliptic to ovate, 2–4cm long, with the margin simply serrate and without glands, pointed at the end and broadly wedge-shaped or rounded at the base
- Stipules long, narrow, pointed and spreading outwards

M_6M_6 Leaflets elliptic to ovate and especially on the underside sparsely to densely covered with soft woolly hairs; margin often bearing glands
Correct, see **N_3** or **N_3N_3**
Wrong, back to **M_6**

N_3 Stipules very small and usually not reaching the middle of the leaf-stalk (Fig. 560)
Correct, see **O**
Wrong, see **N_3N_3**

Rosa – Rose

O

560 Upper side
Apple Rose

Rosa villosa L.
Apple Rose

Fig. 560 – see p. 140/141

- Leaves 4–9cm long
- Leaf-stalk 1–3cm long and usually with stalked glands
- Leaflets elliptic, 1–4cm long, doubly serrate with glandular teeth, shortly pointed at the end and rounded at the base
- Stipules small and narrow

N_3N_3 Stipules reaching over half way up the leaf-stalk or to its end
Correct, see **O_1** or **O_1O_1**
Wrong, back to **N_3**

Rosa – Rose

O_1

561 Upper side
Sweet Briar

Rosa rubiginosa L.
Sweet Briar

Fig. 561 – see p. 140/141

- Leaves 4–7cm long
- Leaf-stalk 0.5–2.5cm long, glabrous or woolly, with stalked glands and small, slightly hooked prickles
- Leaflets elliptic or roundish, 1–2.5cm long, simply serrate/dentate, with numerous stalked glands on the margin, shortly pointed at the end and broadly wedge-shaped or rounded at the base

---

O_1
O_1

562 Upper side
Downy Rose

Rosa tomentosa Sm.
Downy Rose

Fig. 562 – see p. 140/141

- Leaves 5–10cm long
- Leaf-stalk 1–3cm long, woolly, with stalked glands and somewhat prickly
- Leaflets broadly elliptic to roundish, 2–4cm long, simply and doubly serrate, rounded at the end with a small point and wedge-shaped or rounded at the base
- Stipules long and narrow

BB
B Leaves simply pinnate with a terminal leaflet; the 3, 5, 7 or 9 leaflets coarsely dentate to coarsely crenate and partly irregularly 2- or 3-lobed (in 2 or 3 sections) (Fig. 563–565)
Correct, see **C_2**, **C_2C_2** (p. 80) or **$C_2C_2C_2$** (p. 80)
Wrong, back to **B** (p. 74)

Clematis – Clematis

C_2

563 Upper side **Alpine Clematis**

Clematis alpina (L.) Miller
Alpine Clematis

Fig. 563 – see p. 142/143

- Leaves 10–15cm long
- Leaf-stalk 3–7cm long, green, all leaflets stalked
- Lobes of the 3 leaflets narrowly ovate, 2–4cm long, coarsely and deeply serrate, with a long point at the end and rounded or irregularly heart-shaped at the base

C_2
C_2

564 Upper side **Traveller's Joy**

***Clematis vitalba* L.**
Traveller's Joy, Old Man's Beard
Fig. 564 - see p. 142/143

- Leaves 3-10cm long
- Leaf-stalk 1-6cm long, twining and tinged wine-red to purple above
- The 3 or 5 leaflets ovate, 3-5cm long, coarsely toothed in the lower part, rounded, obtuse or shortly pointed at the end and heart-shaped at the base

Acer - Maple

C_2
C_2
C_2

565 Upper side
Ash-leaved Maple

***Acer negundo* L.**
Ash-leaved Maple, Box Elder
Fig. 565 - see p. 142/143

- Leaves 7-15cm long
- Leaf-stalk 5-8cm long, glabrous or finely hairy and often tinged red
- Leaflets narrowly elliptic to ovate, 5-10cm long, often 2- to 3-lobed, coarsely serrate in the upper part and entire below, with a long point at the end and wedge-shaped, truncate or rounded at the base

AA Leaves palmately divided into 3, 5 or 7 leaflets (Fig. 566-577)
Correct, see **B_1** or **B_1B_1** (p. 81)
Wrong, back to **A** (p. 74)

566 Upper side
Horse Chestnut

B_1 Leaves palmately divided into 3 leaflets (Fig. 567-572)
Correct, see **C_3** or **C_3C_3**
Wrong, see **B_1B_1** (p. 81)

C_3 Margin of leaflets with more or less deep incisions and coarsely serrate, dentate or lobed; distinctly bluish grey beneath with brownish hairs on the midrib, terminal leaflet stalked (Fig. 567)
Correct, see **D_2**
Wrong, see **C_3C_3**

Acer - Maple

D_2

567 Under side
Paper-bark Maple

***Acer griseum* (Franch.) Pax**
Paper-bark Maple
Fig. 567 - see p. 142/143

- Leaves 6-10cm long
- Leaf-stalk 1-5cm long, often hairy and usually reddish above
- Leaflets elliptic to obovate, 3-6cm long, coarsely serrate, dentate or lobed, shortly pointed or rounded at the end and wedge-shaped or rounded at the base
- Leaflets bluish grey beneath and with brownish hairs on the midrib

C_3C_3 Leaflets entire, pale, dark or greyish green beneath and without brownish hairs on the midrib
Correct, see **D_3** or **D_3D_3**
Wrong, back to **C_3**

D_3 Leaves at most 5cm long with narrowly obovate leaflets
Correct, see **E_4**
Wrong, see **D_3D_3**

Cytisus - Broom

E_4

568 Upper side **Purple Broom**

***Cytisus purpureus* Scop.**
Purple Broom
Fig. 568 - see p. 142/143

- Leaves 2-5cm long
- Leaf-stalk 1-3cm
- Leaflets narrowly obovate, 1.5-2.5cm long, rounded or obtuse at the end and narrowly wedge-shaped at the base

D_3D_3 Leaves 6-16cm long; leaflets narrowly ovate to narrowly elliptic (Fig. 569) or broadly elliptic to obovate (Fig. 570)
Correct, see **E_5** (p. 81) or **E_5E_5** (p. 81)
Wrong, back to **D_3**

569
Under side
Alpine Laburnum

570
Under side
Common Laburnum

Laburnum – Laburnum

E_5

571 Upper side **Alpine Laburnum**

Laburnum alpinum
(Mill.) Bercht. et J. S. Presl
Alpine Laburnum
Fig. 571 – see p. 144/145

- Leaves 8–16cm long
- Leaf-stalk 5–9cm long, glabrous or with spreading hairs
- Leaflets narrowly ovate to narrowly elliptic, 3–8cm long, acute or obtuse at the end; sometimes with a short, sharp point and wedge-shaped or rounded at the base

E_5
E_5

572 Upper side **Common Laburnum**

Laburnum anagyroides Med.
Common Laburnum
Fig. 572 – see p. 144/145

- Leaves 6–12cm long
- Leaf-stalk 2–7cm long and with appressed silky hairs
- Leaflets broadly elliptic to obovate, 1.5–8cm long, rounded at the end and usually with a small sharp point and broadly wedge-shaped at the base

B_1B_1 Leaves palmately divided into 5 or 7 leaflets (Fig. 573–577) — Correct, see **C_4** or **C_4C_4**; Wrong, back to **B_1** (p. 80)

C_4 Leaf-stalk tinged red above and beneath (Fig. 573) — Correct, see **D_4**; Wrong, see **C_4C_4**

Aesculus – Horse-chestnut

D_4

573 Upper side **Buckeye**

Aesculus parviflora Walt.
Buckeye
Fig. 573 – see p. 144/145

- Leaves 20–30cm long
- Leaf-stalk 10–18cm long and tinged red
- Leaflets narrowly obovate, 9–18cm long, finely pointed at the end and wedge-shaped at the base

C_4C_4 Leaf-stalks green (Fig. 574–577) — Correct, see **D_5**, **D_5D_5** or **$D_5D_5D_5$**; Wrong, back to **C_4**

574
Under side
Horse-chestnut

Aesculus – Horse Chestnut

D_5

575 Upper side **Yellow Buckeye**

Aesculus octandra Marsh.
Yellow Buckeye
Fig. 575 – see p. 144/145

- Leaves 10–30cm long
- Leaf-stalk 5–15cm long
- Leaflets oblong-elliptic, 10–15cm long, finely serrate, usually shortly stalked, pointed at the end and narrowly wedge-shaped at the base

D_5
D_5

576 Upper side **Red Horse Chestnut**

Aesculus carnea Hayne
Red Horse Chestnut
Fig. 576 – see p. 144/145

- Leaves 10–25cm long
- Leaf-stalk 5–15cm long
- Leaflets elliptic (greatest breadth always at the middle), 8–16cm long, simply and in places doubly serrate, pointed at the end and wedge-shaped at the base

D_5
D_5
D_5

577 Under side **Horse Chestnut**

Aesculus hippocastanum L.
Horse-chestnut
Fig. 577 – see p. 144/145

- Leaves 10–30cm long
- Leaf-stalk 5–15cm long and grooved
- Leaflets oblong-obovate, the greatest breadth always in the upper third, 8–20cm long, simply and in places doubly serrate, shortly pointed at the end and wedge-shaped at the base

A Leaves lobed like a maple (Fig. 578–615) — Correct, see **B** or **BB**; Wrong, see **AA** (p. 88)

578
Upper side
Gooseberry

579
Upper side
Norway Maple

B Leaves truncate, emarginate or retuse at the end (Fig. 580) — Correct, see **C**; Wrong, see **BB**

Liriodendron – Tulip Tree

C

580 Under side
Tulip Tree

Liriodendron tulipifera L.
Tulip Tree
Fig. 580 – see p. 146/147

- Leaves 10–25cm long and equally broad, square in outline and with 2 or 4 lobes varying in size
- Truncate, emarginate or retuse at the end
- Leaf-stalk 6–12cm long and slightly thickened at the base
- Medium to dark green and glabrous above; bluish green beneath, glabrous or with hairs arising from small depressions

---

BB Leaves not truncate, emarginate or retuse at the end (Fig. 581) — Correct, see **C_1** or **C_1C_1**; Wrong, back to **B**

581
Oriental Plane

C_1 Leaves with small bristles on the upper side and very rough to the touch; with stiff, appressed hairs beneath or with rough spreading hairs — Correct, see **D** or **DD**; Wrong, see **C_1C_1**

Ficus – Fig

D

582 Upper side
Fig

Ficus carica L.
Fig
Fig. 582 – see p. 146/147

- Leaves 20–30cm long, of varied outline but usually roundish and with 3, 5 or 7 lobes varying in size
- Rounded at the end
- Leaf-stalk 5–8cm long, thickish and usually with an enlarged base
- Dark green and bristly above; paler green and with soft, appressed hairs beneath

---

Morus – Mulberry

DD

583 Upper side
Black Mulberry

Morus nigra L.
Black Mulberry
Fig. 583 – see p. 146/147

- Leaves 5–15cm long, broadly ovate or heart-shaped in outline, with 2 or more lobes, irregularly coarsely serrate
- Tip long and finely pointed
- Leaf-stalk 1–4cm long and often hairy
- Dark green and roughly hairy above; paler green beneath with appressed hairs

---

C_1C_1 Leaves not roughly hairy above — Correct, see **D_1** or **D_1D_1** (p. 83); Wrong, back to **C_1**

D_1 Shrubs up to 5m with prickles or thorns — Correct, see **E**, **EE** (p. 83) or **EEE** (p. 83); Wrong, see **D_1D_1** (p. 83)

Ribes – Currant, Gooseberry

E

584 Under side
Gooseberry

Ribes uva-crispa L.
Gooseberry
Fig. 584 – see p. 146/147

- Leaves 2–6cm long, heart-shaped to roundish in outline and 3- or 5-lobed
- Rounded at the end or with a small point
- Leaf-stalk 1–2cm long and somewhat enlarged at the base
- Shiny dark green above and often slightly hairy; medium green beneath and softly hairy, later becoming glabrous

Crataegus – Hawthorn

EE

585 Upper side
Midland Hawthorn

Crataegus laevigata (Poir.) DC.
Midland Hawthorn
Fig. 585 – see p. 146/147

- Leaves 3–5cm long, varied in outline but usually ovate, obovate or roundish
- Obtuse or flattened at the end and with small teeth
- Leaf-stalk 0.8–1.5cm long and grooved; stipules lanceolate to ovate, serrate with glandular teeth
- Shiny dark green above and pale medium green to pale bluish green beneath

EE
E

586 Upper side
Hawthorn

Crataegus monogyna Jacq.
Hawthorn
Fig. 586 – see p. 146/147

- Leaves 3–6cm long, broadly ovate or rhombic in outline and deeply 3-, 5-, 7- or 9-lobed
- Often flattened at the end and often with the lobes themselves lobed about the middle
- Leaf-stalk 1–2cm long, grooved; stipules crescent-shaped and toothed
- Shiny dark green and glabrous above; bluish green beneath and often slightly hairy in the axils of the veins

D_1D_1	Trees or shrubs without prickles/thorns	Correct, see **E_1** or **E_1E_1** (p. 85) Wrong, back to **D_1** (p. 82)
E_1	Lobes of leaves with one or more finely printed secondary lobes (Fig. 587, 588)	Correct, see **F** or **FF** Wrong, see **E_1E_1** (p. 85)

587
Upper side
Silver Maple

588
Upper side
Norway Maple

F	Leaves conspicuously silvery to white beneath (Fig. 589, 590)	Correct, see **G** Wrong, see **FF**

Acer – Maple

G

589 Under side
Silver Maple

Acer saccharinum L.
Silver Maple
Fig. 589 – see p. 148/149

- Leaves 10–15cm long, broadly ovate in outline and 5-lobed
- Middle lobe with a long point at the end
- Leaf-stalk 4–7cm long, usually reddish above and without milky juice
- Medium to dark green and glabrous above; silvery grey beneath

590 Underside
Silver Maple, Wier's form

Acer saccharinum L.
f. laciniatum (Carr.) Rehd. **'Wieri'**
Silver Maple, Wier's form
Fig. 590 – see p. 148/149

- Leaves 8–15cm long, broadly ovate to roundish in outline and deeply 5-lobed
- Middle lobe with a long point at the end
- Leaf-stalk 4–7cm long, green and without milky juice
- Dark green and glabrous above; silvery grey beneath

FF	Leaves not conspicuously silvery grey or white beneath	Correct, see **G_1** or **G_1G_1** (p. 84) Wrong, back to **F**
G_1	All lobes, or at least the middle one, completely or for the greater part finely to coarsely serrate or dentate	Correct, see **H**, **HH** (p. 84), **HHH** (p. 84), **HHHH** (p. 84), or **HHHHH** (p. 84) Wrong, see **G_1G_1** (p. 84)

Forsythia – Forsythia

H

591 Upper side
Balkan Forsythia

Forsythia europaea Deg. et Bald.
European Forsythia
Fig. 591 – see p. 148/149

- Leaves 4–8cm long, ovate to ovate-lanceolate in outline and very rarely lobed
- Pointed at the end and the tip often slightly curved to one side
- Leaf-stalk 1–3cm long
- Dark green above and pale green beneath; both sides glabrous

Acer – Maple

HH

592 Upper side **Grey-budded Snake-bark Maple**

Acer rufinerve Sieb. et Zucc.
Grey-budded Snake-bark Maple
Fig. 592 – see p. 148/149

- Leaves 5–13cm long, broadly elliptic, roundish or obliquely ovate in outline and usually distinctly 3-lobed
- Middle lobe finely pointed at the end
- Leaf-stalk 2–7cm long, pink to dark red and furrowed
- Dark green to bluish green above; paler green beneath with brownish red hairs along the veins especially on young leaves

---

HH
H

593 Upper side
Smooth Japanese Maple

Acer palmatum Thunb.
Smooth Japanese Maple
Fig. 593 – see p. 148/149

- Leaves 5–10cm long, circular in outline, cut more than halfway towards the centre into 3, 5, 7, 9 or 11 lobes
- Middle lobe finely pointed at the end
- Leaf-stalk 2–6cm long, glabrous or sparsely hairy, green or tinged red
- Medium green and glabrous above; pale green beneath with whitish markings in the axils of the veins

---

HH
HH

594 Upper side
Downy Japanese Maple

Acer japonicum Thunb.
'Aconitifolium'
Downy Japanese Maple
Fig. 594 – see p. 148/149

- Leaves 8–15cm long, roundish in outline and divided almost to the base into 9 or 11 pinnatisect lobes
- Middle lobe finely pointed at the end
- Leaf-stalk 3–6cm long and tinged red especially above
- Medium green above, paler green beneath; silky hairy only when young

---

Liquidambar – Sweet Gum

HH
HH
H

595 Upper side
Sweet Gum

Liquidambar styraciflua L.
Sweet Gum
Fig. 595 – see p. 150/151

- Leaves 10–20cm long, broadly ovate or roundish in outline, 3-lobed on young trees and 5- or 7-lobed on older trees
- Middle lobe pointed at the end
- Leaf-stalk 4–9cm long
- Shiny green and glabrous above; distinctly paler green beneath with white to brownish tufts of hairs

---

G_1G_1 Middle lobe of leaves not finely serrate or dentate — Correct, see **H_1** or **H_1H_1**; Wrong, back to **G_1** (p. 83)

H_1 Leaves very deeply (far beyond the middle) 5- or more rarely 7-lobed; individual lobes always longer than broad (Fig. 596) — Correct, see **I**; Wrong, see **H_1H_1**

Platanus – Plane

I

596 Upper side
Oriental Plane

Platanus orientalis L.
Oriental Plane
Fig. 596 – see p. 150/151

- Leaves 10–20cm long, broadly ovate or roundish in outline and deeply 5- or 7-lobed; only 3-lobed on younger shoots
- Middle lobe with a very long point at the end
- Leaf-stalk 3–7cm long and thickened bulb-like at the base
- Shiny medium green above and pale green beneath; finely and densely hairy when young, later becoming glabrous

---

H_1H_1 The 3, 5 or 7 lobes not or only just reaching halfway towards the centre of the leaf — Correct, see **I_1** or **I_1I_1** (p. 85); Wrong, Back to **H_1**

I_1 Middle lobe of leaves not or only rarely having very coarse teeth — Correct, see **K, KK** (p. 85) or **KKK** (p. 85); Wrong, see **I_1I_1** (p. 85)

Acer – Maple

K

597 Upper side
Cappadocian Maple

Acer cappadocicum Gled.
Cappadocian Maple
Fig. 597 – see p. 150/151

- Leaves 10–20cm long and equally broad, roundish or broadly heart-shaped in outline and with 5 or 7 lobes
- Middle lobe with a fine, long point at the end
- Leaf-stalk 5–15cm long
- Dark green above and paler green beneath, both sides glabrous

Platanus – Plane

KK

598 Upper side **London Plane**

Platanus x acerifolia (Ait.) Willd
Platanus hybrida Brot.
London Plane
Fig. 598 – see p. 150/151

- Leaves 10–25cm long and equally broad, very varied in outline but usually roundish and 3-, 5- or 7-lobed
- Middle lobe pointed at the end
- Leaf-stalk 3–10cm long and thickened bulb-like at the base
- Shiny green and glabrous above; paler green beneath, finely hairy, later becoming glabrous

Catalpa – Catalpa

KK
K

599 Upper side **Yellow Catalpa**

Catalpa ovata G. Don et Zucc.
Yellow Catalpa
Fig. 599 – see p. 150/151

- Leaves 10–25cm long, varied in outline; usuallv broadly ovate or heart-shaped and often 2-, 3- or 5-lobed
- End of leaf shortly pointed
- Leaf-stalk 4–10cm long, often dark red above and green beneath
- Dark green above with very soft hairs; paler to medium green beneath and only slightly rough to the touch

I_1I_1	Middle lobe of leaves with 2 or more clearly visible large, printed teeth (Fig. 600)	Correct, see K_1 or K_1K_1 Wrong, back to I_1 (p. 84)

600 Under side **Norway Maple**

Acer – Maple

K_1

601 Upper side **Norway Maple**

Acer platanoides L.
Norway Maple
Fig. 601 – see p. 150/151

- Leaves 10–20cm long and equally broad, roundish or broadly heart-shaped in outline and with 3, 5 or 7 lobes of varying size
- Middle lobe with a long, fine point at the end
- Leaf-stalk to 15cm long, usually reddish, with milky juice and somewhat thickened at the base
- Dark green and glabrous above; pale green beneath, with tufts of hair in the axils of the veins, later glabrous

K_1
K_1

602 Upper side **Sugar Maple**

Acer saccharum Marsh.
Sugar Maple
Fig. 602 – see p. 152/153

- Leaves 8–15cm long and equally broad, broadly ovate or roundish in outline and with 3 or 5 lobes
- Middle lobe with a long fine point at the end
- Leaf-stalk 5–10cm long and often tinged red
- Medium to dark green and glabrous above; greyish green and glabrous beneath

E_1E_1	Lobes of leaves without finely pointed secondary lobes (Fig. 603–615)	Correct, see F_1, F_1F_1 or $F_1F_1F_1$ (p. 86) Wrong, back to E_1 (p. 83)
F_1	Lobes entire, without secondary lobes	Correct, see G_2 or G_2G_2 Wrong, see F_1F_1 or $F_1F_1F_1$ (p. 86)

Acer – Maple

G_2

Acer monspessulanum L.
Montpelier Maple
Fig. 603 – see p. 152/153

- Leaves 3–6cm long, horizontally elliptic in outline with 3 lobes
- Middle lobe rounded at the end
- Leaf-stalk 1–3cm long and somewhat broadened at the base
- Shiny dark green and glabrous above; bluish grey beneath, hairy at first and later becoming glabrous

603 Upper side **Montpelier Maple**

Hedera – Ivy

G_2
G_2

604 Upper side **Ivy**

Hedera helix L.
Ivy
Fig. 604 – see p. 152/153

- Leaves 4–10cm long, varied in outline; ovate to roundish on non-flowering shoots, 3- or 5-lobed, leathery and evergreen
- Middle lobe obtuse or rounded at the end
- Leaf-stalk 3–7cm long and usually brown to brownish red above
- Dark bluish green above with clearly visible pale yellow veins and glabrous; dull pale green and glabrous beneath

F_1F_1	Lobes with secondary lobes, the latter rounded and entire, more rarely undulate or coarsely crenate-sinuate (Fig. 605)	Correct, see G_3 (p. 86) Wrong, see $F_1F_1F_1$ (p. 86)

Acer – Maple

G_3

605 Upper side
Field Maple

Acer campestre L.
Field Maple
Fig. 605 – see p. 152/153

- Leaves 3-10cm long, roundish to ovate in outline and with 3 or 5 lobes
- Middle lobe obtuse or rounded at the end
- Leaf-stalk 1-5 cm long and usually reddish above
- Dark green and glabrous above; paler green beneath, softly hairy and later becoming glabrous

---

F_1F_1 F_1 Lobes of leaves distinctly finely to coarsely serrate or dentate (Fig. 606–615)
Correct, see **G_4** or **G_4G_4**
Wrong, back to **F_1** (p. 85)

G_4 Leaves conspicuously snow-white beneath with matted woolly hairs (Fig. 606)
Correct, see **H_2**
Wrong, see **G_4G_4**

Populus – Poplar

H_2

606 Under side
White Poplar

Populus alba L.
White Poplar
Fig. 606 – see p. 152/153

- Leaves 5-12cm long and varied in outline; elliptic to ovate on long shoots and suckers and with 3 or 5 lobes
- Middle lobe pointed or slightly rounded at the end
- Leaf-stalk 2-4cm long, flattened and white hairy
- Shiny dark green above, glabrous when mature; remaining densely white-felted beneath; at first both sides covered with matted woolly hairs

---

G_4G_4 Leaves yellow, blue, pale or dark green beneath
Correct, see **H_3**, **H_3H_3** or **$H_3H_3H_3$**
Wrong, back to **G_4**

H_3 Leaves less than 5cm long and the 3 or 5 lobes coarsely doubly serrate (Fig. 607)
Correct, see **I_2**
Wrong, see **H_3H_3**

Ribes – Currant

I_2

607 Upper side
Mountain Currant

Ribes alpinum L.
Mountain Currant
Fig. 607 – see p. 152/153

- Leaves 2-5cm long, broadly ovate to roundish in outline with 3, more rarely 5 lobes
- Middle lobe acute, obtuse or rounded at the end
- Leaf-stalk 1-2cm long with long glandular hairs
- Dark green above with scattered hairs; paler green beneath, shiny and glabrous

---

H_3H_3 Leaves more than 5cm long and lobes only finely simply and doubly toothed
Correct, see **I_3** or **I_3I_3**
Wrong, see **$H_3H_3H_3$**

Ribes – Currant

I_3

608 Upper side
Black Currant

Ribes nigrum L.
Black Currant
Fig. 608 – see p. 154/155

- Leaves 5-10cm long, roundish in outline and with 3 or 5 lobes
- Middle lobe pointed at end
- Leaf-stalk 2-5cm long and broadened at the base
- Medium to dark green above, hairy at first, later becoming glabrous; pale green beneath with yellowish resin glands

---

I_3I_3

609 Upper side
Red Currant

Ribes rubrum L.
Red Currant
Fig. 609 – see p. 154/155

- Leaves 4-7cm long, roundish in outline and with 3 or 5 lobes
- Middle lobe pointed at end
- Leaf-stalk 2-3.5cm long and somewhat thickened at the base
- Dark green above, not shiny; paler green beneath and softly hairy, not dotted with glands, later becoming glabrous

---

H_3H_3 H_3 Leaves more strongly and coarsely serrate or dentate than in the Red and Black Currants and more than 5cm long including the leaf-stalk
Correct, see **I_4** (p. 87) or **I_4I_4** (p. 87)
Wrong, back to **H_3H_3** or **H_3**

I_4 Leaves with a deep, narrow and acute basal sinus (Fig. 610) — Correct, see K_2 / Wrong, see I_4I_4

Vitis – Vine

K_2

610 Under side **Grape-vine**

Vitis vinifera L. ssp. *vinifera*
Grape-vine

Fig. 610 – see p. 154/155

- Leaves 5–15cm long, varied in outline; usually roundish and as a rule deeply 3- or 5-lobed
- Middle lobe with a short point at the end
- Leaf-stalk 4–8cm long
- Dark green above and hairy when young, later becoming glabrous; pale to greyish green beneath and often hairy

I_4I_4 Basal sinus of leaves always shallow; base of leaf-blade truncate, heart-shaped, rounded or broadly wedge-shaped (Fig. 611–615) — Correct, see K_3 or K_3K_3 / Wrong, back to I_4

K_3 Leaf-stalk 2–3cm long, narrowly grooved above, and with 2–4 green concave nectar-glands just below the base of the leaf-blade — Correct, see L_2 / Wrong, see K_3K_3

Viburnum – Viburnum

L_2

611 Upper side **Guelder Rose**

Viburnum opulus L.
Guelder Rose

Fig. 611 – see p. 154/155

- Leaves 4–12cm long, varied in outline; usualy roundish or obliquely elliptic and with 3 or 5 lobes
- Middle lobe shortly pointed or obtuse
- Leaf-stalk 2–3cm long, tinged red and with 2–4 green glands
- Dark green and glabrous above; greyish green beneath, slightly woolly and with very prominent yellowish green veins

K_3K_3 Leaf-stalks without glands at the base of the blade and longer than 2cm — Correct, see L_1, L_1L_1, $L_1L_1L_1$ or $L_1L_1L_1L_1$ / Wrong, back to K_3

Acer – Maple

L_1

612 Upper side **Sycamore**

Acer pseudoplatanus L.
Sycamore

Fig. 612 – see p. 154/155

- Leaves 8–20cm long, broadly elliptic or heart-shaped in outline and 3- or 5-lobed
- Middle lobe shortly pointed, obtuse or rounded at the end
- Leaf-stalk up to 10cm long and tinged red above
- Dark green and glabrous above; pale bluish green beneath, densely hairy at first and later usually becoming glabrous; veins pale green

L_1L_1

613 Under side **Italian Maple**

Acer opalus Mill.
Italian Maple

Fig. 613 – see p. 154/155

- Leaves 4–10cm long, usually a little broader, usually roundish in outline and with usually 5 lobes
- Middle lobe usually obtuse at the end
- Leaf-stalk 3–9cm long and tinged dark red above
- Dark green and glabrous above; bluish green beneath, hairy at first, later becoming glabrous; veins yellowish white

$L_1L_1L_1$

614 Under side **Red Maple**

Acer rubrum L.
Red Maple

Fig. 614 – see p. 156/157

- Leaves 5–10cm long, broadly ovate or roundish in outline and usually with 3 lobes
- Middle lobe pointed at the end
- Leaf-stalk 4–6cm long and coloured red and green above
- Dark green above and greyish green beneath; both sides glabrous or the underside hairy on the veins

Morus – Mulberry

$L_1L_1L_1L_1$

615 Upper side **White Mulberry**

Morus alba L.
White Mulberry

Fig. 615 – see p. 156/157

- Leaves 6–18cm long, varied in outline; without lobes but with a regularly toothed margin or with 3, 5 or 7 lobes
- Middle lobe only very shortly pointed
- Leaf-stalk 2–4cm long, grooved and woolly at first
- Shiny dark green and glabrous above; pale bluish green beneath and hairy on the larger veins; veins pale yellow to whitish

AA	Leaves not lobed like a maple but with 3–10 lobes on each side	Correct, see **B_1** or **B_1B_1** Wrong, back to **A** (p. 82)

B_1	Leaves with 3–4 clearly pointed lobes on each side (Fig. 616)	Correct, see **C_2** Wrong, see **B_1B_1**

Sorbus – Service Tree, Whitebeam

C_2

616 Upper side
Wild Service Tree

Sorbus torminalis (L.) Crantz
Wild Service Tree
Fig. 616 – see p. 156/157

- Leaves 6–10cm long, ovate to roundish in outline and with 3 or 4 pointed lobes on each side
- Middle lobe pointed at the end
- Leaf-stalk 2–5cm long, loosely felted, later glabrous
- Shiny dark green above and at first finely hairy; pale bluish green beneath and loosely felted, later the hairs remaining only in the axils of the veins

B_1B_1	Leaves with more than 4 lobes on each side (Fig. 617–629)	Correct, see **C_3** or **C_3C_3** Wrong, back to **B_1**

C_3	Lobes of leaves finely serrate (Fig. 617–621)	Correct, see **D_2** or **D_2D_2** Wrong, see **C_3C_3**

D_2	Leaves densely white-felted beneath (Fig. 617–618)	Correct, see **E_2** or **E_2E_2** Wrong, see **D_2D_2**

617
Under side
Mougeot's Whitebeam

618
Under side
Swedish Whitebeam

Sorbus – Whitebeam

E_2

619 Upper side
Mougeot's Whitebeam

Sorbus mougeotii Soy.-Will. et Godr.
Mougeot's Whitebeam
Fig. 619 – see p. 156/157

- Leaves 6–10cm long, oblong-elliptic to ovate in outline; the numerous lobes becoming smaller towards the end of the leaf
- Leaf-blade shortly pointed at the end
- Leaf-stalk 1–2cm long
- Dark green above, hairy at first, later becoming glabrous; densely white-felted beneath

E_2
E_2

620 Upper side
Swedish Whitebeam

Sorbus intermedia (Ehrh.) Pers.
Swedish Whitebeam
Fig. 620 – see p. 156/157

- Leaves 6–12cm long, oblong-elliptic to elliptic in outline; the 5–8 lobes on each side becoming smaller towards the end of the leaf
- Leaf-blade very shortly pointed or obtuse at the end
- Leaf-stalk 1–2cm long and grey-felted
- Shiny dark green above; densely white- to grey-felted beneath

D_2D_2	Leaves not densely white-felted beneath (Fig. 621)	Correct, see **E_3** Wrong, back to **D_2**

Sorbus – Whitebeam

E_3

621 Under side
Broad-leaved Whitebeam

Sorbus latifolia (Lam.) Pers.
Broad-leaved Whitebeam
Fig. 621 – see p. 156/157

- Leaves 7–12cm long, ovate to broadly ovate in outline; the 6–9 lobes on each side becoming smaller towards the end of the leaf
- Leaf-blade shortly pointed at the end
- Leaf-stalk 1–3cm long
- Shiny dark green and glabrous above; only slightly grey-felted beneath and appearing greyish green

C_3C_3	Lobes of leaves not serrate; leaves lobed like an Oak (Fig. 623–629)	Correct, see **D_3** (p. 89) or **D_3D_3** (p. 89) Wrong, back to **C_3**

D_3 Leaves with broad, obtuse or rounded lobes (Fig. 623–625)
Correct, see **E_4** or **E_4E_4**
Wrong, see **D_3D_3**

E_4 An auricle (small lobe) on each side of the midrib at the base of the leaf-blade (Fig. 622) and leaf-stalk not more than 7mm long
Correct, see **F_2**
Wrong, see **E_4E_4**

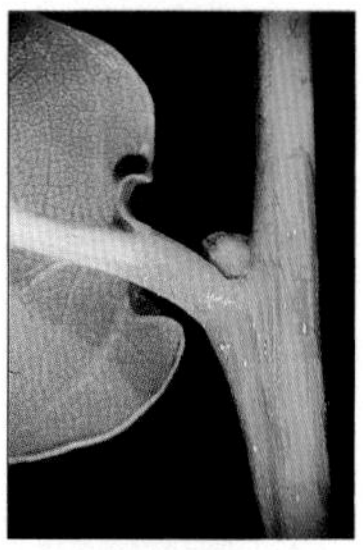

622 Under side
Auricle in Pedunculate Oak

Quercus - Oak

F_2

623 Upper side
Pedunculate Oak

Quercus robur L.
Common Oak, Pedunculate Oak
Fig. 623 - see p. 158/159

- Leaves 5–16cm long, obovate to elliptic, with the greatest breadth in the upper third and with 4 or 5 irregular, rounded lobes on each side
- Middle lobe rounded at end
- Leaf-stalk at most 7mm long
- Shiny dark green and glabrous above; pale to bluish green beneath, rarely with a few hairs

E_4E_4 No auricles (small lobes) present at the base of the leaf-blade and leaf-stalk 7–25mm long (Fig. 624, 625)
Correct, see **F_3** or **F_3F_3**
Wrong, back to **E_4**

Quercus - Oak

F_3

624 Upper side
Downy Oak

Quercus pubescens Willd.
Downy Oak
Fig. 624 - see p. 158/159

- Leaves 5–10cm long, varied in form; usually obovate, with the greatest breadth in the upper third, with 5–7 lobes on each side
- Most lobes obtuse at the end, occasionally with a very small point
- Leaf-stalk 8–12cm long
- Both sides felted at first; later the upper side dark green and glabrous; greyish green beneath because of the hairs

F_3
F_3

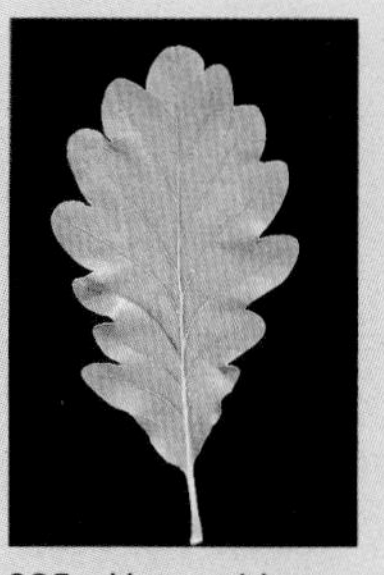

625 Upper side
Sessile Oak

Quercus petraea Liebl.
Sessile Oak
Fig. 625 - see p. 158/159

- Leaves 6–12cm long, obovate, usually broadest in the middle and with 5 to more rarely 9 rounded lobes on each side
- Middle lobe rounded at end
- Leaf-stalk 10–25mm long
- Dull dark green and glabrous above; paler green beneath with very small stellate hairs

D_3D_3 Lobes of leaves with a short or long point
Correct, see **E_5** or **E_5E_5**
Wrong, back to **D_3**

626
Under side
Turkey Oak

627
Under side
Red Oak

Quercus - Oak

E_5

628 Upper side
Turkey Oak

Quercus cerris L.
Turkey Oak
Fig. 628 - see p. 158/159

- Leaves 6–15cm long and varied in form; usually narrowly elliptic, broadest in the upper part, and with 7–9 irregular, often distinctly pointed lobes on each side
- Middle lobe usually shortly pointed at the end
- Leaf-stalk 7–15mm long
- Roughly hairy above at first, later glabrous and shiny; pale green beneath with soft woolly hairs

E_5
E_5

629 Upper side
Red Oak

Quercus rubra L.
Red Oak
Fig. 629 - see p. 158/159

- Leaves 10–20cm long, usually elliptic or obovate with 4–6 lobes on each side tipped by a long bristle or whisker
- Middle lobe ending in a long point
- Leaf-stalk to 5cm long
- Dull to dark green above and glabrous in older leaves; pale yellowish green beneath with stellate hairs in the angles formed by the midrib and lateral veins

A Leaves with numerous, long, widely separated hairs on the margin (Fig. 630, 631) — Correct, see **B** or **BB**; Wrong, see **AA**

Rhododendron – Rhododendron

B

630 Under side **Hairy Alpenrose**

Rhododendron hirsutum L.
Hairy Alpenrose
Fig. 630 – see p. 160/161

- Leaves 1–3.5cm long, oblong-elliptic in outline, thick and leathery
- Obtuse or rounded at the end
- Leaf-stalk 0.3–0.8cm long
- Shiny dark green above, somewhat wrinkled and usually glabrous; pale green beneath with at first whitish and later yellowish brown glandular scales

Erica – Heath, Heather

BB

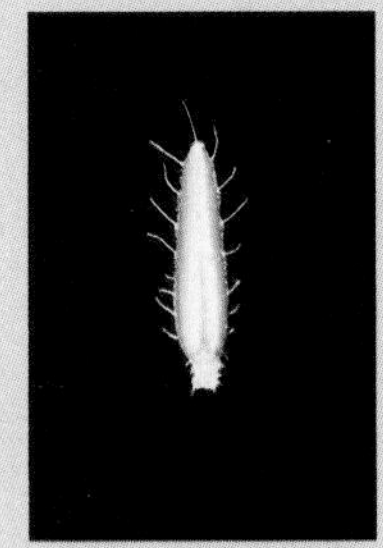

631 Under side **Cross-leaved Heath**

Erica tetralix L.
Cross-leaved Heath, Bog Heather
Fig. 631 – see p. 160/161

- Leaves 3–6mm long, narrowly linear or needle-shaped in outline and with inrolled margins
- Obtuse or rounded at the end
- Leaf-stalk 1–2mm long, very broad and usually woolly hairy
- Dark green surface above under the whitish felt; white beneath with a prominent medium green midrib

AA Leaves without long hairs on the margins — Correct, see **B_1** or **B_1B_1**; Wrong, back to **A**

B_1 Under side of leaves brown because of brownish hairs or spherical glands (especially clear in older leaves) (Fig. 632–634) — Correct, see **C** or **CC**; Wrong, see **B_1B_1**

C Under side of leaves distinctly rust-brown to brown because of crisped hairs (Fig. 632, 633) — Correct, see **D** or **DD**; Wrong, see **CC**

Ledum – Ledum

D

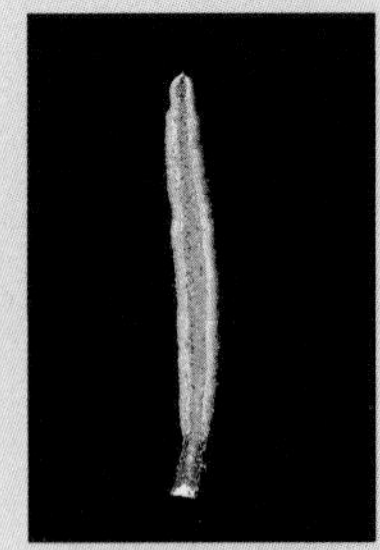

632 Under side **Marsh Ledum**

Ledum palustre L.
Marsh Ledum
Fig. 632 – see p. 160/161

- Leaves 2–5cm long, linear to lanceolate in outline and with strongly recurved margins
- Obtuse or rounded at the end and usually with a fine, short point
- Leaf-stalk 2–3mm long with rusty brown hairs
- Dark green above and distinctly felted; rust-red to brown-felted beneath

DD

633 Under side **Labrador Tea**

Ledum groenlandicum Oed.
Labrador Tea
Fig. 633 – see p. 160/161

- Leaves 2–5cm long, oblong to oblong-ovate in outline and with the margins rolled under
- Obtuse at end
- Leaf-stalk 3–6mm long with brown hairs
- Medium to dark green above with an undulate surface; pale to dark green beneath under the dark brown, crisped hairs

CC Under side of leaves distinctly brown because of brownish spherical glands especially in older leaves (Fig. 634) — Correct, see **D_1**; Wrong, back to **C**

Rhododendron – Rhododendron

D_1

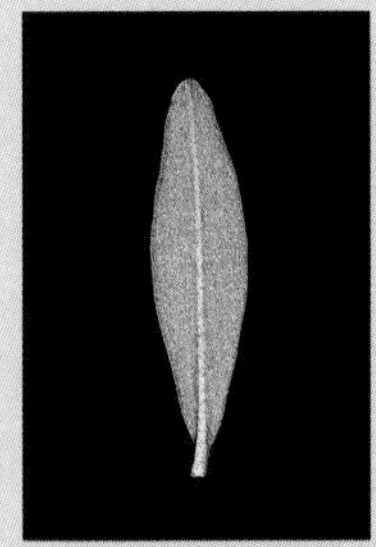

634 Under side **Alpenrose**

Rhododendron ferrugineum L.
Alpenrose
Fig. 634 – see p. 160/161

- Leaves 2–5cm long, oblong-lanceolate to oblong-elliptic in outline, leathery and narrowing into the stalk; margins somewhat recurved
- Rounded or obtuse at the end
- Leaf-stalk up to 6mm long
- Shiny dark green and slightly wrinkled above; brown beneath because of spherical glands

B_1B_1 Under side of leaves not coloured brown because of hairs or spherical glands — Correct, see **C_1** (p. 91), **C_1C_1** (p. 92) or **$C_1C_1C_1$** (p. 92); Wrong, back to **B_1**

C_1 Margins of leaves distinctly inrolled or somewhat recurved (Fig. 635–645)

Correct, see **D_2** or **D_2D_2**
Wrong, see **C_1C_1** (p. 92) or **$C_1C_1C_1$** (p. 92)

D_2 Midrib not visible beneath (Fig. 635, 636); only a white band visible

Correct, see **E** or **EE**
Wrong, see **D_2D_2**

Empetrum – Crowberry

E

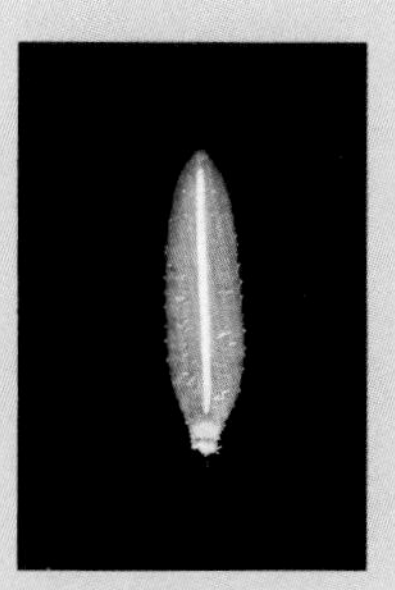

635 Under side
Crowberry

Empetrum nigrum L.
Crowberry

Fig. 635 – see p. 160/161

- Leaves 4–7mm long, narrowly elliptic or linear in outline, leathery and with strongly inrolled margins
- Obtuse or shortly pointed at the end
- Leaf-stalk 1–2mm long, broad and appressed to the shoot
- Dark green and glabrous above; with a white keel and scattered hairs beneath

Erica – Heath, Heather

EE

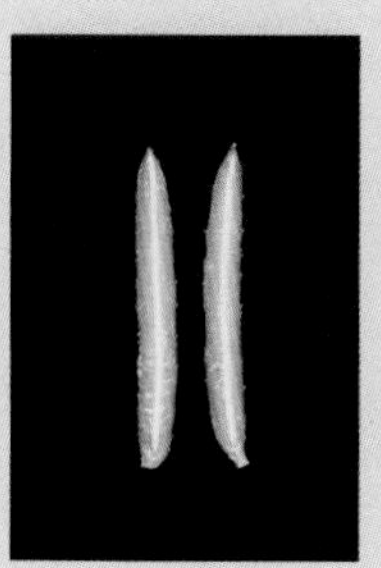

636 Under side
Spring Heath

Erica carnea L.
Spring Heath

Fig. 636 – see p. 162/163

- Leaves 4–8mm long, needle-like or linear in outline and with inrolled margins
- Rounded at the end and usually with a prickly point
- Leaf-stalk 1–2mm long and as broad as the blade
- Medium to dark green, glabrous and shiny above; with a white longitudinal band beneath

D_2D_2 Midrib clearly visible on the under side

Correct, see **E_1** or **E_1E_1**
Wrong, back to **D_2**

E_1 Leaves narrowly elliptic, needle-like or narrowly linear in outline and not longer than 10mm

Correct, see **F**, **FF** or **FFF**
Wrong, see **E_1E_1**

Loiseleuria – Loiselauria

F

637 Upper and under
Trailing Azalea

Loiseleuria procumbens (L.) Desv.
Trailing Azalea

Fig. 637 – see p. 162/163

- Leaves 4–8mm long, narrowly elliptic in outline, with recurved margins and not much broader than the stalk
- Obtuse or shortly pointed at the end
- Leaf-stalk 1–3mm long
- Dark green above with shallow longitudinal furrows; bluish white beneath with very prominent midrib

Erica – Heath, Heather

FF

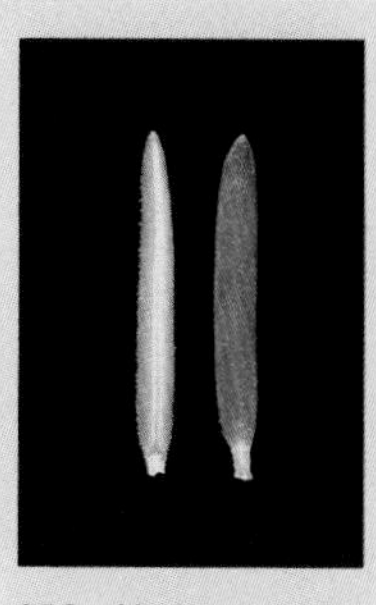

638 Under and upper
Tree Heath

Erica arborea L.
Tree Heath

Fig. 638 – see p. 162/163

- Leaves 4–7mm long, needle-shaped or narrowly linear in outline with the margins strongly inrolled
- Obtuse or rounded at the end
- Leaf-stalk 1–2mm long, whitish and almost as broad as the blade
- Dark green above; whitish beneath between the inrolled margins; midrib clearly visible

FF
F

639 Under side
Cornish Heath

Erica vagans L.
Cornish Heath

Fig. 639 – see p. 162/163

- Leaves 4–10mm long, narrowly linear in outline and not much broader than the stalk
- Obtuse or rounded at the end
- Leaf-stalk 1–2mm long and as broad as the blade
- Dark green above; whitish beneath with a clearly visible dark green midrib

E_1E_1 Leaves elliptic, ovate or oblong-ovate in outline and rarely longer than 10mm (Fig. 640)

Correct, see **F_2** (p. 92)
Wrong, see **$E_1E_1E_1$** (p. 92) or **$E_1E_1E_1E_1$** (p. 92)

640 Upper side
Cranberry

Vaccinium – Vaccinium

F_2

641 Under side
Cranberry

Vaccinium oxycoccus L.
Cranberry

Fig. 641 – see p. 164/165

- Leaves 5–10mm long, elliptic, ovate or oblong-ovate in outline and with recurved margins
- Obtuse or shortly pointed at the end
- Leaf-stalk at most 2mm long
- Shiny dark green above and usually with a slightly impressed midrib; with a bluish green bloom beneath

---

E_1E_1 E_1 Leaves narrowly elliptic to obovate in outline and between 1 and 3cm long (Fig. 642, 643)

Correct, see **F_3** or **F_3F_3**
Wrong, see **$E_1E_1E_1E_1$**

Buxus – Box

F_3

642 Upper side
Box

Buxus sempervirens L.
Box

Fig. 642 – see p. 164/165

- Leaves 1–3cm long, narrowly elliptic to oblong-ovate in outline, leathery and with the margins only slightly recurved
- Usually emarginate at the end
- Leaf-stalk to 2mm long
- Shiny dark green above with an often whitish midrib; pale green beneath with prominent midrib

---

Vaccinium – Vaccinium

F_3
F_3

643 Under side
Cowberry

Vaccinium vitis-idaea L.
Cowberry

Fig. 643 – see p. 164/165

- Leaves 1–3cm long, elliptic to obovate in outline, thick, leathery and with slightly recurved margins
- Usually emarginate at the end
- Leaf-stalk 2–5mm long and woolly hairy
- Dark green above with whitish veins; greyish green beneath with brownish dots

---

E_1E_1 E_1E_1 Leaves narrowly lanceolate in outline and between 1 and 5cm long

Correct, see **F_4** or **F_4F_4**
Wrong, back to **E_1** (p. 91)

Andromeda – Bog Rosemary

F_4

644 Under side
Bog Rosemary

Andromeda polifolia L.
Bog Rosemary

Fig. 644 – see p. 162/163

- Leaves 1–5cm long, narrowly lanceolate in outline, leathery and with strongly recurved margins
- Finely pointed at the end or with a prickly tip
- Leaf-stalk 3–7mm long and usually white
- Shiny dark green above, the surface broken up by white lateral veins; silvery, white or pale bluish green beneath with clearly visible midrib

---

Rosmarinus – Rosemary

F_4
F_4

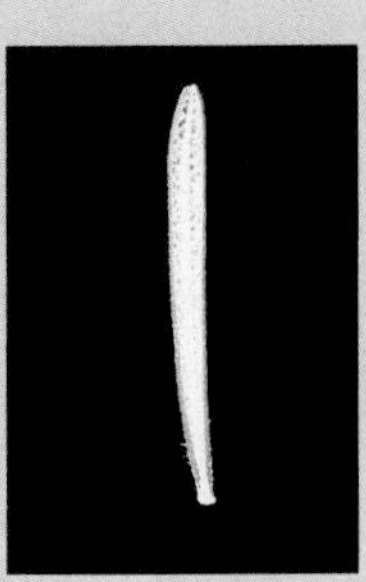

645 Under side
Rosemary

Rosmarinus officinalis L.
Rosemary

Fig. 644 – see p. 162/163

- Leaves 3–5cm long, very narrowly lanceolate in outline, leathery and with inrolled margins
- Obtuse or rounded at the end
- Leaves sessile
- Dark green and slightly wrinkled above; densely white-felted beneath with a very prominent white midrib

---

C_1C_1 Margins of leaves curved upwards; individual leaves 1–3mm long (Fig. 646)

Correct, see **D_3**
Wrong, see **$C_1C_1C_1$**

Calluna – Ling

D_3

646 Upper side
Ling

Calluna vulgaris (L.) Hull
Ling, Heather

Fig. 646 – see p. 164/165

- Leaves 1–3mm long, needle-like or narrowly ovate in outline, scale-like and with the margins curved upwards
- Usually rounded at the end
- Leaves sessile
- Dark green above in summer, brownish red in winter and deeply grooved; keeled beneath

---

C_1C_1 C_1 Margins of leaves not inrolled or curved

Correct, see **D_4** (p. 93), **D_4D_4** (p. 93), **$D_4D_4D_4$** or **$D_4D_4D_4D_4$** (p. 94)
Wrong, back to **C_1** (p. 91)

D_4 Leaves lanceolate to obovate in outline, usually emarginate at the end and 0.3-2cm long (Fig. 647, 648) — Correct, see **E_2** or **E_2E_2**; Wrong, see **D_4D_4**

Genista - Greenweed

E_2

647 Under side **Hairy Greenweed**

Genista pilosa L.
Hairy Greenweed

Fig. 647 - see p. 164/165

- Leaves 3-12mm long, narrowly obovate to lanceolate in outline
- Emarginate or retuse at the end
- Leaves sessile or very shortly stalked
- Dark green and with short appressed hairs on both sides; later becoming glabrous

Daphne - Daphne

E_2
E_2

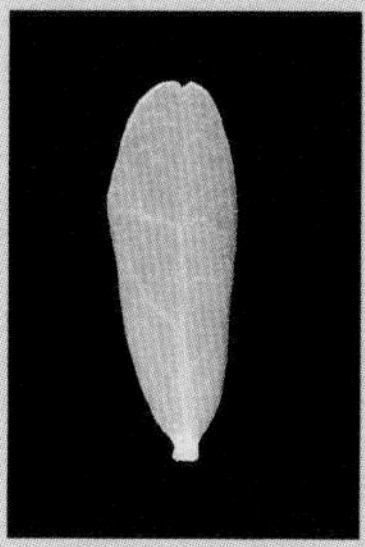

648 Upper side
Garland Flower

Daphne cneorum L.
Garland Flower

Fig. 648 - see p. 164/165

- Leaves 5-20mm long, linear, lanceolate or spathulate in outline and rarely with a slightly recurved margin
- Emarginate or rounded at the end and then often with a small point
- Leaf-stalk very short and broad
- Medium to dark green above; bluish grey beneath with whitish veins

D_4D_4 Leaves fan-shaped in outline and with the upper margin irregularly undulate or deeply cut into several lobes (Fig. 649) — Correct, see **E_3**; Wrong, see **$D_4D_4D_4$**

Ginkgo - Maidenhair Tree

E_3

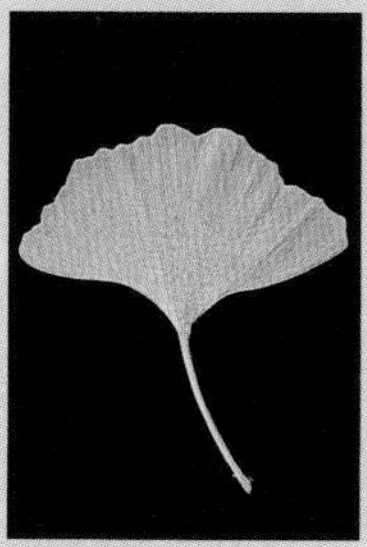

649 Upper side
Maidenhair Tree

Ginkgo biloba L.
Maidenhair Tree

Fig. 649 - see p. 166/167

- Leaves 6-10cm long, fan shaped in outline, with an irregularly undulate margin and fine, forked veins
- End of leaf broadened into the shape of a fan
- Leaf-stalk 2-9cm long
- Both sides glabrous and medium to dark green

D_4D_4
D_4 Leaves roundish or spathulate in outline and rounded or more rarely very slightly emarginate at the end (Fig. 650-653) — Correct, see **E_4** or **E_4E_4**; Wrong, see **$D_4D_4D_4D_4$** (p. 94)

E_4 Leaves 6-11cm long and base of blade deeply heart-shaped (Fig. 650) — Correct, see **F_5**; Wrong, see **E_4E_4**

Cercis - Judas Tree

F_5

650 Upper side
Judas Tree

Cercis siliquastrum L.
Judas Tree

Fig. 650 - see p. 166/167

- Leaves 6-11cm long and equally broad, roundish, and occasionally slightly sinuate along the margin
- Broadly rounded or slightly emarginate at the end
- Leaf-stalk 3-4.5cm long with both sides tinged red
- Dark green above and bluish green beneath; both sides glabrous

E_4E_4 Leaves 0.4-4.5cm long and not deeply heart-shaped at the base of the blade (Fig. 651-653) — Correct, see **F_6** or **F_6F_6**; Wrong, see **$D_4D_4D_4D_4$**

F_6 Veins distinctly impressed on the upper side and leaf-stalk reddish on both sides (Fig. 651) — Correct, see **G**; Wrong, see **F_6F_6** (p. 94)

Salix - Willow

G

651 Upper side
Net-leaved Willow

Salix reticulata L.
Net-leaved Willow

Fig. 651 - see p. 166/167

- Leaves 1÷4.5cm long and broadly elliptic to roundish in outline
- Obtuse or rounded at end
- Leaf-stalk 3-20mm long and reddish on both sides
- Dark green above with the impressed veins forming a network; grey to whitish grey beneath with very prominent veins

F_6F_6 Veins not distinctly impressed on the upper side (Fig. 652, 653)

Correct, see G_1 or G_1G_1
Wrong, back to F_6 (p. 93)

Vaccinium – Vaccinium

G_1

652 Under side
Northern Bilberry

Vaccinium uliginosum L.
Northern Bilberry

Fig. 652 – see p. 166/167

- Leaves 5–20mm long, elliptic, obovate or roundish in outline and thick
- Usually rounded at the end, more rarely slightly retuse or obtuse
- Leaf-stalk 1–2mm long and slightly grooved above
- Medium green above; bluish green beneath with very prominent dark green veins

Salix – Willow

G_1
G_1

653 Upper side
Blunt-leaved Willow

Salix retusa L.
Blunt-leaved Willow

Fig. 653 – see p. 166/167

- Leaves 4–20mm long, obovate to oblong-ovate or spathulate in outline and more rarely with small teeth at the margin
- Rounded, obtuse or emarginate at the end
- Leaf-stalk 2–5mm long
- Shiny medium to dark green and glabrous above; medium to whitish green beneath and slightly hairy when young

D_4D_4 D_4D_4 Leaves different from those in D_4, D_4D_4 or $D_4D_4D_4$ (e.g. Fig. 654, 655)

Correct, see E_5 or E_5E_5
Wrong, back to D_4 (p. 93)

654
Butcher's Broom

655
Oleaster

E_5 Leaves dark purple to black in colour (Fig. 656)

Correct, see F_7
Wrong, see E_5E_5

Fagus – Beech

F_7

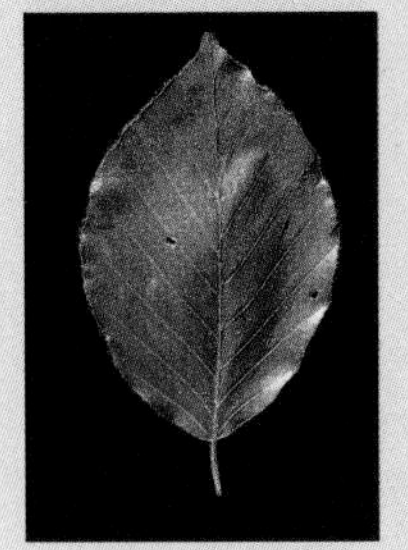

656 Upper side
Copper Beech

Fagus sylvatica L. 'Atropunicea'
Copper Beech

Fig. 656 – see p. 168/169

- Leaves 5–10cm long, broadly elliptic to obovate in outline and with an undulate margin
- Shortly pointed at the end
- Leaf-stalk 2–5mm long and dark red to blackish in colour
- Both sides softly hairy when young and fringed at the margin; dark purple above and dark red to blackish beneath

E_5E_5 Leaves not dark purple in colour

Correct, see F_8 or F_8F_8
Wrong, back to E_5

F_8 'Leaves' long and with a spiny tip (fig. 657)

Correct, see G_2
Wrong, see F_8F_8

Ruscus – Butcher's Broom

G_2

657 Upper side
Butcher's Broom

Ruscus aculeatus L.
Butcher's Broom

Fig. 657 – see p. 166/167

- 'Leaves' (flattened shoots) 1–4cm long, elliptic to ovate tapering towards the end
- With a long, fine point, ending in a spine
- Leaf-stalk 1–3mm long
- Both sides medium green with dark green parallel veins

F_8F_8 Leaves not having a spiny tip

Correct, see G_3, G_3G_3 (p. 95) or $G_3G_3G_3$ (p. 95)
Wrong, back to F_8

G_3 Leaves broadly lanceolate to ovate and bluish green to greyish white beneath (Fig. 658)

Correct, see H (p. 95)
Wrong, see G_3G_3 (p. 95)

Eucalyptus – Gum Tree

H

658 Under side **Blue Gum**

Eucalyptus globulus Labill.
Blue Gum

Fig. 658 – see p. 168/169

- Leaves 7–15cm long and lanceolate to ovate in outline when young
- Pointed or prickly at the end
- Leaf-stalk in young leaves only very short
- Dark green above, often with a pale purple or whitish midrib; dark green or bluish green beneath

---

G_3G_3 Leaves linear to lanceolate and grey or silvery white beneath (Fig. 659, 660)

Correct, see **H_1** or **H_1H_1**
Wrong, see **$G_3G_3G_3$**

Hippophae – Sea Buckthorn

H_1

659 Under side **Sea Buckthorn**

Hippophae rhamnoides L.
Sea Buckthorn

Fig. 659 – see p. 168/169

- Leaves 5–7cm long, linear to lanceolate in outline and occasionally slightly recurved at the margin
- Obtuse or pointed at the end
- Leaf-stalk 1–3mm long and white, or leaves sessile
- With silvery scales on both sides

Elaeagnus – Oleaster

H_1
H_1

660 Under side **Oleaster**

Elaeagnus angustifolia L.
Oleaster

Fig. 660 – see p. 168/169

- Leaves 4–8cm long and narrowly lanceolate in outline
- Slightly pointed, obtuse or rounded at the end
- Leaf-stalk 4–9mm long and white
- With silvery scales on the upper side; densely stellate hairy beneath and therefore appearing greyish white

---

G_3G_3 G_3 Leaves not as in **G_3** (p. 94) and **G_3G_3** (p. 95)

Correct, see **H_2** or **H_2H_2**
Wrong, back to **G_3** (p. 94)

H_2 Leaves narrowly lanceolate, crescent-shaped, thick, and hanging from the twig (Fig. 661)

Correct, see **I**
Wrong, see **H_2H_2**

Eucalyptus – Gum Tree

I

661 Upper side **Blue Gum**

Eucalyptus globulus Labill.
Blue Gum

Fig. 661 – see p. 168/169

- Adult leaves 10–30cm long, somewhat crescent-shaped and narrowly lanceolate in outline
- With a long point at the end
- Leaf-stalk 1–5cm long, often slightly reddish
- Dark green above and somewhat bluish green beneath; both sides glabrous

---

H_2H_2 Leaves narrowly lanceolate to narrowly ovate and not crescent-shaped

Correct, see **I_1**, **I_1I_1** (p. 96) or **$I_1I_1I_1$** (p. 98)
Wrong, back to **H_2**

I_1 Leaves narrowly obovate and with their greatest breadth always above the middle of the blade

Correct, see **K** or **KK** (p. 96)
Wrong, see **I_1I_1** (p. 96) or **$I_1I_1I_1$** (p. 96)

K Leaves 3–8cm long, soft to the touch and medium to dark green beneath (Fig. 662)

Correct, see **L**
Wrong, see **KK** (p. 96)

Daphne – Daphne

L

662 Under side **Mezereon**

Daphne mezereum L.
Mezereon

Fig. 662 – see p. 170.171

- Leaves 3–8cm long, obovate oblong in outline and rarely with slightly recurved margins
- Shortly pointed at the end
- Leaf-stalk 3–5mm long
- Dark green above and greyish green beneath; both sides glabrous

KK Leaves 6–14cm long, somewhat leathery and shiny dark green above (Fig. 663) — Correct, see **L_1** Wrong, back to **K** (p. 95)

Daphne – Daphne

L_1

663 Upper side **Spurge Laurel**

Daphne laureola L.
Spurge Laurel

Fig. 663 – see p. 168/169

- Leaves 6–14cm long and narrowly obovate in outline
- Shortly pointed at the end
- Leaves sessile or with a very short stalk
- Shiny dark green above and pale green beneath; both sides glabrous

I_1I_1 Leaves lanceolate, narrowly elliptic or narrowly obovate and with their greatest breadth at or below (rarely above) the middle of the blade (Fig. 664–676) — Correct, see **K_1** or **K_1K_1** Wrong, back to **I_1** (p. 95)

K_1 Leaves obtuse or rounded at the end (Fig. 664–666) — Correct, see **L_2** or **L_2L_2** Wrong, see **K_1K_1**

L_2 Globular shrubs growing on trees, their leaves with 4–8 parallel veins (Fig. 664) — Correct, see **M** Wrong, see **L_2L_2**

Viscum – Mistletoe

M

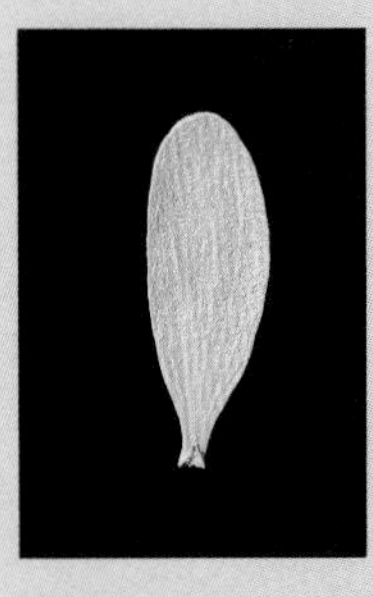

664 Upper side **Mistletoe**

Viscum album L.
Mistletoe

Fig. 664 – see p. 170/171

- Leaves 2–6.5cm long and spathulate, narrowly obovate or narrowly elliptic in outline
- Rounded at the end
- Leaves sessile
- Both sides glabrous, yellowish green and with parallel veins

L_2L_2 Shrubs not growing on trees; underside of leaves with clearly visible midrib and finer lateral veins — Correct, see **M_1** or **M_1M_1** Wrong, back to **L_2**

Daphne – Daphne

M_1

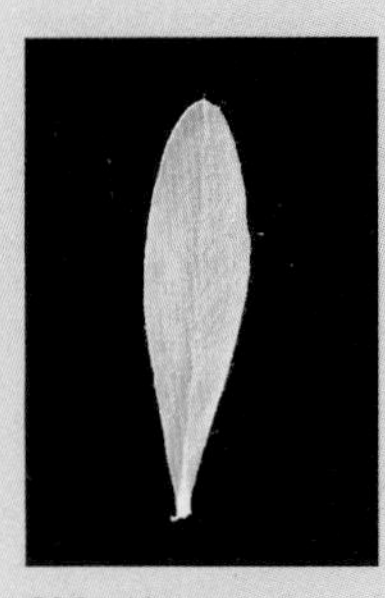

665 Upper side **Alpine Mezereon**

Daphne alpina L.
Alpine Mezereon

Fig. 665 – see p. 170/171

- Leaves 1–5cm long, lanceolate to narrowly obovate in outline and often with their greatest breadth above the middle
- Obtuse or rounded at the end
- Leaves usually sessile
- Both sides hairy when young; dull green to dark green above and greyish green beneath

Punica – Pomegranate

M_1
M_1

666 Upper side **Pomegranate**

Punica granatum L.
Pomegranate

Fig. 666 – see p. 170/171

- Leaves 3–8cm long and oblong-elliptic in outline
- Obtuse or rounded at the end
- Leaf-stalk 1–5mm long and often reddish above
- Dark green above with an impressed midrib; pale green beneath; both sides glabrous

K_1K_1 Leaves pointed at the end — Correct, see **L_3** or **L_3L_3** (p. 97) Wrong, back to **K_1**

L_3 Leaves 6–12cm long, oblong-lanceolate and with a dense fringe of fine hairs on the margin (Fig. 667) — Correct, see **M_2** (p. 97) Wrong, see **L_3L_3** (p. 97)

667 Under side **Yellow Rhododendron**

Rhododendron – Rhododendron

M_2

668 Upper side
Yellow Rhododendron

Rhododendron luteum Sweet
Yellow Rhododendron
Fig. 668 – see p. 170/171

- Leaves 6–12cm long, oblong-lanceolate in outline with fine hairs on the margin
- Pointed at end
- Leaf-stalk 5–15mm long
- Medium green above and slightly undulate; greyish medium green beneath; both sides grey hairy when young

L_3L_3	Leaves without a dense fringe of fine hairs on the margin	Correct, see **M_3, M_3M_3** or **$M_3M_3M_3$** Wrong, back to **L_3** (p. 96)

M_3	Leaves with very long stalks (1–4cm) and with greyish white hairs remaining on the under side; leaf-stalk green (Fig. 669)	Correct, see **N** Wrong, see **M_3M_3**

Pyrus – Pear

N

669 Under side
Willow-leaved Pear

Pyrus salicifolia Pall.
Willow-leaved Pear
Fig. 669 – see p. 172/173

- Leaves 3–9cm long, narrowly elliptic in outline and occasionally with a few small teeth along the margin
- Obtuse or pointed at the end
- Leaf-stalk 1–4cm long
- Both sides with silvery grey hairs when young; later medium to dark green and often glabrous above; remaining greyish white and hairy beneath

M_3M_3	Leaves with a stalk 1–4cm long and usually with a wavy margin; leaf-stalk distinctly tinged red (Fig. 670, 671)	Correct, see **N_1** Wrong, see **$M_3M_3M_3$**

670 Under side
Laurel

Laurus – Laurel

N_1

671 Upper side
Laurel

Laurus nobilis L.
Laurel
Fig. 671 – see p. 172/173

- Leaves 5–12cm long, oblong-lanceolate to narrowly elliptic in outline and often with a slightly wavy margin
- Pointed at the end
- Leaf-stalk 1–4cm long and usually tinged red

Medium to dark green above, pale green beneath, both sides glabrous; lower part of midrib beneath often reddish

$M_3M_3M_3$	Leaves with a stalk 0.2–3cm long and greenish beneath; leaf-stalk green	Correct, see **N_2, N_2N_2** (p. 98) or **$N_2N_2N_2$** (p. 98) Wrong, back to **M_3**

N_2	Leaves tapering to a short point from a broad base; lateral veins far apart (Fig. 672, 673)	Correct, see **O** or **OO** Wrong, see **N_2N_2** (p. 98) or **$N_2N_2N_2$** (p. 98)

Rhododendron – Rhododendron

O

672 Under side
Rhododendron

Rhododendron ponticum L.
Rhododendron
Fig. 672 – see p. 172/173

- Leaves 8–15cm long, oblong-lanceolate to oblong-elliptic in outline and occasionally with slightly recurved margins
- Shortly pointed at the end
- Leaf-stalk from 1–3cm long
- Dark green above with a pale green midrib; pale green beneath with a prominent midrib; both sides glabrous

Prunus – Cherry

OO

673 Under side
Cherry Laurel

Prunus laurocerasus L.
Cherry Laurel
Fig. 673 – see p. 170/171

- Leaves 10–25cm long, oblong-elliptic to oblong-obovate in outline, stiff, leathery and usually with 4 glands in the lower part of the blade
- With a short, narrow point at the end
- Leaf-stalk 5–10mm long
- Shiny dark green above and pale green beneath; both sides glabrous

N_2N_2 Leaves tapering gradually from the middle of the blade towards the tip; lateral veins close together and almost at right angles to the midrib (Fig. 674)

Correct, see O_1
Wrong, see $N_2N_2N_2$

Nerium – Oleander

O_1

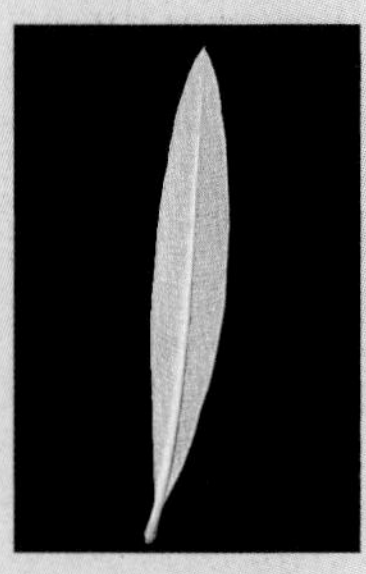

674 Under side **Oleander**

Nerium oleander L.
Oleander
Fig. 674 – see p. 172/173

- Leaves 6–15cm long, linear-lanceolate in outline and more rarely with slightly recurved margins
- Pointed at the end
- Leaf-stalk 3–7mm long; blade narrowing into the stalk
- Medium to dark green and glabrous above; greyish or pale green beneath with prominent midrib and sparsely hairy or glabrous

N_2N_2
N_2 Leaves tapering gradually from the middle of the blade towards the tip; lateral veins not close together (Fig. 675, 676)

Correct, see O_2 or O_2O_2
Wrong, back to N_2 (p. 97)

Ligustrum – Privet

O_2

675 Upper side **Wild Privet**

Ligustrum vulgare L.
Wild Privet
Fig. 675 – see p. 172/173

- Leaves 3–7cm long and lanceolate to oblong-elliptic in outline
- Pointed at the end
- Leaf-stalk 5–15mm long
- Medium to dark green above and somewhat paler green beneath; both sides glabrous

Olea – Olive

O_2
O_2

676 Under side **Olive**

Olea europaea L.
Olive
Fig. 676 – see p. 172/173

- Leaves 4–7cm long, lanceolate in outline, thick, leathery and often with slightly wavy margins
- Pointed at the end; often with a small sharp point
- Leaf-stalk 2–6mm long
- Dull dark green to greyish green above and greyish white to silvery grey beneath

I_1I_1 Leaves elliptic, ovate, broadly elliptic or broadly ovate

Correct, see K_2 or K_2K_2 (p. 99)
Wrong, back to I_1 (p. 95)

K_2 Leaves distinctly heart-shaped at the base of the blade

Correct, see L_4, L_4L_4 or $L_4L_4L_4$
Wrong, see K_2K_2 (p. 99)

Syringa – Lilac

L_4

677 Upper side **Lilac**

Syringa vulgaris L.
Lilac
Fig. 677 – see p. 174/175

- Leaves 5–10cm long and ovate or elliptic in outline with a pointed tip
- With a long point at the end
- Leaf-stalk 1–3cm long
- Dark green above and paler bluish green beneath; both sides glabrous

Catalpa – Catalpa

L_4
L_4

678 Upper side **Indian Bean Tree**

Catalpa bignonioides Walt.
Indian Bean Tree
Fig. 678 – see p. 174/175

- Leaves 10–20cm long and broadly ovate to heart-shaped in outline
- With a long, fine point at the end or with a short point
- Leaf-stalk 7–15cm long
- Medium to dark green above; paler green beneath with short, soft hairs

L_4
L_4
L_4

679 Upper side **Yellow Catalpa**

Catalpa ovata G. Don et Zucc.
Yellow Catalpa
Fig. 679 – see p. 174/175

- Leaves 10–25cm long and varied in outline; usually broadly ovate or heart shaped
- With a short point at the end
- Leaf-stalk 4–10cm long, often darker on the upper side
- Medium to dark green above with very fine hairs; pale to medium green beneath and slightly rough to the touch; with dark red glandular spots in the axils of the veins beneath

K_2K_2 Leaves rounded at the base of the blade or wedge-shaped — Correct, see **L_5**, **L_5L_5** or **$L_5L_5L_5$** Wrong, back to **K_2** (p. 98)

L_5 Leaves 1–3cm long, obovate, leathery and with their greatest breadth above the middle of the blade (Fig. 680) — Correct, see **M_4** Wrong, see **L_5L_5** or **$L_5L_5L_5$**

Arctostaphylos – Bearberry

M_4

680 Under side
Bearberry

Arctostaphylos uva-ursi (L.) Spreng.
Bearberry

Fig. 680 – see p. 174/175

- Leaves 1–3cm long, obovate or obovate-oblong in outline and with dense fine hairs on the margins
- Obtuse at the end or more rarely slightly emarginate
- Leaf-stalk 1–3mm long with white hairs
- Dark green above with a clearly visible, pale green midrib; a close, dark green network of veins beneath

L_5L_5 Leaves 20–40cm long, obovate, and pale bluish green beneath (Fig. 681) — Correct, see **M_5** Wrong, see **$L_5L_5L_5$**

Magnolia – Magnolia

M_5

681 Under side
Japanese Big-leaved Magnolia

Magnolia hypoleuca Sieb. et Zucc.
Japanese Big-leaved Magnolia

Fig. 681 – see p. 174/175

- Leaves 20–40cm long, obovate in outline and gradually narrowing towards the base
- Rounded at the end with a short point
- Leaf-stalk 3–8cm long
- Pale to medium green and glabrous above; paler bluish green and slightly hairy beneath

L_5L_5 L_5 Leaves 2–20cm long and elliptic, ovate or broadly ovate in outline — Correct, see **M_6**, or **M_6M_6** (p. 100) Wrong, back to **L_5**

M_6 Leaves densely felted beneath and so appearing greyish green — Correct, see **N_3**, **N_3N_3** or **$N_3N_3N_3$** Wrong, see **M_6M_6** (p. 100)

N_3 Leaves 5–10cm long, elliptic to broadly ovate in outline, with a stalk 1–2cm long covered in woolly hairs (Fig. 682) — Correct, see **O_3** Wrong, see **N_3N_3**

Cydonia – Quince

O_3

682 Under side
Quince

Cydonia oblonga Mill.
Quince

Fig. 682 – see p. 174/175

- Leaves 5–10cm long, elliptic to broadly ovate in outline and slightly grey-felted on the margins
- Obtuse, shortly rounded or weakly pointed at the end
- Leaf-stalk 1–2cm long covered in woolly hairs
- Dark green and usually glabrous above; grey-felted beneath

N_3N_3 Leaves 6–10cm long, obovate in outline, with a white woollly stalk 1–3cm long (Fig. 683) — Correct, see **O_4** Wrong, see **$N_3N_3N_3$**

Pyrus – Pear

O_4

683 Under side
Snow Pear

Pyrus nivalis Jacq.
Snow Pear

Fig. 683 – see p. 176/177

- Leaves 6–10cm long, obovate in outline and woolly hairy
- Acute at the end or rounded with a short point
- Leaf-stalk 1–3cm long covered with white woolly hairs
- Dark green above and covered with woolly hairs; densely felted beneath and so appearing greyish green

N_3N_3 N_3 Leaves 2–6cm long, ovate, broadly elliptic or roundish in outline, with a hairy stalk 0.2–0.7cm long (Fig. 684, 685) — Correct, see **O_5** or **O_5O_5** (p. 100) Wrong, back to **N_3**

Cotoneaster - Cotoneaster

O_5

684 Upper side
Cotoneaster

Cotoneaster tomentosus (Ait.) Lindl.
Cotoneaster
Fig. 684 - see p. 176/177

- Leaves 3-6cm long and elliptic to broad ovate in outline
- Obtuse at the end, more rarely rounded; occasionally with a small point
- Leaf-stalk 2-7mm long and densely felted
- Dark green and loosely hairy above; densely grey-felted beneath

---

O_5
O_5

685 Upper side
Common Cotoneaster

Cotoneaster integerrimus Medic.
Common Cotoneaster
Fig. 684 - see p. 176/177

- Leaves 2-4cm long, broadly elliptic, ovate or roundish in outline and very finely hairy on the margins
- Obtuse or acute at the end and usually with a prickly point
- Leaf-stalk 3-6mm long and finely hairy
- Dark green and usually glabrous above; densely white or grey-felted beneath

---

M_6M_6	Leaves not woolly felted beneath; the under side whitish, green or bluish green	Correct, see N_4, N_4N_4 or $N_4N_4N_4$ (p. 101) Wrong, back to M_6 (p. 99)

N_4	Leaves with the veins curving towards the tip (see Introduction!) (Fig. 686–688)	Correct, see O_6, O_6O_6 or $O_6O_6O_6$ Wrong, see N_4N_4 or $N_4N_4N_4$ (p. 101)

Cornus - Dogwood

O_6

686 Upper side
Dogwood

Cornus sanguinea L.
Dogwood
Fig. 686 - see p. 176/177

- Leaves 4-10cm long, elliptic to broadly ovate in outline and with 3 or 4 pairs of lateral veins curving towards the tip
- Pointed at the end
- Leaf-stalk 5-15mm long and usually grooved and dark red above
- Both sides sparsely hairy with clearly visible veins of the 1st and 2nd order; medium to dark green above and somewhat paler green beneath

---

O_6
O_6

687 Upper side
Cornelian Cherry

Cornus mas L.
Cornelian Cherry
Fig. 687 - see p. 176/177

- Leaves 4-10cm long, narrowly elliptic or elliptic to ovate in outline, often with a slightly wavy margin and with 3-5 pairs of lateral veins curving towards the tip
- Usually pointed at the end
- Leaf-stalk 3-15mm long, slightly grooved, often also tinged red and with fine whitish hairs
- Both sides with scattered white appressed hairs

O_6
O_6
O_6

688 Under side
Table Dogwood

Cornus controversa Hemsl.
Table Dogwood
Fig. 688 - see p. 176/177

- Leaves 7-12cm long and ovate or broadly ovate in outline
- With a short or long point at the end
- Leaf-stalk 1-3cm long
- Dark green above with clearly visible, impressed veins; bluish grey beneath and finely hairy on the veins; 6-9 pairs of lateral veins

---

N_4N_4	Leaves with the lateral veins running parallel to each other towards the margin (Fig. 689, 690)	Correct, see O_7 or O_7O_7 (p. 101) Wrong, see $N_4N_4N_4$ (p. 101)

O_7	Greatest breadth of leaves always above the middle (Fig. 689)	Correct, see P Wrong, see O_7O_7 (p. 101)

Fagus - Beech

P

689 Under side
Oriental Beech

Fagus orientalis Lipsky
Oriental Beech
Fig. 689 - see p. 178/179

- Leaves 6-12cm long, elliptic or usually obovate in outline and with numerous fine hairs on the margin
- Acute at the end or with a small point
- Leaf-stalk 5-15mm long covered with milky hair
- Dark bluish green and glabrous above with pale yellowish green veins; medium to dark green beneath with brownish hairs on the yellowish green veins

O_7O_7 Greatest breadth of leaves always at or below the middle (Fig. 690) — Correct, see **P_1**; Wrong, back to **O_7** (p. 100)

Fagus - Beech

P_1

690 Under side
Beech

Fagus sylvatica L.
Common Beech
Fig. 690 - see p. 178/179

- Leaves 5-10cm long, elliptic to broadly ovate in outline and with a wavy margin that is fringed with whitish hairs, especially when young
- Usually with a short point at the end
- Leaf-stalk 3-15mm long and often rather dark in colour
- Shiny dark green above and medium green beneath; very prominent lateral veins running parallel to each other

N_4N_4 N_4 Leaves with the veins curved or forming a network — Correct, see **O_8** or **O_8O_8** (p. 102); Wrong, back to **N_4** (p. 100)

O_8 Under side of leaves distinctly pale to dark bluish green — Correct, see **P_1** or **P_1P_1**; Wrong, see **O_8O_8** (p. 102)

P_1 Veins clearly deeply impressed on the upper side of the leaves (Fig. 691, 692) — Correct, see **Q** or **QQ**; Wrong, see **P_1P_1**

Salix - Willow

Q

691 Upper side
Spear-leaved Willow

Salix hastata L.
Spear-leaved Willow
Fig. 691 - see p. 178/179

- Leaves 2-8cm long, elliptic to ovate in outline and usually entire; more rarely with a few teeth wide apart
- Pointed or slightly rounded at the end
- Leaf-stalk 5-12mm long and distinctly grooved above
- Dark green and glabrous above; pale bluish green beneath and hairy at first on the prominent pale green veins

Parrotia - Persian Ironwood

QQ

692 Upper side
Persian Ironwood

Parrotia persica (DC.) C. A. Mey.
Persian Ironwood
Fig. 692 - see p. 178/179

- Leaves 6-10cm long, obovate or almost circular in outline, thick, leathery, and coarsely sinuate above the middle
- Obtuse or rounded at the end
- Leaf-stalk 5-8mm long
- Shiny dark green above and pale bluish green beneath and with whitish veins

P_1P_1 Veins not deeply impressed on the upper side of the leaves (Fig. 693-697) — Correct, see **Q_1** or **Q_1Q_1**; Wrong, back to **P_1**

Q_1 Both sides of the leaves remaining hairy and therefore soft to the touch (Fig. 693) — Correct, see **R**; Wrong, see **Q_1Q_1**

Lonicera - Honeysuckle

R

693 Upper side
Fly Honeysuckle

Lonicera xylosteum L.
Fly Honeysuckle
Fig. 693 - see p. 180/181

- Leaves 2-6cm long, elliptic, broadly ovate or obovate in outline and with the margins fringed by whitish hairs
- Obtuse or pointed at the end
- Leaf-stalk 5-10mm long with dense, appressed hairs
- Medium to dark green above and bluish green beneath; appressed hairs on both sides

Q_1Q_1 Leaves glabrous or only hairy when young and later becoming glabrous (Fig. 694) — Correct, see **R_1** (p. 102), **R_1R_1** (p. 102) or **$R_1R_1R_1$** (p. 102); Wrong, back to **Q_1**

694 Under side
Blue Honeysuckle

Lonicera – Honeysuckle

R_1

695 Upper side
Perfoliate Honeys

Lonicera caprifolium L.
Perfoliate Honeysuckle

Fig. 695 – see p. 180/181

- Leaves 2–10cm long, narrowly ovate to elliptic in outline; the uppermost leaves united to form an elliptic or circular leaf
- Obtuse or occasionally shortly pointed at the end
- Sessile or the lower leaves shortly stalked
- Dark green and glabrous above; bluish grey-green beneath and at first hairy at the base

---

R_1
R_1

696 Upper side
Blue Honeysuckle

Lonicera caerulea L.
Blue Honeysuckle

Fig. 696 – see p. 180/181

- Leaves 2–8cm long and elliptic, oblong-elliptic or obovate in outline
- Usually obtuse or rounded at the end
- Leaf-stalk 1–4mm long, broadened at the base and slightly hairy
- Dark green above, quickly becoming glabrous; bluish green beneath and becoming glabrous except for the leaf-stalk

---

R_1
R_1
R_1

697 Upper side
Honeysuckle

Lonicera periclymenum L.
Honeysuckle

Fig. 697 – see p. 180/181

- Leaves 4–10cm long and elliptic to obovate in outline
- Obtuse or pointed at the end
- Lower leaves with stalks up to 7mm long; the uppermost pair of leaves sessile
- Dark green above; bluish green beneath and only somewhat hairy when young

---

O_8O_8	Under side of leaves distinctly pale to medium green, never bluish green	Correct, see **P_2** or **P_2P_2** Wrong, back to **O_8** (p. 101)
P_2	Leaf-stalks distinctly winged; if only slightly winged then with a long thorn at the junction with the stem (Fig. 698, 699)	Correct, see **Q_1** or **Q_1Q_1** Wrong, see **P_2P_2**

Citrus – Orange, Lemon

Q_1

698 Upper side
Orange

Citrus sinensis (L.) Pers.
Orange

Fig. 698 – see p. 178/179

- Leaves 3–7cm long, elliptic, broadly elliptic or obovate in outline, firm, leathery, and broader than in the Lemon
- Acute at the end or rounded with a small point
- Leaf-stalk 5–20mm long, green and usually distinctly winged
- Shiny dark green above and pale green beneath; both sides glabrous

---

Q_1
Q_1

699 Upper side
Lemon

Citrus limon (L.) Burm.
Lemon

Fig. 699 – see p. 178/179

- Leaves 3–7cm long, narrowly elliptic to elliptic in outline, firm, leathery, very similar to the leaves of the Orange, and more rarely slightly crenate or dentate on the margin
- Pointed at the end
- Leaf-stalk 5–20mm long, often winged and usually with a thorn at its junction with the stem
- Shiny dark green above and pale green beneath; both sides glabrous

---

P_2P_2	Leaf-stalks not winged and without a thorn at the junction with the stem (Fig. 700–712)	Correct, see **Q_2** or **Q_2Q_2** Wrong, back to **P_2**
Q_2	Leaves ovate-rhombic and shiny dark green above (Fig. 700)	Correct, see **R_2** Wrong, see **Q_2Q_2** (p. 103)

Hedera – Ivy

R_2

700 Upper side
Ivy

Hedera helix L.
Ivy

Fig. 700 – see p. 182/183

- Leaves 4–10cm long and varied in outline; ovate-rhombic on flowering shoots, without lobes and leathery
- Shortly pointed at the end
- Leaf-stalk 3–11cm long
- Shiny dark green above with white veins; dull pale green beneath; both sides glabrous

Q_2Q_2 Leaves not ovate-rhombic (Fig. 701–712) — Correct, see **R_3** or **R_3R_3**; Wrong, back to **Q_2** (p. 102)

R_3 Leaves very finely glandular serrate (appearing entire to the naked eye; teeth only clearly visible with a lens) (Fig. 701) — Correct, see **S**; Wrong, see **R_3R_3**

Euonymus – Spindle Tree

S

701 Upper side **Broad-leaved Spindle Tree**

Euonymus latifolius (L.) Mill.
Broad-leaved Spindle Tree
Fig. 701 – see p. 182/183

- Leaves 7–14cm long and elliptic to obovate in outline
- Pointed at the end
- Leaf-stalk 5–10mm long and grooved above
- Dark green above and pale green beneath; both sides glabrous

R_3R_3 Leaves without small teeth — Correct, see **S_1** or **S_1S_1**; Wrong, back to **R_3**

S_1 Leaves 8–20cm long — Correct, see **T** or **TT**; Wrong, see **S_1S_1** (p. 104)

T Underside of leaves with conspicuous rust-red downy hairs (Fig. 702) — Correct, see **U**; Wrong, see **TT**

702 Under side **Evergreen Magnolia**

Magnolia – Magnolia

U

703 Upper side **Evergreen Magnolia**

Magnolia grandiflora L.
Evergreen Magnolia
Fig. 703 – see p. 182/183

- Leaves 8–20cm long, elliptic to broadly elliptic in outline, thick, leathery and falling in the 2nd year
- Obtuse to acute at the end and often with a rounded tip
- Leaf-stalk 20–25mm long and densely covered with rust-brown hairs
- Shiny dark green and glabrous above; paler green beneath with rust-red downy hairs

TT Under side of leaves without conspicuous rust-red, downy hairs (Fig. 704) — Correct, see **U_1** or **U_1U_1** (p. 104); Wrong, back to **T**

704 Under side **Alder Buckthorn**

U_1 Veins on the underside whitish to pale yellow (Fig. 705) — Correct, see **V**; Wrong, see **U_1U_1** (p. 104)

705 Under side **Garden Magnolia**

Magnolia – Magnolia

V

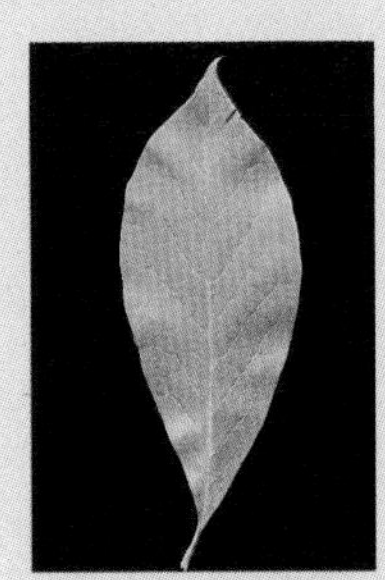

706 Upper side **Garden Magnolia**

Magnolia x soulangeana
Soul.-Bod.
Garden Magnolia
Fig. 706 – see p. 182/183

- Leaves 10–20cm long, oblong-elliptic or usually narrowly obovate in outline and broadest in the upper third
- With a short point at the end
- Leaf-stalk 1–4cm long
- Medium to dark green and glabrous above; paler green beneath and somewhat hairy

U_1U_1 Veins on the under side medium to dark green — Correct, see **V_1**; Wrong, back to **U_1** (p. 103)

Lonicera – Honeysuckle

V_1

707 Under side **Alpine Honeysuckle**

Lonicera alpigena L.
Alpine Honeysuckle
Fig. 707 – see p. 180/181

- Leaves 8–12cm long, elliptic to obovate in outline and with a fringe of fine hairs on the margins when young
- Shortly pointed at the end
- Leaf-stalk 1–2cm long
- Dark green above; paler green and very shiny beneath with fine hairs along the midrib

S_1S_1 Leaves 3–8cm long — Correct, see **T_1** or **T_1T_1**; Wrong, back to **S_1** (p. 103)

T_1 Leaf stalks usually distinctly grooved above (Fig. 708) — Correct, see **U_2** or **U_2U_2**; Wrong, see **T_1T_1**

708 Upper side **European Forsythia**

U_2 Midrib and lateral veins on the under side green and leaf-stalk 1–3cm long (Fig. 709) — Correct, see **V_2**; Wrong, see **U_2U_2**

709 Under side **European Forsythia**

Forsythia – Forsythia

V_2

710 Upper side **European Forsythia**

Forsythia europaea Deg. et Bald.
European Forsythia
Fig. 710 – see p. 182/183

- Leaves 4–8cm long and elliptic, ovate or ovate-lanceolate in outline
- Pointed at the end; the tip often slightly curved to one side
- Leaf-stalk 1–3cm long
- Dark green above and pale green beneath; both sides glabrous

U_2U_2 Midrib and lateral veins on the under side pale yellow and leaf-stalk 3–14mm long — Correct, see **V_3**; Wrong, back to **U_2**

Lonicera – Honeysuckle

V_3

711 Under side **Black-berried Honeysuckle**

Lonicera nigra L.
Black-berried Honeysuckle
Fig. 711 – see p. 180/181

- Leaves 3–8cm long, elliptic, broadly elliptic to obovate in outline and often with slightly wavy margins
- Shortly pointed at the end
- Leaf-stalk 2–8mm long and grooved above
- Medium to dark green and glabrous above; medium green beneath and downy along the midrib

T_1T_1 Leaf-stalks not or only slightly grooved above — Correct, see **U_3**; Wrong, back to **T_1**

Rhamnus – Buckthorn

U_3

712 Upper side **Alder Buckthorn**

Rhamnus frangula L.
Alder Buckthorn
Fig. 712 – see p. 182/183

- Leaves 3–7cm long and elliptic to broadly elliptic in outline
- With a short point at the end
- Leaf-stalk 6–14mm long
- Dark green above and shiny pale green beneath

A	Most leaves transformed into sharp, green spines (Fig. 713) (small, very narrow leaves present only in luxuriant growth or in young plants)	Correct, see **B** Wrong, see **AA** or **AAA**

Ulex – Gorse

B

713 **Gorse**

Ulex europaeus L.
Gorse
Fig. 713 – see p. 184/185

- Typical leaves often absent; most leaves and also the short shoots transformed into spines
- End of the spine sharp
- Leaf-stalks absent; spines with numerous lateral spines
- Stems grooved and often with downy hairs

AA	Margins of leaves with a fringe of sharp spines (Fig. 714), dentate with bristly teeth (Fig. 715) or with several coarse spiny teeth (Fig. 716, 717)	Correct, see B_1, B_1B_1 or $B_1B_1B_1$ Wrong, see **AAA**

B_1	Leaves fringed with sharp spines (Fig. 714)	Correct, see **C** Wrong, see B_1B_1 or $B_1B_1B_1$

Berberis – Barberry

C

714 Upper side **Barberry**

Berberis vulgaris L.
Barberry
Fig. 714 – see p. 184/185

- Leaves 2–4cm long, narrowly obovate to obovate in outline and with the margin fringed by sharp spines
- Rounded or obtuse at the end
- Leaf-stalk 5–15mm long
- Dark green above and whitish green beneath; both sides glabrous

B_1B_1	Leaves dentate with spiny teeth (Fig. 715)	Correct, see C_1 Wrong, see $B_1B_1B_1$

Castanea – Sweet Chestnut

C_1

715 Upper side **Sweet Chestnut**

Castanea sativa Mill.
Sweet Chestnut
Fig. 715 – see p. 184/185

- Leaves 10–30cm long, oblong-lanceolate in outline, thick, leathery and with bristly pointed teeth
- With a short, narrow point at the end
- Leaf-stalk 2–5cm long
- Shiny dark green and glabrous above; pale green beneath and with matted woolly hairs when young; 15–20 pairs of lateral veins

$B_1B_1B_1$	Leaves with several coarse spiny teeth (Fig. 716, 717)	Correct, see C_2 or C_2C_2 Wrong, back to B_1

Ilex – Holly

C_2

716 Upper side **Holly**

Ilex aquifolium L.
Holly
Fig. 716 – see p. 184/185

- Leaves 3–8cm long, elliptic to ovate in outline, thick, leathery and with coarse spiny teeth
- With a long, spiny point at the end
- Leaf-stalk 1cm long and grooved above
- Shiny dark green above and pale green beneath; both sides glabrous

Quercus – Oak

C_2C_2

717 Upper side **Evergreen Oak**

Quercus ilex L.
Evergreen Oak, Holm Oak
Fig. 717 – see p. 184/185

- Leaves 3–8cm long and varied in form; often with 4–7 sharp teeth on each side
- With a sharp, spiny point at the end
- Leaf-stalk 7–15mm long and remaining white-felted until late in the year
- Young leaves hairy on both sides; older leaves shiny dark green and glabrous; grey to whitish beneath because of the dense covering of hair

AAA	Margins of leaves neither fringed with spines, nor dentate with bristly teeth, nor with several coarse spiny teeth, but serrate, dentate or crenate	Correct, see B_2 (p. 106), or B_2B_2 (p. 107) Wrong, back to **A**

B_2 Leaves usually heart-shaped or obliquely heart-shaped (Fig. 718–725) and regularly toothed

Correct, see **C_2** or **C_2C_2**
Wrong, see **B_2B_2** (p. 107)

C_2 Leaves with white or pale grey matted woolly hairs beneath (Fig. 718, 719)

Correct, see **D** or **DD**
Wrong, see **C_2C_2**

Tilia – Lime

D

718 Under side
Silver Lime

Tilia tomentosa Moench
Silver Lime

Fig. 718 – see p. 186/187

- Leaves 6–12cm long, roundish heart-shaped or obliquely heart-shaped in outline and with the margin fairly regularly serrate or dentate
- Shortly pointed at the end
- Leaf-stalk 2–3.5cm long and therefore shorter than in the Weeping Silver Lime
- Dark green above; with white or pale grey matted woolly hairs beneath

---

DD

719 Under side
Weeping Silver Lime

Tilia petiolaris DC.
Weeping Silver Lime

Fig. 719 – see p. 186/187

- Leaves 7–11cm long, obliquely heart-shaped in outline and regularly sharply serrate/dentate (leaf-teeth with a bristle-like tip)
- Shortly pointed at the end
- Leaf-stalk 3–6cm long with matted woolly hairs; leaves pendent
- Dark green above, becoming almost glabrous; felted beneath with white or greyish white stellate hairs

---

C_2C_2 Leaves green or bluish green beneath (Fig. 720–725)

Correct, see **D_1** or **D_1D_1**
Wrong, back to **C_2**

D_1 Leaves green beneath with whitish tufts of hair in the axils of the veins (Fig. 720)

Correct, see **E**
Wrong, see **D_1D_1**

Tilia – Lime

E

720 Under side
Large-leaved Lime

Tilia platyphyllos Scop.
Large-leaved Lime

Fig. 720 – see p. 186/187

- Leaves 7–15cm long, heart-shaped or obliquely heart-shaped in outline and with the margin regularly crenate-serrate
- With a short point at the end
- Leaf-stalk 2–5cm long and often somewhat hairy
- Dark green and somewhat hairy above; paler green beneath with whitish tufts of hair in the axils of the veins

---

D_1D_1 Leaves bluish green beneath and with (Fig. 721, 724) or without (Fig. 722) brownish tufts of hair in the axils of the veins

Correct, see **E_1**, **E_1E_1** or **$E_1E_1E_1$** (p. 107)
Wrong, back to **D_1**

721 Under side
Small-leaved Lime

722 Under side
Katsura Tree

Tilia – Lime

E_1

723 Upper side
Small-leaved Lime

Tilia cordata Mill.
Small-leaved Lime

Fig. 723 – see p. 186/187

- Leaves 4–7cm long, usually heart-shaped in outline (or obliquely heart-shaped) and with the margin finely and sharply serrate
- Shortly pointed at the end
- Leaf-stalk 2–5cm long and glabrous
- Shiny dark green to bluish green above and glabrous; pale bluish green beneath with brownish red tufts of hair in the axils of the veins

---

E_1
E_1

724 Under side
Caucasian Lime

Tilia x euchlora K. Koch
Caucasian Lime

Fig. 724 – see p. 186/187

- Leaves 5–15cm long, obliquely heart-shaped in outline and irregularly toothed; teeth tipped with bristles
- With a bristle-tipped point at the end
- Leaf-stalk 3–6cm long
- Dark bluish green and glabrous above; bluish green beneath with pale yellow veins and pale brown tufts of hair in their axils

Cercidiphyllum – Katsura Tree

E_1
E_1
E_1

725 Upper side
Katsura Tree

Cercidiphyllum japonicum
Sieb. et Zucc. ex Miq.
Katsura Tree
Fig. 725 – see p. 186/187

- Leaves 6–12cm long, broadly ovate to roundish or heart-shaped in outline and with a crenate margin
- Very shortly pointed at the end
- Leaf-stalk 3–6cm long, green with a reddish tinge
- Dull or greyish green above; pale bluish green beneath and like the upper side glabrous

---

B_2B_2 Leaves not heart-shaped; but if slightly heart-shaped then the leaf-margin doubly serrate or doubly serrate/dentate (Fig. 726, 727)

Correct, see **C_3**, **C_3C_3** or **$C_3C_3C_3$** (p. 108)
Wrong, back to **B_2** (p. 106)

C_3 Leaves oblong obovate, broadly ovate, roundish or slightly heart-shaped and doubly serrate/dentate

Correct, see **D_1** or **D_1D_1**
Wrong, see **C_3C_3** or **$C_3C_3C_3$** (p. 108)

Corylus – Hazel

D_1

726 Upper side
Hazel

Corylus avellana L.
Hazel
Fig. 726 – see p. 188/189

- Leaves 5–10cm long, oblong-obovate, roundish or slightly heart-shaped in outline and with the margin doubly serrate/dentate
- With a short point at the end
- Leaf-stalk 5–15mm long and glandular hairy
- Medium green above and pale to medium green beneath; both sides more or less softly hairy

---

D_1
D_1

727 Upper side
Turkish Hazel

Corylus colurna L.
Turkish Hazel
Fig. 727 – see p. 184/185

- Leaves 8–12cm long, broadly ovate to roundish or somewhat heart-shaped in outline, with the greatest breadth above the middle and serrate and with the margin coarsely doubly dentate
- With a fairly long point at the end
- Leaf-stalk 1.5–3cm long
- Shiny dark green above and later glabrous; medium to dark green beneath and hairy on the veins

---

C_3C_3 Leaves triangular, ovate-rhombic or rhombic in outline (Fig. 728–731)

Correct, see **D_2** or **D_2D_2**
Wrong, see **$C_3C_3C_3$** (p. 108)

D_2 Leaf-margin regularly sinuately serrate/dentate, or crenate-serrate (Fig. 728–730)

Correct, see **E_2**, **E_2E_2** or **$E_2E_2E_2$**
Wrong, see **D_2D_2** (p. 108)

Populus – Poplar

E_2

728 Upper side
Lombardy Poplar

Populus nigra L. var. *italica* Muenchh.
Lombardy Poplar
Fig. 728 – see p. 188/189

- Leaves 4–8cm long, lozenge-shaped or rhombic and for the most part sinuately serrate/dentate
- With a long point at the end
- Leaf-stalk 1–3cm long and often tinged with red
- Dark green above and greyish green beneath; both sides glabrous

---

E_2
E_2

729 Under side
Hybrid Black Poplar

Populus x canadensis Moench
Hybrid Black Poplar
Fig. 729 – see p. 188/189

- Leaves 6–10cm long, almost triangular in outline and with a wavy, crenate-serrate margin
- With a short point at the end
- Leaf-stalk 3–8cm long and occasionally somewhat reddish
- Shiny dark green above and paler green beneath; both sides glabrous

---

E_2
E_2
E_2

730 Under side
Black Poplar

Populus nigra L.
Black Poplar
Fig. 730 – see p. 188/189

- Leaves 3–9cm long, triangular to rhombic in outline, reddish at first and with the margin crenate-serrate
- Pointed at the end
- Leaf-stalk 3–6cm long and laterally compressed
- Dark green above and pale bluish green beneath; lateral veins not as strongly branched as in the Hybrid Black Poplar

D_2D_2 Leaf-margin distinctly coarsely doubly serrate/dentate (Fig. 731) — Correct, see **E_3**; Wrong, back to **D_2** (p. 107)

Betula – Birch

E_3

731 Upper side **Silver Birch**

Betula pendula Roth
Silver Birch
Fig. 731 – see p. 188/189

- Leaves 3-7cm long, triangular or ovate-rhombic in outline, often heart-shaped on suckers and usually coarsely doubly serrate/dentate (entire towards the base of the blade)
- With a long point at the end
- Leaf-stalk 2-3cm long
- Dark green above and pale greyish green beneath, both sides glabrous

C_3C_3 Leaves not as in **C_3** or **C_3C_3** — Correct, see **D_3** or **D_3D_3**
C_3

D_3 Leaves distinctly gland-dotted beneath (Fig. 732) — Correct, see **E_4**; Wrong, see **D_3D_3**

Vaccinium – Vaccinium

E_4

732 Under side **Cowberry**

Vaccinium vitis-idaea L.
Cowberry
Fig. 732 – see p. 190/191

- Leaves 1-3cm long, narrowly obovate in outline, leathery, with their greatest breadth always above the middle and with the margin at times slightly crenate and dentate (some parts entire)
- Obtuse or slightly emarginate at the end
- Leaf-stalk 3-5mm and somewhat hairy
- Shiny dark green above; rather pale greyish blue-green beneath

D_3D_3 Leaves not gland-dotted beneath — Correct, see **E_5** or **E_5E_5**; Wrong, back to **D_3**

E_5 Leaves truncate at the end or in most cases emarginate (Fig. 733, 734) — Correct, see **F** or **FF**; Wrong, see **E_5E_5**

Salix – Willow

F

733 Under side **Dwarf Willow**

Salix herbacea L.
Dwarf Willow
Fig. 733 – see p. 190/191

- Leaves 8-20mm long, roundish ovate to circular in outline and with the margin crenate-serrate
- Usually emarginate at the end
- Leaf-stalk 3-6mm long and somewhat broadened at the base
- Medium to bluish green and glabrous on both sides; a clearly visible network of veins

Alnus – Common Alder

FF

734 Upper side **Alder**

Alnus glutinosa (L.) Gaertn.
Alder
Fig. 734 – see p. 188/189

- Leaves 4-10cm long, broadly obovate to roundish in outline, with their greatest breadth above the middle and simply and doubly serrate/dentate
- Usually emarginate at the end, more rarely rounded
- Leaf-stalk 5-15mm long
- Medium to dark green above; paler green beneath with whitish to rust-coloured tufts of hair in the axils of the veins

E_5E_5 Leaves obtuse or pointed at the end — Correct, see **F_1**, **F_1F_1** (p. 109), **$F_1F_1F_1$** (p. 109) or **$F_1F_1F_1F_1$** (p. 109)

F_1 Leaves sinuately dentate, remaining densely white-felted beneath and 5-12cm long (Fig. 735) — Correct, see **G**; Wrong, see **F_1F_1** (p. 109), **$F_1F_1F_1$** (p. 109) or **$F_1F_1F_1F_1$** (p. 109)

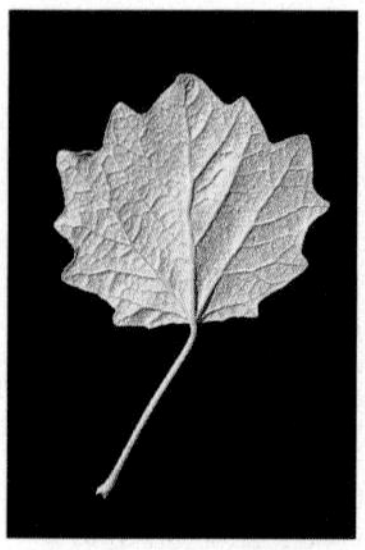

735 Under side **White Poplar**

Populus – Poplar

G

736 Upper side
White Poplar

Populus alba L.
White Poplar
Fig. 736 – see p. 190/191

- Leaves 5–12cm long and varied in outline; often triangular to ovate and sinuately dentate
- Rounded or shortly pointed at the end
- Leaf-stalk 2–4cm long, flattened and covered with white hairs
- Shiny dark green above (covered with matted woolly hairs when young) and remaining densely white-felted beneath

---

F_1F_1 Leaves irregularly coarsely sinuately dentate, greyish blue-green beneath (Fig. 737) and 3–10cm long — Correct, see **G_1** Wrong, see **$F_1F_1F_1$** or **$F_1F_1F_1F_1$**

Populus – Poplar

G_1

737 Under side
Aspen

Populus tremula L.
Aspen
Fig. 737 – see p. 190/191

- Leaves 3–9cm long (up to 15cm on suckers), usually roundish in outline and irregularly sinuately dentate
- Rounded at the end or shortly pointed from a broad base
- Leaf-stalk 3–10cm long, flattened and often somewhat reddish in colour
- Brownish red at first above, later greyish blue-green; pale greyish green beneath

---

F_1F_1
F_1 Leaves regularly coarsely crenate, whitish to pale greyish green beneath with a stalk 0.2–1cm long (Fig. 738) — Correct, see **G_2** Wrong, see **$F_1F_1F_1F_1$**

Dryas – Mountain Avens

G_2

738 Under side
Mountain Avens

Dryas octopetala L.
Mountain Avens
Fig. 738 – see p. 190/191

- Leaves 5–30mm long, oblong-elliptic in outline, leathery and with the margin regularly coarsely crenate and slightly recurved
- Obtuse or shortly pointed at the end
- Leaf-stalk 2–10mm long
- Shiny dark green and glabrous above; silvery white beneath with matted woolly hairs

---

F_1F_1
F_1F_1 Leaf-margin formed in a different way — Correct, see **G_3** or **G_3G_3** (p. 110) Wrong, back to **F_1** (p. 108)

G_3 Halves of the blade clearly differing in size and noticeably unequal at the base (Fig. 739–742) — Correct, see **H**, **HH**, **HHH** or **HHHH** (p. 110) Wrong, see **G_3G_3** (p. 110)

Ulmus – Elm

H

739 Upper side
Fluttering Elm

Ulmus laevis Pall.
Fluttering Elm
Fig. 739 – see p. 192/193

- Leaves 7–12cm long, narrowly elliptic, elliptic or roundish in outline, broadest at the middle and sharply doubly serrate/dentate
- With a short, fine point at the end
- Leaf-stalk only up to 5mm long
- Dull dark green above; greyish green and finely hairy beneath

---

HH

740 Upper side
Wych Elm

Ulmus glabra Huds.
Wych Elm
Fig. 740 – see p. 192/193

- Leaves 5–16cm long, elliptic, ovate or often obovate in outline, sometimes 3-pointed and with the margin coarsely doubly serrate
- Finely pointed at the end
- Leaf-stalk 3–6mm long, often covered by one half of the blade
- Dark green and rough above; medium green beneath and with fine white hairs on the larger veins

---

HH
H

741 Upper side
Smooth-leaved Elm

Ulmus minor Mill.
Smooth-leaved Elm
Fig. 741 – see p. 192/193

- Leaves 3.5–8cm long and varied in outline; usually narrowly obovate or obovate-elliptic
- With a narrow, tapering point at the end
- Leaf-stalk 5–13mm long and usually somewhat hairy
- Dark green and usually glabrous above; paler green beneath and with conspicuous velvety tufts of hairs in the axils of the veins

Celtis – Nettle-tree

HH
HH

742 Upper side **Southern Nettle-tree**

Celtis australis L.
Southern Nettle-tree
Fig. 742 – see p. 192/193

- Leaves 4–15cm long, oblong-elliptic to narrowly ovate in outline and with the margin sharply serrate
- With a slender point at the end
- Leaf-stalk 10–15mm long
- Dark green and roughly hairy above; greyish green and softly hairy beneath

---

H_1H_1 Leaves narrowly elliptic, narrowly ovate to roundish or narrowly obovate and greyish green beneath (Fig. 745–757)

Correct, see **I_1** or **I_1I_1**
Wrong, see **$H_1H_1H_1$** (p. 112) or **$H_1H_1H_1H_1$** (p. 118)

I_1 Leaves narrowly obovate or obovate (with their greatest breadth above the middle of the blade)

Correct, see **K** or **KK**
Wrong, see **I_1I_1**

G_3G_3 Halves of the blade more or less equal in size and attached to the stalk at about the same height

Correct, see **H_1**, **H_1H_1**, **$H_1H_1H_1$** (p. 112) or **$H_1H_1H_1H_1$** (p. 118)
Wrong, back to **G_3** (p. 109)

H_1 Leaves elliptic to ovate and distinctly white beneath (Fig. 743, 744)

Correct, see **I** or **II**
Wrong, see **H_1H_1**, **$H_1H_1H_1$** (p. 112) or **$H_1H_1H_1H_1$** (p. 118)

Populus – Poplar

I

743 Under side
Western Balsam Poplar

Populus trichocarpa
Torr. et A. Gray ex Hook.
Western Balsam Poplar
Fig. 743 – see p. 192/193

- Leaves 8–14cm long, broadly ovate to somewhat rhombic in outline, thick, rather leathery and finely crenate-serrate
- Pointed at the end
- Leaf-stalk 2–5cm long and usually slightly reddish above
- Dark green and glabrous above; whitish or rust-coloured beneath and often with fairly fine downy hairs

---

Sorbus – Whitebeam

II

744 Under side
Whitebeam

Sorbus aria (L.) Crantz
Whitebeam
Fig. 744 – see p. 192/193

- Leaves 6–12cm long, ovate, elliptic or even roundish in outline and simply or doubly serrate/dentate
- Obtuse or rounded at the end with a short point
- Leaf-stalk 1–2cm long with white hairs
- Medium green and somewhat silky-hairy above; always densely white-felted beneath

---

Salix – Willow

K

745 Under side
Eared Willow

Salix aurita L.
Eared Willow
Fig. 745 – see p. 190/191

- Leaves 2–5cm long, narrowly obovate to obovate in outline, with auriculate, persistent stipules and with the margin irregularly coarsely serrate, finely dentate and also wavy
- Broadly rounded at the end with a short, oblique and slightly recurved point
- Leaf-stalk 5–8mm long and hairy
- Greyish green and hairy beneath

Myrica – Bog Myrtle

KK

746 Under side
Bog Myrtle

Myrica gale L.
Bog Myrtle, Sweet Gale
Fig. 746 – see p. 194/195

- Leaves 2–5cm long, oblong-obovate in outline, thickish and coarsely toothed in the upper half
- With a short point at the end
- Leaf-stalk 3–6mm long
- Dull dark green and rather finely hairy above; pale green beneath and finely hairy on the midrib

---

I_1I_1 Greatest breadth of leaves at or below the middle of the blade

Correct, see **K_1** or **K_1K_1** (p. 111)
Wrong, back to **I_1**

K_1 Leaves at most 3cm long (Fig. 747–750)

Correct, see **L**, **LL**, **LLL** or **LLLL** (all p. 111)
Wrong, see **K_1K_1** (p. 111)

Betula – Birch

L

747 Upper side
Dwarf Birch

Betula nana L.
Dwarf Birch
Fig. 747 – see p. 194/195

- Leaves at most 3cm long, usually roundish in outline, the margin simply toothed with broad, blunt teeth
- With a coarse tooth at the end
- Leaf-stalk 1–2mm long and dark red in colour
- Dark green above and somewhat undulate; whitish beneath with a network of dark green veins

---

LL

748 Upper side
Birch

Betula x intermedia (Hartm.) Thomas
Birch
Fig. 748 – see p. 194/195

- Leaves 8–25mm long, elliptic to broadly obovate in outline, and with the margin simply and coarsely serrate
- Rounded at the end with one or several teeth at the tip
- Leaf-stalk 3–7mm long
- Dark green above and greyish green beneath; both sides gland-dotted

---

Nothofagus – Southern Beech

LL
L

749 Upper side
Antarctic Beech

Nothofagus antarctica
(G. Forst.) Oerst.
Antarctic Beech
Fig. 749 – see p. 194/195

- Leaves 1–3cm long, ovate to roundish in outline and with the margin irregularly crenate, serrate and sinuate
- Rounded at the end
- Leaf-stalk 2–4mm long
- Shiny dark green above and often slightly wrinkled; greyish green beneath

---

Rhamnus – Buckthorn

LL
LL

750 Upper side
Rock Buckthorn

Rhamnus saxatilis Jacq.
Rock Buckthorn
Fig. 750 – see p. 194/195

- Leaves 1–3cm long, lanceolate to elliptic in outline, finely and regularly serrate
- Pointed at the end
- Leaf-stalk 2–5mm long
- Dark green above and whitish green beneath with dark green lateral veins; both sides glabrous

---

K_1K_1	Leaves 3–10cm long	Correct, see **L_1** or **L_1L_1** Wrong, back to **K_1** (p. 110)
L_1	Leaves narrowly or broadly lanceolate to ovate (or possibly even weakly obovate) (Fig. 751, 752)	Correct, see **M** or **MM** Wrong, see **L_1L_1**

Salix – Willow

M

751 Upper side
Willow

Salix glabra Scopoli
Willow
Fig. 751 – see p. 194/195

- Leaves 3–9cm long, lanceolate to obovate in outline and with the margin regularly and finely serrate
- Tapering to the end or with a short point
- Leaf-stalk 5–15mm long and somewhat broadened at the base
- Shiny dark-green above and pale bluish-green beneath with a thick waxy bloom

---

MM

752 Under side
Grey Willow

Salix cinerea L.
Grey Willow
Fig. 752 – see p. 196/197

- Leaves 5–9cm long, broadly lanceolate to obovate in outline, with a wavy margin, and irregularly finely to coarsely toothed
- Shortly pointed at the end
- Leaf-stalk 5–20mm long and somewhat broadened at the base
- Dull green, without lustre, and shortly hairy above; covered beneath with greyish green velvety hairs and with prominent veins

---

L_1L_1	Leaves different from those in **L_1**; usually elliptic to roundish (Fig. 753–757)	Correct, see **M_1**, **M_1M_1** (p. 112) or **$M_1M_1M_1$** (p. 112) Wrong, back to **L_1**
M_1	Leaves with doubly serrate margin (Fig. 753)	Correct, see **N** (p. 112) Wrong, see **M_1M_1** or **$M_1M_1M_1$** (p. 112)

Alnus - Alder

N

753 Upper side
Grey Alder

Alnus incana (L.) Moench
Grey Alder
Fig. 753 - see p. 196/197

- Leaves 5-10cm long, broadly ovate to broadly elliptic in outline and with the margin doubly serrate
- Pointed at the end
- Leaf-stalk 7-20mm long
- Dark green and glabrous above and remaining greyish green beneath; both sides softly hairy when young

---

M_1M_1 Leaves with a wavy or coarsely dentate to crenate margin — Correct, see **N_1**; Wrong, see **$M_1M_1M_1$**

Salix - Willow

N_1

754 Under side
Goat Willow

Salix caprea L.
Goat Willow, Pussy Willow
Fig. 754 - see p. 196/197

- Leaves 4-10cm long, broadly elliptic to ovate in outline and with the margin wavy or coarsely dentate to crenate
- With a short, oblique point at the end
- Leaf-stalk 1-2cm long, somewhat broadened at the base, slightly reddish in colour and with downy hairs
- Brownish dark green and glabrous above; greyish green beneath because of the downy covering

---

M_1M_1
M_1 Leaves with finely serrate or serrate/dentate margin (Fig. 755-757) — Correct, see **N_2**, **N_2N_2** or **$N_2N_2N_2$**; Wrong, back to **M_1** (p. 111)

Malus - Apple

N_2

755 Under side
Apple

Malus sylvestris (L.) Mill.
ssp. *domestica* (Borkh.) Mansf.
Apple
Fig. 755 - see p. 196/197

- Leaves 5-9cm long, narrowly elliptic, elliptic to ovate in outline and with the margin regularly serrate
- With a short point at the end
- Leaf-stalk 2-5cm long
- Dark green and often somewhat undulate above; pale greyish green beneath and densely felted at first

Salix - Willow

N_2
N_2

756 Upper side
Spear-leaved Willow

Salix hastata L.
Spear-leaved Willow
Fig. 756 - see p. 196/197

- Leaves 3-8cm long, elliptic to ovate in outline and with the margin finely serrate/dentate
- Shortly pointed at the end
- Leaf-stalk 3-8mm long, somewhat broadened at the base, and tinged reddish above
- Dark green and glabrous above; pale bluish green beneath and hairy only when young

---

Pyrus - Pear

N_2
N_2
N_2

757 Upper side
Pear

Pyrus communis L.
Pear
Fig. 757 - see p. 196/197

- Leaves 3-8cm long, elliptic, ovate or roundish in outline, thick, and with the margin finely serrate and in some parts entire
- With a short, narrow point at the end
- Leaf-stalk 1-8cm long
- Shiny and glabrous above; somewhat hairy beneath at first, later glabrous and slightly paler green

---

H_1H_1
H_1 Leaves elliptic to roundish and green to bluish green beneath — Correct, see **I_2** or **I_2I_2** (p. 113); Wrong, see **$H_1H_1H_1H_1$** (p. 118)

I_2 Leaves without prominent lateral veins beneath — Correct, see **K_2**, **K_2K_2** (p. 113) or **$K_2K_2K_2$** (p. 113); Wrong, see **I_2I_2** (p. 113)

K_2 Leaves 1-3cm long with a 0.5-3mm long stalk (Fig. 758) — Correct, see **L_2**; Wrong, see **K_2K_2** (p. 113) or **$K_2K_2K_2$** (p. 113)

758 Upper side **Bilberry**

Vaccinium – Vaccinium

L_2

759 Upper side **Bilberry**

Vaccinium myrtillus L.
Bilberry

Fig. 758, 759 – see p. 198/199

- Leaves 1–3cm long, oblong-ovate, elliptic or ovate in outline and with the margin finely serrate, dentate or crenate
- Rounded or shortly pointed at the end
- Leaf-stalk 0.5–3mm long
- Medium to dark green above and somewhat paler green beneath

---

K_2K_2 Leaves 2–4.5cm long with an often slightly reddish stalk 1–2cm long (Fig. 760) — Correct, see **L_3**; Wrong, see **$K_2K_2K_2$**

Amelanchier – Service Berry

L_3

760 Upper side **Service Berry**

Amelanchier ovalis Medic.
Service Berry

Fig. 760 – see p. 198/199

- Leaves 2–4.5cm long, ovate to roundish in outline and with the margin finely serrate or dentate; occasionally entire or crenate
- Rounded at the end
- Leaf-stalk 1–2cm long and covered with woolly hairs especially when young
- Dark green and glabrous above; somewhat paler green beneath and woolly when young

---

K_2K_2 K_2 Leaves always more than 5cm long — Correct, see **M_2** or **M_2M_2**; Wrong, back to **K_2** (p. 112)

M_2 Leaves pointed and usually rounded at the base of the blade (Fig. 761) — Correct, see **N_3** or **N_3N_3**; Wrong, see **M_2M_2**

761 Under side **Portugal Laurel**

Prunus – Cherry

N_3

762 Upper side **Portugal Laurel**

Prunus lusitanica L.
Portugal Laurel

Fig. 762 – see p. 200/201

- Leaves 6–12cm long, oblong-ovate in outline, leathery and with the margin irregularly serrate/dentate
- Pointed at the end; often with a slightly rounded top
- Leaf-stalk 10–25mm long, grooved and often tinged red above
- Dark green above and pale green beneath; both sides glabrous

---

N_3
N_3

763 Upper side **Apricot**

Prunus armeniaca L.
Apricot

Fig. 763 – see p. 198/199

- Leaves 5–10cm long, broadly ovate, roundish or slightly heart-shaped in outline and with a finely serrate margin
- Shortly pointed at the end
- Leaf-stalk 3–7cm long and dark red in colour
- Dull green above and somewhat paler green beneath; both sides glabrous

---

M_2M_2 Leaves obtuse at the end, with numerous fine teeth and with the base of the blade wedge-shaped (Fig. 764) — Correct, see **N_4**; Wrong, back to **M_2**

Arbutus – Strawberry Tree

N_4

764 Under side **Strawberry Tree**

Arbutus unedo L.
Strawberry Tree

Fig. 764 – see p. 198/199

- Leaves 5–10cm long, oblong-elliptic in outline and irregularly serrate with teeth of varied length
- Obtuse at the end and with several short teeth or shortly pointed
- Leaf-stalk 5–15mm long, distinctly hairy and often somewhat reddish
- Dark green and shiny above; much paler green beneath with only the midrib prominent

---

I_2I_2 Leaves with midrib and lateral veins prominent beneath — Correct, see **K_3** (p. 114) or **K_3K_3** (p. 115); Wrong, back to **I_2** (p. 112)

K_3 Lateral veins of leaves usually straight and not curving towards the tip; if slightly curved, then only at the end — Correct, see L_4 or L_4L_4; Wrong, see K_3K_3 (p. 115)

L_4 Leaves with 4 or 5 pairs of straight lateral veins, 1-3.5cm long and with the margin irregularly coarsely serrate (Fig. 765) — Correct, see M_3; Wrong, see L_4L_4

Betula - Birch

M_3

765 Under side
Shrubby Birch

Betula humilis Schrank
Shrubby Birch
Fig. 765 - see p. 198/199

- Leaves 1-3.5cm long, elliptic, ovate to roundish in outline and with the margin simply and regularly serrate
- Rather obtuse to weakly pointed at the end
- Leaf-stalk 3-7mm long and often somewhat reddish above
- Shiny dark green and glabrous above; paler green beneath, distinctly net-veined and with 4 or 5 pairs of lateral veins

L_4L_4 Leaves with 5 or more pairs of straight lateral veins and usually longer than 3cm — Correct, see M_4, M_4M_4 or $M_4M_4M_4$; Wrong, back to L_4

M_4 Leaves unequally doubly serrate/dentate and 3-5cm long (Fig. 766) — Correct, see N_5; Wrong, see M_4M_4 or $M_4M_4M_4$

Betula - Birch

N_5

766 Upper side
Downy Birch

Betula pubescens Ehrh.
Downy Birch
Fig. 766 - see p. 198/199

- Leaves 3-5cm long, broadly ovate to rhombic in outline and with the margin unequally doubly serrate/dentate; entire at the base of the blade
- Shortly pointed at the end
- Leaf-stalk 1-2cm long and somewhat hairy
- Dark green above, becoming glabrous; finely downy beneath in the axils of the larger veins

M_4M_4 Leaves very finely serrate and 5-14cm long (Fig. 767) — Correct, see N_6; Wrong, see $M_4M_4M_4$

Rhamnus - Buckthorn

N_6

767 Upper side
Alpine Buckthorn

Rhamnus alpinus L.
ssp. alpinus
Alpine Buckthorn
Fig. 767 - see p. 202/203

- Leaves 5-14cm long, elliptic to ovate in outline and with the margin finely serrate; often crenate in the lower part
- With an abrupt short point at the end
- Leaf-stalk 8-15mm long
- Shiny dark green and glabrous above; somewhat paler green beneath and with 5-20 primary lateral veins on each side of the midrib

$M_4M_4M_4$ Leaves simply and/or doubly serrate and 3-12cm long (Fig. 768-770) — Correct, see N_7, N_7N_7 or $N_7N_7N_7$; Wrong, back to M_4

Alnus - Alder

N_7

768 Under side
Green Alder

Alnus viridis (Chaix) DC.
Green Alder
Fig. 768 - see p. 200/201

- Leaves 3-6cm long, elliptic to broadly ovate in outline and with the margin simply, doubly or irregularly serrate
- Obtuse at the end with small teeth or a point
- Leaf-stalk 1-2cm long and grooved
- Dark green and glabrous above; paler green beneath; with 5-10 clearly visible lateral veins

Carpinus - Hornbeam

N_7N_7

769 Under side
Hornbeam

Carpinus betulus L.
Hornbeam
Fig. 769 - see p. 200/201

- Leaves 4-12cm long, ovate to oblong-ovate in outline and with the margin finely simply and doubly serrate
- Rather obtuse or often pointed at the end
- Leaf-stalk 5-15mm long and often reddish above
- Deep rich green and glabrous above; paler green beneath and slightly hairy in the axils of the veins; folded into pleats between the lateral veins

Ostrya – Hop Hornbeam

N_7
N_7
N_7

770 Under side
Hop Hornbeam

Ostrya carpinifolia Scop.
Hop Hornbeam
Fig. 770 – see p. 200/201

- Leaves 5–12cm long, ovate-oblong or ovate in outline and with the margin sharply simply and doubly serrate
- Pointed at the end
- Leaf-stalk 4–12mm long
- Dark green above; yellowish green beneath and somewhat hairy in the axils of the veins; not undulate between the veins

---

K_3K_3 Lateral veins of the leaves curving towards the tip

Correct, see **L_5** or **L_5L_5**
Wrong, back to **K_3** (p. 114)

L_5 Lateral veins on the under side of the leaves appearing distinctly pale yellow to whitish yellow (Fig. 771, 772)

Correct, see **M_5** or **M_5M_5**
Wrong, see **L_5L_5**

Morus – Mulberry

M_5

771 Under side
White Mulberry

Morus alba L.
White Mulberry
Fig. 771 – see p. 200/201

- Leaves 7–18cm long and varied in outline; often without lobes and therefore broadly ovate
- Shortly pointed at the end or rounded and with a short terminal tooth
- Leaf-stalk 2–5cm long, grooved above and somewhat hairy
- Dark green above and smooth or slightly rough; bluish green beneath and hairy on the veins

---

M_5
M_5

772 Under side
Black Mulberry

Morus nigra L.
Black Mulberry
Fig. 772 – see p. 200/201

- Leaves 6–18cm long and varied in outline; often broadly ovate to heart-shaped and with a coarsely serrate margin
- Tipped by a finer, longer point than in the White Mulberry
- Leaf-stalk 1–2cm long
- Shiny dark green above and very roughly hairy; paler bluish green and hairy beneath

---

L_5L_5 Lateral veins beneath not distinctly pale yellow to whitish yellow, but pale to bluish green

Correct, see **M_6**, **M_6M_6** or **$M_6M_6M_6$** (p. 117)
Wrong, back to **L_5**

M_6 Leaves elliptic to mostly roundish in outline, 2–6cm long and obtuse or with an abrupt short point at the end (Fig. 773, 774)

Correct, see **N_8** or **N_8N_8**
Wrong, see **M_6M_6** or **$M_6M_6M_6$** (p. 117)

Prunus – Cherry

N_8

773 Under side
St Lucie Cherry

Prunus mahaleb L.
St Lucie Cherry
Fig. 773 – see p. 202/203

- Leaves 3–6cm long, broadly ovate to roundish in outline and with a crenate-serrate margin
- Obtuse or shortly pointed at the end
- Leaf-stalk 1–2cm long and usually without glands
- Shiny dark green and glabrous above; bluish green beneath and often somewhat hairy on the midrib

---

Rhamnus – Buckthorn

N_8
N_8

774 Upper side
Dwarf Buckthorn

Rhamnus pumila
(Turra) W. Vent
Dwarf Buckthorn
Fig. 774 – see p. 202/203

- Leaves 2–5cm long, elliptic, obovate or roundish in outline and with the margin very finely crenate-serrate
- With a short abrupt point at the end
- Leaf-stalk 4–9mm long
- Dark green and glabrous above; paler green beneath and somewhat hairy on the veins

---

M_6M_6 Leaves narrowly elliptic to broadly elliptic in outline, 2–12cm long and very shortly pointed, obtuse or rounded at the end

Correct, see **N_9** or **N_9N_9** (P. 116)
Wrong, see **$M_6M_6M_6$** (p. 117)

N_9 Leaves narrowly wedge-shaped at the base of the blade (Fig. 775, 776)

Correct, see **O** (p. 116) or **OO** (p. 116)
Wrong, see **N_9N_9** (p. 116)

Prunus - Cherry

O

775 Upper side
Dwarf Russian Almond

Prunus tenella Batsch
Dwarf Russian Almond
Fig. 775 - see p. 202/203

- Leaves 3-7cm long, narrowly elliptic in outline and with the margin finely and regularly serrate/dentate
- Pointed at the end
- Leaf-stalk 5-15mm long
- Shiny dark green above and pale green beneath; both sides glabrous; only the midrib really prominent

---

OO

776 Upper side
Plum

Prunus domestica L.
ssp. domestica
Plum
Fig. 776 - see p. 202/203

- Leaves 3-10cm long, elliptic or obovate in outline and with the margin finely serrate and crenate
- Rounded, obtuse or pointed at the end
- Leaf-stalk 10-15mm long
- Dark green above and later glabrous; pale green beneath and often remaining hairy for a long time

---

N_9N_9 Leaves broadly wedge-shaped or rounded at the base of the blade — Correct, see **O_1** or **O_1O_1**; Wrong, back to **N_9** (p. 115)

O_1 Leaf-stalk distinctly reddish above (Fig. 777) — Correct, see **P**; Wrong, see **O_1O_1**

Prunus - Cherry

P

777 Upper side
Blackthorn

Prunus spinosa L.
Blackthorn, Sloe
Fig. 777 - see p. 204/205

- Leaves 2-5cm long, broadly lanceolate to oblong-elliptic in outline and with the margin serrate and in places crenate
- Obtuse or shortly pointed at the end
- Leaf-stalk 5-12mm long and often reddish above
- Dark green above and pale green beneath; hairy when young

O_1O_1 Leaf-stalk not or only slightly reddish above — Correct, see **P_1** or **P_1P_1**; Wrong, back to **O_1**

P_1 Leaf-stalk 1-3cm long, glabrous, slightly grooved above, and with the veins very strongly curved towards the tip of the blade (Fig. 778) — Correct, see **Q**; Wrong, see **P_1P_1**

Rhamnus - Buckthorn

Q

778 Upper side
Buckthorn

Rhamnus catharticus L.
Buckthorn
Fig. 778 - see p. 202/203

- Leaves 4-7cm long, elliptic to roundish in outline and with the margin finely crenate-serrate
- Usually with a short point at the end
- Leaf-stalk 1-3cm long and slightly grooved above
- Dull dark green above and medium bluish green beneath; both sides usually glabrous; with 2-4 curved lateral veins each side of the midrib

---

P_1P_1

779 Under side
Wayfaring Tree

Leaf-stalk at most 1cm long; if longer, then densely grey-felted (Fig. 779); veins not as in **P_1**

Correct, see **Q_1**, **Q_1Q_1** (p. 117) or **$Q_1Q_1Q_1$** (p. 117)
Wrong, back to **P_1**

Viburnum - Viburnum

Q_1

780 Upper side
Wayfaring Tree

Viburnum lantara L.
Wayfaring Tree
Fig. 780 - see p. 206/207

- Leaves 5-12cm long, ovate to oblong-ovate in outline and with the margin regularly and finely toothed
- Pointed at the end
- Leaf-stalk up to 15mm long and densely felted
- Medium to dark green above and somewhat wrinkled; medium green beneath and densely covered with stellate hairs

Sorbus - Whitebeam

Q_1
Q_1

781 Upper side
False Medlar

Sorbus chamaemespilus (L.) Crantz
False Medlar

Fig. 781 - see p. 204/205

- Leaves 3-8cm long, narrowly elliptic to elliptic in outline, with their greatest breadth usually below the middle and the margins simply and finely serrate
- Obtuse or weakly pointed at the end
- Leaf-stalk 5-10mm long
- Shiny dark green above and paler green beneath; both sides glabrous; forms with the leaves felted beneath are hybrids

Mespilus - Medlar

Q_1
Q_1
Q_1

782 Upper side
Medlar

Mespilus germanica L.
Medlar

Fig. 782 - see p. 206/207

- Leaves 5-12cm long, oblong-elliptic to obovate in outline and with the margin finely serrate/dentate; in places also entire
- Very shortly pointed at the end
- Leaf-stalk up to 10mm long or the leaf sessile
- Dull green above, somewhat downy and slightly wrinkled; pale to greyish green beneath and with whitish matted woolly hairs; veins above deeply impressed

M_6M_6 M_6	Leaves narrowly to broadly elliptic or ovate in outline, 4-12cm long and usually with a long point at the end (Fig. 785-793)	Correct, see **N_{10}** or **$N_{10}N_{10}$** (p. 118) Wrong, back to **M_6** (p. 115)

N_{10}	Most leaves with 1-4 greenish or reddish nectar-glands on the leaf-stalk (Fig. 783, 784)	Correct, see **O_2**, **O_2O_2** or **$O_2O_2O_2$** Wrong, see **$N_{10}N_{10}$** (p. 118)

783
Nectar-glands
Wild Cherry

784
Nectar-glands
Bird Cherry

O_2	Margins of leaves very finely and regularly serrate; teeth shorter than 0.7mm (Fig. 785)	Correct, see **P_2** Wrong, see **O_2O_2**

Prunus - Cherry

P_2

785 Upper side
Bird Cherry

Prunus padus L.
Bird Cherry

Fig. 785 - see p. 204/205

- Leaves 5-12cm long, oblong-elliptic to obovate in outline and with the margin finely and regularly serrate
- With a fine, slender point at the end
- Leaf-stalk up to 2cm long, red above and with 1-3 usually greenish nectar-glands
- Dull dark green above and pale or bluish green beneath, both sides glabrous

O_2O_2	Margins of leaves finely serrate and in places crenate (Fig. 786)	Correct, see **P_3** Wrong, see **$O_2O_2O_2$**

Prunus - Cherry

P_3

786 Upper side
Sour Cherry

Prunus cerasus L.
Sour Cherry

Fig. 786 - see p. 204/205

- Leaves 4-12cm long, elliptic to ovate in outline, flat, somewhat leathery, and with the margin finely serrate and in places crenate
- Pointed at the end
- Leaf-stalk 1-3cm long and usually with green nectar-glands
- Shiny dark green above and pale green beneath; veins beneath distinctly prominent

O_2O_2 O_2	Margins of leaves regularly or irregularly rather coarsely serrate (Fig. 787, 788)	Correct, see **P_4** or **P_4P_4** (p. 118) Wrong, back to **O_2**

Prunus - Cherry

P_4

787 Upper side
Japanese Cherry

Prunus serrulata Lindl.
Japanese Cherry

Fig. 787 - see p. 204/205

- Leaves 8-14cm long, narrowly ovate in outline and with the margin sharply and irregularly serrate
- With a long point at the end
- Leaf-stalk 2-4cm long, reddish above and usually with 2-4 nectar-glands
- Shiny dark green above and bluish green beneath; both sides glabrous; veins distinctly prominent

P_4
P_4

788 Upper side
Wild Cherry

Prunus avium L.
Wild Cherry
Fig. 788 – see p. 204/205

- Leaves 6–15cm long, oblong-ovate to obovate in outline with an irregularly serrate margin
- With a slender point at the end
- Leaf-stalk 2–4cm long with 2–4 red nectar-glands
- Dark green and glabrous above; green beneath and finely hairy when young; small tufts of hair in the axils of the larger veins

---

N_{10}
N_{10} Leaves without nectar-glands on the leaf-stalk (Fig. 789–793)

Correct, see **O_3**, **O_3O_3**, **$O_3O_3O_3$** or **$O_3O_3O_3O_3$**
Wrong, back to **N_{10}** (p. 117)

789 Under side **Spindle Tree**

Euonymus – Spindle Tree

O_3

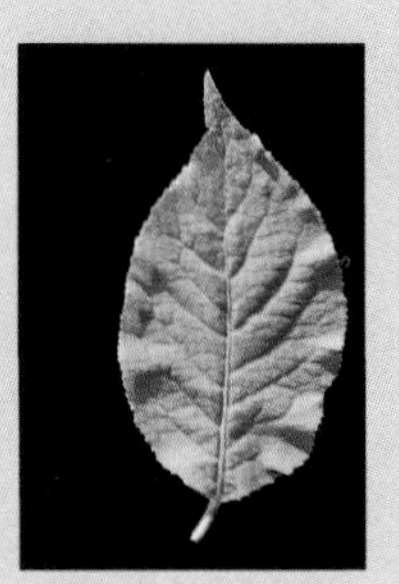

790 Upper side
Spindle Tree

Euonymus (Evonymus) europaeus L.
Spindle Tree
Fig. 790 – see p. 206/207

- Leaves 3–8cm long, elliptic to ovate in outline and very finely and regularly serrate
- Narrowly pointed at the end
- Leaf-stalk 5–9mm long and grooved
- Medium to dark green above and pale bluish green beneath; both sides glabrous

---

Forsythia – Forsythia

O_3
O_3

791 Upper side
Hybrid Forsythia

Forsythia x intermedia Zab.
Hybrid Forsythia
Fig. 791 – see p. 206/207

- Leaves 6–11cm long, lanceolate to oblong-ovate in outline (sometimes also tripartite on luxuriant growth) and with the margin irregularly serrate and dentate
- Pointed at the end
- Leaf-stalk 1–2cm long and usually grooved above
- Dark green above and paler green to pale greyish green beneath; both sides glabrous

---

O_3
O_3
O_3

792 Upper side
European Forsythia

Forsythia europaea Deg. et Bald.
European Forsythia
Fig. 792 – see p. 206/207

- Leaves 5–8cm long, narrowly elliptic to narrowly ovate in outline and usually finely serrate in the upper part
- Pointed at the end
- Leaf-stalk 5–10mm long and grooved above
- Dark green above and paler green beneath; both sides glabrous

---

O_3
O_3
O_3
O_3

793 Upper side
Green Forsythia

Forsythia viridissima Lindl.
Green Forsythia
Fig. 793 – see p. 206/207

- Leaves 4–14cm long, lanceolate to narrowly elliptic in outline and with the margin finely serrate/dentate above the middle
- Pointed at the end
- Leaf-stalk 5–30mm long and usually grooved above
- Dark green above and pale green beneath; both sides glabrous

---

H_1H_1
H_1H_1 Leaves spathulate (1–4cm long), narrowly to broadly lanceolate and white, greyish green or greenish beneath

Correct, see **I_3** or **I_3I_3** (p. 119)
Wrong, back to **H_1** (p. 110)

I_3 Leaves 1–4cm long, very narrowly wedge-shaped at the base and with the margin fringed with spreading, white hairs 0.5–1.5mm in length (Fig. 794)

Correct, see **K_4**
Wrong, see **I_3I_3** (p. 119)

K_4

794 Upper side
Black Bearberry

Arctostaphylos alpinus (L.) Spreng.
Black Bearberry
Fig. 794 – see p. 208/209

- Leaves 1–4cm long, spathulate or narrowly obovate in outline and with the margin finely and closely serrate; entire towards the base
- Obtuse at the end
- Leaf-stalk only a few mm long or the leaf sessile
- Dark green and convex above; whitish green beneath with dark green veins

I_3I_3 Leaves without long, spreading, white hairs along the margin (Fig. 795–799)
Correct, see **K_5** or **K_5K_5**
Wrong, back to **I_3** (p. 118)

K_5 Leaves green to bluish green beneath (Fig. 795, 796)
Correct, see **L_6** or **L_6L_6**
Wrong, see **K_5K_5**

L_6 Midrib on both sides very pale yellowish white and under side of leaf pale bluish green (Fig. 795)
Correct, see **M_7**
Wrong, see **L_6L_6**

Prunus – Cherry

M_7

795 Under side
Almond

Prunus dulcis (Mill.) D. A. Webb
Almond
Fig. 795 – see p. 208/209
- Leaves 4–12cm long, lanceolate to oblong-ovate and with the margin very finely serrate/dentate
- Obtuse or pointed at the end
- Leaf-stalk 10–25mm long
- Medium to dark green above and pale bluish green beneath; both sides glabrous

---

L_6L_6 Midrib on both sides pale green and under side of leaf medium bluish green (Fig. 796)
Correct, see **M_8**
Wrong, back to **L_6**

Prunus – Cherry

M_8

796 Under side
Peach

Prunus persica (L.) Batsch
Peach
Fig. 796 – see p. 208/209
- Leaves 5–15cm long, narrowly to broadly lanceolate in outline and with a finely serrate/dentate margin
- With a long point at the end
- Leaf-stalk 5–15mm long
- Shiny dark green above and medium green to medium bluish green beneath; both sides glabrous

---

K_5K_5 Leaves greyish green or white beneath
Correct, see **L_7** or **L_7L_7**
Wrong, back to **K_5**

L_7 Leaves only serrate in the upper part; entire in the lower part (Fig. 797)
Correct, see **M_9**
Wrong, see **L_7L_7**

Salix – Willow

M_9

797 Under side
Purple Willow

Salix purpurea L.
Purple Willow
Fig. 797 – see p. 208/209
- Leaves 5–10cm long, lanceolate in outline with their greatest breadth usually in the upper third and finely serrate towards the tip; entire in the lower part
- Shortly pointed at the end
- Leaf-stalk 5–8mm long and often tinged red
- Bluish green and glabrous above; pale bluish green beneath and also glabrous

---

L_7L_7 Leaves coarsely sinuate serrate along the whole margin (Fig. 798) or finely and regularly serrate/dentate (Fig. 799)
Correct, see **M_{10}** or **$M_{10}M_{10}$**
Wrong, back to **L_7**

Salix – Willow

M_{10}

798 Under side
Crack Willow

Salix fragilis L.
Crack Willow
Fig. 798 – see p. 208/209
- Leaves 5–16cm long, oblong-lanceolate in outline, usually broadest in the lower third and coarsely sinuately serrate
- With a very long, fine point at the end
- Leaf-stalk up to 1cm long
- Dark green and slightly shiny above; with silky hairs at first beneath, later pale or bluish green

---

M_{10}
M_{10}

799 Under side
White Willow

Salix alba L.
White Willow
Fig. 799 – see p. 208/209
- Leaves 5–10cm long, narrowly lanceolate to lanceolate in outline, the upper part often curved to one side and the margin finely and regularly serrate/dentate
- Narrowly and finely pointed at the end
- Leaf-stalk 5–10mm long
- Both sides with a covering of silvery hairs at first; later dark green and almost glabrous above; remaining silvery white beneath

800 ***Taxus baccata* - Yew**
Evergreen, to 20m high, very slow growing, with green shoots

Taxus baccata L.
Yew (with many forms)
Taxaceae - Yew family p. 65

Size: 1-3cm long and 2-3cm broad

Form of needle: Linear, flattened, decurrent on the twig, slightly crescent-shaped and always standing singly; life-span 3-8 years

Stalk: 2-3mm long and green

End of needle: Finely pointed

Base of needle: Narrowed to the stalk and with the base broadly decurrent on the twig

Margin of needle: Entire

Upper/under side: Shiny dark green above with a prominent midrib; pale or yellowish green beneath, with a clearly visible midrib and on each side of it a broad, rather inconspicuous band of stomata

Arrangement on the shoot: Spirally arranged on long shoots

Distribution: From the colline to the montane zone; usually on steep slopes and in gorges in open to shady beech, fir, ash or maple woods

801 ***Sequoia sempervirens* - Coast Redwood** *Evergreen tree, 65-100m high, with green shoots, irregularly forked*

Sequoia sempervirens
(D. Don) Endl.
Coast Redwood
Taxodiaceae - Swamp Cypress family p. 65

Size: On long shoots 6-10mm long, on short shoots 4-20mm long, and 1-2.5mm broad

Form of needle: Linear to lanceolate, flattened, straight or slightly curved, becoming gradually smaller towards the end of the shoot and with a life-span of 2-4 years

Stalk: Sessile

End of needle: Abruptly pointed

Base of needle: With the whole breadth of the needle decurrent for several mm on the shoot

Margin of needle: Entire

Upper/under side: Dark green above and pale green on the younger short shoots; medium green beneath on the margins and in the middle, with 2 whitish bands of stomata in between

Arrangement on the shoot: Needles arranged spirally

Distribution: Native in the lowlands and hilly areas of the damp, misty coastal region of southern Oregon

802 ***Araucaria araucana* - Chile Pine**
Evergreen conifer up to 30m high, with whorls of thick branches

Araucaria araucana
(Mol.) K. Koch
Chile Pine, Monkey Puzzle
Araucariaceae - Chile Pine family p. 65

Size: 2.5-5cm long and 1-2.5cm broad

Form of needle: Needle-shaped, triangular, stiff, rather coarse, thickish, and pointing towards the end of the shoot; life-span from 10-15 years and later falling with the dead twigs

Stalk: Sessile

End of needle: Ending in a sharp, spiny point

Base of needle: Broadened considerably at the base and somewhat decurrent on the shoot

Margin of needle: Entire

Upper/under side: Both sides shiny dark green, glabrous and with parallel veins

Arrangement on the shoot: Needles spirally arranged and overlapping

Distribution: Native in the Andes of Chile and Argentina; frequently planted as a decorative tree in parks in the Mediterranean region; fine specimens in Ireland and England

803 ***Abies alba* - Common Silver Fir**
Evergreen tree, up to 50m high, with greyish brown, very hairy twigs

Abies alba Mill.
Common Silver Fir
Pinaceae - Pine family p. 58, 59, 66

Size: Up to 3cm long and 2-3cm broad

Form of needle: Flattened, linear, not prickly, without sheaths and, after falling, leaving behind broadly elliptic to circular scars; life-span 7-11 years

Stalk: Sessile

End of needle: Obtuse or distinctly emarginate

Base of needle: Narrowing in the lower part and attached to the twig by a circular base

Margin of needle: Entire

Upper/under side: Dark green above, the fine lines of stomata (if present) only at the tips and with a slightly impressed midrib; pale to medium green beneath with 2 distinct, silvery white bands of stomata; midrib somewhat raised

Arrangement on the shoot: Needles spirally arranged

Distribution: An important forest tree from the hill to the montane zone, forming stands in shady places where the air is very moist

804 ***Abies nordmanniana* - Caucasian Fir**
Evergreen conifer, 30-50m high, with olive-green shoots, grooved at first

Abies nordmanniana
(Stev.) Spach
Caucasian Fir
Pinaceae - Pine family p. 66

Size: 2-3.5cm long and 2-2.5mm broad

Form of needle: Linear, stiff, coarse, pointing slightly towards the end of the short and distinctly furrowed

Stalk: Sessile

End of needle: Obtuse, rounded or slightly emarginate

Base of needle: Narrowing in the lower part of the needle, twisted, and attached to the twig by a broadly elliptic to circular base

Margin of needle: Entire

Upper/under side: Dark green above, without bands of stomata and grooved in the middle; striped beneath (dark green stripes) with 2 broad bands of stomata

Arrangement on the shoot: Needles closely set and arranged spirally

Distribution: In the western Caucasus and mountains of the Pontic region between 900m and 2200m, associated with the Oriental Spruce and Oriental Beech; a valuable park tree in central Europe

805 ***Abies veitchii* - Veitch's Fir**
Evergreen conifer, 15-40m high, with greyish green and very hairy young shoots

Abies veitchii Lindl.
Veitch's Fir
Pinaceae - Pine family p. 66

Size: 1-2.5cm long and up to 2mm broad

Form of needle: Linear, soft, and often pointing diagonally forwards, brush-like, so that the chalky white undersides are visible

Stalk: Sessile

End of needle: Flat and distinctly emarginate

Base of needle: Narrowing in the lower part of the needle, slightly curved, and attached to the twig by an elliptic or circular base

Margin of needle: Entire

Upper/under side: Medium to dark green above, without bands of stomata and slightly grooved in the middle; striped beneath (pale to medium green stripes) and with 2 broad, chalky white bands of stomata

Arrangement on the shoot: Needles arranged spirally

Distribution: Native in Japan; discovered in Japan in 1860 by J. G. Veitch and brought to England in 1861; hardy in Europe and occasionally planted in parks

806 ***Abies procera* - Noble Fir**
Evergreen conifer, up to 80m high in its native country, with olive-green to brown shoots

Abies procera Rehd.
Noble Fir

Pinaceae - Pine family p.66

Size: 2.5-3.5cm long and 1.5mm broad

Form of needle: Linear, coarse, densely crowded and clearly curved upwards

End of needle: Usually obtuse

Base of needle: Needles with their base appressed to the twig and then curving abruptly upwards

Margin of needle: Entire

Upper/under side: Greyish green above, flattened and grooved, with lines of stomata that extend to the base as broad bands; with 2 greyish longitudinal bands beneath

Arrangement on the shoot: Needles densely crowded and arranged spirally

Distribution: Native in Pacific North America; hardy in central Europe; frequently planted in parks and gardens; brought to Europe in 1830

807 ***Pseudotsuga menziesii* - Douglas Fir**
Evergreen conifer, 50-60m high, with yellowish to olive- green, hairy shoots

Pseudotsuga menziesii (Mirbel) Franco
Douglas Fir

Pinaceae - Pine family p. 66

Size: 1.8-3.5cm long and 1-1.5mm broad

Form of needle: Straight or slightly curved, flat, leathery, soft, leaving behind when it falls a raised, cushion-like scar, and smelling of orange when rubbed

Stalk: Small, and standing out at an angle from the twig

End of needle: Obtuse or somewhat pointed

Margin of needle: Entire

Upper/under side: Dull medium to dark green and furrowed above; with 2 narrow silvery grey bands of stomata beneath

Arrangement on the shoot: Needles densely crowded and spirally arranged

Distribution: Native only in the mountains near the western coast of North America; introduced into England in 1827 by D. Douglas; planted in parks and widely cultivated for afforestation

808 ***Juniperus communis* - Common Juniper** *Evergreen, column-shaped shrub or tree up to 15m with triangular shoots*

Juniperus communis L. ssp. *communis*
Common Juniper

Cupressaceae - Cypress family p. 67

Size: 1-2cm long and 1-2mm broad

Form of needle: Linear, straight, not decurrent on the shoot and rather sharp

Stalk: Sessile

End of needle: Sharply pointed

Base of needle: Attached to the twig by a broad base and usually standing out at a right-angle

Margin of needle: Entire

Upper/under side: With a broad, white central band above and slightly grooved; shiny green and keeled beneath

Arrangement on the shoot: Needles arranged in whorls of 3

Distribution: From the hills to the montane zone; frequently on sunny, dry pastures, on rocks, and in open woods and heaths

809 ***Juniperus nana* - Dwarf Juniper**
Evergreen, prostrate, dwarf shrub, 20-50cm high, with short, stout branches

Juniperus communis L. ssp. *alpina* Celak (*J. nana* Willd.)
Dwarf Juniper

Cupressaceae - Cypress family p. 67

Size: 4-8mm long and 1-2mm broad

Form of needle: Usually crescent-shaped, linear and attached to the shoot by a broad base; whorls of needles densely crowded and only about 1-3mm apart

Stalk: Sessile

End of needle: Shortly pointed; not prickly

Margin of needle: Entire

Upper/under side: Dark green on the margins above with a broad band of stomata; dark green and slightly keeled beneath

Arrangement on the shoot: Needles arranged in whorls

Distribution: In the subalpine zone; in dwarf shrub communities, screes and on sunny slopes; a strongly cold-resistant mountain plant

810 ***Juniperus chinensis* - Chinese Juniper**
Evergreen conifer, 5-20m high, originating in China, Japan and Mongolia

Juniperus chinensis L.
Chinese Juniper 'Blaauw'

Cupressaceae - Cypress family p. 67

Size: Juvenile leaves 6-10mm long and 1mm broad; adult leaves 3-5mm long and 1-2.5mm broad

Form of leaves: Juvenile leaves needle-like, spreading at an acute angle; adult leaves scale-like, rhombic, densely crowded and overlapping each other

Stalk: Sessile

End of needle: Juvenile leaves spiny-pointed; adult leaves obtuse or pointed

Margin of needle: Entire

Upper/under side: Juvenile leaves with 2 separate bluish green bands of stomata above and dark green beneath; adult leaves with 2 indistinct stomatic areas at the base

Arrangement on the shoot: Needle-like leaves usually in whorls of 3; but also opposite

Distribution: Brought to England in 1767 by W. Kerr; in England up to 18m high; planted in parks and gardens

811 ***Picea abies* - Norway Spruce**
Evergreen conifer, 30-55m high, with dull reddish brown, fairly stout shoots

Picea abies (L.) Karst. (*P. excelsa* (Lam.) Link)
Norway Spruce

Pinaceae - Pine family p. 58, 59, 67

Size: 0.5-2.5cm long and 1mm broad

Form of needle: Fairly rigid, almost square in cross-section, pointing sideways and upwards from the twig and often curved, crescent-shaped; life-span 5-7 years

Stalk: With a very short, brownish stalk

End of needle: Rather obtuse to pointed

Base of needle: Only slightly narrowed towards the small stalk

Margin of needle: Entire

Upper/under side: Dark green on all sides with fine lines of stomata

Arrangement on the shoot: Needles spirally arranged

Distribution: Originally subalpine; planted in afforestation from the hill to the montane zone; shallow rooting, so likely to be blown down in gales

812 ***Picea orientalis* – Oriental Spruce**
Evergreen conifer, 40–50m high, with pale brown shoots, densely covered with crisped hairs

Picea orientalis (L.) Link
Oriental Spruce
Pinaceae – Pine family p. 67

Size: 5–11mm long and 1–1.3mm broad

Form of needle: 4-angled, almost square in cross-section, densely crowded, straight or somewhat curved and shortly stalked

Stalk: 0.3–0.8mm long, brownish with slightly brownish hairs

End of needle: Obtuse

Base of needle: Narrowed towards the base

Margin of needle: Entire

Colour: Shiny dark green; with white lines of stomata on all sides

Arrangement on the shoot: Spirally arranged

Distribution: Native in the Caucasus and northern Asia Minor between 600m and 2100m; occasionally planted in parks

813 ***Picea omorika* – Serbian Spruce**
Evergreen conifer, 30–35m high, with light brown shoots covered with brown hairs

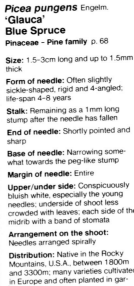

Picea omorika (Panc.) Purk.
Serbian Spruce
Pinaceae – Pine family p. 68

Size: 1–1.9cm long and 1.5–2mm broad

Form of needle: Distinctly flattened, somewhat curved, densely crowded and pointing towards the end of the shoot, keeled above and beneath; life-span 10–12 years

Stalk: Very short and brownish in colour

End of needle: Obtuse or somewhat pointed but not prickly

Base of needle: Rounded

Margin of needle: Entire

Upper/under side: Pale green above at first, later dark green; clearly visible bands of stomata on both sides of the keel beneath

Arrangement on the shoot: Spirally arranged

Distribution: Native in S.E. Europe; seeds first reached central Europe about 1890; planted as an ornamental tree in gardens and parks

814 ***Picea pungens* – Blue Spruce**
Evergreen conifer, 25–35m high, with pale to orange-brown, glabrous shoots

Picea pungens Engelm. 'Glauca'
Blue Spruce
Pinaceae – Pine family p. 68

Size: 1.5–3cm long and up to 1.5mm thick

Form of needle: Often slightly sickle-shaped, rigid and 4-angled; life-span 4–8 years

Stalk: Remaining as a 1mm long stump after the needle has fallen

End of needle: Shortly pointed and sharp

Base of needle: Narrowing somewhat towards the peg-like stump

Margin of needle: Entire

Upper/under side: Conspicuously bluish white, especially the young needles; underside of shoot less crowded with leaves; each side of the midrib with a band of stomata

Arrangement on the shoot: Needles arranged spirally

Distribution: Native in the Rocky Mountains, U.S.A., between 1800m and 3300m; many varieties cultivated in Europe and often planted in gardens and parks

815 ***Tsuga canadensis* – Eastern Hemlock**
Evergreen conifer, 20–30m high, with densely brownish hairy shoots

Tsuga canadensis (L.) Carr.
Eastern Hemlock, Canadian Hemlock
Pinaceae – Pine family p. 68

Size: 7–15mm long and 1.5–2.5mm broad

Form of needle: Flattened, standing out on both sides of the twig, narrowed towards the tip and of varying size; needles of the middle row frequently twisted and smaller than the needles at the side

Stalk: Needles with a distinctly yellowish white stalk, which is usually somewhat appressed to the twig

End of needle: Rounded

Base of needle: Rounded or truncate

Margin of needle: Finely serrate; teeth set far apart

Upper/under side: Shiny dark green above; bluish green beneath with 2 silvery bands of stomata

Arrangement on the shoot: Spirally arranged

Distribution: Native in eastern North America; reached Europe in 1730 and since then has been planted in parks and occasionally woods

816 ***Metasequoia glyptostroboides* – Dawn Redwood** *Deciduous conifer, 10–30m high, with slender, reddish or brownish green shoots*

Metasequoia glyptostroboides Hu et Cheng
Dawn Redwood
Taxodiaceae – Swamp Cypress family p. 68

Size: 1–4cm long and 2–3mm broad

Form of needle: Linear in outline, flattened, noticeably soft; needles on short shoots somewhat curved, practically opposite each other and falling in the autumn with the short shoot; needles on the long shoots falling singly in autumn

Stalk: 0.5–1mm long

End of needle: Rounded or with quite a short point

Base of needle: Rounded

Margin of needle: Entire

Upper/under side: Both sides pale green at first; later dark green above and somewhat paler green beneath; with an indistinct middle band beneath

Arrangement on the shoot: Spirally arranged on long shoots, opposite on short shoots

Distribution: Native in S.W. China; discovered in 1941 and in cultivation in Europe since 1948; planted in parks

817 ***Taxodium distichum* – Swamp Cypress**
Evergreen conifer, 20–50m high, with conspicuously slender shoots

Taxodium distichum (L.) L. C. Rich
Swamp Cypress
Taxodiaceae – Swamp Cypress family p. 68

Size: 1–2cm long and 1–2mm broad

Form of needle: Needles on the short shoots in regular ranks, very shortly stalked or sessile, linear and flattened

Stalk: Sessile or shortly stalked

End of needle: Somewhat pointed

Shoot: Long shoots becoming woody, brown to reddish brown, with a slight bloom, glabrous, needles separate and falling singly in autumn; short shoots green, up to 1mm thick, not becoming woody and falling together with the needles in autumn

Margin of needle: Entire

Upper/under side: Fresh green at first, later pale to medium green and rust-brown in autumn; with fine longitudinal bands beneath

Arrangement on the shoot: Arranged spirally on long shoots and alternately in 2 ranks on short shoots.

Distribution: Native in the Florida and Mississippi region; reached Europe in 1640; has long been planted as a park tree in Europe

818 ***Pinus mugo*** **– Mountain Pine**
An evergreen shrub with one or more stems or a tree up to 25m high

Pinus mugo Turra
Mountain Pine

Pinaceae – Pine family p. 69

Size: 2–8cm long and 1–3mm broad

Form of needle: Stiff, straight or somewhat crescent-shaped, semi-circular in cross-section and densely crowded on the shoot; sheaths at the base of young needles up to 1cm long and brownish white, equally short at the base of needles on older shoots; life-span 5–10 years

Stalk: Sessile

End of needle: Shortly pointed, not prickly

Margin of needle: Needles finely serrate on the margin (somewhat rough to the touch if rubbed towards the base)

Upper/under side: Dark green on both sides with numerous fine lines of stomata

Arrangement on the shoot: Needles on short shoots in pairs which are arranged spirally

Distribution: In the subalpine zone; a species with a wide ecological distribution; on sunny slopes, in shady, north-facing localities with prolonged covering of snow, and one particular form, on raised bogs

819 ***Pinus sylvestris*** **– Scots Pine**
Evergreen conifer up to 40m high with glabrous, light brown, grooved shoots

Pinus sylvestris L.
Scots Pine

Pinaceae – Pine family p. 60, 61, 69

Size: 3–7cm long and up to 2mm broad

Form of needle: Stiff, usually distinctly twisted, in pairs on short shoots, semi-circular in cross-section, somewhat flattened and clustered at the end of the shoot; sheaths at the base 0.3–0.6cm long and persistent; life-span 2–7 years according to variety

Stalk: Sessile

End of needle: Pointed

Margin of needle: Needles finely serrate on the margin (somewhat rough to the touch if rubbed towards the base)

Upper/under side: Bluish or greyish green above and beneath with very fine lines of stomata

Arrangement on the shoot: Needles on short shoots in pairs which are arranged spirally

Distribution: From the hill to the subalpine zone; on the top of cliffs, marly screes, poor stony areas and poor, acid moorland; an important forest tree

820 ***Pinus leucodermis*** **– Bosnian Pine**
Evergreen conifer, 15–20m high, with the shoots glabrous and covered with a bloom at first

Pinus leucodermis Ant.
Bosnian Pine

Pinaceae – Pine family p. 69

Size: 6–10cm long and 1–2mm broad

Form of needle: Robust, often somewhat curved, semi-circular in cross-section, stiff, in pairs on short shoots, and clustered at the ends of the shoots; sheaths at the base of the short shoots 0.5–1.5cm long, dark grey and persistent; life-span 5–7 years

Stalk: Sessile

End of needle: Pointed and only slightly prickly

Margin of needle: Needles with very fine, small teeth on the margin (somewhat rough to the touch if rubbed towards the base)

Upper/under side: Dark green on both sides; bands of stomata over the whole surface

Arrangement on the shoot: Needles on short shoots in pairs which are arranged spirally

Distribution: Widely distributed in the mountain regions (800–2200m) of the Balkans; occasionally planted in central Europe; discovered in 1864 by Fr. Maly, brought to Vienna in 1865

821 ***Pinus pinaster*** **– Maritime Pine**
Evergreen conifer, 20–30m high, with shoots dark brown at first

Pinus pinaster Ait.
Maritime Pine

Pinaceae – Pine family p. 69

Size: 13–25cm long and 1–2mm broad

Form of needle: Coarse, sharp, semi-circular in cross-section and in pairs on short shoots (in threes on younger trees); life-span 3–4 years; dark brown to black sheaths retained until the 3rd or 4th year

Stalk: Sessile

End of needle: Shortly pointed and sharp

Margin of needle: Needles with the pale yellow margin finely serrate (somewhat rough to the touch if rubbed towards the base)

Upper/under side: Dark or greyish green on both sides with numerous fine lines of stomata

Arrangement on the shoot: Needles on short shoots in pairs which are arranged spirally

Distribution: Native and widely distributed in the western Mediterranean region; occasionally planted in parks in central Europe

822 ***Pinus nigra*** **– Austrian Pine**
Evergreen conifer, 20–40m high, with stout, thick shoots

Pinus nigra Arnold ssp. *nigra*
Austrian Pine

Pinaceae – Pine family p. 69

Size: 10–18cm long and 1–2mm broad

Form of needle: Very robust, usually somewhat curved, semi-circular in cross-section, flattened, stiff, and in pairs on short shoots; sheaths at the base of the short shoots 0.8–1.5cm long, dark grey and persistent; life-span 4–8 years

Stalk: Sessile

End of needle: Pointed, fairly sharp

Margin of needle: Needles with fine, small teeth on the margin (rough to the touch if rubbed)

Upper/under side: Dark green on both sides; lines of stomata over the whole surface

Arrangement on the shoot: Needles on short shoots in pairs which are arranged spirally

Distribution: Native in southern and eastern Europe; an important forest-forming tree in the dry parts of the limestone mountains of central and southern Europe; quite commonly found in parks

823 ***Pinus aristata*** **– Bristle-cone Pine**
Evergreen conifer, 13–18m high, with reddish brown shoots

Pinus aristata Engelm.
Bristle-cone Pine

Pinaceae – Pine family p. 70

Size: 2.5–4cm long and 1mm broad

Form of needle: In fives on short shoots, often curved, with white spots of resin, and triangular in cross-section; sheaths at the base of the short shoots becoming torn, and persisting until the 4th year as reflexed lobes; life-span 12–15 years

Stalk: Sessile

End of needle: With a fine, slender point

Margin of needle: Entire

Upper/under side: Dark green above without stomatic lines; the other two sides medium green and with lines of stomata

Arrangement on the shoot: Needles on short shoots in bundles of 5 (more rarely 3 or 4) which are arranged spirally

Distribution: Native in western North America; discovered in 1861 and later brought to Europe; occasionally planted in parks; oldest trees 4700 years old

824 ***Pinus parviflora* - Japanese White Pine**
Evergreen conifer, 15–30m high (in Europe only 10m high), with pale grey shoots

Pinus parviflora Sieb. et Zucc.
Japanese White Pine

Pinaceae - Pine family p. 70

Size: 4–7cm long and 0.5–1cm broad

Form of needle: Distinctly curved and twisted, triangular in cross-section, in fives on short shoots and clustered, brush-like, at the ends of the twigs; sheaths at the base of the short shoots falling in the 1st year

Stalk: Sessile

End of needle: Obtuse

Margin of needle: Needles with the margin finely serrate (rough to the touch if rubbed towards the base)

Upper/under side: Dark bluish green above; the 2 inner surfaces with lines of stomata and therefore appearing bluish white

Arrangement on the shoot: Needles on the short shoots in bundles of 5 which are arranged spirally

Distribution: Native in Japan between 1300m and 1800m; introduced into England in 1861 by J. G. Veitch, planted in parks

825 ***Pinus strobus* - Weymouth Pine**
Evergreen conifer, 30–50m high, with shoots hairy at first

Pinus strobus L.
Weymouth Pine

Pinaceae - Pine family p. 70

Size: 5–12cm long

Form of needle: Rather slender and flexible, triangular in cross-section and in fives on short shoots; basal sheaths filling completely in the 1st year; life-span 3 years

Stalk: Sessile

End of needle: Pointed at the tip, not prickly

Margin of needle: Needles with very fine, small teeth on the margin (somewhat rough to the touch if rubbed towards the base)

Upper/under side: Pale green at first above, dark green in the 2nd year; greyish green on the inner surfaces, each with 2 or 3 bluish white lines of stomata

Arrangement on the shoot: Needles on the short shoots in bundles of 5 which are arranged spirally

Distribution: Native only in eastern North America; this species was introduced into Europe at the end of the 16th century; since then it has been cultivated for afforestation or planted as a park tree

826 ***Pinus cembra* - Arolla Pine**
Evergreen conifer, 10–25m high, with the shoots rust-red felted at first

Pinus cembra L.
Arolla Pine, Swiss Stone Pine

Pinaceae - Pine family p. 60, 61, 70

Size: 5–12cm long and 0.8–1.5mm broad

Form of needle: Fairly straight, triangular in cross-section, stiffly upright, in fives on the short shoots and clustered at the ends of the shoots; basal sheaths falling in the 1st year; life-span 4–6 years

Stalk: Sessile

End of needle: Needles with very fine, small teeth on the margin (somewhat rough to the touch if rubbed towards the base)

Upper/under side: Dark green above; greyish green on the inner surfaces, each with 3–5 bluish white lines of stomata

Arrangement on the shoot: Needles on the short shoots in bundles of 5 which are arranged spirally

Distribution: Native only in the central Alps and Carpathians between 1600m and 3000m; occasionally planted in the lowlands in parks

827 ***Sequoiadendron giganteum* - Sierra Redwood** *Evergreen conifer, 50–100m high, with coarse, very stiff, greenish grey shoots*

Sequoiadendron giganteum (Lindl.) Buchh.
Sierra Redwood, Wellingtonia

Taxodiaceae - Swamp Cypress family p. 71

Size: 3–6mm long (on main shoots up to 12mm) and 0.8–1.2mm broad

Form of needle: Awl-shaped to lanceolate or scale-like, usually spreading as they grow, and smelling of aniseed when rubbed; life-span 3–4 years; needles falling with shoots

Stalk: Sessile

End of needle: Pointed

Base of needle: Attached to the shoot by a broad base

Margin of needle: Entire

Upper/under side: Dark green above and somewhat rounded; dark green beneath and longitudinally furrowed; with fine, white lines of stomata over the whole surface

Arrangement on the shoot: Needles arranged spirally (forming 3 ranks)

Distribution: Native on the western slopes of the Sierra Nevada, California; introduced everywhere in Europe as an ornamental and park tree

828 ***Larix decidua* - European Larch**
Deciduous conifer, 25–40m high, with glabrous, straw-yellow to light brown shoots

Larix decidua Mill.
European Larch

Pinaceae - Pine family p. 36, 37, 70

Size: 1.5–3cm long and 0.5–0.9mm broad

Form of needle: Narrowly linear, soft, flattened, in groups of 30–40 on short shoots, and singly but fairly densely crowded on long shoots

Stalk: Sessile

End of needle: Obtuse or shortly pointed

Base of needle: Attached to the shoot by a broad base

Margin of needle: Entire

Upper/under side: Needles pale to dark green and becoming golden yellow before falling in autumn; 2 paler bands of stomata beneath

Arrangement on the shoot: Spirally arranged on long shoots; in groups of 30–40 on short shoots

Distribution: Native only in the subalpine zone of central European mountains; the characteristic species of the Arolla Pine-Larch woods; also widely distributed nowadays in the lowlands by afforestation

829 ***Larix kaempferi* - Japanese Larch**
Deciduous conifer, up to 30m high, with pale green young shoots covered with a bloom

Larix kaempferi (Lamb.) Carr.
Japanese Larch

Pinaceae - Pine family p. 71

Size: 1.5–3.5cm long and 1–1.5mm broad

Form of needle: Flattened, soft, singly on long shoots and in groups of 20–40 on short shoots

Stalk: Sessile

End of needle: Obtuse or pointed

Base of needle: Attached to the shoot by a broad base

Margin of needle: Entire

Upper/under side: Needles at first pale green, later in the year bluish green and becoming golden yellow before falling in autumn; 2 clearly visible bands of stomata beneath

Arrangement on the shoot: Clustered on the short shoots, spirally arranged on the long shoots

Distribution: Native only in Japan; brought to England in 1861 by J. G. Veitch; completely hardy in central Europe and frequently planted

830 ***Cedrus deodara* - Deodar**
Evergreen tree, up to 40m high, with long shoots rounded to triangular in shape

Cedrus deodara
(D. Don) G. Don
Deodar
Pinaceae - Pine family p. 71

Size: 2-6.5cm long and up to 1mm broad

Form of needle: Roundish or 4-angled in cross-section, soft, and with a life-span of 2-3 years

Stalk: Sessile

End of needle: Finely pointed and rather sharp

Margin of needle: Entire

Upper/under side: Dark green on all sides with fine lines of stomata

Arrangement on the shoot: Needles on the long shoots standing singly and arranged spirally, those on the short shoots in groups of 25-30

Distribution: Native in the western Himalayan region; more frequently planted in gardens and parks south of the Alps than in central Europe

831 ***Cedrus libani* - Cedar of Lebanon**
Evergreen 25-30m high, with short shoots up to 2cm long and lasting for up to 10 years

Cedrus libani A. Rich
Cedar of Lebanon
Pinaceae - Pine family p. 71

Size: 1-3.5cm long and 1-1.2mm broad

Form of needle: Stiff, sharp, triangular to rhombic in cross-section and, because of the flattened surface, always broader than high

Stalk: Sessile

End of needle: Pointed, sharp

Base of needle: Somewhat narrowed towards the base

Margin of needle: Entire

Upper/under side: With quite fine lines of stomata on all sides; needles appearing pale to dark green

Arrangement on the shoot: Needles on the long shoots standing singly and arranged spirally; on the short shoots in a rosette-like group of 10-20

Distribution: Native in Asia Minor and W. Asia (Lebanon, Syria); reached Europe in 1638; since then planted in parks and gardens in districts with a mild winter climate

832 ***Cedrus atlantica* - Atlas Cedar**
Evergreen conifer, 30-40m high, with angular long shoots

Cedrus atlantica
(Endl.) Manetti ex Carr.
Atlas Cedar
Pinaceae - Pine family p. 71

Size: 1-3cm long and 1-1.3mm broad

Form of needle: Rigid, somewhat curved at the end, irregularly 4-angled in cross-section and somewhat thicker and stiffer than those of the Cedar of Lebanon; life-span 4-7 years

Stalk: Sessile

End of needle: Very shortly pointed, not sharp

Base of needle: Narrowed towards the base

Margin of needle: Entire

Upper/under side: With lines of stomata on all sides, therefore appearing whitish blue-green

Arrangement on the shoot: On long shoots standing singly and arranged spirally; on short shoots in a rosette-like group of 10-40

Distribution: Native in N.W. Africa (Algeria, Atlas Mountains); reached Europe in 1839; planted in parks, especially the blue-needled form

833 ***Cupressus sempervirens* - Italian Cypress** *Evergreen conifer, 20-30m high, leaves forming outer surface of shoots*

Cupressus sempervirens
L.
Italian Cypress
Cupresssaceae - Cypress family p. 72

Length: Leaves of the main shoot 2-5mm, those of the lateral shoots 1mm long

Form of leaves: Scale-like, appressed and overlapping each other on the younger shoots and later spreading slightly; life-span 2-3 years and later falling with the shoot

Stalk: Sessile

End of leaf: Pointed, but with a blunt tip on the lateral shoots

Margin of leaf: Entire

Upper/under side: Dark green on both sides; with an oblong, often indistinct gland on the back

Arrangement on the shoot: Leaves opposite, arranged in lateral pairs

Distribution: Native in S.E. Europe; in the Mediterranean region a tree of gardens, avenues and cemeteries

834 ***Juniperus sabina* - Savin**
Evergreen shrub, much-branched, the branches 1-2m long, with green shoots 1-1.5mm thick

Juniperus sabina L.
Savin
Cupressaceae - Cypress family p. 72

Size: Juvenile leaves needle-like, 4-5mm long and 0.5-1mm broad; adult leaves up to 2.5mm long

Form of leaves: Juvenile leaves needle-like and in whorls of 3; adult leaves scale-like and overlapping

Stalk: Sessile

End of leaf: Obtuse or pointed

Margin of leaf: Entire

Upper/under side: Adult leaves of the upper and lower ranks dark green, with an elliptical gland and whitish waxy line; adult leaves of the side ranks dark green with stomatic areas at the sides

Arrangement on the shoot: Adult leaves opposite, arranged in lateral pairs

Distribution: From the hill to the subalpine zone; on hot, dry slopes of the continental inner Alps, in dry, grassy places under pines; often forming large colonies

835 ***Thujopsis dolabrata* - Hiba**
Evergreen tree, up to 35m high, with flat, fan-shaped branchlets

Thujopsis dolabrata (L.f.)
Sieb. et Zucc.
Hiba, Hiba Arbor-vitae
Cupressaceae - Cypress family p. 72

Size: 3-8mm long and 1-4mm broad

Form of the scale-leaves: Leaves of the upper and lower ranks oblong-obovate, somewhat smaller than the leaves of the side ranks, flattened, leathery and overlapping each other; leaves of the side ranks larger then those of the upper and lower ranks and keeled; life-span of the leaves 2-6 years

End of leaf: Leaves of the upper and lower ranks obtuse; those of the side ranks pointed

Margin of leaf: Scale-leaves all entire

Upper/under side: Both types of leaf shiny pale to dark green above; leaves of the upper and lower ranks with 2 narrow, silvery white areas of stomata beneath; leaves of the side ranks with a broad patch of stomata beneath

Arrangement on the shoot: Leaves opposite, arranged opposite, arranged in lateral pairs

Distribution: A tree native in Japan; brought to Europe in 1853 by P. F. Siebold; nowadays planted in many parks; hardy in central Europe

836 ***Thuja orientalis* - Chinese Thuja**
Evergreen shrub or tree up to 10m high with young shoots covered in scale-like leaves

Thuja orientalis L.
Chinese Thuja

Cupressaceae - Cypress family
p. 72

Length: 7–8mm long on main shoots; 1.5–2.5mm long on lateral shoots

Form of leaves: Scale-like, closely appressed to the shoots, dark green and with a weak resinous scent; leaves of the upper and lower ranks with their margins slightly overlapped by the leaves of the side ranks; life-span 1–3 years and later falling with the shoots

Stalk: Sessile

End of leaf: Scale-like leaves obtuse and slightly incurved at the ends

Margin of leaf: Entire

Upper/under side: Both sides the same colour with scattered white stomata; glands on the leaves of the upper and lower ranks inconspicuous

Arrangement on the shoot: Leaves opposite, arranged in lateral pairs

Distribution: Native in China and Korea; planted in Europe at the beginning of the 18th century; many varieties planted in gardens, parks and cemeteries

837 ***Thuja occidentalis* - White Cedar**
Evergreen conifer, 15–20m high, with flattened, greenish shoots

Thuja occidentalis L.
White Cedar

Cupressaceae - Cypress family
p. 73

Length: 4–7mm long on main shoots, otherwise 2–3mm

Form of scale-leaves: Leaves of the upper and lower ranks acutely obovate, appressed to the shoot, distinctly flattened and somewhat overlapped by the elliptic to triangular, keeled leaves of the side ranks; life-span of leaves 2–3 years and falling together with the shoot

End of leaf: Obtuse or shortly pointed

Margin of leaf: Scale-leaves entire

Upper/under side: Shoot dark green above, leaves of the upper and lower ranks with a clearly visible resin-gland; under side of shoot yellowish green; stomata in irregular grey lines or patches; leaves aromatically scented when rubbed

Arrangement on the shoot: Leaves opposite, arranged in lateral pairs

Distribution: Native in eastern North America; introduced into Europe by 1536; many forms planted nowadays as ornamental trees in gardens and parks

838 ***Chamaecyparis lawsoniana* - Lawson Cypress** *Evergreen tree, up to 20m high in Europe, with flattened, green shoots*

Chamaecyparis lawsoniana
(A. Murr.) Parl.
Lawson Cypress

Cupressaceae - Cypress family
p. 73

Length: 1–2.5mm long on lateral shoots, 3–7mm long on main shoots

Form of scale-leaves: Visible part of the leaves of the upper and lower ranks rhombic or narrowly-elliptic and with a conspicuous, oblong resin-gland; leaves of the side ranks with 2 inconspicuous resin-glands

Stalk: Sessile

End of leaf: Obtuse to pointed

Margin of leaf: Entire

Upper/under side: Shoot dark to greyish green above and paler green beneath

Arrangement on the shoot: Leaves opposite, arranged in lateral pairs

Distribution: Originally found only in western North America; in Europe since 1854; nowadays many garden forms planted throughout the whole of Europe as ornamental trees

839 ***Thuja plicata* - Western Red Cedar**
Evergreen conifer, 20–50m high, with shoots green at first

Thuja plicata Donn ex D. Don
Western Red Cedar

Cupressaceae - Cypress family
p. 73

Length: Leaves of the main shoots 6–8mm long, otherwise 2–3mm long

Form of leaves: Scale-like, appressed, overlapping, and aromatically scented when rubbed; leaves of the side ranks covering the margins of the leaves of the upper and lower ranks; life-span 2–3 years

Stalk: Sessile

End of leaf: Leaves of the primary shoots with long, free points; leaves of the lateral shoots rather obtuse or somewhat pointed

Margin of leaf: Entire

Upper/under side: Leaves rich green above, those of the upper and lower ranks with a gland; shoots greyish green beneath with conspicuous stomata in almost triangular silver grey patches

Arrangement on the shoot: Leaves opposite, arranged in lateral pairs

Distribution: Brought to Europe in 1854 by J. Jeffrey from the forests of the coastal mountains of the western United States; planted in parks and large gardens

840 ***Chamaecyparis nootkatensis* - Nootka Cypress** *Evergreen tree, 20–35m high, with flattened green shoots*

Chamaecyparis nootkatensis
(D. Don) Spach
Nootka Cypress

Cupressaceae - Cypress family
p. 73

Length: 5–6mm long on main shoots, otherwise 2–3mm long

Form of the scale-leaves: Visible portion of the leaves of the upper and lower ranks acutely rhombic and overlapping; leaves of the side ranks triangular, somewhat keeled, and with the upper part spreading

Stalk: Sessile

End of leaf: All leaves sharply pointed

Margin of leaf: Scale-leaves entire

Upper/under side: Dark green on both sides; leaves of the upper and lower ranks with a more or less clearly visible glandular furrow on the back

Arrangement on the shoot: Leaves opposite, arranged in lateral pairs

Distribution: Native in Pacific North America; brought to Europe in 1851; used as an ornamental tree in parks but not so frequently as the pendulous form ('Pendula')

841 ***Chamaecyparis obtusa* - Hinoki Cypress** *Evergreen tree, up to 40m high, with flat, green shoots*

Chamaecyparis obtusa
(Sieb. et Zucc.) Sieb. et Zucc. ex Endl.
Hinoki Cypress

Cupressaceae - Cypress family
p. 73

Length: 4–5mm long on main shoots, otherwise only 1.5–2.5mm

Form of the scale-leaves: Leaves of the upper and lower ranks narrowly obovate, thickish, and closely appressed to the shoot; leaves of the side ranks crescent-shaped, closely overlapping and somewhat smaller than those of the other ranks

End of leaf: All leaves obtuse or rounded

Margin of leaf: All leaves entire

Upper/under side: Shiny dark green above, and with a glandular furrow on the leaves of the upper and lower ranks; greyish green beneath with white lines of stomata

Arrangement of the shoot: Leaves opposite, arranged in lateral pairs

Distribution: Native in Japan; this species first reached Europe in 1861; many forms planted nowadays in gardens and parks

842 ***Colutea arborescens*** **- Bladder Senna**
Unarmed, much-branched shrub with green stems, growing 2–4m high

Colutea arborescens L.
Bladder Senna

Leguminosae - Pea family p. 75

Length: 4–10cm

Form: Odd-pinnate, with 3–6 pairs of leaflets; terminal leaflet long-stalked

Stalk: 0.5–1.5cm long

Form of leaflets: Elliptic to obovate, 1–3.5cm long, 0.5–2cm broad and shortly stalked

End of leaflets: Distinctly emarginate

Base of leaflets: Broadly wedge-shaped

Margin of leaflets: Entire

Upper/under side: Glabrous and medium to dark green above; white-felted beneath (becoming glabrous with age) and therefore greyish green

Arrangement on the shoot: Leaves alternate

Distribution: On the edges of Downy Oak woods, in hedges, open woodland and on dry, rocky slopes, especially in S. Europe and N. Africa; centre of distribution in the Mediterranean region

843 ***Coronilla emerus*** **- Scorpion Senna**
Deciduous, much-branched shrub growing 30–100cm high, with angular, green stems

Coronilla emerus L.
Scorpion Senna

Leguminosae - Pea family p. 75

Length: 2–6cm

Form: Odd-pinnate, with 7 or 9 leaflets, the terminal sessile

Stalk: Up to 1cm long

Form of leaflets: Obovate, 1–2cm long, 0.5–1cm broad and shortly stalked or sessile

End of leaflets: Usually emarginate or more rarely rounded with a bristly point

Base of leaflets: Narrowly to broadly wedge-shaped

Margin of leaflets: Entire

Upper/under side: Dark green and glabrous above; greyish green beneath and with appressed hairs when young

Arrangement on the shoot: Leaves alternate

Distribution: On warm, dry, calcareous, rocky slopes and in open oak and pine woods from the hill to the montane zone

844 ***Junglans nigra*** **- Black Walnut**
Deciduous tree, which reaches a height of 50m in eastern North America

Juglans nigra L.
Black Walnut

Juglandaceae - Walnut family p. 74

Length: 30–60cm

Form: Odd-pinnate, with 5–12 pairs of leaflets; terminal leaflet often absent or very small, therefore also 'falsely paripinnate'

Stalk: 1–6cm long and often broadened at the base

Form of leaflets: Lanceolate to narrowly ovate, 6–12cm long, the leaflets of each pair usually not quite opposite each other on the leaf-stalk

End of leaflets: Shortly pointed

Base of leaflets: Regularly or irregularly broadly wedge-shaped or rounded

Margin of leaflets: Irregularly serrate or dentate, usually entire towards the base

Upper/under side: Dark green and glabrous above; somewhat paler green beneath and often hairy on the midrib

Distribution: Planted in parks and gardens

845 ***Ceratonia siliqua*** **- Carob**
Evergreen tree, which reaches a height of 10m in the eastern Mediterranean region

Ceratonia siliqua L.
Carob

Leguminosae - Pea family p. 75

Length: 10–20cm

Form: Even-pinnate, with 2–6 pairs of leaflets

Stalk: 2–5cm long, and tinged red throughout its length

Form of leaflets: Obovate or elliptic to roundish, 3–7cm long and 2–4cm broad, sessile or shortly stalked and leathery; leaflets of each pair usually lying opposite each other

End of leaflets: Rounded, and often emarginate or distinctly incised

Base of leaflets: Broadly wedge-shaped

Margin of leaflets: Entire or slightly undulate

Upper/under side: Both sides glabrous; shiny dark green above; greyish green beneath

Arrangement on the shoot: Leaves alternate

Distribution: In evergreen woods, on dry slopes and stony soils in the Mediterranean region

846 ***Acacia dealbata*** **- Silver Wattle**
Evergreen tree, which in its native country (Australia) reaches a height of 30m.

Acacia dealbata Link
Silver Wattle, Mimosa

Leguminosae - Pea family p. 74

Length: 7–15cm

Form: Doubly even-pinnate, with 15–25 pairs of leaflets, each leaflet with 20–40 pairs of smaller leaflets (leaflets of the 2nd order); pairs of leaflets arranged opposite each other

Stalk: 1–3cm long

Form of leaflets: Narrowly linear, 3–5mm long and sessile

End of leaflets: Rounded or shortly pointed

Base of leaflets: Wedge-shaped or rounded

Margin of leaflets: Entire

Upper/under side: Leaf-axis and leaflets silvery hairy on both sides; more bluish green above; usually paler green beneath

Arrangement on the shoot: Leaves alternate

Distribution: Evergreen tree, which was introduced into France in 1864

847 ***Ailanthus altissima*** **- Tree of Heaven**
Deciduous tree, which reaches a height of 25m in eastern Asia

Ailanthus altissima (Mill.) Swingle
Tree of Heaven

Simaroubaceae - Quassia family p. 74

Length: 40–75cm

Form: Usually odd-pinnate, with 10–18 pairs of leaflets

Stalk: 8–20cm long, broadened at the base, and greenish or distinctly red

Form of leaflets: Oblong-ovate to obliquely elliptic, 5–15cm long and usually shortly stalked; pairs of leaflets rarely lying exactly opposite each other, usually slightly alternately arranged

End of leaflets: Narrowed to a point

Base of leaflets: Broadly wedge-shaped, rounded or more rarely heart-shaped

Margin of leaflets: Entire, except for 1–4 teeth of varying size in the lower part

Upper/under side: Dull dark green above; somewhat paler green beneath

Arrangement on the shoot: Leaves alternate

Distribution: Planted in large gardens and parks; introduced into England from China in 1751

848 ***Pistacia lentiscus* – Mastic Tree**
Evergreen, much-branched shrub growing 4–6m high

Pistacia lentiscus L.
Mastic Tree

Anacardiaceae – Cashew family p. 74

Length: 3–7cm

Form: Even-pinnate or odd-pinnate with 4-12 leaflets

Stalk: 1-3cm long and winged

Form of leaflets: Narrowly elliptic to narrowly obovate, 2–4cm long, leathery, sessile, the leaflets of each pair lying almost or exactly opposite each other on the leaf-stalk

End of leaflets: Usually rounded and with a short point

Base of leaflets: Wedge-shaped

Margin of leaflets: Entire

Upper/under side: Both sides glabrous; dark green above; pale green beneath

Arrangement on the shoot: Leaves alternate

Distribution: In open deciduous and pine woods and on rocky slopes in the Mediterranean region

849 ***Robinia pseudoacacia* – False Acacia**
Deciduous tree, with spiny twigs, growing to a height of 25m

Robinia pseudoacacia L.
False Acacia

Leguminosae – Pea family p. 75

Length: 15–30cm

Form: Odd-pinnate, with 3–12 pairs of leaflets; terminal leaflet long-stalked; stipules converted into stout spines

Stalk: 3–4cm long and enlarged at the base

Form of leaflets: Oblong-elliptic to ovate, 3–6cm long, shortly but distinctly stalked

End of leaflets: Rounded, obtuse, or indistinctly emarginate

Base of leaflets: Broadly wedge-shaped or rounded

Margin of leaflets: Entire

Upper/under side: Dull pale to dark green above, becoming glabrous; greyish green beneath and only hairy at first

Arrangement on the shoot: Leaves alternate

Distribution: Planted in gardens and parks; occasionally escaping and becoming naturalised; introduced into Europe from North America about 1640 by the French botanist Jean Robin

850 ***Rubus idaeus* – Raspberry**
Deciduous shrub, growing to a height of 2m, with suckers arising from the roots

Rubus idaeus L.
Raspberry

Rosaceae – Rose family p. 76

Length: 5–15cm

Form: Odd-pinnate, with 3 (on flowering shoots), 5 or more rarely 7 leaflets; terminal leaflet distinctly stalked

Stalk: 3-8cm long, hairy, and often prickly throughout its length

Form of leaflets: Elliptic to broadly ovate, 6–10cm long and sessile except for the terminal leaflet

End of leaflets: Pointed

Base of leaflets: Heart-shaped, rounded or even broadly wedge-shaped

Margin of leaflets: Simply and often also doubly serrate

Upper/under side: Dark green above, finely hairy, later becoming glabrous; densely silvery white-felted beneath

Arrangement on the shoot: Leaves alternate

Distribution: In open woods, undergrowth, and grassland in tall-herb communities

851 ***Rubus fruticosus* – Blackberry**
Bushy shrub up to 2m high, with reddish stems on the side exposed to the light; numerous forms

Rubus fruticosus L.
Blackberry

(aggregate species)
Rosaceae – Rose family p. 76

Length: 5–15cm

Form: Odd-pinnate, with 3, 5 or 7 leaflets

Stalk: 2–6cm long; numerous prickles pointing towards the base

Form of leaflets: Broadly elliptic to obovate, 2–8cm long and 3–6cm broad, terminal leaflet long-stalked; lateral leaflets narrower and shortly stalked

End of leaflets: Pointed

Base of leaflets: Rounded or shortly truncate

Margin of leaflets: Simply and doubly serrate

Upper/under side: Dark green and somewhat shiny above; greyish green beneath and more or less densely hairy, becoming glabrous; midrib prickly beneath

Arrangement on the shoot: Leaves alternate

Distribution: In deciduous and conifer woods, hedges, and on verges

852 ***Juglans regia* – Common Walnut**
Deciduous tree growing to 30m high with glabrous twigs

Juglans regia L.
Common Walnut

Juglandaceae – Walnut family p. 34, 35, 76

Length: 20–50cm

Form: Odd-pinnate, with 2–4 pairs of leaflets; terminal leaflet long-stalked; leaves strongly aromatic when rubbed

Stalk: Up to 20cm long and thickened at the base

Form of leaflets: Oblong-elliptic to oblong-ovate, 6–15cm long, sessile except for the terminal leaflet

End of leaflets: Pointed

Base of leaflets: Wedge-shaped or rounded

Margin of leaflets: Entire

Upper/under side: Brownish orange in colour at first; later shiny dark green above and glabrous; paler green beneath

Arrangement on the shoot: Leaves alternate

Distribution: A tree native in S. Europe and the Balkans

853 ***Staphylea pinnata* – Bladder-nut**
Deciduous shrub or small tree growing 1.5–5m high with stems green at first

Staphylea pinnata L.
Bladder-nut

Staphyleaceae – Bladder-nut family p. 77

Length: 15–25cm

Form: Odd-pinnate, with 2–3 pairs of leaflets; terminal leaflet long-stalked

Stalk: 5–9cm long

Form of leaflets: Elliptic to narrowly ovate, 6–9cm long, 3–5cm broad, and sessile except for the terminal leaflets

End of leaflets: Shortly pointed

Base of leaflets: Wedge-shaped

Margin of leaflets: Very finely dentate or serrate

Upper/under side: Dark green and glabrous above; bluish to greyish green beneath, with short, whitish hairs on the veins, later becoming glabrous

Arrangement on the shoot: Leaves opposite

Distribution: In the hill zone especially in the Föhn region; found locally on warm slopes, at the edges of woods, and amongst the herbaceous vegetation in beech, maple or oak woods

854 **Fraxinus ornus – Manna Ash**
Deciduous tree, up to 20m high, native in the eastern Mediterranean region

Fraxinus ornus L.
Manna Ash

Oleaceae – Olive family p. 77

Length: 15–30cm

Form: Odd-pinnate, with 3–5 pairs of leaflets; terminal leaflet with a distinctly longer stalk than those of the lateral leaflets

Stalk: 3–8cm long and often finely hairy

Form of leaflets: Oblong-ovate, 3–7cm long, up to 2.5cm broad, and stalked

End of leaflets: Pointed

Base of leaflets: Wedge-shaped or rounded

Margin of leaflets: Irregularly serrate or dentate

Upper/under side: Medium green and glabrous above; paler green beneath with reddish brown or light brown hairs along the midrib

Arrangement on the shoot: Leaves opposite, each pair of leaves on a stem at right angles to the next

Distribution: Predominantly in the hill zone on dry, sunny slopes; planted as an ornamental and street tree, especially in S. Europe

855 **Fraxinus excelsior – Common Ash**
Deciduous tree growing up to 40m high with grey twigs

Fraxinus excelsior L.
Common Ash

Oleaceae – Olive family p. 32, 33, 78

Length: 20–30cm

Form: Odd-pinnate, with 3–7 pairs of leaflets; terminal leaflet stalked

Stalk: 3–6cm long

Form of leaflets: Elliptic to ovate, 4–10cm long, 2–3cm broad, and sessile

End of leaflets: Shortly pointed

Base of leaflets: Narrowly or broadly wedge-shaped, the lowest leaflets often rounded

Margin of leaflets: Unequally serrate; mostly entire in the lowest part

Upper/under side: Dark green and glabrous above; paler green beneath with reddish brown woolly hairs along the veins

Arrangement on the shoot: Leaves opposite, each pair of leaves on a stem at right angles to the next

Distribution: In water-meadows, deciduous woods, valleys, by rivers and on stony slopes

856 **Sorbus aucuparia – Rowan**
Deciduous tree or shrub, of pioneer character, growing 5–20m high

Sorbus aucuparia L.
Rowan, Mountain Ash

Rosaceae – Rose family p. 52, 53, 78

Length: 10–20cm long and 8–11cm broad

Form: Odd-pinnate, with 4–9 pairs of leaflets; terminal leaflet long-stalked

Stalk: 2–3cm long and coloured reddish and greenish above

Form of leaflets: Oblong-lanceolate, 2–6cm long, 1–2.5cm broad, sessile or very shortly stalked

End of leaflets: Pointed

Base of leaflets: The two halves of the leaflet ending at a different point on the midrib

Margin of leaflets: Coarsely serrate and entire in the lower part

Upper/under side: Dark green above, and at first covered with greyish silvery hairs; greyish green felted beneath

Arrangement on the shoot: Leaves alternate

Distribution: In open deciduous, Spruce and Arolla Pine woods; from the hill to the subalpine zone

857 **Sorbus domestica – Service Tree**
Deciduous tree, native mainly in S. Europe, growing 15–20m high

Sorbus domestica L.
Service Tree

Rosaceae – Rose family p. 78

Length: 10–25cm

Form: Odd-pinnate with 5–10 pairs of leaflets

Stalk: 3–5.5cm long

Form of leaflets: Narrowly elliptic, 3–8cm long, up to 2cm broad, sessile or shortly stalked

End of leaflets: Shortly pointed

Base of leaflets: Always narrowly wedge-shaped, the two halves of the leaflet usually symmetrical and ending at the same point of the midrib

Margin of leaflets: Almost entire on the lower third; otherwise simply or very slightly doubly serrate

Upper/under side: Dark green and glabrous above; paler green beneath and softly hairy, especially along the veins

Arrangement on the shoot: Leaves alternate

Distribution: In dry Oak, Hornbeam and Downy Oak woods

858 **Sambucus racemosa – Red-berried Elder** *Deciduous shrub growing to 2m high with thin, smooth stems; pith brown*

Sambucus racemosa L.
Red-berried Elder

Caprifoliaceae – Honeysuckle family p. 77

Length: 10–25cm

Form: Odd-pinnate, with 2–3 pairs of leaflets; terminal leaflet distinctly stalked

Stalk: 7–10cm long; one to several roundish glands at the base

Form of leaflets: Lanceolate to narrowly ovate, 4–8cm long, up to 3.5cm broad

End of leaflets: Long-pointed

Base of leaflets: Obliquely wedge-shaped or rounded

Margin of leaflets: Irregularly serrate

Upper/under side: Dark green and glabrous above; bluish grey-green beneath and hairy at first

Arrangement on the shoot: Leaves opposite

Distribution: In shady woods, on screes and rocks

859 **Sambucus nigra – Elder**
Deciduous shrub or tree up to 7m high with grey stems containing white pith

Sambucus nigra L.
Elder

Caprifoliaceae – Honeysuckle family p. 77

Length: 10–30cm

Form: Odd-pinnate, with usually 2, more rarely 3 pairs of leaflets; terminal leaflet distinctly stalked and much broader than in the Red-berried Elder

Stalk: 4–10cm long and grooved above

Form of leaflets: Elliptic, 10–15cm long and 3–5cm broad; upper pair off leaflets usually sessile, the lower usually stalked

End of leaflets: Shortly pointed

Base of leaflets: Wedge-shaped and rounded; the two halves of the leaflet often asymmetrical

Margin of leaflets: Irregularly coarsely serrate

Upper/under side: Dark green and glabrous above; bluish to greyish green beneath

Arrangement on the shoot: Leaves opposite

Distribution: In damp woods, on river-banks, and on waste ground; hill to montane zone

860 **Rosa pendulina - Alpine Rose**
Shrub, growing 0.5-3m high, with green or reddish shoots

Rosa pendulina L.
Alpine Rose
Rosaceae - Rose family p. 78

Length: 5-10cm

Form: Odd-pinnate, with 9 or 11 leaflets; often 7 leaflets on flowering shoots

Stalk: 1.5-3cm long, with fine, stalked glands; often reddish above and greenish beneath; stipules long, narrow below but broadening upwards, spreading and pointed

Form of leaflets: Oblong-elliptic, more rarely ovate or roundish, 1-4cm long, 0.5-2.5cm broad, sessile or quite shortly stalked

End of leaflets: Shortly pointed

Base of leaflets: Usually wedge-shaped

Margin of leaflets: Usually doubly serrate, rarely simply serrate; teeth finely pointed and with stalked glands

Upper/under side: Both sides usually glabrous; dull dark green above; paler green beneath, often with stalked glands on the midrib

Distribution: In alpine meadows, gorges, on dwarf shrub moorland and tall-herb grassland.

861 **Rosa glauca - Red-leaved Rose**
1-3m high; stems shiny reddish brown; shoots reddish or covered with a bluish bloom

Rosa glauca Pourr.
Red-leaved Rose
Rosaceae - Rose family p. 78

Length: 4-8cm

Form: Odd-pinnate, with 7 or 9 leaflets; sometimes 5 leaflets on flowering shoots

Stalk: 1-4cm long, glabrous, covered with a bluish purple bloom; stipules pointed and usually coloured greenish red to purple

Form of leaflets: Elliptic or oblong-ovate, 1.5-4.5cm long, 1-3cm broad and shortly stalked

End of leaflets: Narrowly pointed

Base of leaflets: Wedge-shaped or rounded

Margin of leaflets: Usually simply toothed; teeth pointing forwards; leaflets often entire in the lower part

Upper/under side: Both sides usually glabrous; bluish green or coppery red above; paler bluish green beneath, often purplish in places

Distribution: In thickets, crevasses, and clearings in the montane and subalpine zones

862 **Rosa canina - Dog Rose**
Shrub, growing 1-3m high, with erect or arching stems

Rosa canina L.
Dog Rose
(variable species)
Rosaceae - Rose family p. 79

Length: 6-11cm

Form: Odd-pinnate, with 5 or 7 leaflets

Stalk: 2-4cm long, somewhat prickly, often with stalked glands and broadened at the base; stipules narrow, pointed, the tips spreading sideways

Form of leaflets: Ovate to elliptic, 2-4cm long, 1-2.5cm broad, sessile or very shortly stalked

End of leaflets: Shortly pointed

Base of leaflets: Broadly wedge-shaped or rounded

Margin of leaflets: More or less regularly simply, or sometimes doubly serrate; pointed teeth directed forwards

Upper/under side: Both sides usually glabrous; dull to dark greyish green above; bluish green beneath, often with fine silky hairs

Distribution: In hedges, glades, and neglected fields and pastures from the hill to the subalpine zone

863 **Rosa villosa - Apple Rose**
Dense shrub, 1.5-2m high, with shoots reddish at first and covered with a bloom

Rosa villosa L.
Apple Rose
Rosaceae - Rose family p. 79

Length: 4-9cm

Form: Odd-pinnate, with 5 or 7 leaflets; more rarely 3 or 9 leaflets

Stalk: 1-3cm long, green and usually with stalked glands; stipules small, narrow, broadened above and curved inwards

Form of leaflets: Elliptic or oblong-elliptic, 1-4cm long, 0.5-2cm broad and sessile

End of leaflets: Shortly pointed

Base of leaflets: Rounded or more rarely somewhat heart-shaped

Margin of leaflets: Doubly serrate; teeth broad and gland-tipped

Upper/under side: Greyish to dark green above with appressed hairs; paler green beneath, with densely appressed hairs, numerous stalked glands and somewhat resinous

Distribution: On rocky slopes and in hedges in the montane and subalpine zones

864 **Rosa rubiginosa - Sweet Briar**
Shrub, growing 2-3m high, with shortly branched and prickly stems

Rosa rubiginosa L.
Sweet Briar
Rosaceae - Rose family p. 79

Length: 4-7cm

Form: Odd-pinnate, with 5, 7, or more rarely 9 leaflets

Stalk: 0.5-2.5cm long, glabrous or downy, with stalked glands and small, hooked prickles; stipules broad, densely fringed with glands, and with the tips pointing forwards or spreading sideways

Form of leaflets: Elliptic or roundish, 1-2.5cm long, 1-2cm broad and sessile

End of leaflets: Rounded or with a small point

Margin of leaflets: Doubly toothed; teeth prominent with numerous stalked glands

Upper/under side: Glabrous or with scattered downy hairs above, dark green, rarely glandular; slightly to densely downy beneath, paler green with numerous reddish stalked glands

Distribution: On moorland meadows, rocky slopes and in hedges from the hill to the subalpine zone

865 **Rosa tomentosa - Downy Rose**
Shrub 0.5-2m high, with arching stems often covered with a bluish bloom

Rosa tomentosa Sm.
Downy Rose
Rosaceae - Rose family p. 79

Length: 5-10cm

Form: Odd-pinnate, with 5 or 7 leaflets

Stalk: 1-3cm long, with matted woolly hairs, with almost sessile glands and several hooked prickles; stipules pointed and somewhat spreading

Form of leaflets: Broadly ovate to elliptic, 2-4cm long, 1-2.5cm broad and sessile or shortly stalked

End of leaflets: Usually rounded, but with a small point

Base of leaflets: Broadly wedge-shaped or rounded

Margin of leaflets: Simply and doubly toothed; teeth very large, broad and pointed

Upper/under side: Dark green above and with appressed hairs; paler green beneath, softly felted, glands present or absent

Distribution: On the edges of woods and in open scrub from the hill to the montane zone

866 **Acer Griseum - Paper-bark Maple**
Tree to 12m high, native in central China, with cinnamon brown bark

Acer griseum (Franch.) Pax
Paper-bark Maple
Aceraceae - Maple family p. 80

Length: 6-10cm

Form: Trifoliolate; terminal leaflet up to 5.5cm long, lateral leaflets up to 3.5cm long

Stalk: 1-5cm long, often hairy and usually reddish above

Form of leaflets: Elliptic to obovate, 3-6cm long and sessile except for the terminal leaflet

End of leaflets: Obtuse or shortly pointed

Base of leaflets: Terminal leaflet narrowly wedge-shaped

Margin of leaflets: Terminal leaflet lobed in the upper half or with 3-5 coarse teeth, otherwise entire; lateral leaflets often irregularly coarsely toothed to below the middle

Upper/under side: Dark green and glabrous above; distinctly bluish green beneath, with brownish hairs on the midribs

Arrangement on the shoot: Leaves opposite

Distribution: Planted in gardens and parks

867 **Cytisus purpureus - Purple Broom**
Deciduous half-shrub with stems curving upwards to a height of 30-75cm

Cytisus purpureus Scop.
Purple Broom
Leguminosae - Pea family p. 80

Length: 2-5cm

Form: Trifoliolate

Stalk: 1-3cm long, glabrous and grooved

Form of leaflets: Narrowly obovate, 1.5-2.5cm long, 0.5-1cm broad and sessile

End of leaflets: Rounded or obtuse

Base of leaflets: Narrowly wedge-shaped

Margin of leaflets: Entire

Upper/under side: Both sides with scattered hairs or glabrous; somewhat darker green above than beneath

Arrangement on the shoot: Leaves alternate

Distribution: On rocky slopes and open woods in central and S. Europe from the hill to the montane zone; cultivated in rock gardens since the 18th century

868 **Clematis vitalba - Traveller's Joy**
Deciduous, quick-growing climber reaching up to 10m in height

Clematis vitalba L.
Traveller's Joy, Old Man's Beard
Ranunculaceae - Buttercup family p. 80

Length: 3-10cm

Form: Odd-pinnate, with 3 or 5 leaflets; the 2 lower ones may also be 3-lobed

Stalk: 1-6cm long, wine red to purple above and twining

Form of leaflets: Ovate and pointed, 3-5cm long, 2-4cm broad and stalked

End of leaflets: Rather obtuse or shortly pointed

Base of leaflets: Heart-shaped

Margin of leaflets: Entire in the upper third, coarsely toothed or lobed in the lower part

Upper/under side: Dark green above and paler green or greyish green beneath

Arrangement on the shoot: Leaves opposite

Distribution: In damp woods and the damp borders of woodland, and on shady slopes

869 **Clematis alpina - Alpine Clematis**
Rather rare deciduous climber, growing up to 3m high

Clematis alpina (L.) Miller
Alpine Clematis
Ranunculaceae - Buttercup family p. 79

Length: 10-15cm

Form: Odd-pinnate, with 3 leaflets, each divided into 2 or 3 parts

Stalk: 3-7cm long

Form of leaflets: Divisions of leaflets narrowly ovate, 2-4cm long and 1-2cm broad

End of leaflets: Divisions sometimes long-pointed

Base of leaflets: Rounded or irregularly heart-shaped

Margin of leaflets: Finely, or even coarsely and deeply serrate

Upper/under side: Medium green above and paler green beneath; hairy on both sides

Arrangement on the shoot: Leaves opposite

Distribution: Among herbaceous plants and shrubs in half-shady conifer woods, on shrubby grassland, in the Alpenrose-Mountain Pine region and on rocks especially in the subalpine zone

870 **Fraxinus americana - White Ash**
Hardy, deciduous tree up to 15m high with always glabrous twigs

Fraxinus americana L.
White Ash
Oleaceae - Olive family p. 77

Length: 15-40cm

Form: Odd-pinnate, with 2-4 pairs of leaflets; all distinctly stalked

Stalk: 5-12cm long

Form of leaflets: Elliptic to narrowly ovate, up to 8cm long; terminal leaflet with a stalk 5-12mm long

End of leaflets: Pointed

Base of leaflets: Terminal leaflet usually wedge-shaped; lateral leaflets rounded

Margin of leaflets: Usually entire

Upper/under side: Dark green and glabrous above; pale greyish green to whitish green beneath and slightly hairy, becoming glabrous

Arrangement on the shoot: Leaves opposite

Distribution: Occasionally planted in parks; growing in swamps in the U.S.A.

871 **Acer negundo - Ash-leaved Maple**
Deciduous tree, often much-branched, growing 10-20m high with usually green twigs

Acer negundo L.
Ash-leaved Maple, Box Elder
Aceraceae - Maple family p. 80

Length: 7-15cm

Form: Odd-pinnate, with 3, 5 or more rarely 7 or 9 leaflets; terminal leaflet with a short or long stalk

Stalk: 5-8cm long, glabrous or finely hairy, and often reddish above

Form of leaflets: Narrowly elliptic to ovate, 5-10cm long, occasionally with 2 or 3 lobes, and sessile or stalked

End of leaflets: Long-pointed

Base of leaflets: Wedge-shaped, truncate or rounded

Margin of leaflets: Coarsely serrate in the upper part, entire in the lower part

Upper/under side: Medium to dark green and glabrous above, greyish green beneath

Arrangement on the shoot: Leaves opposite

Distribution: Native in the U.S.A.; often planted in parks

872 ***Laburnum alpinum* - Alpine Laburnum**
Deciduous shrub or small tree 5m high; cultivated forms up to 10m in height

Laburnum alpinum (Mill.) Bercht et J. S. Presl
Alpine Laburnum
Leguminosae - Pea family p. 81

Length: 8-16cm

Form: With 3 leaflets

Stalk: 5-9cm long and glabrous or with spreading hairs

Form of leaflets: Narrowly ovate to narrowly elliptic, 3-8cm long, 1.5-4.5cm broad and sessile

End of leaflets: Pointed or more rarely obtuse and sometimes with a short, bristly point

Base of leaflets: Wedge-shaped or rounded

Margin of leaflets: Entire, and with hairs 0.5-1mm long when young

Upper/under side: Dark green and usually glabrous above; paler green beneath, and hairy especially on the midrib

Arrangement on the shoot: Leaves on long shoots alternate; arranged in clusters on the lateral short shoots

Distribution: On rocky slopes, in clearings and open woods from the lowlands to the montane (more rarely subalpine) zone in warm but damp places

873 ***Laburnum anagyroides* - Common Laburnum** *Deciduous shrub or tree up to 7m high; cultivated forms up to 9m in height*

Laburnum anagyroides Med.
Common Laburnum
Leguminosae - Pea family p. 81

Length: 6-12cm

Form: With 3 leaflets

Stalk: 2-7cm long with appressed, silky hairs

Form of leaflets: Broadly elliptic to obovate, 1.5-8cm long, 1.5-3cm broad and sessile

End of leaflets: Rounded, and usually with a short, bristly point

Base of leaflets: Usually broadly wedge-shaped

Margin of leaflets: Entire

Upper/under side: Dark green and glabrous above; bluish green or greyish green beneath and with appressed hairs like the leaf-stalk

Arrangement on the shoot: Leaves on long shoots alternate; arranged in tufts on the lateral short shoots

Distribution: On stony slopes, on crags, in open scrub and Pine woods from the lowlands to the montane (more rarely subalpine) zone; poisonous

874 ***Aesculus parviflora* - Buckeye**
Deciduous, suckering shrub up to 4m high with light greyish brown stems

Aesculus parviflora Walt.
Buckeye
Hippocastanaceae - Horse Chestnut family p. 81

Length: 20-30cm

Form: With 5 or 7 leaflets, palmately arranged

Stalk: 10-18cm long and coloured red

Form of leaflets: Narrowly obovate, 9-18cm long; the 3 middle leaflets distinctly stalked, the 2 lower ones with only short stalks

End of leaflets: Long-pointed

Base of leaflets: Narrowly wedge-shaped

Margin of leaflets: Crenate-serrate or finely serrate/dentate

Upper/under side: Medium to dark green above and bluish grey-green beneath; both sides glabrous

Arrangement on the shoot: Leaves alternate

Distribution: Occasionally planted in gardens and parks; native in south-eastern North America

875 ***Aesculus octandra* - Yellow Buckeye**
Deciduous, ornamental tree up to 20m high with greyish brown twigs

Aesculus octandra Marsh. (*A. flava* Ait., *A. lutea* Wangenh.)
Yellow Buckeye
Hippocastanaceae - Horse Chestnut family p. 81

Length: 10-30cm

Form: Usually with 5 leaflets, palmately arranged

Stalk: 3-15cm

Form of leaflets: Oblong-elliptic, 10-15cm long, the 3 middle leaflets distinctly stalked, the 2 lower ones with only short stalks

End of leaflets: Pointed

Base of leaflets: Narrowly wedge-shaped

Margin of leaflets: Finely serrate

Upper/under side: Dark green and glabrous above; yellowish green beneath, hairy at first, later becoming glabrous

Arrangement on the shoot: Leaves opposite

Distribution: Ornamental tree native in eastern North America; often planted with the 2 related species to form a mixed group because of its yellow and pink flowers

876 ***Aesculus hippocastanum* - Horse Chestnut**
Deciduous tree, 20-25m high, native in the mountain forests of the Balkan peninsula

Aesculus hippocastanum L.
Horse Chestnut
Hippocastanaceae - Horse Chestnut family p. 24, 25, 81

Length: 10-30cm long

Form: With 5 or 7 leaflets, palmately arranged

Stalk: 5-15cm long and grooved above

Form of leaflets: Oblong-obovate (greatest breadth always in the upper third), 5-15cm long and sessile; leaflets decreasing in size towards the leaf-base

End of leaflets: Shortly pointed

Base of leaflets: Narrowly wedge-shaped

Margin of leaflets: Irregularly simply and in places doubly serrate

Upper/under side: Dark green and glabrous above; pale to greyish green beneath with brown hairs on the veins when young

Arrangement on the shoot: Leaves opposite

Distribution: Popular shade-tree in parks, gardens, farms and hotel grounds

877 ***Aesculus x carnea* - Red Horse Chestnut**
Deciduous tree, 15-20m high, with greyish brown twigs

Aesculus x carnea Hayne (*A. hippocastanum x A. pavia*)
Red Horse Chestnut
Hippocastanaceae - Horse Chestnut family p. 81

Length: 10-25cm long

Form: Usually with 5 leaflets, palmately arranged

Stalk: 5-15cm long

Form of leaflets: Elliptic (with the greatest breadth in the middle), 6-16cm long and usually sessile; the smallest leaflets pointing towards the leaf-base

End of leaflets: Pointed

Base of leaflets: Wedge-shaped

Margin of leaflets: Irregularly simply toothed and in places doubly serrate

Upper/under side: Dull, dark green and often wrinkled above; yellowish green beneath

Arrangement on the shoot: Leaves opposite

Distribution: The Red Horse-chestnut is a fertile hybrid between the S. European Horse Chestnut and the red-flowered Horse Chestnut native in the U.S.A.; planted as a street tree

878 ***Crataegus monogyna*** **– Hawthorn**
Deciduous, densely branched and thorny shrub or small tree growing 1–8m high

Crataegus monogyna Jacq.
Hawthorn

Rosaceae – Rose family p. 83

Length: 3–6cm

Form of blade: Broadly ovate or rhombic in outline and deeply 3-, 5-, 7- or more rarely 9-lobed

Stalk: 1–2cm long, glabrous or hairy along the groove; stipules crescent-shaped and toothed

Lobes: Long, narrow and shortly pointed; the 2 lower lobes reaching almost to the midrib; sinuses acute

End of leaf: Terminal lobe usually flattened; a small point often present in the middle

Base of blade: Wedge-shaped, truncate or heart-shaped

Margin of leaf: Lobes entire in the lower part, otherwise finely serrate

Upper/under side: Shiny dark green and glabrous above; bluish green beneath and somewhat hairy in the axils of the veins

Arrangement on the shoot: Leaves alternate; arranged in clusters on short shoots; thorns 1–2.5cm long

Distribution: In hedges, deciduous woods, slopes from hill to montane

879 ***Crataegus laevigata*** **– Midland Hawthorn** *Deciduous, very thorny shrub or small tree 2–8m high*

Crataegus laevigata (Poir.) DC.
Midland Hawthorn

Rosaceae – Rose family p. 83

Length: 3–5cm

Form of blade: Usually ovate, obovate or oblong, and 3- or 5-lobed in the upper part

Stalk: 0.8–1.5cm long, glabrous or sparingly hairy and grooved; stipules lanceolate to ovate, glandular serrate and glabrous

Lobes: Short, broadly rounded or shortly pointed; sinuses only reaching half-way towards the midrib

End of leaf: Obtuse or flattened and with small teeth

Base of blade: Wedge-shaped

Margin of leaf: Lobes irregularly serrate; lowest part of leaf entire

Upper/under side: Shiny dark green above, whitish green beneath

Arrangement on the shoot: Leaves alternate; arranged in clusters on short shoots; thorns 6–15cm long

Distribution: In hedges, on the edges of woods, and as a pioneer tree in fields and vineyards; up to the montane zone

880 ***Ribes uva-crispa*** **– Gooseberry**
Deciduous shrub 60–150cm high with greyish brown stems

Ribes uva-crispa L.
Gooseberry

Saxifragaceae – Saxifrage family p. 82

Length: 2–6cm long and equally broad

Form of blade: Heart-shaped to oblong in outline and 3- or 5-lobed

Stalk: 1–2cm long and somewhat broadened at the base

End of leaf: Terminal lobe rounded or with a short point

Lobes: Usually 3; roundish and only shortly pointed at the end; sinuses between the lobes acute

Base of blade: Weakly heart-shaped or truncate

Margin of leaf: Lobes deeply crenate and serrate above the sinuses

Upper/under side: Dark green, shiny, and often slightly hairy above; medium green and softly hairy beneath

Arrangement on the shoot: Leaves alternate on long shoots; arranged in clusters on short shoots

Distribution: In hedges, open woods, damp woodland and valleys and by fences

881 ***Liriodendron tulipifera*** **– Tulip Tree**
Deciduous tree, native in the eastern U.S.A., and reaching a height of 35m in Europe

Liriodendron tulipifera L.
Tulip Tree

Magnoliaceae – Magnolia family p. 82

Length: 10–25cm

Form of blade: Square in outline; blade with 2 or 4 lobes, unequal in size, their long sides almost parallel (the leaf-shape is unmistakable!)

Stalk: 6–12cm long and slightly thickened at the base

Lobes: 2 or 4, unequal in size, pointed; on young trees the leaves may be 4- or 6-lobed; sinuses between the lobes rounded and forming an obtuse angle

End of leaf: Terminal lobe truncate, emarginate or distinctly incised

Base of blade: Heart-shaped, rounded or truncate

Margin of leaf: Lobes entire

Upper/under side: Medium to dark green and glabrous above; bluish green beneath with hairy or glabrous depressions in the axils of the veins

Distribution: Cultivated in Europe since 1688; planted in parks and gardens

882 ***Morus nigra*** **– Black Mulberry**
Deciduous tree, growing to a height of 10–20m; cultivated especially in vine-growing regions

Morus nigra L.
Black Mulberry

Moraceae – Mulberry family p. 82

Length: 5–15cm

Form of blade: Broadly ovate or heart-shaped in outline, unequally coarsely serrate or with 2 or more irregular lobes

Stalk: 1–4cm long and often hairy

Lobes: Lateral lobes rounded and of unequal size; terminal lobe long and finely pointed, its base narrower than the middle

End of leaf: Terminal lobe long and finely pointed

Base of blade: Deeply heart-shaped

Margin of leaf: Lobes unequally coarsely serrate as far as the sinuses; entire in the acute or rounded sinuses

Upper/under side: Dark green above and rough to the touch because of the appressed hairs; paler green beneath with very prominent pale yellow veins and soft, appressed hairs

Arrangement on the shoot: Leaves alternate

Distribution: Planted in gardens in warmer districts

883 ***Ficus carica*** **– Fig**
Small, deciduous tree up to 6m high; in plantations in warm countries

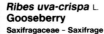

Ficus carica L.
Fig

Moraceae – Mulberry family p. 82

Length: 20–30cm

Form of blade: With varied outline; usually roundish with 3, 5 or 7 lobes of unequal size

Stalk: 5–8cm long, thickish and usually with a broadened base

Lobes: Usually obovate, 6–12cm long, rounded or more rarely shortly pointed at the end; terminal lobe always narrower in the lower part than higher up

End of leaf: Terminal lobe usually rounded

Base of blade: Mostly heart-shaped

Margin of leaf: Entire, undulate, and also irregularly toothed

Upper/under side: Dark green above and roughly bristly; paler green beneath with pale yellow veins and soft, appressed hairs

Arrangement on the shoot: Leaves alternate

Distribution: On warm, dry, sunny slopes

884 ***Forsythia europaea* - European Forsythia** *Deciduous shrub, growing 1.5–2.5m high; native in N. Albania and S.W. Yugoslavia*

Forsythia europaea
Deg. et Bald.
European Forsythia
Oleaceae – Olive family p. 83

Length: 4–8cm

Form of blade: Ovate to ovate-lanceolate in outline; very rarely lobed

Stalk: 1–3cm long and usually grooved above

Lobes: When present, narrow and pointed, sinuses between the lobes acute

End of leaf: Pointed; tip often somewhat curved to one side

Base of blade: Narrowly or broadly wedge-shaped

Margin of leaf: Entire in the lower part, otherwise distinctly serrate

Upper/under side: Dark green above and pale green beneath; both sides glabrous

Arrangement on the shoot: Leaves opposite

Distribution: Planted in gardens; but horticulturally unimportant

885 ***Acer rufinerve* - Grey-budded Snake-bark Maple** *Deciduous tree, up to 10m high, native in the mountain forests of Japan*

Acer rufinerve Sieb et Zucc.
Grey-budded Snake-bark Maple
Aceraceae – Maple family p. 84

Length: 5–13cm

Form of blade: Broadly ovate in outline; often broader than long; distinctly 3-lobed

Stalk: 2–7cm long, pink to dark red above and furrowed

Lobes: Middle lobe broadly triangular or ovate and finely pointed; side lobes smaller than the middle lobe and spreading

End of leaf: Middle lobe finely pointed

Base of blade: Weakly heart-shaped or truncate

Margin of leaf: Lobes consistently unequally sharply serrate

Upper/under side: Dark to bluish green above; paler green beneath and with brownish red hairs along the veins especially when young

Arrangement on the shoot: Leaves opposite; each pair of leaves at right-angles to the next

Distribution: Often planted in gardens for autumn colour

886 ***Acer saccharinum* - Silver Maple**
A deciduous tree, native in the river valleys of Atlantic U.S.A., and growing up to 40m high

Acer saccharinum L.
Silver Maple
Aceraceae – Maple family p. 83

Length: 10–15cm

Form of blade: Broadly ovate in outline and 5-lobed (often only obscurely 5-lobed); middle lobe often 3-lobed

Stalk: 4–7cm long, usually reddish above, without milky juice

Lobes: Of unequal size and pointed; the middle lobe only reaching half-way down the blade

End of leaf: Terminal lobe long-pointed

Base of blade: Heart-shaped or truncate

Margin of leaf: Lobes at the base and at the sinuses entire, otherwise coarsely serrate and dentate

Upper/under side: Medium to dark green and glabrous above; conspicuously silvery grey to bluish grey beneath

Arrangement on the shoot: Leaves opposite; each pair of leaves at right-angles to the next

Distribution: Cultivated in Europe since the beginning of the 18th century as a hardy ornamental tree

887 ***Acer saccharinum 'Wieri'* - Silver Maple**
Tree up to 20m high with pendulous branches, native in Atlantic U.S.A.

Acer saccharinum L. *'laciniatum'* (Carr.) Rehd. **'Wieri'**
Silver Maple, Wier's form
Aceraceae – Maple family p. 83

Length: 8–15cm

Form of blade: Broadly ovate to roundish in outline and deeply 5-lobed

Stalk: 4–7cm long, green, without milky juice

Lobes: Of unequal size (the 2 lowest the smallest), very narrow, deeply incised, and narrower in the lower part than in the middle; middle lobe 3-lobed; sinuses between the lobes obtuse or rounded

End of leaf: Terminal lobe long-pointed

Base of blade: Broadly arrow-shaped

Margin of leaf: Lobes entire in the lower quarter, otherwise with numerous smaller, pointed lobes

Upper/under side: Dark green and glabrous above; conspicuously silvery grey to bluish grey beneath

Arrangement on the shoot: Leaves opposite

Distribution: Found by Wier in 1873; a hardy park tree

888 ***Acer palmatum* - Smooth Japanese Maple**
Deciduous shrub or small tree, 3–8m high, native in Japan

Acer palmatum Thunb.
Smooth Japanese Maple
Aceraceae – Maple family p. 84

Length: 5–10cm

Form of blade: Circular in outline and with 3, 5, 7, 9 or 11 lobes reaching more than halfway towards the base

Stalk: 4–7cm long, usually reddish above, without milky juice

Lobes: Ovate-lanceolate and pointed; lowermost lobe sometimes at an acute angle with the leaf-stalk and much smaller than the others; sinuses between the lobes acute

End of leaf: Terminal lobe finely pointed

Base of blade: Arrow-shaped, heart-shaped or truncate

Margin of leaf: Simply and doubly serrate

Upper/under side: Medium green and glabrous above; pale green beneath and with tufts of whitish hairs in the axils of the veins

Arrangement on the shoot: Leaves opposite; stems of many forms bright red; each pair of leaves at right-angles to the next

Distribution: Numerous forms are often planted in gardens and parks

889 ***Acer japonicum* - Downy Japanese Maple**
Small, deciduous tree, 5–7m high, native in the mountain forests of N. Japan

Acer japonicum Thunb. *'Aconitifolium'*
Downy Japanese Maple
Aceraceae – Maple family p. 84

Length: 8–15cm

Form of blade: Roundish in outline and divided almost to the base into 9 or 11 pinnatisect lobes

Stalk: 3–6cm long and red in colour

Lobes: Narrowly obovate, pinnatisect, and usually long pointed; sinuses between the lobes acute

End of leaf: Terminal lobe finely pointed

Base of blade: Arrow-shaped or deeply heart-shaped

Margin of leaf: Lobes simply or doubly serrate

Upper/under side: Medium green above and paler green beneath; silky hairy only when young

Arrangement on the shoot: Leaves opposite; each pair of leaves at right-angles to the next

Distribution: Frequently planted in gardens and parks

890 **Liquidambar styraciflua - Sweet Gum**
Conical, deciduous tree, up to 45m high, often with corky wings on the branchlets

Liquidambar styraciflua L.
Sweet Gum

Hamamelidaceae - Witch-hazel family p. 84

Length: 10-20cm long and equally broad

Form of blade: Broadly ovate or roundish in outline; leaves on young trees only 3-lobed, on older trees 5- or 7-lobed

Stalk: 4-9cm long

Lobes: Narrowly triangular and pointed; sinuses between the lobes acute or obtuse

End of leaf: Terminal lobe pointed

Base of blade: Arrow-shaped, heart-shaped or truncate

Margin of leaf: Lobes finely serrate

Upper/under side: Shiny dark green above; distinctly paler green beneath with tufts of long hairs in the axils of the veins

Arrangement on the shoot: Leaves alternate

Distribution: Often dominant in the damp woods of Atlantic N. America; planted in Europe since 1688 as an ornamental tree in parks

891 **Catalpa ovata - Yellow Catalpa**
Deciduous tree up to 10m high, native in China, with predominantly glabrous twigs

Catalpa ovata
Yellow Catalpa

Bignoniaceae - Bignonia family p. 85

Length: 10-25cm

Form of blade: Varied in outline; broadly ovate or heart-shaped and often with 2, 3 or 5 lobes

Stalk: 4-10cm, hairy at first, later becoming glabrous, often dark red above and green beneath

Lobes: When present, broadly triangular, unequal in size, entire and printed; sinuses between the lobes obtuse and rounded

End of leaf: Shortly pointed

Base of blade: Rounded or heart-shaped

Margin of leaf: Entire and fringed with very fine hairs

Upper/under side: Dark green above and very soft to the touch; pale to medium green beneath and only slightly rough; veins yellowish green and distinctly prominent; reddish black glands in the axils of the veins

Arrangement on the shoot: Leaves opposite

Distribution: Planted as an ornamental tree in parks

892 **Acer platanoides - Norway Maple**
Deciduous tree, 25-30m high, with a broad crown and glabrous brown twigs

Acer platanoides L.
Norway Maple

Aceraceae - Maple family p. 20, 21, 85

Length: 10-20cm long and broad

Form of blade: Roundish or broadly heart-shaped in outline and with 3, 5 or 7 lobes of unequal size

Stalk: Up to 15cm long, usually reddish, containing a milky juice and somewhat thickened at the base

Lobes: Usually 5 (more rarely 3 or 7); of unequal size and with several very long, slender teeth; sinuses between the lobes obtuse or rounded

End of leaf: Middle lobe with a long, fine point

Base of blade: Usually heart-shaped

Margin of leaf: Entire between the 3-5 long teeth on each lobe

Upper/under side: Dark green and glabrous above; pale green beneath and with tufts of hairs in the axils of the veins, later becoming glabrous

Arrangement on the shoot: Leaves opposite; each pair of leaves at right-angles to the next

Distribution: Throughout Europe in beech and mixed deciduous woods (especially damp oak, hornbeam)

893 **Acer cappadocicum - Cappadocian Maple** *Deciduous tree, 10-15m high, with distinctly smooth, green twigs*

Acer cappadocicum Gled.
Cappadocian Maple

Aceraceae - Maple family p. 84

Length: 10-20cm long and equally broad

Form of blade: Roundish or broadly heart-shaped in outline and with 5 or 7 lobes

Stalk: 5-15cm long

Lobes: Usually 5 lobes; broadly triangular, of unequal size, and sometimes ending in a long, fine point; sinuses between the lobes obtuse or rounded; lowest lobes pointing diagonally downwards

End of leaf: Middle lobe ending abruptly in a long, fine point

Base of blade: Heart-shaped

Margin of leaf: Entire; sometimes slightly undulate

Upper/under side: Dark green above and paler green beneath; both sides glabrous

Arrangement on the shoot: Leaves opposite; each pair at right-angles to the next

Distribution: Planted only in large gardens and parks in central Europe; native in the Caucasus and W. Asia

894 **Platanus x acerifolia - London Plane**
Deciduous tree, up to 40m high, its pale green crown formed like a high dome

Platanus x *acerifolia*
(Ait.) Willd.
London Plane

Platanaceae - Plane family p. 85

Length: 10-25cm long and equally broad

Form of blade: With a varied outline; usually roundish and with 3, 5 or 7 lobes of unequal size, which at most reach the middle of the blade

Stalk: 3-10cm long, thickened and bulbous at the base

Lobes: Usually 5 (3 on younger shoots); broadly triangular, coarsely toothed and pointed; sinuses between the lobes rounded, obtuse or acute

End of leaf: Middle lobe pointed

Base of blade: Usually truncate or weakly heart-shaped

Margin of leaf: Lobes entire except for the coarse teeth

Upper/under side: Shiny green and glabrous above; paler green beneath and becoming glabrous later

Arrangement on the shoot: Leaves alternate

Distribution: Often planted as a park or street tree in central Europe; thrives in the very dry air of towns; origin unknown

895 **Platanus orientalis - Oriental Plane**
Deciduous tree, native in W. Asia, growing to a height of over 25m

Platanus orientalis L.
Oriental Plane

Platanaceae - Plane family p. 84

Length: 10-20cm

Form of blade: Broadly ovate or roundish and deeply 5- or 7-lobed; may be 3-lobed on younger shoots

Stalk: 3-7cm long, thickened and bulbous at the base

Lobes: Of unequal size, much longer than broad, often with smaller lobes and long-pointed; sinuses between the lobes rounded; middle lobe much longer than its width at the base

End of leaf: Terminal lobe with a very long point

Base of blade: Usually wedge-shaped

Margin of leaf: Lobes sinuately dentate and entire towards the base

Upper/under side: Shiny medium green above and pale green beneath; with dense, fine hairs when young, later becoming glabrous

Arrangement on the shoot: Leaves alternate

Distribution: Grows in very damp places in its native habitat; occasionally planted in parks in central Europe

896 **Populus alba - White Poplar**
Deciduous, broad-crowned tree, 10-30m high, with long shoots white- to grey-felted

Populus alba L.
White Poplar

Salicaceae - Willow family p. 40, 41, 86

Length: 5-12cm

Form of blade: Varied in outline; on long shoots and suckers elliptic to ovate and with 3-5 large lobes

Stalk: 2-4cm long, flattened and with white hairs

Lobes: 3-5, of unequal size, triangular, pointed and often sinuately dentate; sinuses between the lobes obtuse or rounded

End of leaf: Middle lobe pointed or slightly rounded

Base of blade: Rounded, slightly heart-shaped or truncate

Margin of leaf: Lobes sinuately dentate

Upper/under side: Both sides woolly felted at first; later shiny dark green above and becoming glabrous; remaining densely white-felted beneath

Arrangement on the shoot: Leaves alternate

Distribution: On the edge of damp woods, in waste places, and by water; ascending to 1500m

897 **Ribes alpinum - Mountain Currant**
Deciduous, much-branched, non-spiny shrub 1-2m in height

Ribes alpinum L.
Mountain Currant

Saxifragaceae - Saxifrage family p. 86

Length: 2-5cm long and broad

Form of blade: Broadly ovate to roundish in outline, with 3 or more rarely 5 lobes

Stalk: 1-2cm long, fringed with long glandular hairs

Lobes: 3, more rarely 5, broadly triangular, with coarse, deeply cut teeth, and pointed or obtuse at end

End of leaf: Middle lobe pointed, obtuse or rounded

Base of blade: Lobes coarsely and deeply serrate; teeth only shortly pointed

Upper/under side: Dark green above with scattered hairs; paler green beneath, shiny and usually glabrous

Arrangement on the shoot: Leaves alternate

Distribution: Scattered amongst the luxuriant vegetation of mixed woods, in gorges, on grassland with tall-herb communities, and in open pine woods in the montane and subalpine zones; also damp woods in hill zone

898 **Acer monspessulanum - Montpelier Maple** *Deciduous, 6-10m high, native in Mediterranean region, brownish green branchlets*

Acer monspessulanum L.
Montpelier Maple

Aceraceae - Maple family p. 85

Length: 3-6cm

Form of blade: Horizontally elliptic in outline with 3 lobes

Stalk: 1-3cm long and somewhat broadened at the base

Lobes: 3 (more rarely 5), thick, leathery, broadly triangular, rounded, and of similar size; lateral lobes spreading more or less horizontally; sinuses between the lobes usually forming a right-angle

End of leaf: Middle lobe rounded

Base of blade: Weakly heart-shaped or rounded

Margin of leaf: Lobes entire; more rarely somewhat wavy

Upper/under side: Shiny dark green and glabrous above; bluish green beneath, softly hairy at first, later glabrous

Arrangement on the shoot: Leaves opposite; each pair of leaves at right-angles to the next

Distribution: On sunny rock slopes, in sunny oak woods; ascending to 1700m in the Caucasus

899 **Acer campestre - Field Maple**
Deciduous tree, 10-15m high, with a rounded crown and corky wings on the twigs

Acer campestre L.
Field Maple

Aceraceae - Maple family p. 86

Length: 3-10cm long and often equally broad

Form of blade: Roundish to ovate in outline, with 3 or 5 lobes

Stalk: 1-5cm long, usually reddish above and containing a milky juice

Lobes: 3 or 5, of unequal size, obtuse or rounded, coarsely sinuate or entire; lobes becoming smaller towards the base

End of leaf: Middle lobe obtuse or rounded

Base of blade: Heart-shaped

Margin of leaf: Lobes entire, except for the coarse, rounded teeth

Upper/under side: Dark green and glabrous above; paler green beneath and softly hairy when young, later becoming glabrous

Arrangement on the shoot: Leaves opposite; each pair of leaves at right-angles to the next

Distribution: In thickets, hedges, and in damp oak and hornbeam woods with luxuriant vegetation from the hill to the montane zone

900 **Hedera helix - Ivy**
Evergreen climber up to 20m high with brownish green shoots rooting near the leaves

Hedera helix L.
Ivy

Araliaceae - Ivy family p. 85

Length: 4-10cm

Form of blade: Varied in outline; on non-flowering stems ovate to roundish, 3- or 5-lobed, leathery and evergreen (lasting 3 years)

Stalk: 3-7cm long and usually brown to brownish red above

Lobes: 3 (more rarely 5), of unequal size, broadly triangular and obtuse or rounded; lateral lobes spreading horizontally; sinuses between the lobes obtuse-angled or rounded

End of leaf: Middle lobe obtuse or rounded

Base of blade: Heart-shaped

Margin of leaf: Lobes entire; occasionally slightly wavy

Upper/under side: Dark bluish green and glabrous above with prominent pale yellow veins; dull pale green and glabrous beneath

Arrangement on the shoot: Leaves alternate

Distribution: Trailing on the ground or climbing on trees and walls in deciduous mixed woods, parks and on rocks

901 **Acer saccharum - Sugar Maple**
Deciduous tree from U.S.A., up to 40m high in its native habitat, with brownish yellow twigs

Acer saccharum Marsh.
Sugar Maple

Aceraceae - Maple family p. 85

Length: 8-15cm long and equally broad

Form of blade: Roundish or broadly heart-shaped in outline, with 3 or 5 lobes

Stalk: 5-10cm long and often reddish in colour

Lobes: Usually 5, of unequal size, broadly triangular, long-pointed and often also with 1 or 2 large pointed teeth

End of leaf: Middle lobe with a long, fine point

Base of blade: Weakly heart-shaped

Margin of leaf: Lobes entire between the teeth

Upper/under side: Medium to dark green and glabrous above; greyish green and glabrous beneath

Arrangement on the shoot: Leaves opposite; each pair of leaves at right-angles to the next

Distribution: Planted in Europe in large gardens and parks; often cultivated in the U.S.A. for the sugar obtained from its sap; the leaf is a feature of the Canadian national flag

902 **Ribes nigrum - Black Currant**
Deciduous shrub, 1-2m high, with young shoots finely hairy, and greyish to reddish brown

Ribes nigrum L.
Black Currant

Saxifragaceae Saxifrage family p. 86

Length: 5-10cm long and equally broad

Form of blade: Roundish in outline and 3- or 5-lobed

Stalk: 2-5cm long and broadened at the base

Lobes: 3 or 5, very broadly triangular, doubly serrate, and strongly scented; sinuses between the lobes acute

End of leaf: Middle lobe pointed

Base of blade: Heart-shaped

Margin of leaf: Lobes doubly serrate

Upper/under side: Medium to dark green above, hairy at first, later becoming glabrous; pale green beneath dotted with yellowish resin glands (magnifying glass required!)

Arrangement on the shoot: Leaves alternate

Distribution: In damp woods, thickets and alder groves; now only rarely found wild; first cultivated in 16th century; nowadays an important plant of cultivation with numerous large-fruited varieties

903 **Ribes rubrum - Red Currant**
Deciduous, non-spiny shrub, 1-2m high, with red berries

Ribes rubrum L.
Red Currant

Saxifragaceae - Saxifrage family p. 86

Length: 4-7cm

Form of blade: Roundish in outline and with 3 or 5 lobes

Stalk: 2-3.5cm long and somewhat thickened at the base

Lobes: 3 or 5, moderately to broadly triangular and pointed; sinuses between the lobes acute

End of leaf: Middle lobe pointed

Base of blade: Heart-shaped or truncate

Margin of leaf: Lobes doubly serrate and/or crenately toothed

Upper/under side: Dark green and dull above; paler green and softly hairy beneath, later becoming glabrous; not gland-dotted

Arrangement on the shoot: Leaves alternate

Distribution: Cultivated in gardens, and derived from wild European species. Its parents are mainly the Wild Red Currant, *R. spicatum*, and the Rock Red Currant, *R. petraeum*.

904 **Vitis vinifera - Grape-vine**
Deciduous climber with greyish to reddish brown fibrous bark

Vitis vinifera L. ssp. *vinifera*
Grape-vine

Vitaceae - Vine family p. 87

Length: 5-15cm long and broad

Form of blade: Varied in outline; usually roundish and as a rule moderately to deeply 3- or 5-lobed

Stalk: 4-8cm long

Lobes: 3 or 5, of varied size, triangular, pointed

End of leaf: Middle lobe with a short point

Base of blade: Deeply and narrowly heart-shaped or with a very narrow sinus where the blade joins the stalk

Margin of leaf: Lobes broadly toothed in the middle and upper parts; entire in the lower part and by the sinus

Upper/under side: Dark green above and hairy when young, later becoming glabrous; pale to greyish green beneath and often felted, more rarely becoming glabrous

Arrangement on the shoot: Leaves alternate

Distribution: Numerous varieties cultivated in the hill zone

905 **Viburnum opulus - Guelder Rose**
Quick-growing, deciduous shrub, 1-4m high, with glabrous, angular stems

Viburnum opulus L.
Guelder Rose

Caprifoliaceae - Honeysuckle family p. 87

Length: 4-12cm long and equally broad or broader

Form of blade: Varied in outline; usually roundish or horizontally elliptic with 3 or 5 lobes

Stalk: 2-3cm long with 2-6 linear, gland-tipped appendages at the base and 2-4 green, concave nectar-glands just below the blade

Lobes: Lateral lobes broadly triangular, pointed or obtuse; terminal lobe often rectangular

End of leaf: Middle lobe shortly pointed or obtuse

Base of blade: Heart-shaped or truncate

Margin of leaf: Lobes irregularly coarsely toothed except sinuses and lower parts of the lateral lobes

Upper/under side: Dark green and glabrous above; greyish green beneath, somewhat downy

Arrangement on shoot: Lvs opposite

Distribution: Damp woods, hedges, on wood-margins and the banks of streams; hill to montane zone

906 **Acer pseudoplatanus - Sycamore**
Deciduous tree, 30-40m high, developing to an impressive size, especially when free-standing

Acer pseudoplatanus L.
Sycamore

Aceraceae - Maple family p. 22, 23, 87

Length: 8-20cm long and up to 16cm broad

Form of blade: Broadly ovate, heart-shaped or roundish in outline and 3- or 5-lobed

Stalk: Up to 10cm long, red above

Lobes: 5, more rarely 3, of unequal size (the lowest always small), broadly triangular and pointed; sinuses between the lobes acute

End of leaf: Middle lobe shortly pointed, obtuse or rounded

Base of blade: Heart-shaped

Margin of leaf: Lobes irregularly coarsely serrate and dentate; entire in the sinuses and at the base of the blade

Upper/under side: Dark green and glabrous above; pale bluish green beneath, densely hairy at first and becoming glabrous later except between the veins; veins pale green

Arrangement on the shoot: Leaves opposite

Distribution: On the banks of streams, on waste ground, in gorges and mixed beech woods

907 **Acer opalus - Italian Maple**
Deciduous shrub or tree up to 20m high with light brown bark

Acer opalus Mill.
Italian Maple

Aceraceae - Maple family p. 87

Length: 4-10cm and usually a little broader

Form of blade: Usually roundish in outline and with 5 lobes (the 2 lower lobes often only indicated)

Stalk: 3-9cm long and dark red above

Lobes: Very broadly triangular, much shorter than in the Sycamore and usually obtuse at the end; sinuses between the lobes rounded, obtuse or acute

End of leaf: Middle lobe usually obtuse

Base of blade: Heart-shaped or truncate

Margin of leaf: Lobes irregularly crenate and dentate; only short sections in the sinuses entire

Upper/under side: Dark green and glabrous above; bluish green beneath and hairy at first, soon becoming glabrous

Arrangement on the shoot: Leaves opposite

Distribution: On south-facing slopes and, south of the Alps, in the mountains of the W. Mediterranean region

908 ***Acer rubrum*** **- Red Maple**
Deciduous tree, up to 40m high in its native habitat, with bright red shoots in the 1st year

Acer rubrum L.
Red Maple
Aceraceae - Maple family p. 87

Length: 5-10cm

Form of blade: Broadly ovate or roundish in outline and usually with 3 lobes (more rarely 5-lobed)

Stalk: 4-6cm long and dark red and green above

Lobes: Very broadly triangular and pointed; terminal lobe larger than the lateral lobes; sinuses between the lobes obtuse

End of leaf: Middle lobe pointed

Base of blade: Truncate or rounded

Margin of leaf: Lobes coarsely serrate and dentate; entire at the sinuses

Upper/under side: Dark green above, bluish grey beneath; both sides glabrous or hairy on the veins beneath

Arrangement on the shoot: Leaves opposite; each pair of leaves at right-angles to the next

Distribution: Native in eastern N. America; suitable for swampy areas of parks; sometimes planted for its splendid wine-red autumn colouring

909 ***Morus alba*** **- White Mulberry**
Much-branched, deciduous tree, up to 20m high, native in China and Korea

Morus alba L.
White Mulberry
Moraceae - Mulberry family p. 87

Length: 6-18cm

Form of blade: Varied in outline; unlobed and with an irregularly serrate margin or with 3, 5 or 7 lobes

Stalk: 2-4cm long, grooved and downy at first

Lobes: 3, 5 or 7; of unequal size, irregularly formed and rounded or shortly pointed; sinuses between the lobes acute, obtuse or rounded

End of leaf: Middle lobe only very shortly pointed

Base of blade: Equally or unequally heart-shaped or truncate

Margin of leaf: Irregularly serrate; entire in the lower part of the lobes and at the sinuses

Upper/under side: Shiny dark green and glabrous above; pale bluish green beneath, almost glabrous or hairy on the larger veins

Arrangement on the shoot: Leaves alternate

Distribution: Occasionally planted in gardens

910 ***Sorbus torminalis*** **- Wild Service Tree**
Large, deciduous shrub or tree, 5-20m high, with shiny brown, glabrous branchlets

Sorbus torminalis (L.) Crantz
Wild Service Tree
Rosaceae - Rose family p. 88

Length: 6-10cm long and almost equally broad

Form of blade: Ovate to roundish in outline and with 3 or 4 pointed lobes on each side

Stalk: 2-5cm long and loosely felted; later glabrous

Lobes: Narrowly to broadly triangular and pointed; lower lobes larger and usually spreading horizontally

End of leaf: Middle lobe pointed

Base of blade: Truncate or rounded

Margin of leaf: Simply and doubly serrate; entire or undulate at the base of the blade

Upper/under side: Shiny dark green above, and finely hairy for a time, but later becoming glabrous; pale bluish green and loosely felted, hairs persisting only between veins

Arrangement on the shoot: Leaves alternate

Distribution: In hornbeam, oak and beech woods; hill zone

911 ***Sorbus mougeotii*** **- Mougeot's Whitebeam** *Deciduous shrub or tree, 4-20m high, with brownish red branchlets*

Sorbus mougeotii
Soy.-Willem. et Godr.
Mougeot's Whitebeam
Rosaceae - Rose family p. 88

Length: 6-10cm

Form of blade: Oblong-elliptic to ovate in outline with a number of irregular lobes on each side, becoming smaller towards the tip

Stalk: 1-2cm long

Lobes: With about 10 lobes on each side; lobes fairly shallow, very shortly pointed and becoming smaller towards the tip

End of leaf: Shortly pointed

Base of blade: Lobes irregularly finely serrate

Upper/under side: Dark green above and later becoming glabrous; densely white-felted beneath and therefore appearing pale grey; veins pale greyish green; 8-12 pairs of lateral veins

Arrangement on the shoot: Leaves alternate

Distribution: On fairly dry, calcareous stony soils on warm, shady places; found here and there in deciduous mixed woods; hill to subalpine zone

912 ***Sorbus intermedia*** **- Swedish Whitebeam**
Deciduous shrub or tree up to 15m high with olive green to brown branchlets

Sorbus intermedia (Ehrh.) Pers.
Swedish Whitebeam
Rosaceae - Rose family p. 88

Length: 6-12cm

Form of blade: Oblong-elliptic to elliptic in outline and with 5-8 short lobes on each side; only serrate in the upper part

Stalk: 1-2cm long and grey-felted

Lobes: 5-8 on each side, fairly shallow and only shortly pointed; sinuses between the lobes acute

End of leaf: Shortly pointed

Base of blade: Broadly wedge-shaped or rounded

Margin of leaf: Lobes irregularly serrate

Upper/under side: Shiny dark green above; remaining grey-felted beneath, but finally becoming somewhat glabrous; 6-9 pairs of lateral veins

Arrangement on the shoot: Leaves alternate

Distribution: Native in Scandinavia; often planted along streets and in parks in Sweden, Denmark and N.E. Germany because of its resistance to air pollution

913 ***Sorbus latifolia*** **- Broad-leaved Whitebeam**
Deciduous tree up to 28m high with greyish brown to olive brown branchlets

Sorbus latifolia (Lam.) Pers.
Broad-leaved Whitebeam
Rosaceae - Rose family p. 88

Length: 7-12cm long and up to 10cm broad in the lower third

Form of blade: Ovate to broadly ovate in outline with 6-9 lobes on each side; only serrate but no longer lobed towards the tip

Stalk: 1-3cm long

Lobes: 6-9 on each side, broadly triangular, pointed, and becoming progressively smaller towards the tip; sinuses between the lobes acute

End of leaf: Shortly pointed

Base of blade: Irregularly or regularly broadly wedge-shaped or rounded

Margin of leaf: Lobes irregularly finely serrate

Upper/under side: Shiny dark green and glabrous above; somewhat grey-felted beneath and therefore appearing pale greyish green; veins pale yellowish green

Arrangement on the shoot: Leaves alternate

Distribution: In warmer parts of the hill zone in oak-hornbeam woods; more rarely montane

914 **Quercus robur - Common Oak, Pedunculate Oak** *Deciduous tree, native in Europe, growing up to 50m high, with light brown branchlets*

Quercus robur L. Common Oak, Pedunculate Oak

Fagaceae - Beech family p. 48, 49, 89

Length: 5-16cm

Form of blade: Obovate to elliptic in outline; the greatest breadth in the upper third; with 4 or 5 irregular lobes of unequal size on each side

Stalk: Usually small; at most 7mm long

Lobes: 4 or 5 on each side, irregular, entire, rounded, and often reaching halfway towards the midrib; sinuses between the lobes rounded

End of leaf: Middle lobe rounded

Base of blade: Usually somewhat heart-shaped and with 2 clearly visible auricles (small lobes)

Margin of leaf: Lobes entire

Upper/under side: Shiny dark green and glabrous above; dull pale to bluish green beneath; rarely slightly hairy

Arrangement on the shoot: Leaves alternate

Distribution: From the hill to the lower montane zone where winters are mild and damp

915 **Quercus pubescens - Downy Oak** *Deciduous tree, 3-20m high, with young stems densely felted at first with downy hairs*

Quercus pubescens Willd. Downy Oak

Fagaceae - beech family p. 89

Length: 5-10cm

Form of blade: Outline varying in shape, but usually obovate with the greatest breadth in the upper third; 5-7 unequal lobes on each side

Stalk: 8-12cm long

Lobes: 5-7 on each side, obtuse or occasionally with a small point at the end; sinuses between the lobes usually rounded

End of leaf: Middle lobe with 2+ obtuse or shortly pointed sections

Base of blade: Often rounded; the 2 halves of the blade not always ending at the same point on the midrib

Margin of leaf: Lobes and their sections entire

Upper/under side: Both sides felted at first; later glabrous and dark green above; pale greyish green beneath because of the hairy covering

Arrangement: Leaves alternate

Distribution: Hill zone, more rarely montane; sunny hillsides, warm and stony slopes; deciduous and pine woods

916 **Quercus petraea - Sessile Oak** *Deciduous tree, growing 20-45m high, with glabrous olive green to brown branchlets*

Quercus petraea Liebl. Sessile Oak

Fagaceae - Beech family p. 89

Length: 6-12cm

Form of blade: Obovate in outline, broadest in the middle, and with 5-9 lobes on each side

Stalk: 10-25mm long

Lobes: 5-9 on each side, rounded, entire, and more or less equal in size; sinuses between the lobes usually acute

End of leaf: Middle lobe obtuse or rounded

Base of blade: Regularly or irregularly wedge-shaped or rounded

Margin of leaf: Lobes entire

Upper/under side: Dull dark green and glabrous above; paler green beneath with very small and scattered stellate hairs

Arrangement on the shoot: Leaves alternate

Distribution: From the hill to the lower montane zone in areas mild in winter; in beech and oak-hornbeam woods; up to 1600m in the southern Alps

917 **Quercus cerris - Turkey Oak** *Deciduous shrub or tree up to 30m high, with branchlets olive green and red at first*

Quercus cerris L. Turkey Oak

Fagaceae - Beech family p. 89

Length: 6-15cm

Form of blade: Varied in outline; usually narrowly elliptic with the greatest breadth in the upper third; 7-9 lobes of unequal size on each side

Stalk: 7-15mm long

Lobes: 7-9 on each side, rather obtuse or more often pointed at the end; sinuses between the lobes rounded or acute

End of leaf: Middle lobe finely pointed, other sections also pointed

Base of blade: Wedge-shaped

Margin of leaf: Lobes and any other pointed sections entire

Upper/under side: Roughly hairy above at first, later glabrous and shiny dark green; pale green beneath, the very long, soft, downy hairs persistent

Arrangement on the shoot: Leaves alternate

Distribution: In hot parts of the hill zone; found here and there especially in Downy Oak woods and on stony slopes

918 **Quercus rubra - Red Oak** *Deciduous tree, 20-35m high, with reddish brown branchlets*

Quercus rubra L. Red Oak

Fagaceae - Beech family p. 89

Length: 10-20cm

Form of blade: Usually elliptic or obovate with 4-6 lobes on each side

Stalk: Up to 5cm long

Lobes: 4-6 on each side, themselves partially lobed; lobes and additional smaller lobes with a strong point, often ending in a bristle-like tip

End of leaf: Middle lobe with additional smaller lobes, all sections long-pointed and usually tipped by a long bristle

Base of blade: Rounded or broadly wedge-shaped

Margin of leaf: Lobes and additional smaller lobes entire

Upper/under side: Dull to dark green and glabrous above; pale yellowish green beneath, with stellate hairs between the midrib and lateral veins

Arrangement on the shoot: Leaves alternate

Distribution: Native in the eastern United States; introduced into Europe a long time ago and used for afforestation; often planted in large gardens and parks as an ornamental tree

919 **Quercus ilex - Evergreen Oak** *Evergreen tree up to 25m high, with grey-felted branchlets that only gradually become glabrous*

Quercus ilex L. Evergreen Oak, Holm Oak

Fagaceae - Beech family p. 105

Length: 3-8cm

Form of blade: Varied in outline; usually oblong-ovate to ovate with 4-7 sharp teeth on each side; often also lobed

Stalk: 7-15mm long and covered with long, white, matted hairs

Lobes: Sharply pointed, entire or undulate, leathery and thick

End of leaf: Sharply pointed

Base of blade: Broadly wedge-shaped or rounded

Margin of leaf: Lobes entire or undulate

Upper/under side: Young leaves hairy on both sides, older leaves shiny dark green and glabrous above; appearing grey to whitish beneath because of the dense covering of hairs

Arrangement on the shoot: Leaves alternate

Distribution: Widespread in the Mediterranean region; often the dominant tree in evergreen woods; planted in parks in areas with a mild winter climate as an ornamental tree

920 **Rhododendron hirsutum - Hairy Alpenrose** *Evergreen shrub up to 1m high with stems green and hairy at first*

Rhododendron hirsutum L.
Hairy Alpenrose

Ericaceae - Heath family p. 90

Length 1-3.5cm

Form of blade: Oblong-elliptic in outline; thick and leathery

Stalk: 0.3-0.8cm long

End of leaf: Obtuse or rounded

Base of blade: Narrowly wedge-shaped

Margin of leaf: Entire, often wavy in places; with 1-2mm long, bristly, spreading hairs

Upper/under side: Shiny dark green above, somewhat wrinkled, glabrous, and with scattered glandular scales; pale green beneath, dotted with glands which are whitish at first, later yellowish brown

Arrangement on the shoot: Leaves alternate

Distribution: In the subalpine zone; always on calcareous subsoil in scree, clefts in rocks, and shady places covered with snow for long periods

921 **Erica tetralix - Cross-leaved Heath** *Prostrate, evergreen, dwarf shrub up to 50cm high with numerous branched stems*

Erica tetralix L.
Cross-leaved Heath, Bog Heather

Ericaceae - Heath family p. 90

Length: 3-6mm

Form of blade: Narrowly linear or needle-like in outline

Stalk: Very short, 1-2mm long, usually felted and very broad

End of leaf: Obtuse or rounded

Base of blade: Very slightly narrowed into the broad stalk

Margin of leaf: Inrolled, with 0.5-1mm long, spreading, white hairs

Upper/under side: With a dark green surface above, but appearing whitish in places because of fine matted hairs; white beneath with a prominent medium green midrib

Arrangement on the shoot: Leaves arranged in whorls of 4, more rarely in whorls of 3

Distribution: From the lowlands to the montane zone; in peat bogs, on heaths and acid, humus-rich, sandy soils and in boggy woods

922 **Ledum groenlandicum - Labrador Tea** *Evergreen shrub, up to 1m high, with erect, brown-felted stems*

Ledum groenlandicum Oed.
(L. palustre ssp. *groenlandicum)*
Labrador Tea

Ericaceae - Heath family p. 90

Length: 2-5cm

Form of blade: Oblong to oblong-elliptic in outline

Stalk: 0.3-0.6cm long with brown hairs

End of leaf: Obtuse

Base of blade: Wedge-shaped or rounded

Margin of leaf: Entire, the whole margin rolled under

Upper/under side: Medium to dark green above with an undulate surface; pale to dark green beneath, in places densely covered with medium to dark brown crisped hairs; midrib pale yellow and prominent

Arrangement on the shoot: Leaves alternate

Distribution: Abundant in N. Europe, on cold peat moors and in bogs; leaves used in time of need as a substitute for tea

923 **Rhododendron ferrugineum - Alpenrose** *Roundish, much-branched, evergreen shrub up to 1m in height*

Rhododendron ferrugineum L.
Alpenrose

Ericaceae - Heath family p. 90

Length: 2-5cm

Form of blade: Oblong-lanceolate to oblong-elliptic in outline, leathery, and narrowed 2-6mm stalk

Stalk: Very short, up to 6mm long

End of leaf: Rounded or obtuse

Base of blade: Narrowly wedge-shaped

Margin of leaf: Entire; margin somewhat recurved

Upper/under side: Shiny dark green above and slightly wrinkled; brown beneath because of the dense covering of overlapping, spherical glands; young leaves with pale yellow glands beneath; scales overlapping

Arrangement on the shoot: Leaves alternate

Distribution: In the subalpine zone; more rarely montane and alpine; on thick layers of acid raw humus amongst pines and larches above or in the forest zone

924 **Ledum palustre - Marsh Ledum** *Evergreen shrub, 1-1.5m high, with stems hairy at first*

Ledum palustre L.
Marsh Ledum

Ericaceae - Heath family p. 90

Length: 2-5cm

Form of blade: Linear to lanceolate in outline

Stalk: 2-3mm long with some brownish hairs; often as broad as the blade

End of leaf: Obtuse or rounded and usually with a short, fine point

Base of blade: Slightly wedge-shaped; base of blade and stalk often as broad as each other

Margin of leaf: Entire; margins strongly recurved to within 1-2mm of each other

Upper/under side: Dark green and distinctly felted above, later often becoming glabrous; rust red to brown-felted beneath

Arrangement on the shoot: Leaves alternate

Distribution: In the hill zone; in N. Europe especially in raised bogs and transitional moorland, wooded bogs, and acid, peaty soils lacking in nutrients

925 **Empetrum nigrum - Crowberry** *Prostrate, evergreen, creeping dwarf shrub, 10-45cm high, forming tufts*

Empetrum nigrum L. ssp. *hermaphroditum* (Hagerup) Böcher
Crowberry

Empetraceae - Crowberry family p. 91

Length: 4-7mm long

Form of blade: Narrowly elliptic or linear in outline and leathery

Stalk: 1-2mm long, broad, dark green and appressed to the shoot

End of leaf: Obtuse or shortly pointed

Base of blade: Wedge-shaped, narrowing slightly to the broad base

Margin of leaf: Entire, margins rolled under, their fringes of white hairs touching each other, resulting in a longitudinal furrow

Upper/under side: Dark green and glabrous above; with a white keel beneath and sparsely hairy; margins dark green

Arrangement on the shoot: Leaves in irregular whorls

Distribution: In damp areas of the montane and subalpine zone and in the Arctic; on sunny slopes and acid soils in the Alps, in association with the Bilberry, Alpenrose, etc.

926 **Erica carnea - Spring Heath**
Evergreen dwarf shrub up to 30cm high, with 4-angled stems forming dense mats

Erica carnea L.
(*E. herbacea* L.)
Spring Heath
Ericaceae - Heath family p. 91

Length: 4-8mm

Form of blade: Needle-like or linear in outline

Stalk: 1-2mm long, brownish white in colour and almost as broad as the blade

End of leaf: Rounded and usually with a short, sharp point

Base of blade: Rounded into the leaf-stalk

Margin of leaf: Margins rolled under; marginal glands far apart

Upper/under side: Medium to dark green above, glabrous and shiny; groove between the margins beneath appearing white

Arrangement on the shoot: Leaves in whorls of 3 or 4

Distribution: In the montane and subalpine zone in Pine woods, on sunny, warm hillsides, in open larch and spruce woods and on moorland

927 **Erica arborea - Tree Heath**
Evergreen shrub up to 5m in height with erect and hairy young stems

Erica arborea L.
Tree Heath
Ericaceae- Heath family p. 91

Length: 4-7mm

Form of blade: Needle-like or narrowly linear in outline

Stalk: 1-2mm long, whitish and almost as broad as the blade

End of leaf: Obtuse or rounded

Base of blade: Abruptly narrowed

Margin of leaf: Entire; margins rolled under leaving only a narrow groove; glandular hairy

Upper/under side: Dark green above and whitish beneath between the inrolled margins; midrib pale green and clearly visible

Arrangement on the shoot: Leaves in whorls of 3 or 4

Distribution: Distributed especially throughout S. Europe, the Caucasus and N. Africa; the famous French bruyère pipes are made from the wood

928 **Erica vagans - Cornish Heath**
Evergreen dwarf shrub 30-80cm high, luxuriant in growth and with light brown stems

Erica vagans L.
Cornish Heath
Ericaceae - Heath family p. 91

Length: 4-10mm

Form of blade: Narrowly linear in outline

Stalk: 1-2mm, white, and almost as broad as the blade

End of leaf: Rounded or obtuse

Base of blade: Slightly narrowed at the sides

Margin of leaf: Entire; with glands far apart; margins rolled under

Upper/under side: Dark green and glabrous above; white beneath with a very prominent dark green midrib

Arrangement on the shoot: Leaves in whorls of 4 or 5

Distribution: In the hill zone; on the edges of woods and shrubby places especially in W. Europe (from Ireland to Portugal)

929 **Loiseleuria procumbens - Trailing Azalea** *Prostrate, evergreen dwarf shrub forming tufts, with stems 15-40cm in length*

Loiseleuria procumbens
(L.) Desv.
Trailing Azalea
Ericaceae - Heath family p. 91

Length: 4-8cm

Form of blade: Narrowly elliptic in outline and not much broader than the stalk

Stalk: 1-3mm; usually pale yellowish white in colour

End of leaf: Obtuse or shortly pointed

Base of blade: Slightly wedge-shaped

Margin of leaf: Entire; margins rolled under

Upper/under side: Dark green above, hairy at first, later glabrous, with a shallow groove along the middle; bluish white to white and glabrous beneath with a distinctly prominent, broad midrib

Arrangement on the shoot: Leaves opposite; each pair of leaves at right-angles to the next

Distribution: In the subalpine and alpine zone; on scree, rocks, ridges exposed to the wind, and on moors dominated by dwarf shrubs; a calcifuge mountain plant

930 **Andromeda polifolia - Bog Rosemary**
Evergreen shrub, 10-20cm high, with creeping stems growing into the tussocks on raised bogs

Andromeda polifolia L.
Bog Rosemary
Ericaceae - Heath family p. 92

Length: 1-5cm

Form of blade: Narrowly lanceolate or narrowly linear in outline and leathery

Stalk: 0.3-0.7cm long and usually white

End of leaf: With a fine or sharp point

Base of blade: Narrowly wedge-shaped

Margin of leaf: Entire; margins rolled under

Upper/under side: Shiny dark green above, with an irregular pattern of white lateral veins; silvery white or pale bluish green beneath with a prominent white midrib

Arrangement on the shoot: Leaves alternate

Distribution: From the hill to the subalpine zone; on raised bogs and wet, acid peat moors lacking in nutrients; a plant characteristic of peat-bogs and moorland

931 **Rosmarinus officinalis - Rosemary**
Evergreen, sweetly scented shrub, with grey-felted stems growing up to 1.5m high

Rosmarinus officinalis L.
Rosemary
Labiatae - Mint family p. 92

Length: 3-5cm

Form of blade: Very narrowly lanceolate or linear in outline and leathery

Stalk: Leaf sessile or very shortly stalked; stalk densely felted with stellate hairs

End of leaf: Obtuse or rounded

Base of blade: Narrowly wedge-shaped

Margin of leaf: Entire; margins rolled under

Upper/under side: Dark green above and slightly wrinkled; densely white-felted beneath; midrib prominent and white

Arrangement on the shoot: Leaves opposite, each pair at right-angles to the next

Distribution: In the warmer parts of the hill zone with a mild winter climate; a plant typical of the maquis and rocky steppes; particularly abundant in the Mediterranean region; Rosemary has been known since ancient times as an aromatic culinary and medicinal plant

932 ***Vaccinium oxycoccus* - Cranberry**
Prostrate, evergreen half-shrub with creeping stems up to 80cm long and becoming woody

Vaccinium oxycoccus L.
Cranberry

Ericaceae - Heath family p. 92

Length: 0.5-1cm (at most 1.5cm)

Form of blade: Elliptic, ovate or oblong-ovate in outline

Stalk: At most 2mm long

End of leaf: Obtuse or shortly pointed

Base of blade: Rounded or weakly heart-shaped

Margin of leaf: Entire; margins recurved

Upper/under side: Shiny dark green above, glabrous, and usually with a pale green, slightly impressed midrib; with a bluish green bloom beneath

Arrangement on the shoot: Leaves alternate

Distribution: From the hill to the montane zone; forming the surface covering of raised bogs; particularly on the tussocks on peat-moors where it grows with Bog Rosemary and Sundew

933 ***Calluna vulgaris* - Ling**
Evergreen, much-branched shrub 20-60cm high, with stems 4-angled at first

Calluna vulgaris (L.) Hull
Ling, Heather

Ericaceae - Heath family p. 92

Length: 1-3mm long

Form of blade: Needle-like or narrowly ovate in outline, or scale-like

Stalk: Leaves sessile

End of leaf: Usually rounded

Base of blade: Clasping the stem, and with 2 pointed auricles, glandular on the margin and pointing downwards

Margin of leaf: Entire; margins curved upwards, the fringe of short hairs forming a white band

Upper/under side: Dark green in summer, brownish red in winter; deeply grooved above, keeled beneath and glabrous or slightly hairy

Arrangement on the shoot: Leaves opposite, each pair at right-angles to the next; overlapping each other and forming 4 longitudinal rows

Distribution: From the hill up into the alpine zone; characteristic of European heaths and moorlands; on moors and heaths, in dry and open woods and on sandy dunes

934 ***Genista pilosa* - Hairy Greenweed**
Deciduous dwarf shrub, 10-30cm high, with finely hairy, angular stems

Genista pilosa L.
Hairy Greenweed

Leguminosae - Pea family p. 93

Length: 0.3-1.2cm long

Form of blade: Narrowly obovate to lanceolate in outline

Stalk: Leaf sessile or very shortly stalked

End of leaf: Emarginate or retuse

Base of blade: Wedge-shaped

Margin of leaf: Entire

Upper/under side: Dark green on both sides with short, appressed hairs; older leaves sometimes glabrous; midrib beneath pale green in colour

Arrangement on the shoot: Leaves alternate

Distribution: In the hill zone; on sandy, stony and sunny heaths on poor soils usually lacking in calcium, in open woods, on crags and at the edges of woods; especially in sunny, dry places, warm in summer; ascending to 1100m in the Black Forest

935 ***Daphne cneorum* - Garland Flower**
Evergreen shrub, 10-40cm high, with creeping stems and hairy young shoots

Daphne cneorum L.
Garland Flower

Thymelaeaceae - Daphne family p. 93

Length: 0.5-2cm

Form of blade: Linear, lanceolate or spathulate in outline

Stalk: Very short and broad

End of leaf: Emarginate, or rounded with a small point

Base of blade: Wedge-shaped

Margin of leaf: Entire; slightly recurved

Upper/under side: Both sides glabrous; medium to dark green above with pale yellowish green veins; bluish grey beneath; midrib dark green and prominent, lateral veins whitish

Arrangement on the shoot: Leaves alternate

Distribution: From the hill to the montane zone, more rarely subalpine; on the edges of woods, on stony slopes, in open, dry pine woods, and in alpine meadows

936 ***Vaccinium vitis-idaea* - Cowberry**
Evergreen, dwarf shrub, 10-30cm high, with creeping, scaly, underground stems

Vaccinium vitis-idaea L.
Cowberry

Ericaceae - Heath family p. 92

Length: 1-3cm

Form of blade: Elliptic to obovate in outline; leaves thick and leathery

Stalk: 0.2-0.5cm long, with downy hairs

End of leaf: Usually emarginate

Base of blade: Obtuse or wedge-shaped

Margin of leaf: Entire; margins slightly recurved; also finely dentate or crenate

Upper/under side: Dark green above with whitish veins; greyish green beneath with small, brown glandular hairs (therefore appearing dotted)

Arrangement on the shoot: Leaves alternate

Distribution: From the hill to the alpine zone; on raw humus in open Spruce, Pine and Larch woods, Juniper thickets, dwarf shrub communities, heaths and moors

937 ***Buxus sempervirens* - Box**
Evergreen, densely branched shrub or tree up to 16m high with stems 4-angled at first

Buxus sempervirens L.
Box

Buxaceae - Box family p. 92

Length: 1-3cm

Form of blade: Narrowly elliptic to oblong-ovate; broadest at or slightly below the middle; blade leathery

Stalk: Up to 2mm long, often slightly winged because of the narrowed base of the blade

End of leaf: Usually emarginate, more rarely rounded

Base of blade: Wedge-shaped

Margin of leaf: Entire; margins slightly recurved

Upper/under side: Shiny dark green above and the midrib often whitish and impressed; pale green beneath and midrib prominent

Arrangement on the shoot: Leaves opposite

Distribution: From the hill to the montane zone; ascending to 2000m in Greece; found here and there in warm places such as mixed deciduous woods and dry meadows; widely cultivated as a park and garden plant

938 ***Salix reticulata* - Net-leaved Willow**
Deciduous, mat-forming dwarf shrub with round stems 5–30cm long

Salix reticulata L.
Net-leaved Willow

Salicaceae - Willow family p. 93

Length: 1–4.5cm

Form of blade: Broadly elliptic to roundish in outline

Stalk: 0.3–2cm long and both sides reddish in colour

End of leaf: Obtuse or rounded

Base of blade: Broadly wedge-shaped or rounded

Margin of leaf: Entire

Upper/under side: Dark green above, hairy at first, later glabrous, with impressed veins forming a network; grey to whitish green beneath with prominent veins; margins slightly recurved

Arrangement on the shoot: Leaves alternate

Distribution: In the subalpine and alpine zone on mountain ledges and rocks, and in snow-hollows; also in the lowlands of N. Europe; a pioneer shrub

939 ***Vaccinium uliginosum* - Northern Bilberry** *Deciduous shrub, 15–90cm high, with stems creeping underground in raw humus*

Vaccinium uliginosum L.
Northern Bilberry

Ericaceae - Heath family p. 94

Length: 0.5–2cm

Form of blade: Elliptic, obovate or roundish in outline, and thick

Stalk: 1–2mm long and often slightly grooved above

End of leaf: Usually rounded; more rarely weakly retuse or obtuse

Base of blade: Rounded or broadly wedge-shaped

Margin of leaf: Entire

Upper/under side: Both sides glabrous; medium green above and bluish green beneath, with prominent dark green veins and slightly hairy at first

Arrangement on the shoot: Leaves alternate

Distribution: From the hill to the subalpine zone, on moors together with birches, pines and heather, in open conifer woods and in dwarf shrub communities on high mountains

940 ***Salix retusa* - Blunt-leaved Willow**
Deciduous, low-growing shrub, with creeping stems 5–30cm long

Salix retusa L.
Blunt-leaved Willow

Salicaceae - Willow family p. 94

Length: 0.4–2cm

Form of blade: Obovate to oblong-ovate or spathulate in outline

Stalk: 2–5mm long

End of leaf: Rounded, obtuse or emarginate

Base of blade: Wedge-shaped

Margin of leaf: Entire; more rarely with a few small teeth

Upper/under side: Shiny medium to dark green above and glabrous; slightly hairy beneath when young, later glabrous and shiny medium to whitish green

Arrangement on the shoot: Leaves alternate

Distribution: In the subalpine and alpine zone, on damp rock-ledges, on boulders, alluvial land, and in north-facing places with 8–10 months' snow-cover (a characteristic plant of wetland communities)

941 ***Ruscus aculeatus* - Butcher's Broom**
Spiny, evergreen shrub, 40–80cm high, with green stems

Ruscus aculeatus L.
Butcher's Broom

Liliaceae - Lily family p. 94

Length: Flattened shoot (cladode) 1–4cm long

Form of blade: True leaves only a few mm long, scale-like, soon withering but remaining on the plant; cladode pointed elliptic to pointed ovate in outline

Stalk: Base of cladode 1–3mm long

End of leaf: Tip of cladode long and finely pointed, ending in a spine

Base of blade: Base of cladode wedge-shaped

Margin of leaf: Entire

Upper/under side: Both sides medium green with dark green parallel veins; very often keeled beneath

Arrangement on the shoot: Leaf-like shoots alternately arranged

Distribution: In the hill and montane zone; on south-facing slopes in the warmest parts of the foothills of the Jura, in the southern Alps and in the Mediterranean region

942 ***Ginkgo biloba* - Maidenhair Tree**
Deciduous, 30–40m high, with several more or less erect branches forming acute angle with trunk

Ginkgo biloba L.
Maidenhair tree

Ginkgoaceae - Ginkgo family p. 93

Length: 6–10cm

Form of blade: Fan-shaped in outline, the upper edge irregularly waved or deeply divided into several lobes

Stalk: 2–9cm long

End of leaf: Fan-shaped, with an irregularly undulate margin

Base of blade: Obtuse or broadly wedge-shaped

Margin of leaf: Entire; upper edge wavy

Upper/under side: Both sides glabrous and medium to dark green; veins finely forked

Arrangement on the shoot: Rosette-like clusters of 3–6 on short shoots, alternately arranged on long shoots

Distribution: Decorative park and street tree, native in China; all the trees planted in Europe (since 1730) are derived from trees in E. Asian temple gardens

943 ***Cercis siliquastrum* - Judas Tree**
Deciduous tree up to 10m high (in gardens and parks sometimes only forming a shrub)

Cercis siliquastrum L.
Judas Tree

Leguminosae - Pea family p. 93

Length: 6–11cm long and equally broad

Form of blade: Almost circular in outline

Stalk: 3–4.5cm long and coloured red on both sides

End of leaf: Rounded or weakly emarginate

Base of blade: Heart-shaped

Margin of leaf: Entire; occasionally with shallow sinuses

Upper/under side: Both sides glabrous; dark green above and bluish green beneath; main veins pale green beneath and prominent

Arrangement on the shoot: Leaves alternate

Distribution: In the hill zone; in Hop Hornbeam and Oriental Hornbeam woods and in wooded parts of south-facing slopes; found wild especially in the Mediterranean region; also planted there as a street tree

944 ***Fagus sylvatica 'Atropunicea'* - Copper Beech** *Deciduous tree up to 40m high with dark brown twigs*

Fagus sylvatica L. 'Atropunicea' Copper Beech

Fagaceae - Beech family p. 94

Length: 5-10cm

Form of blade: Broadly elliptic to obovate in outline; broadest at or above the middle

Stalk: 0.2-0.5cm long and dark red to blackish in colour

End of leaf: Shortly pointed

Base of blade: Broadly wedge-shaped or rounded

Margin of leaf: Entire, often slightly undulate

Upper/under side: Softly hairy when young and fringed with hairs on the margin; older leaves often glabrous; dark purple to black above and dark greenish purple to blackish beneath; veins prominent; lateral veins more or less parallel to each other

Arrangement on the shoot: Leaves alternate (fomring 2 ranks)

Distribution: Planted in large gardens and parks

945 ***Eucalyptus globulus* - Blue Gum** *Evergreen tree up to 45m high with slender shoots, somewhat angular in cross-section*

Eucalyptus globulus Labill. Blue Gum

Myrtaceae - Myrtle family p. 95

Length: 7-15cm

Form of blade: Juvenile leaves broadly lanceolate to ovate in outline and usually spreading

Stalk: Juvenile leaves sessile or very shortly stalked

End of leaf: Pointed, sometimes sharply

Base of blade: Weakly heart-shaped

Margin of leaf: Entire

Upper/under side: Juvenile leaves glabrous on both sides; dark green to bluish green above and often with a pale purple or whitish midrib; dark green to bluish grey beneath

Arrangement on the shoot: Juvenile leaves on young shoots opposite and spreading horizontally; adult leaves arranged alternately and hanging down

Distribution: Planted in the whole Mediterranean region, largely for the drainage of wet areas; grows up to 36m high in southern England

946 ***Hippophae rhamnoides* - Sea Buckthorn** *Deciduous, spiny, densely branched shrub or tree up to 8m in height*

Hippophae rhamnoides L. Sea Buckthorn

Elaeagnaceae - Oleaster family p. 95

Length: 5-7cm

Form of blade: Linear to lanceolate in outline

Stalk: Leaf sessile or with a white stalk 1-3mm long

End of leaf: Obtuse or pointed

Base of blade: Wedge-shaped

Margin of leaf: Entire; often slightly recurved

Upper/under side: Shiny, silvery scales on both sides; greyish green above with scattered scales; silvery white beneath; lateral veins barely or only indistinctly visible

Arrangement on the shoot: Leaves alternate

Distribution: From the hill to the montane zone; on warm slopes, on river-banks, by pathways, in gravel-pits, open pine woods and on scree; a pioneer shrub of open places

947 ***Elaeagnus angustifolia* - Oleaster** *Deciduous, somewhat spiny shrub or small tree, 2-7m high*

Elaeagnus angustifolia L. Oleaster

Elaeagnaceae - Oleaster family p. 95

Length: 4-8cm

Form of blade: Narrowly lanceolate in outline

Stalk: 4-9mm long, white

End of leaf: Somewhat pointed, obtuse or rounded

Base of blade: Wedge-shaped; often slightly rounded

Margin of leaf: Entire

Uper/under side: Dull to dark green above with silvery scales; densely stellate-hairy beneath and therefore appearing greyish white

Arrangement on the shoot: Leaves alternate and close together

Distribution: In the hill zone on the banks of rivers and lakes, on coasts, stony hills, river-beds, dunes and damp woods; often in association with Sea Buckthorn and Tamarisk; an ornamental shrub in W. and central Europe

948 ***Eucalyptus globulus* - Blue Gum** *Evergreen tree up to 45m high (up to 65m in its native habitat) with pendent adult leaves*

Eucalyptus globulus Labill. Blue Gum

Myrtaceae - Myrtle family p. 95

Length: Adult leaves 10-30cm

Form of blade: Adult leaves narrowly lanceolate in outline, slightly crescent-shaped, thick and pendent

Stalk: 1-5cm long and often slightly reddish

End of leaf: With a long point

Base of blade: Broadly wedge-shaped or rounded

Margin of leaf: Entire

Upper/under side: Both sides glabrous; dark green above and often somewhat bluish green beneath

Arrangement on the shoot: Leaves alternate; juvenile leaves, by contrast, opposite

Distribution: Used for afforestation in tropical America, S. China, California, Australia and New Zealand; planted in the Mediterranean region because of its rapid growth (3-10m per year according to the climate); wood not very hard

949 ***Daphne laureola* - Spurge Laurel** *Deciduous shrub up to 1.2m high, only slightly branched, with shoots green at first*

Daphne laureola L. Spurge Laurel

Thymelaeaceae - Daphne family p. 96

Length: 6-14cm

Form of blade: Narrowly obovate in outline with the greatest breadth always above the middle

Stalk: Without a stalk, or with only a very short one

End of leaf: Shortly pointed

Base of blade: Wedge-shaped and narrowed downwards so that the stalk is often suppressed

Margin of leaf: Entire

Upper/under side: Shiny dark green above with the midrib clearly impressed; pale green beneath with the midrib distinctly prominent; both sides glabrous

Arrangement on the shoot: Leaves alternate

Distribution: From the hill to the montane zone; in fairly warm, not too dry places which are mild in winter; in beech, oak and mixed oak-hornbeam woods with luxuriant vegetation

950 ***Daphne mezereum* - Mezereon**
Deciduous, weakly branched shrub, 30-120cm high; young shoots with silvery hairs

Daphne mezereum L.
Mezereon

Thymelaeaceae - Daphne family p. 95

Length: 3-8cm

Form of blade: Oblanceolate in outline; with the greatest breadth above the middle; leaves soft to the touch

Stalk: Very small, between 0.3cm and 0.5cm long

End of leaf: Shortly pointed

Base of blade: Wedge-shaped, narrowing in the short stalk

Margin of leaf: Entire; margins level or slightly recurved, glabrous or slightly hairy

Upper/under side: Both sides glabrous; dark green above and greyish green beneath

Arrangement on the shoot: Leaves alternate, and clustered at the ends of the stems

Distribution: From the hill to the subalpine zone; in mixed beech woods with rich vegetation, on grassland with tall-herb communities, in clearings, on scree and by watercourses

951 ***Daphne alpina* - Alpine Mezereon**
Deciduous shrub, 15-120cm high, with twigs finely hairy at first

Daphne alpina L.
Alpine Mezereon

Thymelaeaceae - Daphne family p. 96

Length: 1-5cm

Form of blade: Lanceolate to narrowly obovate in outline; with the greatest breadth at or above the middle

Stalk: Leaves usually sessile

End of leaf: Obtuse or rounded

Base of blade: Narrowly wedge-shaped narrowing to the leaf-base

Margin of leaf: Entire; finely hairy

Upper/under side: Both sides hairy when young and therefore soft to the touch; later dull dark green above with only a few appressed hairs remaining; greyish green beneath, remaining slightly hairy

Arrangement on the shoot: Leaves clustered at the ends of the stems

Distribution: From the hill to the subalpine zone; in the warmer places on crags, rocks and walls

952 ***Viscum album* - Mistletoe**
Evergreen shrub, almost globular, up to 1m across, with forked stems

Viscum album L.
Mistletoe

Loranthaceae - Mistletoe family p. 96

Length: 2-6.5cm

Form of blade: Spathulate, narrowly obovate or narrowly elliptic in outline

Stalk: Leaves sessile

End of leaf: Rounded

Base of blade: Wedge-shaped

Margin of leaf: Entire

Upper/under side: Both sides yellowish green, glabrous and parallel-veined; leaves more yellowish in winter

Arrangement on the shoot: Leaves opposite, at the ends of the forked stems

Distribution: Growing on trees; from the hill to the montane zone

1st form: On deciduous trees such as poplar, willow, birch, hornbeam, chestnut and lime

2nd form: On fir

3rd form: On pine and spruce

953 ***Punica granatum* - Pomegranate**
Deciduous, spiny shrub or tree 1-5m high with shoots 4-angled at first

Punica granatum L.
Pomegranate

Punicaceae - Pomegranate family p. 96

Length: 3-8cm

Form of blade: Oblong-elliptic in outline

Stalk: 0.1-0.5cm long and usually reddish above

End of leaf: Obtuse or rounded

Base of blade: Wedge-shaped

Margin of leaf: Entire

Upper/under side: Both sides glabrous; dark green above and with a clearly impressed midrib; pale green beneath with the midrib distinctly prominent

Arrangement on the shoot: Leaves opposite; sometimes alternate on young shoots

Distribution: On sunny, stony slopes in mixed Oriental Beech woods in S.E. Europe; native in Iran and adjacent countries and cultivated since ancient times; found today in the whole of the Mediterranean region north to the Valais and S. Tyrol

954 ***Prunus laurocerasus* - Cherry Laurel**
Evergreen shrub or small tree, 2-8m high, young shoots glabrous and green

Prunus laurocerasus L.
Cherry Laurel

Rosaceae - Rose family p. 97

Length: 10-25cm

Form of blade: Oblong-elliptic to oblong-obovate in outline; stiff, leathery and thick; usually with 4 glands in the lower part of the blade

Stalk: 0.5-1cm long

End of leaf: With a short, narrow point

Base of blade: Narrowly wedge-shaped

Margin of leaf: Entire; margins slightly recurved

Upper/under side: Both sides glabrous dark green above and shiny as if varnished; pale green beneath

Arrangement on the shoot: Leaves alternate

Distribution: In the hill zone; planted in gardens, parks and cemeteries; cultivated in central Europe since the 15th century; as undergrowth in open oak woods, in thickets, on stony slopes and walls; native in S.E. Europe

955 ***Rhododendron luteum* - Yellow Rhododendron**
Deciduous shrub, 1-4m high and broad; young growth sticky with matted glandular hairs

Rhododendron luteum Sweet
Yellow Rhododendron

Ericaceae - Heath family p. 97

Length: 6-12cm

Form of blade: Oblong-lanceolate in outline

Stalk: 0.5-1.5cm long

End of leaf: Pointed

Base of blade: Narrowly wedge-shaped

Margin of leaf: Entire; fringed with fine hairs

Upper/under side: With grey hairs on both sides when young; medium green above and slightly undulate; greyish medium green beneath and later only sparingly hairy

Arrangement on the shoot: Leaves alternate

Distribution: Native in E. Europe; planted in gardens and parks; a vigorous, hardy plant of great value; one of the parents of numerous garden hybrids

956 **Ligustrum vulgare - Wild Privet**
Deciduous shrub, 4-7m high, with the young shoots finely hairy

Ligustrum vulgare L.
Wild Privet
Oleaceae - Olive family p. 98

Length: 3-7cm

Form of blade: Lanceolate to oblong-elliptic in outline

Stalk: 0.5-1.5cm long

End of leaf: Pointed

Base of blade: Wedge-shaped

Margin of leaf: Entire

Upper/under side: Both sides glabrous; medium to dark green above; somewhat paler green beneath with a distinctly prominent midrib

Arrangement on the shoot: Leaves opposite or in whorls of 3

Distribution: In the hill zone; in open deciduous and Pine woods, thickets, hedges, in sunny groves, on the edges of woods, banks, walls and in fields on poor soils; the genus is mainly distributed in S. and E. Asia; the only species native in Europe is the Wild Privet

957 **Olea europaea - Olive**
Evergreen shrub or small tree, 2-10m high, with greyish green branchlets

Olea europaea L.
Olive
Oleaceae - Olive family p. 98

Length: 4-7cm

Form of blade: Lanceolate in outline, thick and leathery

Stalk: 0.2-0.6cm long

End of leaf: Tapering often to a small, sharp point

Base of blade: Wedge-shaped

Margin of leaf: Entire; margins often slightly wavy

Upper/under side: Dull dark green to greyish green above and almost glabrous; greyish white to silvery grey beneath; covered with scale-like hairs

Arrangement on the shoot: Leaves opposite

Distribution: Originally a Mediterranean plant; spread by cultivation throughout all the warmer regions of the world. Since ancient times the Olive has played an important part in religious rites. The cultivation of the Olive is thought to have originated with the Semitic-Hamitic races

958 **Pyrus salicifolia - Willow-leaved Pear**
Deciduous, 5-8m high, with pendent branches and young branchlets densely grey-felted

Pyrus salicifolia Pall.
Willow-leaved Pear
Rosaceae - Rose family p. 97

Length: 3-9cm

Form of blade: Narrowly elliptic in outline

Stalk: 1-4cm long

End of leaf: Obtuse or pointed

Base of blade: Narrowly wedge-shaped

Margin of leaf: Entire as a rule; occasionally with a few small teeth

Upper/under side: With silvery grey hairs on both sides when young; later medium to dark green above and more or less glabrous; greyish white hairs remaining beneath

Arrangement on the shoot: Leaves alternate; clustered on short shoots; short shoots often ending in a spine

Distribution: Native in mixed deciduous woods in the Caucasus and Asia Minor; often planted in European gardens as an ornamental tree

959 **Nerium oleander - Oleander**
Erect, bushy, evergreen shrub, 2-6m high, with dark green stems

Nerium oleander L.
Oleander
Apocynaceae - Periwinkle family p. 98

Length: 6-15cm

Form of blade: Linear-lanceolate in outline

Stalk: 0.3-0.7cm long; blade narrowed into the stalk

End of leaf: Pointed

Base of blade: Wedge-shaped

Margin of leaf: Entire; margins slightly recurved

Upper/under side: Medium to dark green and glabrous above; greyish or pale green beneath, sparsely hairy or glabrous and with a distinctly prominent midrib; lateral veins numerous, close together, and parallel to each other

Arrangement on the shoot: Leaves in whorls of 3 or 4; more rarely opposite

Distribution: Frequent in dry river-beds, on gravel soils, and on stony slopes in the Mediterranean region; cultivation of the Oleander is only possible in the mildest areas; a winter temperature of 5-8°C is necessary for proper flower-formation

960 **Rhododendron ponticum - Rhododendron**
Evergreen shrub or small tree 3-5m high, with young branchlets covered with sticky hairs

Rhododendron ponticum L.
Rhododendron
Ericaceae - Heath family p. 97

Length: 8-15cm

Form of blade: Oblong-lanceolate to oblong-elliptic in outline

Stalk: 1-3cm long

End of leaf: Shortly pointed

Base of blade: Narrowly wedge-shaped

Margin of leaf: Entire; margins often slightly recurved

Upper/under side: Dark green above with a pale green midrib; pale green beneath with a distinctly prominent midrib; both sides glabrous

Arrangement on the shoot: Leaves alternate

Distribution: Native from Spain and Portugal to Asia Minor; used as a rootstock in hybridisation; hardy, and therefore occasionally planted in parks and gardens in central Europe

961 **Laurus nobilis - Laurel**
Evergreen shrub or tree, 1-8m high, with young shoots reddish green and glabrous

Laurus nobilis L.
Laurel
Lauraceae - Laurel family p. 97

Length: 5-12cm

Form of blade: Oblong-lanceolate to narrowly elliptic in outline

Stalk: 1-4cm long and usually reddish in colour

End of leaf: Pointed

Base of blade: Wedge-shaped

Margin of leaf: Entire, with margins slightly wavy; more rarely slightly crenate

Upper/under side: Both sides glabrous; medium to dark green above and pale green beneath; lower part of midrib beneath often reddish

Arrangement on the shoot: Leaves alternate

Distribution: In the hill zone: on stony slopes and in open woods; cultivated especially in the Mediterranean region; native in Asia Minor; a dominant species in evergreen woods in the Mediterranean region; cultivated in entrance halls and winter gardens since the time of Louis XIV

962 **Arctostaphylos ura-ursi - Bearberry**
Evergreen, much branched dwarf shrub, forming large, dense mats

Arctostaphylos uva-ursi (L.) Spreng.
Bearberry
Ericaceae - Heath family p. 99

Length: 1-3cm

Form of blade: Obovate or obovate-oblong in outline, with the greatest breadth above the middle, leathery and thick

Stalk: 1-3mm long with white hairs

End of leaf: Obtuse or more rarely slightly emarginate

Base of blade: Wedge-shaped

Margin of leaf: Entire, and densely fringed with fine white hairs

Upper/under side: Both sides glabrous with an indistinct network of veins; dark green above with a clearly visible pale green midrib; with a dense network of dark green veins beneath

Arrangement on the shoot: Leaves alternate

Distribution: From the hill to the alpine zone; in open pine woods, on loamy soils in association with heather and above the tree-line into the dwarf shrub region

963 **Syringa vulgaris - Lilac**
Deciduous shrub or small tree, 2-8m high, with straight, glabrous, olive green stems

Syringa vulgaris L.
Lilac
Oleaceae - Olive family p. 98

Length: 5-10cm

Form of blade: Pointed ovate or pointed elliptic in outline

Stalk: 1-3cm long

End of leaf: With a long point

Base of blade: Truncate or heart-shaped

Margin of leaf: Entire

Upper/under side: Both sides glabrous; dark green above, paler bluish green beneath

Arrangement on the shoot: Leaves opposite

Distribution: From the hill to the montane zone; many forms and hybrids cultivated in Europe since the 16th century; found in S.E. Europe on rocky slopes in sun or half shade, in thickets, in open woods and on the edges of woods; the Common Lilac was brought from Constantinople to Vienna about 1560 by the ambassador Busbecq, and spread quickly throughout central Europe

964 **Catalpa bignonioides - Indian Bean Tree** *Deciduous tree up to 15m high with a short, cylindrical trunk*

Catalpa bignonioides Walt.
Indian Bean Tree
Bignoniaceae - Bignonia family p. 98

Length: 10-20cm long and often equally broad

Form of blade: Broadly ovate to heart-shaped

Stalk: 7-15cm long

End of leaf: With a long, fine point on a short, abrupt point

Base of blade: Weakly heart-shaped or truncate

Margin of leaf: Entire; more rarely with indistinct lateral lobes

Upper/under side: Medium to dark green above; paler green beneath and softly hairy; pleasantly scented when rubbed; veins beneath distinctly prominent

Arrangement on the shoot: Leaves opposite or in whorls of 3

Distribution: Native only in S.E. United States; frequently planted as an ornamental tree in large gardens and parks

965 **Catalpa ovata - Yellow Catalpa**
Deciduous tree, native in China, up to 10m high, with mainly glabrous branchlets

Catalpa ovata G. Don et Zucc.
Yellow catalpa
Bignoniaceae - Bignonia family p. 98

Length: 10-25cm

Form of blade: Varied in outline; broadly ovate or heart-shaped

Stalk: 4-10cm long, hairy at first, later becoming glabrous; often darker coloured above; green beneath

End of leaf: With a tapering point or a short, abrupt point

Base of blade: Usually heart-shaped

Margin of leaf: Entire, and usually fringed with fine hairs

Upper/under side: Medium to dark green above with fine, soft hairs; pale to medium green beneath and only slightly rough to the touch; veins distinctly yellowish green and prominent; reddish black glandular spots in the axils of the veins

Arrangement on the shoot: Leaves opposite or alternate

Distribution: Planted as an ornamental tree in large gardens and parks

966 **Magnolia hypoleuca - Japanese Big-leaved Magnolia**
Deciduous tree up to 30m high with a broad crown and light to dark brown branchlets

Magnolia hypoleuca Sieb. et Zucc. (*M. obovata* Thunb.)
Japanese Big-leaved Magnolia
Magnoliaceae - Magnolia family p. 99

Length: 20-40cm

Form of blade: Obovate in outline gradually narrowing to the base

Stalk: 3-8cm long

End of leaf: Rounded with a short, abrupt point

Base of blade: Wedge-shaped, often somewhat rounded at the base

Margin of leaf: Entire

Upper/under side: Pale to medium green and glabrous above, pale bluish green and slightly hairy beneath

Arrangement on the shoot: Leaves alternate, but clustered at the ends of the shoots

Distribution: A large-leaved Magnolia, native in Japan, occasionally planted in European gardens and parks

967 **Cydonia oblonga - Quince**
Deciduous shrub or small tree, 1-8m high; young branchlets felted

Cydonia oblonga Mill.
Quince
Rosaceae - Rose family p. 99

Length: 5-10cm

Form of blade: Elliptic to broadly ovate in outline

Stalk: 1-2cm long and felted

End of leaf: Obtuse, shortly rounded or weakly pointed

Base of blade: Usually rounded, more rarely heart-shaped

Margin of leaf: Entire; slightly grey-felted on the margins

Upper/under side: Dark green and usually glabrous above; grey-felted beneath, with the hairs densely interwoven

Arrangement on the shoot: Leaves alternate

Distribution: From the hill to the montane zone; a valuable fruit-tree, numerous large-fruited forms being cultivated in gardens, parks and orchards, rarely escaping and becoming naturalised on sunny slopes, at the edges of woods and in thickets; the quince prefers deep, dry, calcareous soils

968 ***Cotoneaster integerrimus* - Common Cotoneaster** *Deciduous, bushy, much-branched shrub, 1-2m high; shoots hairy at first*

Cotoneaster integerrimus Medic.
Common Cotoneaster

Rosaceae - Rose family p. 100

Length: 2-4cm

Form of blade: Broadly elliptic, ovate or roundish in outline

Stalk: 0.3-0.6mm long and finely hairy

End of leaf: Obtuse or pointed; usually with a sharp point

Base of blade: Wedge-shaped, obtuse or rounded

Margin of leaf: Entire; margins with very long, fine hairs

Upper/under side: Dark green and glabrous above; with dense white or yellowish grey matted hairs beneath and therefore appearing greyish green in colour

Arrangement on the shoot: Leaves alternate

Distribution: From the lowlands up into the subalpine zone; in the warmer places in rock crevices, woods, thickets, on sunny crags and in dwarf shrub communities

969 ***Cotoneaster tomentosus* - Cotoneaster** *Deciduous, only moderately branched shrub with stems up to 5m long, grey-felted at first*

Cotoneaster tomentosus (Ait.) Lindl.
Cotoneaster

Rosaceae - Rose family p. 100

Length: 3-6cm; slightly larger than the leaves of the Common Cotoneaster

Form of blade: Elliptic to broadly ovate in outline

Stalk: 0.2-0.7mm long and densely felted

End of leaf: Obtuse, more rarely rounded; occasionally with a small point

Base of blade: Weakly heart-shaped, rounded or obtuse

Margin of leaf: Entire

Upper/under side: Dark green and loosely hairy above; densely felted beneath and therefore appearing grey to white

Arrangement on the shoot: Leaves alternate

Distribution: From the lowlands up into the subalpine zone; on the edges of woods and thickets, in half shaded or sunny places in open oak and mixed woods which are warm in summer

970 ***Pyrus nivalis* - Snow Pear**
Deciduous tree up to 10m high with young shoots white-felted

Pyrus nivalis Jacq.
Snow Pear

Rosaceae - Rose family p. 99

Length: 6-10cm

Form of blade: Obovate in outline

Stalk: 1-3cm long and covered in a white felt

End of leaf: Pointed, or rounded and with a short, abrupt point

Base of blade: Wedge-shaped

Margin of leaf: Entire and fringed with downy hairs

Upper/under side: Dark green above with matted hairs; veins white and clearly visible; densely felted beneath and therefore appearing greyish green

Arrangement on the shoot: Leaves alternate

Distribution: From the hill to the montane zone; in places mild in winter; distributed especially in S. Europe

971 ***Cornus controversa* - Table Dogwood**
Deciduous tree up to 20m high (sometimes a shrub) with shoots brownish green at first

Cornus controversa Hemsl.
Table Dogwood

Cornaceae - Dogwood family p. 100

Length: 7-12cm

Form of blade: Ovate or broadly ovate in outline

Stalk: 1-3cm long

End of leaf: With a short or long point

Base of blade: Wedge-shaped, truncate or rounded

Margin of leaf: Entire

Upper/under side: Dark green above with impressed, clearly visible, primary or secondary veins; bluish grey beneath and finely hairy on the distinctly prominent veins; 6-9 pairs of lateral veins

Arrangement on the shoot: Leaves alternate

Distribution: A tree native in Japan and China; planted in Europe in parks and large gardens

972 ***Cornus sanguinea* - Dogwood**
Deciduous shrub, 1-5m high, stems tinged red on the side exposed to the sun

Cornus sanguinea L.
Dogwood

Cornaceae - Dogwood family p. 100

Length: 4-10cm

Form of blade: Elliptic to broadly ovate in outline

Stalk: 0.5-1.5cm long, usually dark red above and grooved

End of leaf: Pointed, often with a short abrupt point

Base of blade: Usually rounded, more rarely truncate or wedge-shaped

Margin of leaf: Entire; often slightly wavy; with 3 or 4 pairs of secondary veins; margins often slightly reddish in colour

Upper/under side: With scattered hairs on both sides; medium to dark green above and with clearly visible, pale green, primary and secondary veins; paler green beneath; hairs not in tufts but finely crisped; with distinctly prominent, pale green veins

Arrangement on the shoot: Leaves opposite

Distribution: Mainly in the hill zone, more rarely montane: in hedges, open mixed deciduous woods, damp woods, on slopes warm and dry in summer, and on the edges of woods

973 ***Cornus mas* - Cornelian Cherry**
Deciduous shrub or small tree, 3-6m high; stems tinged red on the side exposed to the sun

Cornus mas L.
Cornelian Cherry

Cornaceae - Dogwood family p. 100

Length: 4-10cm

Form of blade: Narrowly elliptic, elliptic to ovate in outline

Stalk: 0.3-1.5cm long, slightly grooved, often reddish in colour and with fine whitish hairs

End of leaf: Pointed, or the two halves of the leaf converging and rounded

Base of blade: Wedge-shaped or rounded

Margin of leaf: Entire; often slightly undulate; with 3-5 pairs of secondary veins

Upper/under side: With scattered, white, appressed hairs on both sides; medium to dark green above with only the primary lateral veins prominent; pale to medium green beneath with the midrib and lateral veins distinctly prominent; often with tufts of white hairs in the axils of the veins

Arrangement on the shoot: Leaves opposite

Distribution: In the hill zone, more rarely montane; in dry, mixed deciduous woods, in hedges, on dry slopes warm in summer, and on the edges of woods

974 **Fagus orientalis - Oriental Beech**
Deciduous tree, up to 40m high in its native habitat, with stems olive green and hairy at first

Fagus orientalis Lipsky
Oriental Beech

Fagaceae - Beech family p. 100

Length: 6-12cm

Form of blade: Elliptic or obovate in outline; always broadest above the middle

Stalk: 0.5-1.5cm long and covered with matted, milky hairs

End of leaf: With a short, abrupt point or a tapering point

Base of blade: Wedge-shaped or rounded

Margin of leaf: Entire, wavy, and densely fringed with very long, fine hairs

Upper/under side: Dark bluish green above, glabrous, and with pale yellowish green veins; dark green beneath with conspicuous brownish hairs on the prominent, pale yellowish green veins

Arrangement on the shoot: Leaves alternate

Distribution: Species native in Aisa Minor, the Caucasus, and N. Iran; occasionally planted in parks in central Europe

975 **Fagus sylvatica - Beech**
Deciduous, much-branched tree, up to 40m high, with young shoots hairy

Fagus sylvatica L.
Common Beech

Fagaceae - Beech family p. 30, 31, 101

Length: 5-10cm

Form of blade: Elliptic to broadly ovate in outline; greatest breadth at or below the middle

Stalk: 0.3-1.5cm long and often dark in colour

End of leaf: With a short, tapering or abrupt point

Base of blade: Wedge-shaped or rounded

Margin of leaf: Entire and undulate; fringed with whitish hairs when young

Upper/under side: Softly hairy when young and fringed at the margin; older leaves usually glabrous; shiny dark green above and medium green beneath; veins prominent; lateral veins running parallel to each other

Arrangement on the shoot: Leaves alternate (arranged in 2 rows)

Distribution: From the hill to the montane zone; a constituent part of various types of wood

976 **Salix hastata - Spear-leaved Willow**
Deciduous shrub, barely more than 1m high, with reddish brown stems hairy at first

Salix hastata L.
Spear-leaved Willow

Salicaceae - Willow family p. 101

Length: 2-8cm

Form of blade: Elliptic to ovate in outline

Stalk: 0.5-1.2cm long and grooved above

End of leaf: Pointed or slightly rounded

Base of blade: Rounded or weakly heart-shaped

Margin of leaf: Entire or with a few small teeth up to 5mm apart

Upper/under side: Dark green and glabrous above; pale bluish green beneath and hairy on the veins at first; veins pale green and prominent

Arrangement on the shoot: Leaves alternate

Distribution: Especially in the montane and subalpine zone; on continuously wet alluvial land by rivers and streams, in alpine alder thickets, in scrub and on scree

977 **Parrotia persica - Persian Ironwood**
Deciduous shrub or tree up to 10m high with young twigs brownish green

Parrotia persica (DC.) C. A. Mey.
Persian Ironwood

Hamamelidaceae - Witch-hazel family p. 101

Length: 6-10cm

Form of blade: Obovate or almost circular in outline; leaves fairly thick and leathery

Stalk: 0.5-0.8cm long

End of leaf: Obtuse or rounded

Base of blade: Rounded or wedge-shaped

Margin of leaf: Entire; coarsely sinuate to crenate-dentate above the middle

Upper/under side: Shiny dark green above with clearly impressed veins of a similar colour; pale bluish green beneath with whitish green, distinctly prominent veins; with fine, brownish hairs at first

Arrangement on the shoot: Leaves alternate; 2 or more together on short shoots

Distribution: Native in N. Iran and the Caucasus; planted in large parks and botanic gardens

978 **Citrus sinensis - Orange**
Evergreen tree, 5-10m high, with twigs green and spiny at first

Citrus sinensis (L.) Pers.
Orange

Rutaceae - Citrus family p. 102

Length: 3-7cm

Form of blade: Elliptic, broadly elliptic or obovate in outline, firm and leathery; broader than that of the lemon

Stalk: 0.5-2cm long and with prominent green wings

End of leaf: Rounded at the end with a tapering or short abrupt point

Base of blade: Wedge-shaped

Margin of leaf: Entire

Upper/under side: Both sides glabrous; shiny dark green above and pale green beneath; the midrib particularly prominent

Arrangement on the shoot: Leaves alternate

Distribution: The orange is native in E. Asia, but is now planted widely throughout the Mediterranean region

979 **Citrus limon - Lemc ı**
Evergreen tree, 5-10m high, with twigs green and spiny at first

Citrus limon (L.) Burm.
Lemon

Rutaceae - Citrus family p. 102

Length: 3-7cm

Form of blade: Narrowly elliptic to elliptic in outline, firm and leathery; very similar to the leaves of the orange

Stalk: 0.5-2cm long and often winged; a thorn often present where the stalk joins the shoot

End of leaf: Pointed

Base of blade: Wedge-shaped

Margin of leaf: Entire or very slightly crenate or dentate

Upper/under side: Shiny dark green above and pale green beneath; midrib and lateral veins prominent; both sides glabrous

Arrangement on the shoot: Leaves alternate

Distribution: Numerous varieties planted in the Mediterranean region and areas with a similar climate

980 **Lonicera xylosteum - Fly Honeysuckle** *Deciduous shrub, 1-3m high, with stems greyish brown and softly hairy at first*

Lonicera xylosteum L. Fly Honeysuckle

Caprifoliacae - Honeysuckle family p. 101

Length: 2-6cm

Form of blade: Elliptic, broadly ovate or obovate in outline

Stalk: 0.5-1cm long, often reddish above and with densely appressed hairs

End of leaf: Obtuse or pointed

Base of blade: Wedge-shaped or rounded

Margin of leaf: Entire; margins sparsely fringed with whitish hairs

Upper/under side: With appressed hairs on both sides; medium to dark green above and bluish green beneath; veins beneath distinctly prominent

Arrangement on the shoot: Leaves opposite

Distribution: From the hill to the montane zone; amongst the luxuriant vegetation in Oak woods, in hedges, mixed Beech and conifer woods, open Pine woods, clearings, on the edges of woods and by fences; widely distributed and common in central Europe except N.W. Germany

981 **Lonicera nigra - Black-berried Honeysuckle** *Deciducous shrub, 1-2m high, with yellowish brown to reddish stems*

Lonicera nigra L. Black-berried Honeysuckle

Caprifoliacae - Honeysuckle family p. 104

Length: 3-8cm

Form of blade: Elliptic, broadly elliptic to obovate in outline

Stalk: 0.2-0.8cm long and grooved above

End of leaf: Shortly pointed

Base of blade: Rounded, truncate or wedge-shaped

Margin of leaf: Entire; margins often slightly undulate

Upper/under side: Medium to dark green and glabrous above; medium green beneath and downy along the midrib; veins pale yellowish green and distinctly prominent

Arrangement on the shoot: Leaves opposite

Distribution: In the montane and subalpine zone; in mixed woods with rich vegetation, on the edges of woods and between rocks; in the undergrowth of mountain woods and on uncultivated damp or stony soils; not very common

982 **Lonicera caprifolium - Perfoliate Honeysuckle** *Deciduous climber up to 5m, stems tinged red on side exposed to sun*

Lonicera caprifolium L. Perfoliate Honeysuckle

Caprifoliacae - Honeysuckle family p. 102

Length: 2-10cm

Form of blade: Narrowly ovate to elliptic in outline and with the lower leaves shortly stalked; leaves towards the ends of the stems united in pairs by their bases; uppermost leaves united and forming an elliptic or circular structure

Stalk: Shortly stalked or sessile

End of leaf: Usually obtuse, occasionally shortly pointed

Base of blade: Wedge-shaped, rounded or heart-shaped

Margin of leaf: Entire, glabrous

Upper/under side: Dark green and glabrous above; bluish to greyish green beneath and hairy at the base at first, but soon becoming glabrous; midrib beneath distinctly prominent

Arrangement on the shoot: Leaves opposite

Distribution: Hill zone; often cultivated in gardens, sometimes escaping and becoming naturalised; found wild in sunny hedges and in oak woods; twines clockwise

983 **Lonicera caerulea - Blue Honeysuckle** *Deciduous shrub, up to 1.5m, stems reddish brown at first, covered with bluish bloom*

Lonicera caerulea L. Blue Honeysuckle

Caprifoliacae - Honeysuckle family p. 102

Length: 2-8cm

Form of blade: Elliptic, oblong-elliptic, or obovate in outline

Stalk: 1-4mm long, slightly hairy, and somewhat broadened at the base

End of leaf: Obtuse or rounded and occasionally with a short, fine point

Base of blade: Rounded

Margin of leaf: Entire

Upper/under side: Both sides hairy when young; dark green above and quickly becoming glabrous; bluish green beneath, becoming glabrous except on the leaf-stalk; veins pale yellowish green and prominent

Arrangement on the shoot: Leaves opposite

Distribution: From the montane to the subalpine zone; on pine moors, in Mountain Pine woods, Alpenrose communities, and in stony places with acid raw humus

984 **Lonicera periclymenum - Honeysuckle** *Deciduous climber, turning clockwise up to 5m high with stems tinged red on the side exposed to the sun*

Lonicera periclymenum L. Honeysuckle

Caprifoliaceae - Honeysuckle family p. 102

Length: 4-10cm

Form of blade: Elliptic to obovate in outline

Stalk: Lower leaves with a stalk up to 0.7cm long; uppermost pair of leaves sessile

End of leaf: Obtuse or pointed

Base of blade: Wedge-shaped

Margin of leaf: Entire

Upper/under side: Both sides glabrous; dark green above, bluish green beneath and only slightly hairy when young

Arrnagement on the shoot: Leaves opposite

Distribution: In the hill zone; in mixed oak and beech woods, in alder groves, hedges and clearings; prefers a climate warm in summer and mild in winter; the centre of distribution lies in atlantic Europe

985 **Lonicera alpigena - Alpine Honeysuckle** *Deciduous shrub up to 2m high with young shoots greyish brown*

Lonicera alpigena L. Alpine Honeysuckle

Caprifoliaceae - Honeysuckle family p. 104

Length: 8-12cm

Form of blade: Elliptic or obovate in outline

Stalk: 1-2cm long

End of leaf: Shortly pointed

Base of blade: Truncate or wedge-shaped

Margin of leaf: Entire; younger leaves with a regular fringe of fine hairs

Upper/under side: Both sides glabrous; dark green above with clearly impressed veins; paler green beneath, distinctly shiny, with fine hairs along the midrib; veins pale or dark green and prominent

Arrnagement on the shoot: Leaves opposite

Distribution: In the montane and subalpine zone; amongst the rich vegetation of beech and mixed woods, in gorges, clearings, on the edges of woods and on bushy slopes

986 **Hedera helix - Ivy**
Evergreen climber up to 20m high with stems bearing adhesive roots

Hedera helix L.
Ivy
Araliaceae - Ivy family p. 102

Length: 4–10cm
Form of blade: Varied in outline; leaves on flowering shoots ovate-rhombic in shape and not lobed, leathery and lasting for 3 years
Stalk: 3–11cm long
End of leaf: Shortly pointed
Base of blade: Obtuse or truncate
Margin of leaf: Entire
Upper/under side: Shiny dark green above with white veins; dull pale green beneath; both sides glabrous
Arrangement on the shoot: Leaves alternate
Distribution: From the hill to the montane zone; creeping along the ground or climbing on trees, walls and rocks; prefers damp places mild in winter; found mainly in beech and oak woods and in damp woods

987 ***Rhamnus frangula* - Alder Buckthorn**
Deciduous shrub 1–3m high, or tree up to 7m with grey to reddish brown branchlets

Rhamnus frangula L.
(*Frangula alnus* Mill.)
Alder Buckthorn
Rhamnaceae - Buckthorn family p. 104

Length: 3–7cm
Form of blade: Elliptic to broadly elliptic in outline
Stalk: 0.6–1.4cm long
End of leaf: With a short, abrupt point
Base of blade: Truncate or wedge-shaped
Margin of leaf: Entire
Upper/under side: Both sides glabrous; dark green above and shiny pale green beneath with prominent, pale yellowish green veins
Arrangement on the shoot: Leaves alternate
Distribution: From the hill to the montane zone; in damp woods, alder groves, birch moors, open woods with wet soils and boggy land; found mainly with Alder, Grey Alder, Bird Cherry and Guelder Rose

988 ***Euonymus latifolius* - Broad-leaved Spindle Tree** *Deciduous shrub 2–5m; young branchlets 4-angled to rounded in cross-section*

Euonymus latifolius (L.) Mill.
Broad-leaved Spindle Tree
Celastraceae - Spindle Tree family p. 103

Length: 7–14cm
Form of blade: Elliptic to obovate in outline
Stalk: 0.5–1cm long and grooved above
End of leaf: Pointed
Base of blade: Truncate or wedge-shaped
Margin of leaf: Appearing entire to the naked eye; with a lens obviously finely and evenly serrate
Upper/under side: Both sides glabrous; dark green above and pale green beneath; veins prominent
Arrangement on the shoot: Leaves opposite
Distribution: From the hill to the montane zone; in warm, damp places amongst the rich vegetation of mixed deciduous words and on the edges of woodland

989 ***Forsythia europaea* - European Forsythia** *Deciduous shrub, 1.5–2.5m high; native in N. Albania and S.W. Yugoslavia*

Forsythia europaea
Deg. et Bald.
European Forsythia
Oleaceae - Olive family p. 104

Length: 4–8cm
Form of blade: Elliptic, ovate or ovate-lanceolate in outline
Stalk: 1–3cm long and usually grooved above
End of leaf: Pointed; tip curved to one side
Base of blade: Truncate or wedge-shaped
Margin of leaf: Entire
Upper/under side: Dark green above and pale green beneath; both sides glabrous; veins medium green and prominent
Arrangement on the shoot: Leaves opposite
Distribution: Planted in gardens but not of great horticultural value

990 ***Magnolia x sonlangeana* - Garden Magnolia**
Deciduous shrub or tree up to 5m high with greyish green young shoots

Magnolia x sonlangeana
Sonl.-Bod.
Garden Magnolia
Magnoliaccae - Magnolia family p. 103

Length: 10–20cm
Form of blade: Oblong-elliptic or usually narrowly obovate in outline; always broadest in the upper third
Stalk: 1–4cm long
End of leaf: With a short, abrupt point
Base of blade: Wedge-shaped
Margin of leaf: Entire
Upper/under side: Medium to dark green and glabrous above; paler green beneath, slightly hairy, and with prominent yellowish white veins
Arrangement on the shoot: Leaves alternate
Distribution: Raised by Soulange-Bodin at Fromont near Paris in 1820; first flowered in 1826; numerous forms planted nowadays in gardens and parks

991 ***Magnolia grandiflora* - Evergreen Magnolia**
Evergreen tree up to 25m high with young shoots densely reddish brown felted

Magnolia grandiflora L.
Evergreen Magnolia
Magnoliaceae - Magnolia family p. 103

Length: 8–20cm
Form of blade: Elliptic to broadly elliptic in outline; leaves thick, leathery, and falling in the 2nd year
Stalk: 2–2.5cm long, stout, and densely covered with rust brown to brownish red hairs
End of leaf: Obtuse to bluntly pointed
Base of blade: Wedge-shaped
Margin of leaf: Entire
Upper/under side: Shiny dark green and glabrous above; paler green beneath with conspicuous, rust-red, downy hairs
Arrangement on the shoot: Leaves alternate
Distribution: Native in the S.E. United States; planted nowadays as an ornamental tree especially in the Mediterranean region

992 ***Quercus ilex*** **- Evergreen Oak**
Evergreen tree up to 25m high with grey-felted twigs that only gradually become glabrous

Quercus ilex L.
Evergreen Oak, Holm Oak

Fagaceae - Beech family p. 105

Length: 3-8cm

Form of blade: Varied in outline; usually oblong-ovate to ovate and with 4-7 sharp teeth on each side; often lobed also

Stalk: 7-15mm long and remaining felted with long white hairs

Lobes: Sharply pointed, entire or undulate, leathery and thick

End of leaf: Sharply pointed

Base of blade: Broadly wedge-shaped or rounded

Margin of leaf: Lobes entire or undulate and spiny-toothed

Upper/under side: Young leaves hairy on both sides; older leaves shiny dark green and glabrous above; appearing grey or whitish beneath because of the dense covering of hairs

Arrangement on the shoot: Leaves alternate

Distribution: Widely distributed in the Mediterranean region; forms Evergreen Oak woods; planted as an ornamental tree in parks where the winters are mild

993 ***Ilex aquifolium*** **- Holly**
Evergreen shrub or tree up to 15m high with pale or dark green twigs

Ilex aquifolium L.
Holly

Aquifoliaceae - Holly family p. 105

Length: 3-8cm

Form of blade: Elliptic to ovate in outline; in some forms the margin is entire and without any teeth; blade thick and leathery

Stalk: 1cm long and grooved above

End of leaf: With a long spiny point

Base of blade: Wedge-shaped

Margin of leaf: Undulate and coarsely spiny toothed; the number and kind of teeth vary according to age or garden form

Upper/under side: Shiny dark green above and pale green beneath; both sides glabrous

Arrangement on the shoot: Leaves alternate

Distribution: From the hill to the montane zone; especially in areas with an oceanic climate; forming the lower tree-layer in beech, beech-fir, and oak-hornbeam woods; occasionally in hedges

994 ***Castanea sativa*** **- Sweet Chestnut**
Deciduous tree up to 35m high with angular, glabrous twigs

Castanea sativa Mill.
Sweet Chestnut

Fagaceae - Beech Family p. 105

Length: 10-30cm

Form of blade: Oblong-lanceolate in outline, with sharp teeth; blade thick and leathery

Stalk: 2-5cm long

End of leaf: Ending in a short, narrow point

Base of blade: Broadly wedge-shaped, rounded or more rarely heart-shaped

Margin of leaf: With very large, sharp teeth, resembling those of a saw and pointing forwards; each of the lateral veins ends in a stout pointed tooth

Upper/under side: Shiny dark green and glabrous above; dull pale green beneath, at first felted, later becoming glabrous; with 15-20 pairs of prominent lateral veins beneath

Arrangement on the shoot: Leaves alternate

Distribution: In the hill zone, more rarely montane; forming woods in the mountains of the S. Alps; planted in the N. Alps in wine region and valleys warmed by the Föhn wind

995 ***Berberis vulgaris*** **- Barberry**
Deciduous shrub up to 3m high with angular, greyish brown stems

Berberis vulgaris L.
Barberry

Berberidaceae - Barberry family p. 105

Length: 2-4cm and narrowed into the stalk

Form of blade: Narrowly obovate to obovate in outline

Stalk: 0.5-1.5cm long

End of leaf: Rounded or obtuse

Base of blade: Narrowly wedge-shaped

Margin of leaf: Fringed with sharp spines

Upper/under side: Both sides glabrous; dark green above and whitish green beneath

Arrangement on the shoot: Leaves in clusters from the axils of 3-parted spines; clusters alternately arranged; leaves converted into single or divided spines, 1-2cm long, on long shoots

Distribution: From the hill to the subalpine zone; in sunny places on the edges of woods, in open oak and pine woods, hedges, and in shrub communities on dry soils

996 ***Corylus colurna*** **- Turkish Hazel**
Deciduous tree up to 20m high occasionally planted in gardens

Corylus colurna L.
Turkish Hazel

Betulaceae - Birch family p. 107

Length: 8-12cm

Form of blade: Broadly ovate to roundish or heart-shaped in outline; greatest breadth usually in the upper third

Stalk: 1.5-3cm long

End of leaf: With an abrupt point of moderate size

Base of blade: Usually heart-shaped or obliquely heart-shaped

Margin of leaf: Serrate and coarsely doubly toothed

Upper/under side: Shiny dark green above and later glabrous; medium to dark green beneath and hairy on the veins; veins of the 2nd and 3rd order not very prominent

Arrangement on the shoot: Leaves alternate

Distribution: In the hill zone; native in S.E. Europe but naturalised in Lower Austria

997 ***Ulex europaeus*** **- Gorse**
Very spiny shrub, 0.5-2m high, with numerous spiny short shoots up to 25mm long

Ulex europaeus L.
Gorse

Leguminosae - Pea family p. 105

Form of blade: Leaves only small and narrow, and only found occasionally on very lush growth or on young plants; often absent; all later leaves converted into sharp, green spines, 4-10mm long; short shoots also spiny. The shrub appears to consist entirely of green stems and spines

Upper/under side: Stems grooved and downy; spines with many lateral spines and also downy

Arrangement on the shoot: Spines alternately arranged

Distribution: A plant characteristic of Atlantic moorland; found in central Europe in mild parts of the lowlands; on shrubby slopes, on moors, and in open oak and pine woods in coastal regions

998 ***Tilia tomentosa* - Silver Lime**
Deciduous tree up to 30m high with stiffly erect branches and grey-felted young shoots

Tilia tomentosa Moench
Silver Lime
Tiliaceae - Lime family p. 106

Length: 6-12cm

Form of blade: Roundish heart-shaped or obliquely heart-shaped in outline

Stalk: 2-3.5cm long, much shorter than in the Weeping Silver Lime

End of leaf: Shortly pointed; with a slender, abrupt point

Base of blade: Usually heart-shaped to obliquely heart-shaped (with a deeper sinus than the Weeping Silver Lime)

Margin of leaf: Fairly regularly serrate/dentate; teeth not ending in a bristle, but more triangular in shape

Upper/under side: Dark green above with the midrib and lateral veins clearly visible; white or pale grey-felted beneath

Arrangement on the shoot: Leaves alternate

Distribution: Native in S.E. Europe and northern Asia Minor; first planted in central Europe about 1770; a favourite street-tree in towns because of its tolerance of smoke-pollution

999 ***Tilia petiolaris* - Weeping Silver Lime**
Deciduous tree, reaching a height of 30m, with pendulous branches

Tilia petiolaris DC. *T. alba*
(K. Koch non Ait.)
Weeping Silver Lime
Tiliaceae - Lime family p. 106

Length: 7-11cm

Form of blade: Obliquely heart-shaped in outline

Stalk: 3-6cm long and felted; leaves pendant

End of leaf: Shortly pointed

Base of blade: Obliquely heart-shaped or obliquely truncate

Margin of leaf: Regularly and sharply serrate/dentate; with teeth ending in a bristle

Upper/under side: Hairy above at first, later almost glabrous and dark green; white or greyish white beneath because of stellate hairs; midrib and lateral veins not very noticeable above

Arrangement on the shoot: Leaves alternate (arranged in 2 rows)

Distribution: Closely related to the Silver Lime, and often planted, especially in parks

1000 ***Tilia platyphyllos* - Large-leaved Lime**
Deciduous tree up to 40m high with young shoots reddish brown and hairy

Tilia platyphyllos Scop.
Large-leaved Lime
Tiliaceae - Lime family
p. 54, 55, 106

Length: 7-15cm

Form of blade: Heart-shaped or obliquely heart-shaped in outline

Stalk: 2-5cm long and often hairy; shorter than the blade

End of leaf: With a short, abrupt point

Base of blade: Obliquely heart-shaped or obliquely truncate

Margin of leaf: Regularly crenate-serrate: teeth all pointing forwards and not bristle-tipped

Upper/under side: Both sides hairy; dark green above and pale green beneath with tufts of whitish hairs in the axils of the veins; all veins hairy and prominent beneath

Arrangement on the shoot: Leaves alternate (arranged in 2 rows)

Distribution: In the hill zone; on steep slopes and below crags in places warm in summer; planted on hills

1001 ***Tilia x euchlora* - Caucasian Lime**
Deciduous tree up to 15m high with arching branches and pendulous shoots

Tilia x euchlora K. Koch
(*T. cordata* x *T. dasystyla*)
Caucasian Lime
Tiliaceae - Lime family p. 106

Length: 5-15cm

Form of blade: Obliquely heart-shaped in outline

Stalk: 3-6cm long and usually glabrous

End of leaf: Pointed, with a bristle at the tip

Base of blade: Usually obliquely heart-shaped

Margin of leaf: Irregularly toothed; all teeth tipped with a bristle

Upper/under side: Shiny dark green to bluish green above and glabrous; somewhat paler bluish green beneath with distinctly prominent veins; with tufts of usually light to medium brown, occasionally whitish hairs in the axils of the veins

Arrangement on the shoot: Leaves alternate

Distribution: Native from the Caucasus to N. Iran: planted in central Europe particularly in avenues and parks

1002 ***Tilia cordata* - Small-leaved Lime**
Deciduous tree up to 30m high with young branchlets olive green and finely hairy

Tilia cordata Mill.
Small-leaved Lime
Tiliaceae - Lime family p. 106

Length: 4-7cm

Form of blade: Heart-shaped in outline

Stalk: 2-5cm long and glabrous

End of leaf: With a short, abrupt point

Base of blade: Regular or obliquely heart-shaped; more rarely truncate

Margin of leaf: Finely and sharply serrate; teeth not tipped with a bristle

Upper/under side: Shiny dark green to bluish green and glabrous above; pale bluish green beneath with tufts of brownish red hairs in the axils of the veins (sometimes whitish in very young leaves); veins beneath not very prominent

Arrangement on the shoot: Leaves alternate (arranged in 2 rows)

Distribution: In the hill zone, more rarely montane; on steep slopes, below crags in mixed deciduous woods and thickets, in gorges, in mild places, warm in summer

1003 ***Cercidiphyllum japonicum* - Katsura Tree**
Deciduous tree, reaching a height of up to 20m, with a high domed crown

Cercidiphyllum japonicum
Sieb. et Zucc. ex Miq.
Katsura Tree
Cercidiphylloucae - Katsura family
p. 107

Length: 6-12cm

Form of blade: Broadly ovate to roundish or heart-shaped in outline

Stalk: 3-6cm long and green or tinged red

End of leaf: Very shortly pointed

Base of blade: Heart-shaped

Margin of leaf: Crenate

Upper/under side: Dull or greyish green above; pale bluish green beneath and also glabrous; leaves of long shoots with pinnate veins, those on short shoots with veins palmately arranged

Arrangement on the shoot: Leaves opposite (on long shoots); those on short shoots alternate

Distribution: Native in Japan and China; planted during the last 100 years in the parks and larger gardens of Europe as an ornamental tree

1004 ***Populus x canadensis* - Hybrid Black Poplar** *Deciduous, quick-growing tree up to 30m high with light greyish brown, glabrous twigs*

Populus x canadensis Moench
Hybrid Black Poplar
(a cross between a European and an American species)
Salicaceae - Willow family p. 107

Length: 6-10cm, larger than the leaves of the Black Poplar

Form of blade: With an almost triangular outline

Stalk: 3-8cm long, occasionally slightly reddish

End of leaf: With an abrupt point

Base of blade: Truncate or weakly heart-shaped

Margin of leaf: Undulate and crenate-serrate; entire on the short point

Upper/under side: Shiny dark green above and paler green beneath; both sides glabrous; lateral veins more clearly branched than in the Black Poplar

Arrangement on the shoot: Leaves alternate

Distribution: Arose spontaneously in France about 1750; various forms planted throughout Europe along streets and in parks

1005 ***Populus nigra* - Black Poplar** *Deciduous, broad-crowned tree up to 30m high with shiny yellowish brown twigs*

Populus nigra L.
Black Poplar
Salicaceae - Willow family p. 107

Length: 4-9cm on long shoots, slightly smaller on short shoots

Form of blade: Rounded triangular to rhombic in outline and reddish at first

Stalk: 3-6cm long and laterally compressed

End of leaf: Pointed

Base of blade: Truncate or broadly wedge-shaped

Margin of leaf: Crenate and serrate; teeth usually rounded

Upper/under side: Dark green above and pale bluish green beneath; both sides glabrous; lateral veins not so strongly branched as those of the Hybrid Black Poplar

Arrangement on the shoot: Leaves alternate

Distribution: In the lowlands in damp woods and by lakes and rivers; associated especially with willows and with other species of poplar; prefers open ground

1006 ***Populus nigra var. italica* - Lombardy Poplar** *Deciduous, narrowly cone-shaped tree up to 30m high*

Populus nigra L. var. *italica* Muenchh.
(*P. nigra* var. *pyramidalis* (Roz.) Spach)
Lombardy Poplar
Salicaceae - Willow family
p. 42, 43, 107

Length: 4-8cm

Form of blade: Lozenge-shaped or rhombic in outline

Stalk: 1-3cm long and often with a reddish tinge

End of leaf: Long pointed

Base of blade: Broadly wedge-shaped

Margin of leaf: Sinuately serrate/dentate; tip and base of blade entire

Upper/under side: Dark green above and greyish green beneath; both sides glabrous

Arrangement on the shoot: Leaves alternate

Distribution: From the lowlands to the montane zone; frequent on river-banks, by roads, farms and monasteries; native in Iran or Turkestan; grown in Europe since the middle of the 18th century

1007 ***Betula pendula* - Silver Birch** *Deciduous tree 5-25m high; twigs with warty resin-glands.*

Betula pendula Roth
Silver Birch
Betulaceae - Birch family
p. 28, 29, 108

Length: 3-7cm

Form of blade: Triangular, ovate-rhombic or more rarely roundish in outline; sticky when young; blades of suckers larger and often heart-shaped

Stalk: 2-3cm long

End of leaf: Usually long pointed

Base of blade: Wedge-shaped

Margin of leaf: Usually coarsely doubly serrate/dentate; entire towards the base of the blade

Upper/under side: Both sides glabrous; dark green above and pale greyish green beneath

Arrangement on the shoot: Leaves alternate

Distribution: From the hill to the subalpine zone; in the lowlands in oak and birch woods, at higher altitudes on moors, in alpine meadows and on heaths; valuable in providing protection for young timber-trees

1008 ***Corylus avellana* - Hazel** *Deciduous shrub, many-stemmed from the base, 2-5m high; stems glandular hairy*

Corylus avellana L.
Hazel
Betulaceae - Birch family p. 107

Length: 5-10cm

Form of blade: Oblong-obovate, roundish or heart-shaped in outline

Stalk: 0.5-1.5cm long and glandular hairy

End of leaf: With a short, abrupt point

Base of blade: Weakly heart-shaped or rounded

Margins of leaf: Doubly serrate/dentate

Upper/under side: Both sides more or less softly hairy; medium green above and pale to medium green beneath; veins of the 2nd and 3rd order distinctly prominent

Arrangement on the shoot: Leaves alternate (usually in 2 rows); on strong shoots arranged all round the twig

Distribution: From the hill to the subalpine zone as undergrowth in woods, in hedges, meadows and pastures, on the banks of streams, the edges of woods, on steep slopes and by paths; a pioneer plant

1009 ***Alnus glutinosa* - Common Alder** *Deciduous tree up to 20m high with shiny, olive green twigs later becoming greenish brown*

Alnus glutinosa (L.) Gaertn.
Common Alder
Betulaceae - Birch family
p. 26, 27, 108

Length: 4-10cm

Form of blade: Broadly obovate to roundish in outline and sticky when young; greatest breadth of blade above the middle

Stalk: 0.5-1.5cm long

End of leaf: Rounded or usually emarginate

Base of blade: Usually broadly wedge-shaped

Margin of leaf: Simply or doubly serrate/dentate; almost all teeth broader than long

Upper/under side: Medium to dark green above; paler green beneath with tufts of whitish to rust-coloured hairs in the axils of the veins; midrib and lateral veins beneath distinctly prominent

Arrangement on the shoot: Leaves opposite

Distribution: From the hill to the montane, more rarely the subalpine zone; by mountain springs, in alder groves, on river-banks and as a pioneer plant in marshes and fens

1010 ***Vaccinium vitis-idaea* - Cowberry**
Dwarf, evergreen shrub, up to 30cm high, with erect shoots, and creeping rhizomes

Vaccinium vitis-idaea L.
Cowberry

Ericaceae - Heath family p. 108

Length: 1-3cm

Form of blade: Narrowly obovate, smooth, leathery and with the greatest breadth always above the middle; life-span of leaves 3 years

Stalk: 0.3-0.5cm with downy hairs

End of leaf: Obtuse or slightly rounded

Base of blade: Wedge-shaped

Margin of leaf: Margins slightly recurved, weakly crenate and dentate, entire in places

Upper/under side: Shiny dark green above with prominent white veins; pale greyish or bluish green beneath and gland-dotted (important character!)

Arrangement on the shoot: Leaves alternate

Distribution: From the montane to the alpine zone usually on raw humus in open spruce and pine-larch woods, dwarf shrub communities, transitional moorland and juniper scrub

1011 ***Salix herbacea* - Dwarf Willow**
Deciduous, dwarf shrub up to 5cm high, with creeping stems up to 15cm in length

Salix herbacea L.
Dwarf Willow

Salicaceae - Willow family p. 108

Length: 0.8-2cm

Form of blade: Roundish ovate to circular in outline

Stalk: 0.3-0.6cm long and somewhat broadened at the base

End of leaf: Emarginate

Base of blade: Heart-shaped or truncate

Margin of leaf: Crenate-serrate; teeth 0.1-0.2mm long and as a rule broadly rounded

Upper/under side: Both sides medium to bluish green and glabrous; distinctly net-veined

Arrangement on the shoot: Leaves alternate

Distribution: In the alpine zone; more rarely extending down into the subalpine and montane zones; especially in snow-hollows; as a pioneer on grassy mountain ridges; on base-rich, usually calcareous soils or on bare rock

1012 ***Populus alba* - White Poplar**
Deciduous, broad-crowned tree, 10-30m high, with white to grey-felted long shoots

Populus alba L.
White Poplar

Salicaceae - Willow family p. 40, 41, 109

Length: 5-12cm

Form of blade: Varied in outline; often triangular to ovate and sinuately toothed; on some twigs almost circular

Stalk: 2-4cm long, flattened and with white hairs

End of leaf: Rounded or shortly pointed

Base of blade: Rounded, weakly heart-shaped or truncate

Margin of leaf: Sinuately toothed; teeth rounded or obtuse, sinuses between them rounded

Upper/under side: Both sides felted at first with woolly hairs; later shiny dark green above and usually becoming glabrous; remaining densely white-felted beneath

Arrangement on the shoot: Leaves alternate

Distribution: On the edge of damp woods, on scree, in thickets on river-banks mainly in the hill zone; found in the Alps up to a height of 1500m; often planted in N. Europe

1013 ***Dryas octopetala* - Mountain Avens**
Evergreen, strongly creeping undershrub, with long, much-branched stems

Dryas octopetala L.
Mountain Avens

Rosaceae - Rose family p. 109

Length: 0.5-3cm

Form of blade: Oblong-elliptic in outline and regularly coarsely crenate; blade leathery and wrinkled

Stalk: 0.2-1cm long

End of leaf: Obtuse or shortly pointed

Base of blade: Truncate or weakly heart-shaped

Margin of leaf: Regularly coarsely crenate and often slightly recurved

Upper/under side: Shiny dark green and glabrous above; felted beneath with silvery white hairs

Arrangement on the shoot: Leaves alternate

Distribution: From the montane up into the alpine zone; on calcareous scree, rocks, moraines, in strong alpine meadows and in open pine woods

1014 ***Salix aurita* - Eared Willow**
Small, much-branched, deciduous shrub, 0.5-3m high with brownish twigs

Salix aurita L.
Eared Willow

Salicaceae - Willow family p. 110

Length: 2-5cm

Form of blade: Narrowly ovate to obovate in outline; stipules auriculate, large and remaining for a long time

Stalk: 0.5-0.8cm long and slightly hairy

End of leaf: Broadly rounded, with a short, obliquely twisted tip

Base of blade: Wedge-shaped

Margin of leaf: Irregularly coarsely serrate to unevenly toothed and often also undulate

Upper/under side: Dull green, glabrous and slightly undulate above; greyish green and densely downy beneath; veins whitish yellow and distinctly prominent

Arrangement on the shoot: Leaves alternate

Distribution: From the hill to the subalpine zone; on wet moorland, on the banks of lakes and streams and in alder groves

1015 ***Populus tremula* - Aspen**
Deciduous shrub or tree up to 10m high with roundish leaves on short shoots

Populus tremula L.
Aspen

Salicaceae - Willow family p. 109

Length: 3-9cm; up to 15cm long on sucker growth

Form of blade: Ovate in outline (on suckers) or roundish; at the ends of shoots the blades are similar to those of the Black Poplar

Stalk: 3-10cm long, flattened, and often slightly reddish in colour

End of leaf: Rounded or shortly pointed from a broad base

Base of blade: Truncate or weakly heart-shaped

Margin of leaf: Irregularly sinuately dentate

Upper/under side: With matted silky hairs at first, later glabrous, dull, and greyish or bluish green above; pale greyish green beneath

Arrangement on the shoot: Leaves alternate

Distribution: From the hill to the subalpine zone; found in open woods, by paths, in clearings, water-meadows, on moorland and in sunny places in the mountains

1016 ***Ulmus glabra* - Wych Elm**
Deciduous, broad-crowned tree, 30-40m high; twigs hairy and reddish brown at first

Ulmus glabra Huds. emend. Moss
(*U. scabra* Mill.)
Wych Elm
Ulmaceae - Elm family
p. 56, 57, 109

Length: 5-16cm

Form of blade: Elliptic, ovate or obovate in outline; broadest in the upper third; occasionally with 3 tips

Stalk: 3-6mm; often covered by one half of the blade

End of leaf: Finely pointed

Base of blade: Only slightly asymmetrical; the 2 halves of the blade not ending at the same point

Margin of leaf: Coarsely doubly serrate, simply serrate in the lower part; double teeth curving forwards

Upper/under side: Dark green and rough above; medium green beneath with fine white hairs on the larger veins; the 13-20 lateral veins on each side usually forked

Arrangement on the shoot: Leaves alternate (arranged in 2 rows)

Distribution: Mainly in the hill and montane zones on the edges of water-meadows, in gorges, on shady slopes and on grassland

1017 ***Ulmus laeris* - Fluttering Elm**
Deciduous tree up to 30m high with twigs densely covered with soft hairs at first

Ulmus laeris Pall.
Fluttering Elm
Ulmaceae - Elm family p. 109

Length: 7-12cm

Form of blade: Narrowly elliptic, elliptic or roundish in outline; broadest in the middle

Stalk: Only very short, up to 5mm long

End of leaf: With a short, fine point

Base of blade: Conspicuously oblique and asymmetrical

Margin of leaf: Sharply doubly serrate/dentate; main teeth directed forwards

Upper/under side: Dull dark green above; greyish green beneath with fine hairs; 12-19 primary lateral veins on each side (2 or 3 more in the longer half of the blade); lateral veins in the upper third of the leaf very rarely forked

Arrangement on the shoot: Leaves alternate (arranged in 2 rows)

Distribution: In the hill zone mainly in water-meadows, in damp mixed woods and on the edges of woodland; suitable as an avenue and street-tree

1018 ***Ulmus minor* - Smooth-leaved Elm**
Deciduous, much-branched tree up to 40m high with twigs reddish brown at first

Ulmus minor Mill.
U. campestris (auct. non L.)
Smooth-leaved Elm
Ulmaceae - Elm family p. 109

Length: 3.5-8cm

Form of blade: Varied in outline; usually narrowly obovate or obovate-elliptic with the greatest breadth in the middle

Stalk: 0.5-1.3cm long and usually somewhat hairy

End of leaf: With a long, slender tip

Base of blade: Unequal; wedge-shaped or rounded

Margin of leaf: Simply or doubly serrate; teeth pointing towards the tip

Upper/under side: Dark green and glabrous above; paler green beneath with conspicuous tufts of velvety hairs in the axils of the veins; with 9-12 pairs of lateral veins, prominent, and ending in the teeth

Arrangement on the shoot: Leaves alternate (arranged in 2 rows)

Distribution: In the hill zone by water-meadows, in woods on sunny slopes and on the edges of woodland

1019 ***Celtis australis* - Southern Nettle-tree**
Deciduous tree up to 20m high, young shoots greenish and very long

Celtis australis L.
Southern Nettle-tree
Ulmaceae - Elm family p. 110

Length: 4-15cm

Form of blade: Obliquely oblong-ovate to narrowly ovate in outline

Stalk: 1-1.5cm long

End of leaf: With a slender tip

Base of blade: Obliquely truncate or obliquely rounded

Margin of leaf: Sharply serrate; teeth pointing towards the tip and ending in a slender point

Upper/under side: Dark green and roughly hairy above; greyish green and softly hairy beneath; on each side of the leaf a strong lateral vein extends from the base of the midrib to the middle of the blade

Arrangement on the shoot: Leaves alternate (arranged in 2 rows)

Distribution: In the hill zone; prefers warm situations; on dry and rocky slopes

1020 ***Populus trichocarpa* - Western Balsam Poplar**
Deciduous tree up to 30m high with slightly angular, olive green young shoots

Populus trichocarpa
Torr. et A. Gray ex Hook.
Western Balsam Poplar
Salicaceae - Willow family p. 110

Length: 8-14cm; up to 25cm on strong shoots

Form of blade: Broadly ovate to rhombic in outline and broadest below the middle; blade thick and rather leathery

Stalk: 2-5cm long and usually reddish above

End of leaf: Pointed

Base of blade: Rounded or truncate; more rarely heart-shaped

Margin of leaf: Finely crenate-serrate

Upper/under side: Dark green and glabrous above; whitish or rust-coloured beneath and glabrous to finely downy

Arrangement on the shoot: Leaves alternate

Distribution: Native in N. America; often planted in parks or in areas of afforestation

1021 ***Sorbus aria* - Whitebeam**
Deciduous, often many-stemmed shrub or tree up to 15m high; twigs reddish on the side exposed to the sun

Sorbus aria (L.) Crantz
Whitebeam
Rosaceae - Rose family p. 110

Length: 6-12cm and up to 8cm broad

Form of blade: Ovate, elliptic or more rarely almost circular in outline

Stalk: 1-2cm long, with white woolly hairs

End of leaf: Obtuse or rounded and with a short point

Base of blade: Broadly wedge-shaped

Margin of leaf: Simply or doubly serrate/dentate; more rarely slightly lobed

Upper/under side: Medium green above and somewhat milky hairy, later becoming glabrous; densely white-felted beneath and therefore appearing pale grey to white; 10-14 pairs of prominent lateral veins beneath

Arrangement on the shoot: Leaves alternate (on long shoots); opposite or in whorls of 3 on short shoots

Distribution: On sunny, fairly dry, south-facing slopes, on crags, scree, in open deciduous and mixed deciduous woods and thickets from the hill to the subalpine zone

1022 **Betula nana - Dwarf Birch**
Deciduous, much-branched, dwarf shrub, 50–100cm high, with young twigs finely felted

Betula nana L.
Dwarf Birch
Betulaceae – Birch family p. 111

Length: Most leaves smaller than 3cm (Usually 1–1.5cm)

Form of blade: Usually roundish in outline and also broader than long; somewhat sticky when young

Stalk: 1–2mm long and dark red in colour

End of leaf: Ending in a coarse tooth

Base of blade: Truncate to weakly heart-shaped

Margin of leaf: Simply serrate; teeth broad and obtuse

Upper/under side: Dark green above, glabrous and slightly undulate; whitish beneath with a dark green network of veins

Arrangement on the shoot: Leaves alternate

Distribution: In northern, arctic, and north-eastern Europe on damp moorland and in dwarf shrub communities; on open raised bogs and pine moors

1023 **Betula x intermedia - Birch**
Deciduous shrub 1–2m high with young shoots slightly hairy

Betula x intermedia (Hartm.) Thomas (*B. nana* x *B. pubescens*)
Birch
Betulaceae – Birch family p. 111

Length: 0.8–2.5cm

Form of blade: Elliptic to broadly obovate or rhombic in outline

Stalk: 0.3–0.7cm long

End of leaf: Rounded and ending with the uppermost tooth or with 2 or more teeth

Base of blade: Broadly wedge-shaped

Margin of leaf: Coarsely simply serrate; teeth broad, rounded or shortly pointed

Upper/under side: Both sides dotted with glands; dark green above and greyish green beneath with dark green veins of the 2nd and subsequent orders

Arrangement on the shoot: Leaves alternate

Distribution: In N. Europe especially by lakes and rivers and on moorland

1024 **Nothofagus antarctica - Antarctic Beech** *Deciduous tree, up to 35m high in its native country, Chile; twigs hairy at first*

Nothofagus antarctica (G. Forst.) Oerst.
Antarctic Beech
Fagaceae – Beech family p. 111

Length: 1–3cm

Form of blade: Ovate to roundish in outline

Stalk: 2–4mm long

End of leaf: Rounded

Base of blade: Regularly or irregularly truncate or heart-shaped

Margin of leaf: Irregularly crenate, serrate and sinuate; teeth rounded or pointed

Upper/under side: Shiny dark green above and often slightly wrinkled; greyish green and glabrous beneath; midrib and primary lateral veins pale brownish green; other lateral veins dark green and clearly visible

Arrangement on the shoot: Leaves conspicuously arranged in 2 rows

Distribution: Rarely taller than 6m in central Europe; occasionally planted in parks; in Britain and Ireland grown experimentally for afforestation

1025 **Rhammus saxatilis - Rock Buckthorn**
Deciduous, much-branched, very thorny shrub up to 1m high with greyish brown stems

Rhamnus saxatilis Jacq.
Rock Buckthorn
Rhamnaceae – Buckthorn family p. 111

Length: 1–3cm

Form of blade: Lanceolate to elliptic in outline

Stalk: 0.2–0.5mm long

End of leaf: Pointed

Base of blade: Wedge-shaped

Margin of leaf: Finely and irregularly serrate

Upper/under side: Dark green above and whitish green beneath; dark green curved lateral veins; both sides glabrous

Arrangement on the shoot: Leaves opposite or almost opposite; sometimes in clusters on short shoots

Distribution: From the hill to the montane zone in open, sunny pine woods, thickets, on the edges of woods and rocky slopes; found wild in S. Germany, southern central Europe and in S. Europe

1026 **Myrica gale - Bog Myrtle**
Deciduous, much-branched shrub, 50–125cm high; young twigs downy

Myrica gale L.
Bog Myrtle, Sweet Gale
Myricaceae – Bog Myrtle family p. 110

Length: 2–5cm

Form of blade: Oblong obovate in outline and rather thick

Stalk: 0.3–0.6mm long

End of leaf: With a very short, abrupt point

Base of blade: Narrowly wedge-shaped tapering into the stalk

Margin of leaf: Coarsely toothed in the upper half, entire below and often undulate

Upper/under side: Dull dark green above with rather fine hairs; pale green beneath and finely hairy on the prominent midrib; yellowish resin-glands on both sides

Arrangement on the shoot: Leaves alternate

Distribution: From N. Germany northwards to 69° latitude, on heather moors, in peat bogs and pine woods, wet pastures and on sandy moorland

1027 **Salix glabra - Willow**
Deciduous shrub, 80–150cm high, with greyish brown, glabrous twigs

Salix glabra Scopoli
Willow
Salicaceae – Willow family p. 111

Length: 3–9cm

Form of blade: Lanceolate to obovate in outline

Stalk: 0.5–1.5cm long and somewhat broadened at the base

End of leaf: With a tapering or short abrupt point

Base of blade: Wedge-shaped

Margin of leaf: Regularly finely serrate

Upper/under side: Shiny dark green above and whitish blue-green beneath with a thick, waxy covering; both sides glabrous

Arrangement on the shoot: Leaves alternate

Distribution: In the high montane and subalpine zones on stony pastures and damp grassland; not common

1028 ***Salix hastata*** **- Spear-leaved Willow**
Deciduous shrub, 0.5-1.5m high, with stems curving upwards

Salix hastata L.
Spear-leaved Willow
Salicaceae - Willow family p. 112

Length: 3-8cm

Form of blade: Elliptic to ovate in outline

Stalk: 3-8mm long, somewhat broadened at the base and slightly reddish above

End of leaf: Shortly pointed

Base of blade: Heart-shaped

Margin of leaf: Finely serrate/dentate

Upper/under side: Dark green and glabrous above; pale greyish or bluish green beneath and hairy only at first; somewhat waxy to the touch; midrib beneath distinctly prominent

Arrangement on the shoot: Leaves alternate

Distribution: In the montane and subalpine zone; on stony and grassy slopes, on damp soils and on continuously wet alluvial ground by rivers and streams

1029 ***Salix cinerea*** **- Grey Willow**
Deciduous, erect shrub up to 5m high with stems grey at first

Salix cinerea L.
Grey Willow
Salicaceae - Willow family p. 111

Length: 5-9cm

Form of blade: Broadly lanceolate to obovate in outline

Stalk: 0.5-2cm long and somewhat broadened at the base

End of leaf: Shortly pointed

Base of blade: Wedge-shaped

Margin of leaf: Undulate, and irregularly finely to coarsely toothed

Upper/under side: Dull green and shortly hairy above; greyish green and velvety beneath; veins beneath distinctly prominent

Arrangement on the shoot: Leaves alternate

Distribution: From the hill to the montane zone on moors and in wet meadows, on damp fringes of woods, by ponds and in damp, acid soils; the Grey Willow is easily recognised by its low, spreading habit

1030 ***Salix caprea*** **- Goat Willow**
Deciduous shrub or tree up to 9m high with young shoots greyish green and hairy

Salix caprea L.
Goat Willow, Pussy Willow
Salicaceae - Willow family p. 112

Length: 4-10cm

Form of blade: Broadly elliptic to ovate in outline

Stalk: 1-2cm long, somewhat broadened at the base, slightly reddish tinged and downy

End of leaf: With a short point, bent to one side

Base of blade: Wedge-shaped

Margin of leaf: Undulate or coarsely dentate to crenate

Upper/under side: Brownish dark green and glabrous above; greyish green beneath because of the downy hairs; veins distinctly prominent

Arrangement on the shoot: Leaves alternate

Distribution: From the hill to the subalpine zone; one of the first colonisers in clearings, on fallow land and in gravel pits; also by lakes, on river-banks, in damp woodland, on the edges of woods, on scree and amongst rocks

1031 ***Malus sylvestris ssp. domestica*** **- Apple** *Deciduous shrub or tree, up to 10m high, with reddish brown, thornless twigs*

Malus sylvestris (L.) Mill. ssp. *domestica* (Borkh.) Mansf.
Apple
Rosaceae - Rose family
p. 38, 39, 112

Length: 5-9cm

Form of blade: Narrowly elliptic, elliptic to ovate in outline

Stalk: 2-5cm long

End of leaf: With a short, abrupt point

Base of blade: Wedge-shaped, rounded or truncate

Margin of leaf: Regularly serrate; teeth usually more than 0.5mm long and mostly pointing towards the tip; more coarsely serrate than the leaves of the pear

Upper/under side: Dark green above, often slightly undulate and glabrous; pale greyish green beneath and densely felted at first

Arrangement on the shoot: Leaves alternate

Distribution: Numerous varieties cultivated for their fruit from the hill to the montane zone; in gardens and orchards

1032 ***Pyrus communis*** **- Pear**
Deciduous shrub (e.g. espalier Pear) or tree up to 20m with brown twigs

Pyrus communis L.
Pear
Rosaceae - Rose family
p. 44, 45, 112

Length: 3-8cm

Form of blade: Elliptic, ovate or roundish in outline, and thick

Stalk: 1-8cm; as long as or slightly shorter than the blade

End of leaf: With a short, slender point

Base of blade: Wedge shaped or weakly rounded

Margin of leaf: Finely serrate, and entire in places; teeth on adult leaves 0.2-0.5mm long and not sharply pointed

Upper/under side: Shiny and glabrous above, somewhat hairy beneath at first, later almost or completely glabrous and somewhat paler green

Arrangement on the shoot: Leaves alternate

Distribution: From the hill to the montane zone; in gardens and orchards in regions with mild winters; numerous varieties are grown

1033 ***Alnus incana*** **- Grey Alder**
Deciduous, many-stemmed shrub or a tree up to 25m high; young twigs reddish brown

Alnus incana (L.) Moench
Grey Alder
Betulaceae - Birch family p. 112

Length: 5-10cm

Form of blade: Broadly ovate to broadly elliptic in outline

Stalk: 0.7-2cm long

End of leaf: Shortly pointed

Base of blade: Broadly wedge-shaped

Margin of leaf: Doubly serrate; all teeth much broader than long

Upper/under side: Both sides softly hairy when young; later almost glabrous and dark green above; remaining greyish green beneath, hairy to felted; only hairy on the veins towards the end of the period of growth

Arrangement on the shoot: Leaves alternate

Distribution: From the hill to the montane zone, more rarely in the subalpine zone; used as a pioneer plant to consolidate the ground in wet woods, on river-banks and on unstable slopes; continuously wet situations are avoided but places with trickling water or occasional flooding are tolerated

1034 ***Vaccinium myrtillus* - Bilberry**
Deciduous, stiffly erect shrub, 30–50cm high; stems green, glabrous and sharply angled

Vaccinium myrtillus L.
Bilberry
Ericaceae - Heath family p. 113

Length: 1–3cm

Form of blade: Oblong-ovate, elliptic or ovate in outline with the greatest breadth usually below the middle

Stalk: Very short, 0.5–3mm long

End of leaf: Rounded or shortly pointed

Base of blade: Broadly wedge-shaped or truncate

Margin of leaf: Finely serrate, dentate or crenate; teeth 0.1–0.3mm long, pointing forwards, often glandular, and shallow

Upper/under side: Dark green above and paler green beneath; both sides glabrous

Arrangement on the shoot: Leaves alternate

Distribution: From the hill to the subalpine zone; forming communities in deciduous and coniferous woods where only a few species are represented; also on poor pastures, acid woodland soils, moors and dwarf shrub heaths

1035 ***Betula humilis* - Shrubby Birch**
Deciduous shrub up to 3m high, with greyish brown stems and whitish lenticels

Betula humilis Schrank
Shrubby Birch
Betulaceae - Birch family p. 114

Length: 1–3.5cm

Form of blade: Elliptic, ovate to roundish in outline

Stalk: 0.3–0.7cm long and often slightly reddish above

End of leaf: Rather obtuse to weakly pointed

Base of blade: Wedge-shaped

Margin of leaf: Simply and irregularly serrate

Upper/under side: Shiny dark green and glabrous above; paler green beneath with a distinct network of veins and with 4 or 5 pairs of lateral veins

Arrangement on the shoot: Leaves alternate

Distribution: From the hill to the montane zone: on open raised bogs and pine moors, acid valley bogs, in open birch woods, shrubby pastures and alder thickets

1036 ***Amelanchier ovalis* - Service Berry**
Deciduous shrub, 1–3m high, with young shoots covered with white woolly hairs

Amelanchier ovalis Medic.
Service Berry
Rosaceae - Rose family p. 113

Length: 2–4.5cm

Form of blade: Ovate to roundish in outline

Stalk: 1–2cm long and felted, especially when young

End of leaf: Rounded

Base of blade: Rounded or weakly heart-shaped

Margin of leaf: Finely serrate or dentate; in places entire or crenate

Upper/under side: Dark green and glabrous; only slightly paler green beneath, and downy when young, later becoming glabrous

Arrangement on the shoot: Leaves alternate

Distribution: From the hill to the subalpine zone; on warm, steep slopes, in rock-crevices, oak and pine woods, open scrub, and in shrubby Mountain Pine communities in the Alps

1037 ***Betula pubescens* - Downy Birch**
Large, deciduous shrub or tree up to 30m high; shoots densely downy at first

Betula pubescens Ehrh.
Downy Birch
Betulaceae - Birch family p. 114

Length: 3–5cm

Form of blade: Broadly ovate to rhombic; with an aromatic scent when young; broadest in the middle of the blade

Stalk: 1–2cm long and somewhat hairy

End of leaf: Shortly pointed

Base of blade: Broadly wedge-shaped or rounded

Margin of leaf: Unequally doubly serrate/dentate; entire at the base of the blade

Upper/under side: Both sides more or less hairy; dark green above and becoming glabrous; with fine, downy hairs in the axils of the larger veins beneath

Arrangement on the shoot: Leaves alternate

Distribution: Found here and there from the hill to the subalpine zone in bogs and wet woodland, on transition moors, and in alder groves and thickets

1038 ***Prunus armeniaca* - Apricot**
Deciduous shrub or tree up to 10m high with twigs reddish brown at first

Prunus armeniaca L.
Apricot
Rosaceae - Rose family p. 113

Length: 5–10cm

Form of blade: Broadly ovate, roundish or weakly heart-shaped in outline

Stalk: 3–7cm long and dark red in colour; usually with 2 glandular tubercles

End of leaf: Shortly pointed

Base of blade: Broadly wedge-shaped, rounded or truncate

Margin of leaf: Finely serrate

Upper/under side: Both sides glabrous; dull green above and slightly paler green beneath

Arrangement on the shoot: Leaves alternate

Distribution: Cultivated in vine-growing regions; prefers sunny situations protected from the cold

1039 ***Arbutus unedo* - Strawberry Tree**
Evergreen tree up to 10m high with a dense, distinctly rounded, domed crown

Arbutus unedo L.
Strawberry Tree
Ericaceae - Heath family p. 113

Length: 5–10cm

Form of blade: Oblong-elliptic in outline

Stalk: 0.5–1.5cm long, distinctly hairy and often somewhat reddish

End of leaf: Obtuse and with several short teeth or shortly pointed

Base of blade: Wedge-shaped

Margin of leaf: Irregularly serrate with teeth of unequal length; teeth at the tip distinctly tinged reddish; entire towards the base of the blade

Upper/under side: Glabrous above, and dark green alternating with pale green areas; much paler green and glabrous beneath, with only the midrib prominent

Arrangement on the shoot: Leaves alternate

Distribution: Found especially amongst the evergreen shrubby vegetation and margins in the Mediterranean region; along the Atlantic coast (as far as Ireland); often planted as an ornamental tree in gardens and parks

1040 ***Prunus lusitanica*** **- Portugal Laurel**
Evergreen shrub or tree up to 20m high with glabrous, red twigs

Prunus lusitanica L.
Portugal Laurel
Rosaceae - Rosé family p.113

Length: 6-12cm

Form of blade: Oblong-ovate in outline, thin and leathery

Stalk: 1-2.5cm long, often distinctly reddish and grooved above

End of leaf: Pointed; tip often slightly rounded

Base of blade: Usually rounded

Margin of leaf: Irregularly serrate/ dentate and wavy in places

Upper/under side: Shiny dark green above and pale green beneath; both sides glabrous; only the midrib prominent

Arrangement on the shoot: Leaves alternate

Distribution: A native tree in Spain and Portugal; planted in gardens in the warmer parts of central Europe

1041 ***Alnus viridis*** **- Green Alder**
Deciduous, many-stemmed shrub, 0.5-2.5m high with reddish brown twigs

Alnus viridis (Chaix) DC. ssp. *viridis*
Green Alder
Betulaceae - Birch family p. 114

Length: 3-6cm

Form of blade: Elliptic to broadly ovate in outline

Stalk: 1-2cm long and grooved, sometimes reddish tinged above in the lower part

End of leaf: Obtuse with small teeth or pointed

Base of blade: Broadly wedge-shaped, rounded or more rarely truncate or heart-shaped

Margin of leaf: Simply or doubly serrate or irregularly serrate; most teeth longer than broad

Upper/under side: Dark green and glabrous above; paler green beneath and glabrous except for possible tufts of hairs in the axils of the veins; with 10-15 pairs of distinctly prominent lateral veins

Arrangement on the shoot: Leaves alternate

Distribution: In the montane and subalpine zones, more rarely the hill zone; on damp, shady slopes, by streams, ditches, ravines, pastures

1042 ***Carpinus betulus*** **- Hornbeam**
Deciduous tree up to 20m high with shoots hairy at first, later becoming glabrous

Carpinus betulus L.
Hornbeam
Betulaceae - Birch family p. 114

Length: 4-12cm

Form of blade: Ovate to oblong-ovate in outline

Stalk: 0.5-1.5cm long; often reddish above

End of leaf: Rather obtuse or more often pointed

Base of blade: Regularly or obliquely rounded to heart-shaped

Margin of leaf: Simply or doubly serrate; individual teeth very small

Upper/side under: Rich green and glabrous above; paler green beneath and sparingly hairy in the axils of the veins; lateral veins running to the margin, very prominent and straight; planted between the lateral veins on both sides

Arrangement on the shoot: Leaves alternate; arranged in 2 distinct rows

Distribution: In the hill zone, more rarely montane; in oak woods, as the dominant species in hornbeam woods, on the fringes of woodland, and often planted round the edges of large gardens and parks

1043 ***Ostrya carpinifolia*** **- Hop Hornbeam**
Deciduous tree up to 20m high with young shoots covered with brownish hairs

Ostrya carpinifolia Scop.
Hop Hornbeam
Betulaceae - Birch family p. 115

Length: 5-12cm

Form of blade: Ovate-oblong or ovate in outline; leaves slightly folded in the young state

Stalk: 4-12mm long

End of leaf: Pointed

Base of blade: Broadly wedge-shaped or rounded

Margin of leaf: Sharply, and simply or doubly serrate; teeth longer and more finely pointed than in the hornbeam

Upper/under side: Only slightly hairy on both sides; dark green and smooth above; yellowish green beneath and slightly hairy in the axils of the veins; 11-15 pairs of lateral veins; not undulate between the veins; lower lateral veins slightly curved at the midrib

Arrangement on the shoot: Leaves alternate (arranged in 2 rows)

Distribution: In the hill and montane zone on shrubby, strong, sunny hillsides, crags, on south-facing slopes in the Downy Oakwood zone; centre in eastern Mediterranean region

1044 ***Morus alba*** **- White Mulberry**
Deciduous shrub or tree up to 15m high with shoots pale brownish yellow at first

Morus alba L.
White Mulberry
Moraceae - Mulberry family p. 115

Length: 7-18cm

Form of blade: Varied in outline; often without lobes and then broadly ovate

Stalk: 2-5cm long, slightly hairy (later glabrous) and grooved above

End of leaf: Rounded and with a short tooth or shortly pointed

Base of blade: Truncate or weakly heart-shaped

Margin of leaf: Unequally serrate; teeth not so long as in the Black Mulberry and often rounded also

Upper/under side: Shiny dark green above and smooth or slightly rough; bluish green beneath and only hairy on the veins; veins whitish yellow and quite prominent

Arrangement on the shoot: Leaves alternate (usually arranged in 2 rows)

Distribution: Native in China and Korea and grown for 4600 years as a food-plant for silkworm and caterpillars; cultivated in S. Europe since the 11th century; naturalised here and there in the hill zone

1045 ***Morus nigra*** **- Black Mulberry**
Deciduous, much-branched tree 15-20m high; leaves sometimes lobed

Morus nigra L.
Black Mulberry
Moraceae - Mulberry family p. 115

Length: 6-18cm

Form of blade: Varied in outline; often broadly ovate to heart-shaped

Stalk: 1-2cm long

End of leaf: Finely pointed; the tip much more slender than in the White Mulberry

Base of blade: Truncate, heart-shaped to obliquely heart-shaped

Margin of leaf: Coarsely serrate

Upper/under side: Shiny dark green above and very roughly hairy; paler bluish green and hairy beneath; veins whitish yellow and distinctly prominent

Arrangement on the shoot: Leaves alternate

Distribution: Tree cultivated since ancient times; grown since the 16th century especially in the vine-growing region, and frequently found in monastery gardens; more commonly found in Tessin, Carinthia, Styria and the Tyrol; the tree was well-known to the Greeks and Romans

1046 ***Prunus mahaleb* - St Lucie Cherry** *Deciduous tree 5-10m high with young shoots finely hairy; flowering twigs very fragrant*

Prunus mahaleb L.
St Lucie Cherry

Rosaceae - Rose family p. 115

Length: 3-6cm

Form of blade: Broadly ovate to roundish in outline

Stalk: 1-2cm long and usually without glands

End of leaf: Obtuse or shortly pointed

Base of blade: Truncate, rounded or weakly heart-shaped

Margin of leaf: Crenate-serrate

Upper/under side: Shiny dark green and glabrous above; bluish green beneath and often somewhat hairy on the midrib; only the midrib particularly prominent beneath

Arrangement on the shoot: Leaves alternate

Distribution: In warm places in the hill and montane zones; especially on warm, dry slopes, in open oak and pine woods, in thickets and hedges

1047 ***Rhamnus pumila* - Dwarf Buckthorn** *Deciduous, low-growing shrub, only 10-20cm high*

Rhamnus pumila (Turra) W. Vent
Dwarf Buckthorn

Rhamnaceae - Buckthorn family p. 115

Length: 2-5cm

Form of blade: Elliptic, obovate or roundish in outline

Stalk: 4-9mm long

End of leaf: With a short, abrupt point

Base of blade: Usually wedge-shaped

Margin of leaf: Very finely crenate-serrate

Upper/under side: Dark green and glabrous above; paler green beneath and somewhat hairy on the veins, later becoming glabrous; with 4-9 (12) pairs of curved and distinctly prominent lateral veins

Arrangement on the shoot: Leaves alternate

Distribution: Mainly in the subalpine and alpine zones on bare rocks and in rock-crevices; very suitable for the rock-garden; the stems spread out evenly on rocks like lattice-work

1048 ***Prunus tenella* - Dwarf Russian Almond** *Deciduous, slender-stemmed, erect shrub 1-1.5m high*

Prunus tenella Batsch
Dwarf Russian Almond

Rosaceae - Rose family p. 116

Length: 3-7cm

Form of blade: Narrowly-elliptic in outline

Stalk: 0.5-1.5cm long

End of leaf: Pointed

Base of blade: Wedge-shaped, narrowing into the stalk

Margin of leaf: Finely and regularly serrate/dentate

Upper/under side: Shiny dark green above and pale green beneath; both sides glabrous; midrib distinctly prominent

Arrangement on the shoot: Leaves alternate

Distribution: In the hill zone; amongst deciduous shrubs on dry soils, on dry grassland and in vineyards; distributed from E. Siberia to Hungary and Lower Austria; eating the seeds may produce symptoms of poisoning

1049 ***Prunus domestica* - Plum** *Deciduous tree, native in W. Asia, growing up to 10m high; young shoots reddish brown*

Prunus domestica L. ssp. *domestica*
Plum

Rosaceae - Rose family p. 116

Length: 3-10cm

Form of blade: Elliptic in outline, or obovate, in which case the greatest breadth is above the middle

Stalk: 1-1.5cm long

End of leaf: Rounded, obtuse or pointed

Base of blade: Narrowly wedge-shaped or at least narrowed

Margin of leaf: Finely serrate and crenate

Upper/under side: Both sides hairy when young; dark green above and later glabrous; pale green beneath, the long hairs often persistent, and with a prominent midrib

Arrangement on the shoot: Alternate on long shoots and arranged in clusters on short shoots

Distribution: Planted in gardens in the hill zone

1050 ***Rhamnus catharticus* - Buckthorn** *Deciduous shrub up to 3m high with grey to greyish brown stems*

Rhamnus catharticus L.
Buckthorn

Rhamnaceae - Buckthorn family p. 116

Length: 4-7cm

Form of blade: Elliptic to roundish in outline

Stalk: 1-3cm long and slightly grooved above

End of leaf: Usually with a short, abrupt point

Base of blade: Broadly wedge-shaped, truncate or rounded

Margin of leaf: Finely crenate-serrate

Upper/under side: Both sides usually glabrous; dull dark green above and medium bluish green beneath; 2-4 curved lateral veins each side of the midrib

Arrangement on the shoot: Leaves opposite or obliquely opposite; each pair at right angles to the next

Distribution: From the hill to the montane zone; in sunny hedges, on dry shrubby slopes, on poor pastures and on dry boundaries of woodland

1051 ***Rhamnus alpinus* - Alpine Buckthorn** *Deciduous shrub up to 3m high with glabrous, greyish brown stems*

Rhamnus alpinus L. ssp. *alpinus*
Alpine Buckthorn

Rhamnaceae - Buckthorn family p. 114

Length: 5-14cm

Form of blade: Elliptic to ovate in outline

Stalk: 0.8-1.5cm long

End of leaf: With a short, abrupt point

Base of blade: Rounded or weakly heart-shaped

Margin of leaf: Finely serrate; usually crenate in the lower part; teeth in the upper part pointing towards the tip

Upper/under side: Shiny dark green and glabrous above; only slightly paler green beneath and usually glabrous; veins beneath distinctly prominent; with 5-20 primary lateral veins on each side of the midrib, curving upwards slightly at the end

Arrangement on the shoot: Leaves alternate

Distribution: In the montane zone; more rarely in the hill and subalpine zones; in open woods, on rocks, on scree, and in hedges in sunny places

1052 ***Prunus serrulata*** **- Japanese Cherry**
Deciduous tree up to 10m high, with stiffly spreading, glabrous twigs

Prunus serrulata Lindl.
Japanese Cherry
Rosaceae - Rose family p. 117

Length: 8-14cm

Form of blade: Narrowly ovate in outline

Stalk: 2-4cm long, reddish above, with 2-4 greenish glands just below the point where it joins the blade

End of leaf: With a long point

Base of blade: Wedge-shaped

Margin of leaf: Sharply and regularly serrate

Upper/under side: Both sides glabrous; shiny dark green above and bluish green beneath; veins distinctly prominent

Arrangement on the shoot: Leaves alternate

Distribution: Tree native in China, Korea and Japan, very often planted in gardens

1053 ***Prunus padus*** **- Bird Cherry**
Deciduous shrub or tree up to 6m high with glabrous, greyish brown twigs

Prunus padus L.
Bird Cherry
Rosaceae - Rose family p. 117

Length: 5-12cm

Form of blade: Oblong-elliptic to obovate in outline

Stalk: Up to 2cm long, red above, and with 1-3 greenish nectar-glands

End of leaf: With a fine, slender tip

Base of blade: Usually rounded, more rarely truncate or wedge-shaped

Margin of leaf: Finely and regularly serrate; teeth shorter than 0.7mm

Upper/under side: Both sides glabrous; dull dark green above and pale or bluish green beneath

Arrangement on the shoot: Leaves alternate

Distribution: From the hill to the montane zone; in damp thickets and woods, gorges, hedges, by rivers and on marshy ground; often associated with ashes, alders and elms

1054 ***Prunus cerasus*** **- Sour Cherry**
Deciduous tree, 5-10m high, with young shoots green, later becoming greyish brown

Prunus cerasus L.
Sour Cherry
Rosaceae - Rose family p. 117

Length: 4-12cm

Form of blade: Elliptic to ovate in outline, flat and slightly leathery

Stalk: 1-3cm long, with or without green nectar-glands

End of leaf: Pointed

Base of blade: Broadly wedge-shaped or rounded

Margin of leaf: Finely serrate and in places crenate

Upper/under side: Shiny dark green and glabrous above; pale green beneath, somewhat hairy and later becoming glabrous; veins distinctly prominent

Arrangement on the shoot: Leaves alternate

Distribution: Brought into central Europe by the Romans; planted in gardens, often escaping and becoming naturalised; native in S.E. Asia and nowadays with many varieties in cultivation

1055 ***Prunus avium*** **- Wild Cherry**
Deciduous tree up to 25m high; twigs brown, roundish, and with corky lenticels

Prunus avium L.
Wild Cherry, Gean
Rosaceae - Rose family
p. 46, 47, 118

Length: 6-15cm

Form of blade: Oblong-elliptic to obovate in outline

Stalk: 2-4cm long, with 2-4 red-coloured nectar-glands just below the point where it joins the blade

End of leaf: Slender, abrupt point

Base of blade: Broadly wedge-shaped, truncate or rounded

Margin of leaf: Irregularly serrate

Upper/under side: Dark green above, usually somewhat wrinkled and glabrous; paler green beneath and finely hairy when young; with small tufts of hairs in the axils of the larger veins; veins distinctly prominent

Arrangement on the shoot: Leaves alternate

Distribution: In the hill zone; on the edges of woodland, in mixed deciduous woods, in hedges, deserted vineyards, or on uncultivated meadows and pastures; several varieties known already to the ancient Greeks

1056 ***Sorbus chamaemespilus*** **- False Medlar**
Small, deciduous shrub, 1-3m high; stems felted at first

Sorbus chamaemespilus (L.) Crantz
False Medlar
Rosaceae - Rose family p. 117

Length: 3-8cm

Form of blade: Narrowly elliptic to elliptic in outline and with the greatest breadth usually below the middle

Stalk: 0.5-1cm long

End of leaf: Obtuse or slightly pointed

Base of blade: Broadly wedge-shaped or rounded

Margin of leaf: Simply and finely serrate; teeth about 1mm long

Upper/under side: Shiny dark green above; paler green beneath; both sides glabrous; forms with leaves felted beneath are hybrids; lateral veins not obviously ending in the teeth; veins distinctly prominent

Arrangement on the shoot: Leaves alternate

Distribution: In the subalpine zone, more rarely montane; a pioneer shrub; on rocks, scree, pastures, in Mountain Pine, Arolla Pine and Larch woods and in Alpenrose and Green Alder thickets

1057 ***Prunus spinosa*** **- Blackthorn**
Deciduous, stiffly branched, very thorny shrub with young shoots softly hairy

Prunus spinosa L.
Blackthorn, Sloe
Rosaceae - Rose family p. 116

Length: 2-5cm

Form of blade: Broadly lanceolate to oblong-elliptic in outline

Stalk: 0.5-1.2cm long and often tinged red above

End of leaf: Obtuse or shortly pointed

Base of blade: Serrate and in places crenate

Upper/under side: Hairy when young, later glabrous; dark green above and pale green beneath

Arrangement on the shoot: Leaves alternate; short shoots ending in a thorn

Distribution: From the hill zone ascending to the montane zone; on sunny rock and scree slopes, the edges of woods, by fences, in vineyards, meadows, hedges and as a pioneer shrub on uncultivated pastures

1058 ***Forsythia x intermedia* - Hybrid Forsythia** *Deciduous shrub, 2-3m high, with greenish yellow stems*

Forsythia x intermedia Zab.

(*F. suspensa x F. viridissima*)

Hybrid Forsythia

Oleaceae - Olive family p. 118

Length: 6-11cm

Form of blade: Lanceolate to oblong-ovate in outline; sometimes divided into three parts on vigorous long shoots

Stalk: 1-2cm long and usually grooved above

End of leaf: Pointed

Base of blade: Wedge-shaped

Margin of leaf: Irregularly serrate or dentate

Upper/under side: Dark green above and paler green to pale bluish green beneath; midrib distinctly prominent

Arrangement on the shoot: Leaves opposite; stems with layers of pith; solid at the nodes

Distribution: Found in Göttingen Botanic Garden in 1878; many forms planted in gardens and parks

1059 ***Forsythia europaea* - European Forsythia** *Deciduous shrub, 1.5-2.5m high, with stiffly erect, glabrous stems*

Forsythia europaea Deg. et Bald.

European Forsythia

Oleaceae - Olive family p. 118

Length: 5-8cm

Form of blade: Narrowly elliptic to narrowly ovate in outline

Stalk: 0.5-1cm long and grooved above

End of leaf: Pointed

Base of blade: Wedge-shaped or rounded

Margin of leaf: Finely serrate in the upper part except for the tip; usually entire in the lower part

Upper/under side: Both sides glabrous; dark green above and paler green beneath

Arrangement on the shoot: Leaves opposite; stems with layers of pith

Distribution: Shrub, native in N. Albania and S.W. Yugoslavia; horticulturally unimportant and therefore only occasionally planted in gardens

1060 ***Forsythia viridissima* - Green Forsythia** *Erect, deciduous shrub, up to 3m high, with greenish, 4-angled stems*

Forsythia viridissima Lindl.

Green Forsythia

Oleaceae - Olive family p. 118

Length: 4-14cm

Form of blade: Lanceolate to narrowly elliptic in outline

Stalk: 0.5-3cm long and usually grooved above

End of leaf: Pointed

Base of blade: Wedge-shaped

Margin of leaf: Usually finely serrate/dentate only in the upper third; otherwise entire

Upper/under side: Both sides glabrous; dark green above and pale green beneath

Arrangement on the shoot: Leaves opposite; stems with layers of pith throughout

Distribution: Ornamental shrub native in China; planted in gardens and parks; not common

1061 ***Euonymus europaeus* - Spindle Tree** *Deciduous shrub, 3-7m high, with green, angular stems which later become greyish brown*

Euonymus (*Evonymus*) ***europaeus*** L.

Spindle Tree

Celastraceae - Spindle Tree family p.118

Length: 3-8cm; 3.5-5cm long on flowering and fruiting stems

Form of blade: Elliptic to ovate in outline; greatest breadth in the middle

Stalk: 0.5-0.9cm long and grooved

End of leaf: With a narrow point

Base of blade: Narrowly or broadly wedge-shaped or rounded

Margin of leaf: Very finely and regularly serrate; teeth often rounded, therefore the margin appearing crenate in places

Upper/under side: Both sides glabrous; medium to dark green above and pale bluish green beneath

Arrangement on the shoot: Leaves opposite

Distribution: From the hill to the montane zone; in damp and mixed deciduous woods, on the borders of woodland, in hedges, by fences and on the verges of paths

1062 ***Viburnum lantana* - Wayfaring Tree** *Deciduous shrub, 3-5m high, with young stems densely felted*

Viburnum lantana L.

Wayfaring Tree

Caprifoliaceae - Honeysuckle family p. 116

Length: 5-12cm

Form of blade: Ovate to oblong-ovate in outline

Stalk: Up to 1.5cm long and densely grey-felted

End of leaf: Pointed

Base of blade: Rounded or weakly heart-shaped

Margin of leaf: Regularly and finely toothed

Upper/under side: Slightly wrinkled above, medium to dark green and with the veins clearly visible; medium green beneath and densely covered with stellate hairs; both sides rough to the touch; veins beneath distinctly prominent; primary veins ending in the leaf-teeth

Arrangement on the shoot: Leaves opposite

Distribution: From the hill to the montane zone; in sunny places in hedges, on the edges of woods, and in open oak and pine woods

1063 ***Mespilus germanica* - Medlar** *Deciduous, thorny shrub, up to 3m high, with young branchlets loosely felted*

Mespilus germanica L.

Medlar

Rosaceae - Rose family p. 117

Length: 5-12cm

Form of blade: Oblong-elliptic to obovate in outline

Stalk: Sessile or up to 1cm long

End of leaf: Very shortly pointed

Base of blade: Usually rounded

Margin of leaf: Finely dentate/serrate and in places entire

Upper/under side: Dull green above, somewhat downy and slightly wrinkled; pale to greyish green beneath with matted whitish hairs; veins deeply impressed above

Arrangement on the shoot: Leaves alternate

Distribution: In the hill zone; escaping and becoming naturalised on sunny slopes, in hedges and open woods with Turkey Oak and Downy Oak, or in woodland communities of Hop Hornbeam and Oriental Hornbeam; a shrub with a preference for warm, moist and open situations; the Medlar was used as a fruit-tree by the Greeks

1064 ***Arctostaphylos alpinus* - Black Bearberry** *Deciduous, creeping and mat-forming dwarf shrub with stems up to 60cm long*

Arctostaphylos alpinus (L.) Spreng.
Black Bearberry
Ericaceae - Heath family p. 118

Length: 1-4cm

Form of blade: Spathulate or narrowly obovate in outline and narrowed into the stalk

Stalk: Only very shortly stalked

End of leaf: Obtuse

Base of blade: Very narrowly wedge-shaped

Margin of leaf: Finely and closely serrate, entire towards the base; fringed with spreading, white hairs, 0.5-1.5mm long

Upper/under side: Dark green above and undulate between the veins; whitish green beneath, with a network of dark green veins

Arrangement on the shoot: Leaves alternate

Distribution: In the subalpine and alpine zone on dwarf shrub heaths, in Mountain Pine woods, on rocks and on scree

1065 ***Salix purpurea* - Purple Willow** *Deciduous shrub, up to 3m high, with young stems reddish brown*

Salix purpurea L.
Purple Willow
Salicaceae - Willow family p. 119

Length: 5-10cm

Form of blade: Lanceolate in outline; greatest breadth usually in the upper third

Stalk: 0.5-0.8cm long and often tinged reddish

End of leaf: Shortly pointed

Base of blade: Wedge-shaped and often also slightly rounded

Margin of leaf: Finely serrate towards the tip; entire in the lower part; teeth pointing towards the leaf-tip; margin not recurved

Upper/under side: Bluish green above, glabrous and with a clearly visible midrib; pale bluish green and glabrous beneath

Arrangement on the shoot: Leaves alternate; often also opposite

Distribution: From the hill to the subalpine zone; beside paths and on the edges of woods, in thickets, by watercourses, on sandbanks in Alpine rivers and in open pine woods; a pioneer shrub of fresh, wet ground

1066 ***Salix alba* - White Willow** *Deciduous tree 10-20m high; twigs at first yellowish brown and with appressed hairs*

Salix alba L.
White Willow
Salicaceae - Willow family p. 50, 51, 119

Length: 5-10cm

Form of blade: Narrowly lanceolate to lanceolate in outline and with narrow stipules at first; uppermost part of blade often curved to one side

Stalk: 0.5-1cm long

End of leaf: With a fine, slender point

Base of blade: Narrowly wedge-shaped

Margin of leaf: Finely and regularly serrate/dentate

Upper/under side: Both sides covered with dense, appressed, silvery hairs when young; later dark green above and usually glabrous; silvery white hairs remaining beneath; lateral veins rather inconspicuous above

Arrangement on the shoot: Leaves alternate

Distribution: In the hill zone; in association with poplars, alders and other willows by rivers, streams and lakes, and in damp woods; also on intermittently flooded ground

1067 ***Salix fragilis* - Crack Willow** *Deciduous shrub or tree up to 15m high; twigs readily breaking off*

Salix fragilis L.
Crack Willow
Salicaceae - Willow family p. 119

Length: 5-16cm

Form of blade: Oblong-lanceolate in outline; sticky when young; usually broadest in the lower third

Stalk: Up to 1cm long and with 2-4 glands

End of leaf: With a very long, fine point

Base of blade: Narrowly or broadly wedge-shaped

Margin of leaf: Coarsely sinuate-serrate; teeth curving inwards; in the typical form the glands are close against the sinuses

Upper/under side: Dark green and slightly shiny above; with silky hairs at first beneath, later pale or bluish green and the midrib distinctly prominent; later in the year completely glabrous

Arrangement on the shoot: Leaves alternate

Distribution: By rivers and in the water-meadows of the hill zone; avoids summer flooding

1068 ***Prunus dulcis* - Almond** *Erect, deciduous shrub or tree up to 10m high with young shoots reddish on the side exposed to the sun*

Prunus dulcis (Mill.) D. A. Webb
Almond
Rosaceae - Rose family p. 119

Length: 4-12cm

Form of blade: Lanceolate to oblong-elliptic in outline

Stalk: 1-2.5cm long

End of leaf: Obtuse or pointed

Base of blade: Wedge-shaped or rounded

Margin of leaf: Very finely serrate/dentate

Upper/under side: Medium to dark green above and pale bluish green beneath; both sides glabrous; only the midrib really prominent

Arrangement on the shoot: Leaves alternate

Distribution: In the hill zone in full sun; one of the oldest cultivated plants in the Mediterranean region; various forms and varieties were already known to the Greeks and Romans; reached China in the 11th century B.C. and Greece about 500 B.C.; main producing countries are Spain, Italy and the U.S.A.

1069 ***Prunus persica* - Peach** *Deciduous shrub or small tree, 3-8m high, with shoots red on the side exposed to the sun*

Prunus persica (L.) Batsch
Peach
Rosaceae - Rose family p. 119

Length: 5-15cm

Form of blade: Narrowly to broadly lanceolate in outline

Stalk: 0.5-1.5cm long, occasionally with glands

End of leaf: With a long point

Base of blade: Wedge-shaped

Margin of leaf: Finely serrate/dentate

Upper/under side: Shiny dark green above and medium green beneath; both sides glabrous; only the midrib beneath distinctly prominent

Arrangement on the shoot: Leaves alternate

Distribution: Many varieties cultivated in vine-growing regions; prefers warm, dry soils in sunny, sheltered places; the wild form is presumed to have been native in China or western central Asia; grown nowadays in large plantations especially in the Mediterranean region

Glossary of Botanical Terms

Technical terms that cannot be replaced with more elementary language are defined in this Glossary, or interpreted in the Introduction to this book, in which case only a page-reference is given here.

achene: a dry, one-seeded fruit
acuminate: see p. 15
acute: see p. 15
adult: see p. 18
alpine: see p. 62
alternate: see p. 18
anisophylly: see p. 18
anther: the pollen-bearing organ forming at the end of a stamen
apiculate: see p. 15
appressed: lying flat and close to
asymmetrical: see p. 16
attenuate: gradually tapering
auricle: an ear-shaped extension at the base of a leaf
auriculate: see p. 16
axil: the angle between a shoot and a leaf, or between a midrib and a vein
axillary tuft: see p. 17
axis: see p. 17

base: see pp. 11, 16
bast: phloem
bisexual: hermaphrodite, having both male and female organs in the same flower
bract: see p. 11
bristle-toothed: see p. 15

calcareous (of soil): rich in calcium carbonate (lime)
calyx: the sepals collectively
cambium: layer of dividing cells between xylem and phloem in a stem
capsule: a dry fruit composed of several carpels
carpel: the female part of a flower: the ovary, style and stigma collectively
catkin: a hanging spike of small, unisexual flowers
cellulose: the principal component of plant cell walls
ciliate: see p. 15
cladode: see p. 11
colline: see p. 62
compound (of leaf): see p. 17
cone: the reproductive structure of a coniferous plant
connate: see p. 16
coppice: trees whose trunks have been cut off near ground level and which have then grown multiple stems
corolla: the petals collectively
cortex: cell tissue in a stem or root between the outer cell layer and the vascular tissue
cotyledon: see p. 18
crenate: see p. 15
crenate-serrate: see p. 14
cuneate: see p. 16
cupule: a cup formed by fused bracts, e.g. acorn cup
cuspidate: narrowing abruptly to a point
cyme: an often flat or convex inflorescence in which the terminal flower opens first

deciduous: see p. 11
decumbent (of stems): resting flat on the ground but with the tip rising
decurrent: see p. 16
decussate: see p. 19
dentate: see p. 14
digitate: see p. 14
dioecious: having male and female flowers on separate plants
disc: the fleshy, sometimes nectar-secreting portion of the receptacle
doubly serrate: see p.14

elliptic: see p. 12
emarginate: see p. 15
entire: see p. 14
evergreen: see p. 11

fascicled: see p. 18
felted: see p. 17
fimbriate: having a fringed margin
foliage leaf: see p. 11
forked: see p. 19

glabrous: without hairs
glandular: see p. 14

hairy: see p. 17
heart-shaped: see pp. 13, 16
heartwood: the central core of wood which is dead, even in the living tree
hermaphrodite: having both male and female organs in the same flower
heterophylly: see p. 18
heterostyly: variation in the length of stamens and styles in different flowers within a species
hill-zone: see p. 62
humus: plant and animal remains in the soil that have lost their cell structure through decomposition

imbricate: see p. 19
imparipinnate: see p. 17
indented: see p. 15
indigenous: native
inflorescence: flower-cluster

juvenile: see p. 18

kidney-shaped: see p. 13

lamina: see p. 11
lanceolate: see p. 12
leaf: see p. 11
leaf base: see p. 11
leaf blade: see p. 11
leaf stalk: see p. 16
leaflet: a leaf-like part of a compound leaf
lenticel: a pore in the corky covering of woody stems
linear: see p. 12
loamy (of soil): containing an even mixture of different-sized particles
lobed: see pp. 15, 17

margin: see p. 14
medulla: pith
medullary ray: the region in a stem where the outer pith meets the inner cortex
midrib: see p. 13
montane: see p. 62
mucronate: see p. 15

nectary: a nectar-secreting gland
needle: see p. 19
net: see p. 13
node: see p. 18
nodule: a swelling on a root, containing bacteria

oblanceolate: see p. 13
oblique: see p. 16
oblong: see p. 12
obovate: see p. 13
obtuse: see p. 15
opposite: see pp. 18, 19

orbicular: see p. 12
ovary: the part of the carpel of a flower that contains the ovules
ovate: see p. 12 (egg-shaped in 2 dimensions)
ovoid: egg-shaped in 3 dimensions
ovule: the structure which becomes the seed when fertilised

palmate: see pp. 14, 17
panicle: a much-branched inflorescence (*cf* raceme, umbel)
parallel: see p. 13
paripinnate: see p. 17
perigon or **perianth**: a collective term for the corolla plus the calyx
perigynous: having the sepals, petals and stamens inserted round the ovary on a concave structure developed from the receptacle
petal: one of the parts of a flower that surrounds the reproductive organs, collectively known as the corolla
petiole: see p. 16
phloem: vascular tissue which conducts nutrients made by the leaves to other parts of the plant
pinnate: see p. 13
pinnatifid: see p. 17
pinnatipartite: see p. 17
pinnatisect: see p. 17
pith: the central tissue of the stems of non-woody plants
pollard: a tree whose trunk has been cut off well above ground level (*cf* coppice), and which has then grown multiple stems
pollen: minute grains, produced within the anther, each of which gives rise to a male sex cell
pollination: the transfer of pollen from male to female reproductive organs
pore (in wood): a small hole
pseudocarp: a false fruit
pulvinus: a swelling on a shoot from which a leaf or its stalk arises

quadrangular: see p. 13

raceme: an unbranched inflorescence with stalked flowers opening from the base upwards (*cf* panicle, umbel)
rachis: the central stalk of a compound leaf, or of an inflorescence
receptacle: the swelling at the end of a stalk which bears the flower-parts
recurved: see p. 15
reniform: kidney-shaped
reticulate: marked with a network pattern
retuse: see p. 15
rounded: see pp. 15, 16

sapwood: young secondary xylem which after some years becomes heartwood
scale: see p. 11
scale-leaf: see p. 11
schizocarp: a fruit which breaks into several pieces, each usually one-seeded
sepal: one of the parts of a flower, collectively known as the calyx, growing outside the petals
serrate: see p. 14
sessile: see pp. 11, 16
shoot: see pp. 11, 18
silky: see p. 17
simple: see p. 17
sinuate: see pp. 14, 17
sinuately dentate: see p. 14
sinus: see p. 14
spathulate: spatula-shaped, with a broad rounded end and tapering gradually towards the base
spine: see p. 16
spring-toothed: see p. 15
stamen: one of the male organs of a flower, comprising a filament (stalk) and an anther
staminode: an imperfectly developed stamen, incapable of producing pollen
stellate: branching like a star
stigma: the part at the end of the style, on which the pollen alights and germinates
stipule: see p. 16
stoma: a pore on the surface of a leaf
style: the part of a flower which grows from the ovary and carries the stigma
subalpine: see p. 62
sucker (*verb*): to put up new and separate shoots from existing roots

terminal leaflet: see p. 17
triangular: see p. 13
trifoliolate: see p. 17
truncate: see p. 15, 16

umbel: an inflorescence whose flowers are borne on stalks growing from about the same point on the stem, resulting in an umbrella shape (*cf* raceme, panicle)
undulate: see p. 15

vascular (tissue): xylen plus phloem
vascular bundles: strands of primary vascular tissue, sandwiched with parenchyma (photosynthetic tissue)
veining: see p. 13
venation: see p. 13
villous: covered with long, soft hairs

wedge-shaped: see p. 16
whorled: see p. 19
winter-green: see p. 19
woolly: see p. 17

xeromorphic: see p. 19
xylem: vascular tissue conducting water and nutrients from roots to other parts of the plant

Index of Vernacular Names of Trees

Index of Scientific Names of Trees

FIELD GUIDE TO THE TREES OF BRITAIN AND NORTHERN EUROPE

By Alan Mitchell

40 colour plates by Preben Dahlstron and Ebbe Sunesen and 640 line drawings by Christine Darter

The definitive hardback field guide to 800 species and varieties of trees. The most thorough and respected guide available today, it allows the user to identify with accuracy and become acquainted in the greatest detail with any cultivated or wild tree growing in Europe north of the Mediterranean littoral.

ISBN 0 00 219213 6

"Superb . . . informative, succinct, clear and magnificently illustrated." The Times

TREES OF BRITAIN AND NORTHERN EUROPE

By Alan Mitchell

Illustrated by John Wilkinson

The complete paperback pocket tree guide - 288 pages of description and colour illustration, featuring every tree - wild or planted, in woods, hedges and fields, in town streets, parks and gardens - which the reader is likely to find in Britain and Northern Europe. Over 600 species and varieties, with information on every aspect, including the finest specimens of each to be found in the British Isles.

ISBN 0 00 219857 6

COLLINS GEM GUIDE TO TREES

By Alistair Fitter

Illustrated by David More

One of the many titles in the Collins *Gem Nature Guides* series. Nearly 200 trees and shrubs covered, with details of leaf, fruit and bark. Liberally illustrated accounts providing a basic botanical introduction to common species of Britain and Northern Europe. Designed to fit comfortably into even the smallest pocket!

ISBN 0 00 458803 7